Compliance with Judgments of the European Court of Human Rights

International Studies in Human Rights

VOLUME 143

The titles published in this series are listed at brill.com/*ishr*

Compliance with Judgments of the European Court of Human Rights

States on a Spectrum of Democratisation

By

Ramute Remezaite

BRILL

LEIDEN | BOSTON

Library of Congress Cataloging-in-Publication Data

Names: Remezaite, Ramute, author.
Title: Compliance with judgments of the European Court of Human Rights : States on a Spectrum of Democratisation / Ramute Remezaite.
Description: Leiden ; Boston : Brill/Nijhoff, 2024. | Series: International studies in human rights, 0924-4751 ; vol. 143 | Includes bibliographical references and index.
Identifiers: LCCN 2023031360 (print) | LCCN 2023031361 (ebook) | ISBN 9789004538207 (hardback) | ISBN 9789004538214 (ebook)
Subjects: LCSH: European Court of Human Rights. | International Court of Justice. | Human rights–Europe. | Civil rights–Europe. | Democratization–Europe.
Classification: LCC KJC5138 .R47 2024 (print) | LCC KJC5138 (ebook) | DDC 341.5/52–dc23/eng/20230914
LC record available at https://lccn.loc.gov/2023031360
LC ebook record available at https://lccn.loc.gov/2023031361

Typeface for the Latin, Greek, and Cyrillic scripts: "Brill". See and download: brill.com/brill-typeface.

ISSN 0924-4751
ISBN 978-90-04-53820-7 (hardback)
ISBN 978-90-04-53821-4 (e-book)
DOI 10.1163/9789004538214

This book is printed on acid-free paper and produced in a sustainable manner.

Contents

Acknowledgments

> To those courageously defending values of freedom, democracy and human rights in the South Caucasus region.

This book is the result of years of research and knowledge gathered on the topic, which would not have been possible without the support of many wonderful people I had the privilege to enjoy throughout the process. It started as a PhD research in the School of Law of the Middlesex University in London in 2014, followed by implementation of multiple civil society and academic projects aimed to enhance compliance with judgments of the European Court of Human Rights (ECtHR) across the Council of Europe, as well as litigation of human rights cases from the South Caucasus as the focus region before the Court. It has greatly contributed to the richness of the research in that it has provided in-depth insights into the particular domestic, often challenging, contexts that the implementation takes place in practice.

I therefore want to first express my deep gratitude to my interlocutors in Baku, Tbilisi, Yerevan, Strasbourg and London for their time and assistance in better understanding the implementation of the ECtHR judgments in the South Caucasus states, and the efforts taken and challenges faced by the Council of Europe supervision system. Thanks to them, the book is largely based on the enriching empirical research that I was able to undertake, along the desk research. I am particularly grateful to my colleagues and friends, human rights defenders in the South Caucasus states whose devotion to striving for better and freer lives for their societies I observe with deep respect. I am forever grateful to my supervisors, Professor Philip Leach and Dr Alice Donald, for their guidance, support and friendship – without it this research would not be a book today. Finally, I wish to express my admiration to my colleagues at the European Human Rights Advocacy Centre, based within the Law School of the Middlesex University, whose professionalism and dedication to the cause of human rights inspire me every day.

Figures

CHAPTER 1

Introduction

1.1 Background and Problem Statement

> We've moved from a backlog crisis [with the Court] to an implementation crisis.[1]
>
> NILS MUIŽNIEKS, Commissioner of Human Rights of the Council of Europe, December 2016

The European Court of Human Rights (ECtHR), which serves as a judicial review mechanism for the protection and promotion of human rights, established in the European Convention for the Protection of Human Rights and Fundamental Freedoms (ECHR), is often seen as the world's leading human rights court. Established in the wake of the devastation of the Second World War, it has issued more than 24,500 judgments and exerted enormous influence on the development of human rights law across all 47 member states of the Council of Europe (CoE) and around the world.[2] Over 670 million inhabitants in Europe can benefit from the protection of the ECtHR in seeking justice for violations that their domestic authorities fail to remedy (which has decreased from round 820 million after the Convention ceased applying to the Russian Federation in September 2022, following its expulsion from the CoE). While the existence of the ECtHR represents a great European achievement in seeking to provide effective remedies for human rights abuses, it poses increasing challenges in regard to effective implementation of ECtHR judgments. Although a recognition of a violation of rights of victims of human rights abuses can be a great success and often does some justice to individuals affected by violations, states often fail to fully and effectively implement judgments so that it leads to a change on the ground for victims and societies affected by those violations. Ineffective implementation of ECtHR judgments has been a growing problem for the European human rights community, with the past years raising issues of dilatory, partial and even contested compliance by certain states.

1 'EIN launch event: a strong call for collective responsibility over implementation of ECtHR judgments' (*European Implementation Network*, 6 December 2016), accessed 28 September 2017.

2 'ECtHR Overview 1959–2021, European Court of Human Rights', accessed 1 January 2022, 3.

 | DOI:10.1163/9789004538214_002

Compliance with ECtHR judgments varies considerably across the CoE member states, and more than 5,500 unimplemented cases, among those 1300 'leading' cases (those identifying systemic, structural problems) remain under the supervision of the Committee of Ministers (CM), the CoE's political body responsible for supervising the implementation process as of 31 December 2021.[3] Some new member states of the CoE, committed to respect the CoE values and principles, that have been showing signs of democratic progress since the end of the Cold War, are now displaying serious vulnerabilities in their fragile domestic systems in securing those values. Some of the main challenges emerged after the accession of post-Soviet states to the CoE, as these states often lack political will and/or institutional capacity to fully and effectively implement ECtHR judgments. Some of these countries, such as Russia or Azerbaijan, do not only continue to lag behind with its democratic development, but also increasingly demonstrate regressive authoritarian tendencies and tremendous regression in their commitment to respect human rights in their domestic contexts in the last years.[4] Worryingly, selective approach of such established democracies as the United Kingdom and its challenging of the ECtHR's authority serves as a green light to the regimes of those new vulnerable democracies to not abide by ECtHR rulings that go against their interests.[5]

Many of these newly emerged aspiring democracies do not only stand behind a major part of unimplemented ECtHR judgments (Figure 1); they are among the 'leading' states in terms of highest numbers of applications pending before the ECtHR. As of 30 November 2022, out of all 75,700 applications pending before the ECtHR at the time, such countries as Azerbaijan accounted for 2,9% (2200 applications), Armenia for 1,7% (1250 applications), Russia for 22,1% (16750 applications) and Ukraine for 14% (10600 applications).[6]

---

3 Committee of Ministers 15th Annual report on Supervision of the Execution of Judgments and Decisions of the European Court of Human Rights (2021) 43.

4 Freedom House, 'Freedom in the World 2020, Freedom House Interactive Map' Azerbaijan and Russia ranked as 'Not Free', accessed 19 June 2020; Human Rights Watch 'World Report 2016: Azerbaijan, Events of 2015'; 'World Report 2016: Russia, Events of 2015'; Amnesty International Report 2017/2018, The State of the World's Human Rights, 82, 310.

5 Philip Leach and Alice Donald, 'Russia Defies Strasbourg: Is Contagion Spreading?' (*EJIL:Talk! Blog of the European Journal of International Law*, 19 December 2015), accessed 9 September 2018; 'Ali Hasanov: Azerbaijan travelled a long distance to develop democratic society and no one can deny it' (AzerTac, 4 November 2014).

6 European Court of Human Rights, Pending Applications allocated to a Judicial Formation, 30 November 2022.

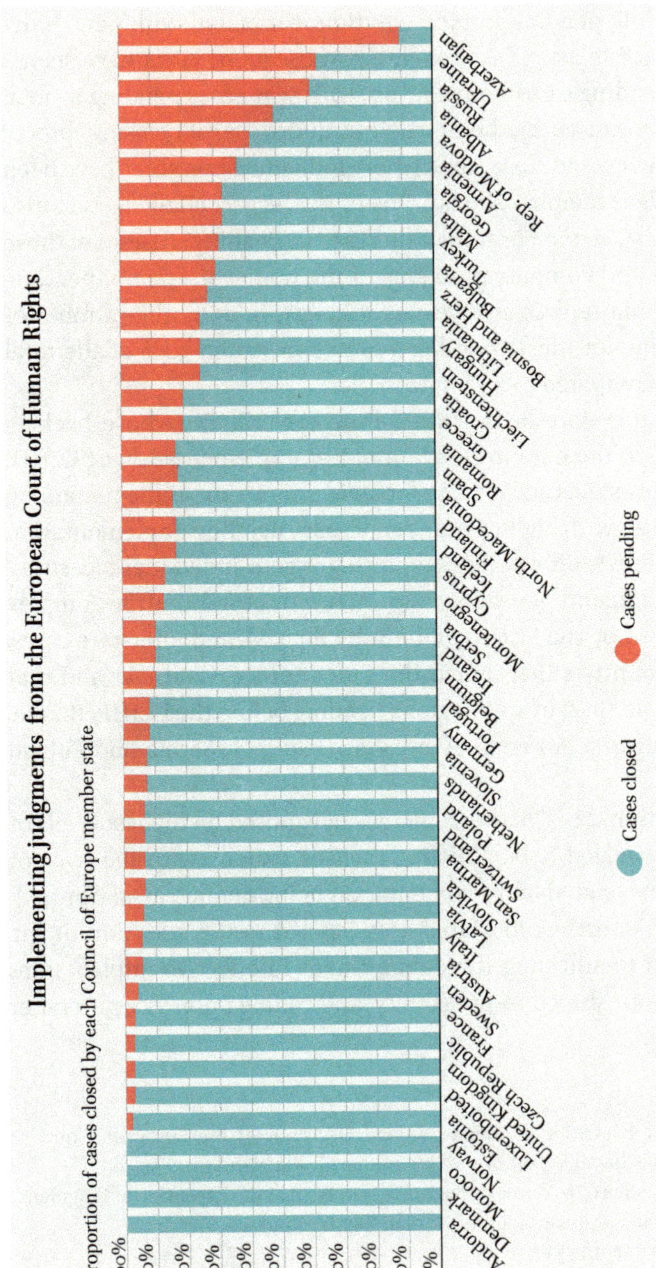

FIGURE 1 Implementation of ECtHR judgments by CoE member states
SOURCE: COUNCIL OF EUROPE, UPDATED 31/12/2018

The gradual decrease of the ECtHR's backlog has been followed by a steady increase of judgments pending implementation before the CM. In 2015, there were 10,652 judgments pending implementation, compared with 9899 judgments in 2010 or 7328 in 2008.[7] Although the subsequent years have seen a sharp decrease in pending cases from 2017 on, with 5533 cases pending in 2021, this has been largely caused by the newly introduced 'partial closure' procedure by the CM allowing it to close cases where individual measures have been adopted by respondent member states.[8] One of the biggest challenges, as also recognised by the CM, is the continued increase of 'leading' cases, i.e. those revealing structural and complex problems in the domestic system, pending implementation for more than five years. Strikingly, in 2019, the number of leading cases pending for more than five years represented 50% of the total 1300 leading cases (compared to 20% in 2011).[9]

The burden has therefore been shifted from the ECtHR (whose backlog remains significant) to the CM entitled to monitor implementation of ECtHR judgments, with a few states accounting for a big proportion of the remaining backlog. Out of 9 states with highest number of cases pending implementation under enhanced supervision, i.e. cases requiring urgent individual measures, pilot judgments, judgments revealing important structural and/or complex problems as identified by the ECtHR and / or by the CM, and interstate cases, eight of them are countries that joined the CoE after the Cold War and that also account for a major part of applications pending before the ECtHR: Russia, Ukraine, Turkey, Bulgaria, Romania, Azerbaijan, Hungary, Serbia and Poland (see Figure 2).[10]

This implementation crisis has been increasingly raised on highest levels of the CoE and acknowledged to be afflicting the CoE system, with the scale of outstanding problems related to implementation being defined as 'alarming'.[11] The high level CM conference in March 2015 has led to the adoption of the Brussels Declaration re-affirming the commitment to effective implementation of the ECHR as 'our shared responsibility' and calling upon all 47 member

7 Supervision of the Execution of Judgments and Decisions of the European Court of Human Rights, 9th Annual Report of the Committee of Ministers (2015) 51, 56.

8 Committee of Ministers 13th Annual report on Supervision of the Execution of Judgments and Decisions of the European Court of Human Rights (2019) 91.

9 CM Annual Report 2021 (n 3) 65.

10 Ibid 63.

11 Parliamentary Assembly of the Council of Europe, Committee on Legal Affairs and Human Rights, 'Implementation of judgments of the European Court of Human Rights', (Council of Europe, 9 September 2015) [46].

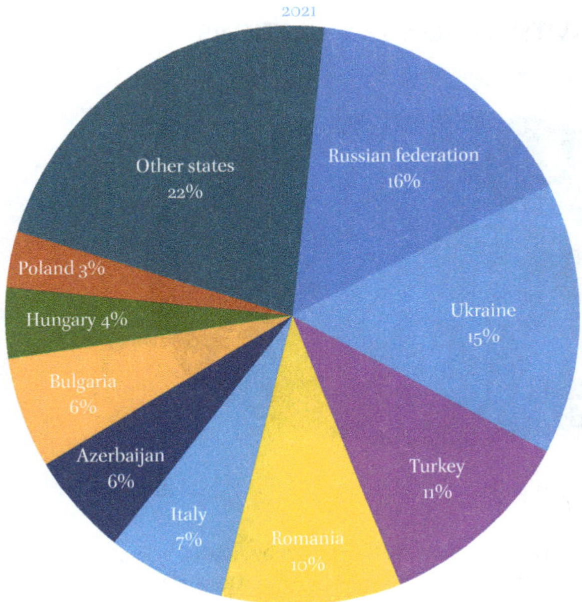

FIGURE 2 States with the highest number of pending cases under enhanced supervision
SOURCE: 15TH ANNUAL REPORT OF THE COMMITTEE OF MINISTERS (2021)

states to put increased efforts towards that end.[12] Although the Declaration entails a rather strong commitment, Europe's civil society expressed concern that the Declaration did not set out any specific measures that states and the CM should take to improve the situation with the implementation of ECtHR judgments.[13] 2017 has further seen the first ECtHR case being referred back to the Court by the CM under 'infringement proceedings' as a result of Azerbaijan's failure to comply with the CM's repeated calls to release the unlawfully imprisoned opposition figure Ilgar Mammadov.[14] These proceedings, triggered by the CM under Article (46)4 of the ECHR, for the first time in the CoE history,

12 Brussels Declaration on the 'Implementation of the European Convention on Human Rights, our shared responsibility' (Committee of Ministers, 27 March 2015), accessed on 3 April 2015.

13 Joint NGO Response to the draft Brussels Declaration on the 'Implementation of the European Convention on Human Rights, our shared responsibility', 27 March 2015.

14 Ramute Remezaite and Jack Dahlsen, 'Explainer: Council of Europe Infringement Proceedings against Azerbaijan' (European Human Rights Advocacy Centre, 26 February 2018), accessed 27 August 2019.

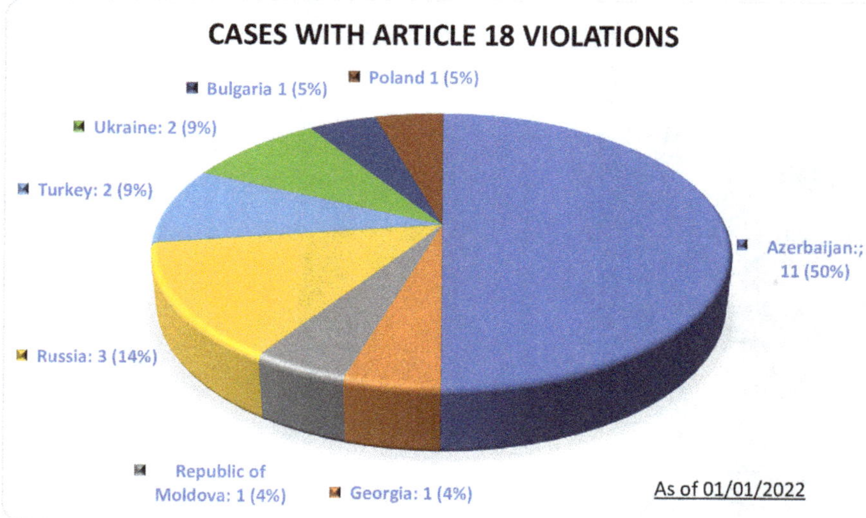

FIGURE 3 ECtHR cases finding violations of article 18 of ECHR by states
SOURCE FOR DATA: HUDOC DATABASE, AS OF 1 JANUARY 2022

have led to the return of the judgment back to the Court for it to decide if Azerbaijan has failed to comply with its obligation to comply with an ECtHR judgment – which the ECtHR found positive.[15] The recent years have also seen a sharp increase in 'bad faith' cases finding a number of states restricting individual rights, in violation of Article 18 of the ECHR, for unauthorised, ulterior purposes with Azerbaijan being the absolute leader, followed by Russia, Turkey and Ukraine (Figure 3).

Such a critical situation largely caused by low performance of the new member states of the CoE not only raises doubts about their genuine commitment to abide by the ECHR but also puts the credibility of the whole CoE system at risk. The failure of it's member states to promptly and effectively implement their obligations under the ECHR diminishes the ECtHR's ability to provide redress for victims and, ultimately, questions its legitimate authority. With the deepening non-implementation crisis in the CoE and the political discourse on the authority deficit of the ECtHR in the UK, Russia (before its expulsion) or Azerbaijan, there is an increasing need to study the respective states' behaviour

15 Interim Resolution of the Committee of Ministers on the execution of the judgment of the European Court of Human Rights in the case of *Ilgar Mammadov v Azerbaijan*, CM/ResDH(2017)429, 5 December 2017; *Ilgar Mammadov v Azerbaijan*, Appl. no. 15172/13 (ECtHR 29 May 2019).

to understand the underlying reasons for such challenges, and to look for the optimal solutions to the situation. The new member states of the CoE that were invited to join the CoE with a *promise* to abide by the ECHR norms and the ECtHR case law rather than a proven record of human rights, rule of law and democratic principles, as many of them emerged from the Soviet Union with weak legal and political systems requires qualitative research of their domestic contexts within which implementation takes place in order to explain the growing challenge for Europe. As Dean Spielmann, the former President of the ECtHR put it, emerging democratic systems committed to join the CoE and integrate its human rights norms and values 'as a part of their transition process and not as a reward for it', which entailed immense challenges to both sides.[16] Prof. Sadurski argued that the accession of emergent new democracies was 'both a threat and a promise' to the European system.[17] His identified *threat* refers to a sharp jump from 23 to 47 states with many new members featuring 'widely inadequate standards of human rights' and 'systemic defects and malfunctions in the legal systems'.[18] Against this context, new member states of the CoE as democratising states, or those displaying regressive totalitarian tendencies, may have had and continue having various other motivations for accessing the CoE. This begs for the analysis of their behaviour, motivation and attitude towards the ECtHR and compliance with its judgments, and how it influences their responsiveness to the socialisation effect of the CM supervision system (see 2.3 for modalities of the CM supervision system).

1.2 Key Aims and Research Questions of the Book

The book seeks to provide substantive insights into compliance with ECtHR judgments in states on the spectrum of democratisation as primary 'culprits' of the growing concern over deepening lack of timely and comprehensive compliance with ECtHR judgments. It does so by looking in indepth into the cases of the three South Caucasus states, Armenia, Azerbaijan and Georgia that feature significantly less in compliance literature than some of the bigger states

16 Dean Spielmann, President of the European Court of Human Rights (2012–2015), 'Foreword', in Iulia Motoc and Ineta Ziemele (eds.), *The Impact of the ECHR in Democratic Change in Central and Eastern Europe* (CUP 2016), xxv.

17 W. Sadurski, 'Partnering with Strasbourg: Constitutionalisation of the European Court of Human Rights, the Accession of Central and East European States to the Council of Europe, and the Idea of Pilot Judgments' (2009) Human Rights Law Review 397–453.

18 Ibid 451.

such as Russia, Turkey or Ukraine. In particular, the book analyses *how* and *why* such states implement, or do not implement, ECtHR judgments. The analysis is done on the basis of the extensive empirical studies, involving dozens of interviews with CoE and domestic actors, and the process tracing of the implementation of specific judgments that have provided invaluable insights into these matters. The selected cases concern a wide spectrum of human rights issues addressed by the ECtHR: from violations of civil and political rights, to cases challenging traditional, national 'values', often linked to systemic discrimination, to abuse of official powers by the authorities and cases addressing the dysfunction of the domestic legal systems, such as the inability of the system to ensure effective investigatory mechanisms, as well as cases emerging in conflict context that bring an additional factor to be taken into consideration. As all the selected cases are 'leading' cases (i.e. disclosing structural, systemic issues in domestic systems), they require structural reforms and are of significant importance to shaping human rights policies in the selected countries and potentially affect their wider societies. The process tracing of implementation of these cases included an in-depth analysis of lifespans of these cases since their transfer to the CM for its supervision until 1 January 2022 allowing to assess compliance as a non-dichotomous concept.

This book fills a gap in academic literature since newer CoE states, particularly smaller states in the region, are significantly less researched than the longer-established Western European member states of the CoE. The book specifically aims:

- To explain the particularities of the domestic contexts of states on the spectrum of democratisation within which compliance with ECtHR judgments takes place and which determines the authorities' actions or inactions;
- To identify key actors in compliance process, both domestically and on the CoE level, and analyse their significance, effectiveness and/or weaknesses;
- To explain the underlying reasons and conditions for states' (non)compliance behaviour;
- To revive and advance the so far limited scholarly debate on the concept of partial compliance in the context of international human rights law, and ECtHR human rights judgments in particular;
- To analyse the wider impact of ECtHR judgments in states on the spectrum of democratisation and introduce an all-encompassing concept of impact, and it's identified forms.

For the purposes of the research in this book, I adopted the definitions of the terms 'implementation' and 'compliance', which overlap and are often inconsistently used in relation to ECtHR judgments and the CoE system. As my research focuses on the effect of ECtHR judgments, I view *implementation* as a process of adopting measures taken by domestic authorities to address human rights issues raised in judgments, whereas *compliance* is seen as an outcome of the implementation when a state implements a judgment in order to be compliant with judgments (i.e. there is a causal link between measures taken and ECtHR judgments). Finally, I also discuss *impact* of ECtHR judgments as examples of positive change that goes beyond the conventional material impact directly deriving from the findings of the judgments and include cases where compliance is not yet achieved.

The hypothesis of this book stems from the presumption that compliance with ECtHR judgments in new democracies of the CoE is a complex matter and is widely dependent on states' political will and capacities, the absence of which often hinders effective implementation (at 2.2). The research also implies the presumption that in new democracies such as the three South Caucasus countries compliance with ECtHR judgments is further fostered by certain material or other incentives. These can include states' intention to 'lock in' their democracies, as suggested by Moravcsik,[19] or the regime's aim to be considered as a part of a 'democratic club' by old democracies of the CoE or states' interest to advance its progress in the process of associating with the European Union or other international partners.[20]

My research hypothesis relies on the synthesis of two prevailing compliance theories – *constructivism* and *rational choice* – which I discuss in greater detail in Chapter 2 (see 2.2). Although earlier seen as competing theories, their synergy receives the increasing support among compliance scholars (see 2.2). *Constructivism* focuses on the way in which international law 'socialises' states by their exposure to and interaction with human rights norms and institutions,[21] whereas the *rational choice* theory, focusing on material incentives and self-interests of governments.[22] I argue that such a synergy is particularly relevant to democratizing states such as the three South Caucasus countries where the political will of the regimes and their 'socialisation' with international mechanisms and norms, followed by additional incentives play a crucial role in states' performance relating to compliance with ECtHR judgments.

19 Andrew Moravcsik, 'The Origins of International Human Rights Regimes: Democratic Delegation in Postwar Europe', (2000) *International Organizations* 217–252.

20 Sharanbir Grewal and Erik Voeten, 'Are New Democracies Better Human Rights Compliers?' (2012) SSRN e-Library, accessed on 3 July 2016.

21 Ryan Goodman and Derek Jinks, *Socializing States: Promoting Human Rights Through International Law* (OUP 2013); Jutta Brunee and Stephen J. Toope, Legitimacy and Legality in International Law: An Interactional Account (CUP 2010) AJIL.

22 Jack L. Goldsmith and Eric A. Posner, *The Limits of International Law*, (OUP 2005); Andrew T. Guzman, *How International Law Works: A Rational Choice Theory* (OUP 2010).

As I discuss in Chapter 2, new democracies feature considerably less that stable democracies in the scholarly work on compliance, including the South Caucasus states. The research will therefore contribute to the growing literature on the degree to which, and under what conditions, the South Caucasus states as new democracies of the CoE comply with human rights judgments and on the processes within and between domestic actors in that regard.

The research hypothesis further relies on the finding suggested by the scholarship on compliance that ECtHR judgments are often partially complied with, rather than followed by a full or non-compliance.[23] It hypothesises that this may be of relevance to new democracies where, as mentioned above, the political will, states' capacities and various incentives influence the compliance with ECtHR judgments. The research therefore looks to explaining the reasons for challenges to full and timely compliance and prevalence of partial compliance.

To test the two compliance theories, I put particular focus on the role and impact of the supervision process of the CM as a significant player in the implementation process. I examine the impact of the reforms stemming from Protocol 14 of the ECHR, which enhanced the supervision process of the implementation of ECtHR judgments by expanding the supervisory powers of the CM and allowing more access to the process for other actors, such as non-governmental organisations (NGOs) or national human rights institutions (NHRI).[24] The research also addresses the ways and conditions under which the CM and its Secretariat, the Department for Execution of Judgments of the European Court of Human Rights (DEJ) engages in the implementation process with the selected countries. It particularly aims to assess the effectiveness of the CM supervision system and identify factors that lead to the influence of the CM work. It allows testing the constructivist approach, which places emphasis on the way the institutions 'socialise' states, on the three new democracies of the CoE, and establish any existing incentives that may arise from such interaction.

The existing literature suggests that ECtHR judgments may have an agenda-setting effect that catalyses domestic mobilisation in favor of legislative

23 Darren Hawkins and Wade Jacoby, 'Partial compliance. A Comparison of the European and Inter-American Courts of Human Rights' (2010) Volume 6, Journal of International Law and International Relations 35.

24 Protocol No 14 to the Convention for the Protection of Human Rights and Fundamental Freedoms, amending the Control System of the Convention, CETS No. 194, entered into force on 1 June 2010.

changes.[25] Civil society and NHRIs may well serve as strong implementation partners, along with all state institutions (executive, legislative and judiciary) that hold the primary obligation to abide by ECtHR judgments. The book therefore assesses what impact on compliance with ECtHR judgments civil society actors and NHRIs may bring as ECtHR judgments can foster domestic constituencies to mobilise to push for change. In some of the researched countries like Georgia, civil society has more space to engage in the implementation process whereas in Azerbaijan, for example, the dialogue between the government and human rights groups is very scarce if existent at all, and much of the input of the civil society to the implementation process is directed through the CM and other CoE bodies.[26] Furthermore, in the researched countries such as Azerbaijan, the role that NHRIs can play in promoting domestic implementation of ECtHR judgments is often taken over by civil society. Armenia is another interesting test case following its Velvet Revolution in 2018 leading to first fair and free elections and change of power, which appears to have created more space for the civil society to participate in the development of domestic human rights policies. Both NGOs and NHRIs are relatively new on the scene; they were however given a stronger formal role to play in the supervision process with the CM, which has already praised civil society's notable efforts in that regard.[27] Empirical study has enabled the analysis as to what extent the civil society and NHRIs can enhance compliance with ECtHR judgments in the three countries.

1.3 Research Methodology

1.3.1 *Country and Case Selection*

This book critically assesses and explains compliance with ECtHR judgments by Armenia, Azerbaijan and Georgia as new democracies of the CoE, or those displaying totalitarian practices. A number of variables allowing differentiating all three countries from other 'new democracies' of the CoE, such as Ukraine, Russia or Moldova, have been taken into consideration in deciding

25 Laurence R. Helfer and Erik Voeten, 'Do European Court of Human Rights Judgments Promote Legal and Policy Change?' (University of Chicago 2010).

26 Media Rights Institute, 'Execution of Judgments of the European Court of Human Rights in Azerbaijan. Status Quo Upon Azerbaijan's Chairmanship of the Committee of Ministers of the Council of Europe', May 2014, 6.

27 Supervision of the Execution of Judgments and Decisions of the European Court of Human Rights, 6th Annual Report of the Committee of Ministers (2012), 19.

on the selection of research countries. These variables ensure both the comparability and the diversity of the three countries to allow the research to answer its questions on the impact of ECtHR judgments and identify factors that influence such outcome.

All three countries constitute a separate geographical region in the eastern part of the CoE area, the South Caucasus, which is also referred to as such in the geopolitical terms by the international community. They all share a number of fundamental background characteristics, including the historical trajectories of the last century, i.e. they all were part of the Soviet Union, which led to similar legal systems and democratic identity-building after the breakdown of the Union. Yet, what separates from the Russian Federation in that regard is their size, and the economical and geopolitical power in the region: all three states are small states geopolitically dependent or influenced by Russia's regional power, and balancing between their interests and *real politik* with Russia as their neighbor of closest proximity, and the Western partners. They all joined the CoE around the same time, in 1999–2001,[28] around half a decade later than Russia or Ukraine, and can be categorised as 'new member states' of the CoE. All three countries joined the CoE in the midst of their transition to democracy, availing themselves of CoE's relevant expertise and efforts towards that goal.[29] Furthermore, Azerbaijan and Armenia saw the CoE as the mediator for the solution of their conflict over Nagorno Karabakh.[30] Since their independence from the Soviet Union, all three countries had similar political systems with weak separation of powers stemming from the Soviet heritage and low respect for civil and political freedoms, with Georgia currently being ahead of the spectrum of the post Soviet states and Azerbaijan ranking on the other end of the spectrum for its increasingly re-occurring authoritarian tendencies in that regard.[31] All three countries were among ten countries with the highest number of pending applications before the ECtHR in 2019, with Azerbaijan and Armenia remaining on this list in 2020 and 2021.[32] They all have judgments

28 Georgia became a member of the Council of Europe on 27 April 1999, Azerbaijan and Armenia joined it on 25 January 2001.

29 PACE Opinion No. 222. (2000) Azerbaijan's application for membership in the Council of Europe; PACE Opinion No. 221 (2000) Armenia's application for membership in the Council of Europe; PACE Doc. 8296, Georgia's application for membership in the Council of Europe, 12 January 1999.

30 Ibid.

31 Ibid [3–4]; Corruption Perceptions Index 2019 by Transparency International ranking Azerbaijan 126th, Armenia 77th and Georgia 44th out of 180 countries.

32 European Court of Human Rights Analysis of statistics 2019 8, accessed 8 March 2020; European Court of Human Rights Analysis of statistics 2021 8, accessed January 2022.

recognising violations of wide spectrum of human rights enshrined in the ECHR under enhanced supervision, meaning these are the cases 'revealing systemic and structural problems'.[33] Azerbaijan has been among 10 countries with the highest number of ECtHR cases under enhanced supervision since 2012.[34] Many judgments exposing structural or systemic domestic problems that are not fully implemented by the states concern civil and political rights that challenge – directly or indirectly – the ruling system and the existing state organization policies (e.g. freedom of expression, excessive use of force by law enforcement in custody, elections cases in Azerbaijan) or are in conflict with strong national cultural/traditional values (e.g. LGBTI rights in Georgia, religious minority rights in Armenia).

The feasibility of my experience in the South Caucasus region and access to research material has also contributed to the country choice for my research. My residence in Azerbaijan and Georgia in 2013–2014, and extensive work with litigating human rights lawyers and civil society organisations on cases before the ECtHR has provided me with invaluable knowledge and networks on the related human rights issues and the status of implementation of ECtHR judgments in the region. The initiation and coordination of the first regional project focused on capacity building of litigating lawyers and NGOs from all five Eastern Partnership countries (the South Caucasus states, Ukraine and Moldova) and Russia in 2013 has further expanded my related knowledge and contacts, and the better understanding of implementation related problems in Armenia and other neighboring countries. It was the good understanding of the existing implementation status of ECtHR judgments but not of the underlying causes for such a status quo that led me to select the three South Caucasus states for my research. My choice was further influenced by the realization that there has been more attention placed on the related situation in, for example, Russia and Ukraine than the smaller South Caucasus states, both by the domestic and outside actors in the academia, the international human rights community and the civil society, to analyse and explain the underlying implementation problem. The size of these three countries and, relatedly, smaller number of ECtHR judgments against them has enabled me to choose several countries for the research and at the same time ensure a wide enough spectrum of human rights issues addressed by ECtHR judgments covered by the research – which would have been much more difficult in the case of Russia or

33 CM Annual Report 2015 (n 7) 65.

34 CM Annual Report 2019 (n 8) 72; Supervision of the Execution of Judgments and Decisions of the European Court of Human Rights, 12th Annual Report of the Committee of Ministers (2018) 71; CM Annual Report 2012 (n 27) 63.

Ukraine where the numbers of cases outgrow the South Caucasus states manifold.[35] For example, in 2019, 189 cases against Azerbaijan, 38, against Armenia, 47 against Georgia were pending implementation before the CM compared to 1663 cases against Russia and 591 against Ukraine.

The three countries feature various diversity variables that allow analysing how they influence the implementation process and the states' compliance with their Convention obligations. The three countries have different domestic structures and processes for implementation of ECtHR judgments, led by different domestic actors, which are discussed in further detail in each country chapter (see 3.2.2, 4.2.1, 5.2). For example, in Azerbaijan, the implementation process of ECtHR judgments is organized and overseen by the Presidential Administration; in Georgia, it is under the responsibility of the Ministry of Justice, and in Armenia it is under the auspices of the Office of the Prime Minister since 2019, formerly under the Ministry of Justice. They feature rather different political systems with different levels of leverage of the executive power over judiciary and dialogues with civil society, with Azerbaijan featuring deepening authoritarian policies, and Armenia and Georgia on the other end of the spectrum of 'democratising' CoE member states in the region (see 3.1.1, 4.1, 5.1).

Five cases, or groups of cases from each country have been selected for the research, the analysis of the implementation process of which allowed me to derive more generalized findings on the states' compliance with ECtHR judgments. I limit my study to what the CM categorises as 'leading cases' that are the first ones to reveal "a new structural/general problem in a respondent state and which thus require the adoption of new general measures" and are mainly examined under the enhanced supervision.[36] General measures are aimed at preventing similar violations in the future that may require legislative or policy reforms, or other more complex types of reforms. Depending on the nature of the case, the level of political willingness to take necessary reforms and their complexity, the implementation process of such measures may take much longer than the one of individual measures. This is further influenced by the fact that the ECtHR does not normally indicate any general measures in its judgments (with very rare exceptions) leaving it at the discretion of the responsible states to decide what measures they deem necessary.[37] States may

35 CM Annual Report 2019 (n 8) 61–62.

36 Supervision of the Execution of Judgments and Decisions of the European Court of Human Rights, 4th Annual Report of the Committee of Ministers (2010) 29.

37 Alice Donald, Anne-Katrin Speck, 'The European Court of Human Rights' Remedial Practice and its Impact on the Execution of Judgments' (2019) Volume 19, Issue 1, 83.

be unwilling to adopt certain measures or unable to do so due to lack of sufficient political will, capacities or resources, or clarity on what general measures are needed for full and effective implementation of ECtHR judgments. As a result, the selected cases include cases that remain pending implementation, including those pending for longer periods of time, varying between five to ten years, and those that have been closed as implemented. This allowed exploring the different reasons for states' delay in taking measures and assess how it compares among the three states and depending on the extent of involvement of the CM supervision and other actors, such as civil society and NHRIs. The selected cases also vary in the Court indicating the specific measures in order to secure effective implementation: at least in one or two selected cases per country the Court specified what steps were needed in that regard. The absence of the specific remedies in the judgments gave me an opportunity to research how states, in dialogue with the CM, arrive, or fail to arrive, at Convention-compatible remedies at the domestic level.

The selected cases concern a wide spectrum of human rights issues addressed by the ECtHR: cases that concern violations of civil and political rights, cases challenging traditional, national 'values', often linked to systemic discrimination, abuse of official powers by the authorities and cases addressing the dysfunction of the domestic legal systems, such as the inability of the system to ensure effective investigatory mechanisms, as well as cases emerging in conflict context that bring an additional factor to be taken into consideration. As all the selected cases are 'leading cases', they require structural reforms and are of significant importance to shaping human rights policies in the selected countries and potentially affect their wider societies, which allow for comparison between states' commitment to adopt individual and general measures, and the assessment of their broader systemic impact.

The below listed cases have been selected for the research, the implementation of which have been tracked using a systematic approach. Some other cases concerning the three states are also referred to throughout the book where relevant.

List of ECtHR cases analysed in this book

Case/Case Group Name	Brief Description	Violated ECHR Arts.	No of Cases
Azerbaijan			
Ilgar Mammadov group Appl. no. 15172/13, 22 May 2014	Abuse of power through arbitrary engagement of criminal proceedings implying use of arrest and detention	Arts 5 and 18	9
Mahmudov and Agazade group Appl. no. 35877/04, 18 December 2008	Unjustified convictions and prison sentence as sanction for defamation, notably against journalists	Art 10	2
Muradova, Mammadov (Jalaloglu) and Mikayil group Appl. no. 34445/05, 11 January 2007	Ill-treatment and/or torture during arrest and police custody Ineffective investigations into actions of security forces	Arts 2, 3, 5, 6, 10, 11, 34	21
Ramazanova and Others group Appl. no. 44363/05, 1 February 2007	Failure of the authorities to apply properly the national legislation regulating the registration / the dissolution of the associations.	Art 11	7
Sargsyan case App. No. 40167/06, 15 June 2015	Impossibility for displaced persons to gain access, in the context of the Nagorno-Karabakh conflict, to their homes and properties, and relatives' graves	Arts 8 and 13, Art 1 of Protocol No.1	1
Armenia			
Ashot Harutyunyan group Appl. No. 34334/04, 15 June 2010	Denial of adequate medical care to prisoners suffering from various diseases	Arts 3, 6	3
Bayatyan group Appl. No. 23459/03, 7 July 2011	Failure to secure alternative service for conscientious objectors	Art 9	5

Case/Case Group Name	Brief Description	Violated ECHR Arts.	No of Cases
Chiragov and Others case Appl. No. 13216/05, 16 June 2015	Impossibility for displaced persons to gain access, in the context of the Nagorno-Karabakh conflict, to their homes and properties	Arts 8, 13, Art 1 of Protocol No .1	1
Mkrtchyan case Appl. no. 6562/03, 11 January 2007	Unlawful administrative penalty imposed for breach of rules on holding demonstrations	Article 11	1
Virabyan group Appl. No. 40094/05, 2 October 2012	Ill-treatment and/or torture in police custody; ineffective investigations into allegations of such acts and into possible discrimination based on political motivations	Arts 3, 6, 14	4
Georgia			
Gorelishvili group Appl. 12979/04, 5 June 2007	Lack of a distinction between statements of fact and value judgments in domestic law at the material time	Article 10	1
Ghavtadze group Appl.no. 23204/07, 30 March 2009	Structural inadequacy of medical care in prisons	Article 3 Article 46	6
Identoba and Others case Appl. No. 73235/12, 12 May 2015	State's failure to protect demonstrators from homophobic violence and to launch effective investigation	Articles 3 and 14	2
Klaus and Yuri Kiladze group Appl. 7975/06, 2 February 2010	Legislative gap preventing victims of Soviet political repression from effectively asserting their rights to compensation	Art 1 of Protocol No.1 Article 46	1

Case/Case Group Name	Brief Description	Violated ECHR Arts.	No of Cases
Tsintsabadze group Appl. no. 35403/06, 18 March 2011 (formerly Gharibashvili group, Appl. no. 11830/03, 15 February 2011)	Excessive use of force by the police during arrest and/or custody Lack of effective investigations into allegations of violations of the right to life and of ill-treatment	Articles 2 and 3	24

Source for description of cases HUDOC database, as of 1 January 2022

The process tracking of implementation of these cases and the states' compliance with the respective ECtHR judgments included an in-depth analysis of lifespans of these cases since their transfer to the CM for its supervision until 1 January 2022 (as a selected end point for the research). It consisted both of the desk research of all the information provided by respondent states to the CM as to the progress of the cases, such as action plans and reports, and other updates, as well as CM official responses through its decisions and resolutions, and notes prepared after CM meetings on each case, or group of cases. The analysis also included written submissions by applicants, NGOs and NHRIs allowing for 'alternative' assessment of the states' progress, as well as various other reports published by NGOs and NHRIs on human rights issues addressed by the judgments – allowing for assessment of the issues in the most recent domestic context. I also analysed reports and other material produced by other CoE bodies relating to Azerbaijan and human rights issues addressed by the Court in its judgments. I further relied on the information obtained through semi-structured interviews with various international and domestic actors, such as DEJ staff and CM representatives, Court and PACE representatives, Government representatives, members of national parliaments, litigating lawyers, NGOs and NHRIs. It allowed analysing some of the motivational and attitudinal aspects of the context within which implementation related decisions have been taken and served as a significant source of information for assessing impact of ECtHR judgments, including where full compliance was not (yet) in place. I mitigated the limited access to certain Government officials in Azerbaijan who did not respond to my requests for interviews with the analysis of official documentary sources produced by the authorities, both those submitted to the CM or other CoE bodies, and those published domestically.

1.3.2 *Research Methods*

In order to test the hypotheses and examine and explain the selected states' compliance with ECtHR human rights judgments, I employ a number of qualitative research methods. It includes desk research of the existing political science and legal scholarship on compliance with international human rights law and country specific literature, which I overview in Section 2.1; review of the selected ECtHR judgments, as well as others relevant to the research available on the Court's HUDOC database; documents related to implementation of specific cases available on the CM's HUDOC EXEC database, such as action plans and reports provided by respondent member states as to what steps they are to take to comply with the judgments; CM decisions and resolutions assessing the authorities' progress, submissions by NGOs and NHRIs, also known as 'Rule 9' submissions. I also analysed documents produced by other CoE bodies that either address implementation issues or concern human rights issues addressed in the analysed ECtHR judgments, such as PACE, CPT, Venice Commission reports, speeches and press releases by CoE officials or representatives of the selected states in various CoE platforms.

To better understand and analyse the domestic contexts of the three countries within which implementation takes place, and their wider human rights policies and environments, I have also reviewed and relied on relevant national laws and other relevant official documents, statements and press releases of state officials, as well as the coverage of ECtHR judgments and human rights issues that they address in the national media, reports produced by the civil society, both domestic and international, and the NHRIs. I reviewed such invaluable material available both in English and Russian (which is a commonly used language in each country after the native language), however, I recognize the limitations in not reviewing the material in native languages of the three selected countries. I remedied some of this reservation by advising domestic actors on relevant issues.

For my empirical study, I employed the qualitative interviewing technique that provided me with rich data explaining the attitudes and motivations of various actors of selected states behind the implementation and compliance with the ECtHR judgments. It allowed for a debate on underlying beliefs about compliance and implementation and states' own performance as compliers and better understanding of the domestic contexts within which implementation takes place. Furthermore, given that the implementation dialogue with the CM takes place behind closed doors, interviewing is an essential method for data collection, particularly on the political dimension of the issue. The interviews with the civil society, litigating lawyers and applicants and allow me to identify compliance expectations of those who bring human rights cases before the ECtHR and their sense of contribution to the implementation process. Much of the empirical literature on compliance of ECtHR judgments is quantitative and little of it covers the new member states of the CoE, including my selected states.[38] My empirical evidence is therefore of significant importance in explaining the respective states' behaviour and the positive impact that the ECtHR judgments have led to so far.

In my empirical study, I focus on the following types of actors both on the national and CoE level: a) government representatives, parliament members and staff, judiciary, lawyers, civil society, national human rights institutions, academics and other relevant stakeholders, b) representatives of the CM, Department for Execution of Judgments, PACE Rapporteur on implementation of ECtHR judgments, other relevant CoE bodies and representatives.

During the period of 2015–2020, I conducted 40 interviews in total, with approximately ten in each country, and a similar number of actors in Strasbourg (both in CoE bodies and state representations to the CoE). The interviewed domestic actors included applicants, their lawyers, Government representatives responsible or otherwise involve in the implementation process, including former Government Agents before the ECtHR, members of national parliaments, judges, representatives to the CoE, NHRIs, civil society organisations. This diversity of views allowed to establish a spectrum of views on human rights issues and the implementation process as wide and possible, to triangulate the data and compare it against the documentary sources where discrepancies among the different interviewees' accounts occurred. The limitations in accessing relevant Azerbaijani Government officials who did not respond to interview requests were remedied through interviews with more in-depth discussions with CM delegates of like-minded states and DEJ

---

38 Among those are: Alice Donald and Anne-Katrin Speck, 'The Dynamics of Domestic Human Rights Implementation: Lessons from Qualitative Research in Europe' (2020), Volume 12 Issue 1, Journal of Human Rights Practice 1–23; Alice Donald, Debra Long, and Anne-Katrin Speck, 'Identifying and Assessing the Implementation of Human Rights Decisions' (2020), Volume 12 Issue 1, Journal of Human Rights Practice, 1–24; Rachel Murray and Christian De Vos, 'Behind the State: Domestic Mechanisms and Procedures for the Implementation of Human Rights Judgments and Decisions' (2020), Volume 12 Issue 1, Journal of Human Rights Practice, 1–26; Alice Donald and Philip Leach, *Parliaments and the European Court of Human Rights* (OUP 2016); Basak Çali, Anne Koch, 'Foxes Guarding the Foxes? The Peer Review of Human Rights Judgments by the Committee of Ministers of the Council of Europe' (2014) Volume 14, Issue 2, Human Rights Law Review 301–325.

representatives on their interactions with the Azerbaijani delegation, and the latter's reactions to it, which are not always translated into written positions. Due to the significant political changes in Armenia that followed the Velvet Revolution in 2018, given that vast majority of my interviews have been conducted pre-2018, I conducted several additional interviews in 2019 and 2020, including with the newly created Office of the Government Agent, to ensure the completeness of the material obtained through interviews. Although it may be too early to assess the impact of the new political environment on implementation of ECtHR judgments, the recent interviews allowed for better understanding and comparison of views of state representatives in charge of implementation towards this issue.

1.3.3 *Structure of the Book*

The subsequent chapters of the book address compliance with ECtHR judgments in each South Caucasus state, and the underlying factors that define and explain the status quo. Chapter 2 provides an overview of the existing compliance literature both in political science and legal scholarship and introduces the theories and definitions that I test and apply in my book. In the same chapter, I provide a brief overview of the existing CoE implementation framework, primarily the CM supervision system, under which the domestic implementation of ECtHR judgments is overseen.

As highlighted in sections on the problem statement and research questions (see 1.1 and 1.2), compliance takes place domestically, which requires qualitative analysis of the domestic contexts that shape and pre-determine the environment for compliance. In Chapters Three, Four and Five as 'country chapters' I therefore shift from doctrine and existing CoE procedures to national-level practice of the states where I analyse and discuss the particularities of each domestic system in the South Caucasus states and how it influences the implementation process. I provide a historical overview of each state's accession to the CoE and the challenging political, legal and social contexts within which they joined the CoE, then moving on to some contemporary issues that the CoE identifies with regard to these states today. I then analyse their domestic implementation systems and their effectiveness in enhancing compliance as an inclusive process and provide some recommendations as to their improvement. Then follows an in-depth analysis of the implementation of the selected judgments and the conclusions that this analysis offers as to the factors that define the successes or the challenges of the process. Among them, I analyse the particularities of the CM and DEJ engagement with the three states on the selected cases and propose some insights as to its effectiveness. It also discusses the role that other domestic actors such as the civil society or NHRIS play in the process.

In Chapter 6, following on the country-level and case-level analysis, I argue that partial compliance as a form of compliance is highly relevant to the South Caucasus states and deserves more attention in compliance literature. Endorsing the categorization of partial compliance proposed by Hawkins and Jacoby in 2010, I discuss the types of partial compliance that derive from the particular contexts of the South Caucasus states, offering further insights into this theory.

Chapter 7 explores the concept of impact and its existence in the compliance context of the South Caucasus states. I argue that impact is identifiable even in cases of partial compliance or non-implemented case and that it varies from material and clearly tangible to non-material impact that ECtHR judgments may have that may not derive directly from the text of the rulings.

In the final Chapter, I offer several conclusions arising out of this research.

CHAPTER 2

Defining Compliance

2.1 Defining and Measuring Compliance

The legal scholarship on compliance has contributed greatly to the legal definition of compliance. Compliance as a legal concept has been developed to assess the conformity between legal requirements and state behaviour subject to those requirements. In its most basic definition, compliance is *conformity to rules.*[1] Neyer and Wolf offer one of the most comprehensive definitions of compliance (emphasis added):

'Compliance needs to be distinguished from the concepts of implementation and effectiveness. Unlike those two concepts, compliance focuses neither on the effort to administer authoritatively public policy directives and the changes they undergo during this administrative process (implementation) nor on the efficacy of a given regulation to solve the political problem that preceded its formulation (effectiveness) ... *Assessing compliance is restricted to the description of the discrepancy between the (legal) text of regulation and the actions and behaviors of its addresses.*'[2]

Legal scholarship puts particular emphasis on the typology of compliance and the methodology to measure compliance. While many scholars initially saw compliance as dichotomous, all or nothing, there is an increasing recognition of the need to see compliance as a spectrum. For example, in their comparative study on the European Court of Human Rights (ECtHR) and the Inter-American Court of Human Rights, Hawkins and Jacoby dismissed the former notion and suggested that *partial compliance* is the most common outcome in both human rights regimes.[3] This is particularly relevant for the European system as the ECtHR does not envisage any specific remedies (with some exceptions) save monetary compensations and leaves it at the discretion of member

1 Jana von Stein, 'The Engines of Compliance', in Dunoff and Pollack, *Interdisciplinary Perspectives on International Law and International Relations* (CUP 2012) 477–501.

2 Jurgen Neyer and Dieter Wolf, 'The Analysis of Compliance with International Rules: Definitions, Variables and Methodology' in Michael Zurn and Christian Joerges (eds.), *Law and Governance in Postnational Europe: Compliance beyond the Nation-State* (CUP 2005) 41–42.

3 Darren Hawkins and Wade Jacoby, 'Partial compliance. A Comparison of the European and Inter-American Courts of Human Rights' (2010) Volume 6, Journal of International Law and International Relations 35.

 | DOI:10.1163/9789004538214_003

states to decide what measures are to be taken to remedy violations found in its judgments and prevent similar violations in the future.[4] Hawkins and Jacoby's study showed that compliance is higher when required measures are rather straightforward and clear, and statistical data shows that Council of Europe (CoE) members, including the three selected states, normally comply with just satisfaction ordered by the ECtHR. General measures aimed at preventing similar violations in the future often require legislative or policy reforms, or other more complex changes, particularly in new democracies, which makes partial compliance all the more relevant in explaining how and why states comply with human rights judgments.

Hawkins and Jacoby suggested 4 forms of partial compliance: 1) split decisions (states comply with part of the judgment but not with all parts) 2) state substitution (state offers a different response than the one the court ordered), 3) slow motion compliance (slow, delayed steps towards compliance), 4) ambiguous compliance amid complexity.[5]

Against this backdrop, my research employs the notion of partial compliance in analysing and explaining compliance in the three selected new democracies (Chapter 7). I started my analysis with the typology suggested by Hawkins and Jacoby but also arrived with some suggestions to this typology in the context of the researched countries. I propose three forms of partial compliance, minimalistic, dilatory and contested compliance, and introduce methodological considerations allowing to identify partial compliance. The typology of contested compliance is particularly novel, as a new form of partial compliance, in light of growing instances of 'bad faith' cases in the CoE region, including in Azerbaijan and Georgia.

2.2 Compliance Theories

The recent decades have witnessed a sharp increase in literature on compliance theories, and it continues evolving. Scholarship developed by political scientists has greatly contributed to the literature on compliance by offering a strand of compliance theories that seek to explain why states comply with international human rights law. The legal scholarship has been mainly focusing on conceptualising and defining compliance, with an increasing but careful

4 With the rare exception of pilot judgments and judgments referring to specific measures in accordance to Article 46 of the ECHR.

5 Hawkins and Jacoby (n 3) 35.

interaction with theoretical approaches adopted by political scientists.[6] This Chapter provides a selective overview of both disciplines, and later explains how the existing literature shaped the approach of my research, which is aimed to contribute to the scholarship of compliance in new democracies.

The political science scholarship offers a diverse strand of theoretical approaches to compliance. Such a diverse typology of compliance theories has seemingly synthesized into two distinct yet not exclusive theories, prevailing in the compliance literature:[7] *constructivism*, which places emphasis on the way in which international law 'socialises' states by their exposure to and interaction with human rights norms and institutions,[8] and the *rational choice* theory, focusing on material incentives such as inter-state explanations and self-interests of governments.[9]

The constructivist theory has increasingly contributed to the existing literature on human rights compliance. It focuses on repeated interaction with states and their exposure to international human rights norms in a non-coercive way, and the internalization of those norms by states. The constructivist approach argues that 'repeated interactions, argumentation and exposure to norms characterize and construct state practice'.[10] It sees a state as a group of actors and provides a diverse spectrum of accounts as to how states come to comply with the international human rights norms. Constructivism places great emphasis on the role that norms, institutions, identities and ideas play in influencing states' behavior. For example, Goodman and Jinks argue that a great importance should be given to *acculturation* as cognitive and social pressures to conform to an in-group.[11] They see compliance with international human rights norms as a matter of a relationship between domestic processes and international acculturation. Hillbrecht focuses on the domestic processes and interaction among various domestic actors, government branches, judiciary and civil society actors, influenced by international norms.[12]

---

6 Lisa. L. Martin, 'Against Compliance', in Dunoff and Pollack, *Interdisciplinary Perspectives on International Law and International Relations* (CUP 2013) 600–605.

7 Elizabeth Stubbins Bates, 'Sophisticated Constructivism in Human Rights Compliance Theory' (2014) Vol. 25 No.4 EJIL 1169–1182.

8 Ryan Goodman and Derek Jinks, *Socializing States: Promoting Human Rights Through International Law* (OUP 2013); Jutta Brunee and Stephen J. Toope, Legitimacy and Legality in International Law: An Interactional Account (CUP 2010) AJIL.

9 Jack L. Goldsmith and Eric A. Posner, *The Limits of International Law* (OUP 2005); Andrew T. Guzman, 'How International Law Works: A Rational Choice Theory' (OUP 2010).

10 Bates (n 7) 1170.

11 Goodman and Jinks, (n 8), p. 101.

12 Courtney Hillebrecht, Domestic Politics and International Human Rights Tribunals: The Problem of Compliance. New York: Cambridge University Press, 2014.

There is an emerging consensus among scholars, including Hillebrecht,[13] Risse, Ropp and Sikkink,[14] and Goodman and Jinks,[15] that constructivist approaches are now in ascendancy but with the integration of insights from the rationalist approach where the two theories are no longer dueling.[16] In re-evaluating their five stage constructivist 'spiral model' that explains states' progress from repression to rule-consistent behavior, Risse, Ropp and Sikkink recognised the need to integrate the rational choice perspective and see the constructivism as a context which includes coercion, incentives, persuasion and capacity building.[17] Goodman and Jinks converge both approaches by insisting on an integrated theory to determine the role of acculturation, persuasion and material inducement.[18] Hillbrecht puts a stronger focus on incentives and political costs in her constructivist approach discussing socialization mechanisms as to the compliance with human rights judgments, yet recognising that the synthesis of the two theories allows for a more comprehensive insight into human rights compliance. This synthesis serves as evidence of modern constructivism's sophistication and methodological breath.[19]

Other approaches that correlate with the constructivism approach include the *managerial* theory, supposing that most states comply with their international legal obligations, most of the time, hence non-compliance results from lack of capacity rather than lack of will;[20] *liberal theories*, that emphasise that there is a strong relationship between evolution of legal norms and national institutions and interests concerning compliance, and focuses on the effect of variations in state-society relations in the context of transnational interdependence;[21] *institutionalism*[22] or *normative approach*[23] that strongly resonate with the constructivism theory.

---

13 Ibid.

14 Thomas Risse, Stephen C. Ropp, and Kathryn Sikkink (eds), The Persistent Power of Human Rights: From Commitment to Compliance. Cambridge: Cambridge University Press, 2013.

15 Bates (n 7).

16 Ibid 1170.

17 Ibid.

18 Ibid.

19 Ibid 1170–1171.

20 Abram Chayes and Antonia Handler Chayes, 'On Compliance', *International Organization*, 47 (2) (1993) 175–205.

21 Andrew Moravcsik, 'Liberal Theories of International Law', in Dunoff and Pollack, *Interdisciplinary Perspectives on International Law and International Relations* (CUP 2013).

22 Barbara Koremenos, 'Institutionalism and International Law' in Dunoff and Pollack (eds) (n 59) 59–60.

23 Thomas M. Franck, *The Power of Legitimacy among Nations* (OUP 1990).

The compliance scholarship has been increasingly focusing on analysing the distinctive features and reasons of stable and new democracies relating to their human rights compliance. New members of the CoE have however featured considerably less than stable democracies in the existing scholarly work.[24] Simmons finds that human rights agreements have improved rights primarily in those countries that are neither stable autocracies nor stable democracies.[25] Grewal and Voeten find that democratising states are more likely to implement similar judgments more quickly than stable democracies but this effect diminishes as judgments remain pending longer.[26] They further suggest that both the political will of the leadership and effective institutional mechanisms are instrumental in democratising states' efforts to comply with human rights judgments. Differently from stable democracies, bureaucratic capacities alone will not secure compliance with a judgment where there is no political will to do so as their institutional mechanisms, including strong judicial institutions, are often too poor to rectify the government's obstruction. Their scholarship suggests that democratising states are more likely to receive judgments against them that are more difficult to implement as they often concern several violations and have more follow cases and involve more serious human rights violations. Such cases require extensive reforms, which makes it more difficult to remedy and to implement.

The hypothesis of my research integrates elements of two prevailing theories in the compliance literature: the dominant constructivist theory, which integrates rational choice perspectives, with an insight into the theory of reputational concerns.[27] With his three 'Rs' theory, Guzman argues that it is necessary to determine if and when international norms influence the behavior of states and that compliance relies on reputation, reciprocity and retaliation.[28] The reputational concern, which my research explores in relation to all three states, is of particular relevance to new democracies where the compliance with human rights judgments is widely dependent on the regime design and political will and states may want to portray themselves as credible members

24 Başak Çalı and Alice Wyss, 'Why Do Democracies Comply with Human Rights Judgments? A Comparative Analysis of the UK, Ireland and Germany' (2009), SSRN e-Library; Andreas von Staden, 'Shaping Human Rights Policy in Liberal Democracies. Assessing and Explaining Compliance with the Judgments of the European Court of Human Rights', PhD dissertation, (Princeton University 2009); Grewal and Voeten (n 20).

25 Beth Simmons, *Mobilizing for Human Rights* (CUP 2009).

26 Sharanbir Grewal and Erik Voeten, 'Are New Democracies Better Human Rights Compliers?' (2012) SSRN e-Library, accessed on 3 July 2016.

27 Section 2.2 of this book.

28 Andrew T. Guzman, *How International Law Works: A Rational Choice Theory* (OUP 2010).

of the democratic club (i.e. the CoE). The hypothesis is also drawn upon the assumption that certain incentives play a crucial role on compliance by new democracies where there is willingness to comply with international legal obligations but there is variation in states' capacity to do so. Such an assumption draws from some accounts of the rational choice theory set forth by Grewal and Voeten, and Moravcsik who suggest that new democracies are more likely to implement similar judgments more quickly than stable democracies, subject to presence of certain political incentives to signal states' commitment to human rights reform.[29] They suggest several incentives that may encourage new democracies to implement human rights judgments:

- Emerging democracies may want to *'lock in' their democracies* by making binding commitments and their leaders may be eager to implement judgments being fearful of what their successors might do (Moravcsik theory).[30]
- They may also want to do it for the purpose of *convincing a skeptical domestic public* that a government is indeed seriously committed to respecting human rights. This is particularly relevant for countries in democratic transitions when society is not sure about the sincerity of commitments of its leadership for reforms, with less secure system of checks and balances. Grewal and Voeten argue that in democratising countries (as opposed to stable autocracies and stable democracies) human rights treaties enable domestic mobilization that can bring human rights issues on the public agenda and help civil society hold leaders accountable to their promises to improve their human rights commitments.[31]
- Human rights judgments may similarly be more likely to help put human rights issues on the political, including the legislative agenda, in democratising states where there is space for civil society to engage and participate in political processes.[32]
- Democratising states may want to demonstrate a credible *commitment to human rights for international audiences* with the intention to be regarded as an equal and reliable partner in the international arena, particularly among stable democracies.[33]

29 Grewal and Voeten (n 26); Andrew Moravcsik, 'The Origins of International Human Rights Regimes: Democratic Delegation in Postwar Europe', *International Organization* 54 (2) (2000) 217–52.
30 Grewal and Voeten (n 26) 4.
31 Ibid.
32 Ibid.
33 Ibid.

- There may also be *material incentives* that may motivate states to comply with human rights judgments. Grewal and Voeten argue that the increasing attention of donors, aid agencies, international institutions and trading partners to human rights practices may result in higher and quicker rates of compliance for democratising countries under scrutiny.[34]

As not much scholarly work to support such assumptions has been done yet, Simmons and Nielsen' suggestion to have a better look into how democratising (or 'nonwestern') states think about international law and what their domestic considerations for ratification and compliance are, which would allow better understand states' strategies.[35] Their study into the 'reward-for-ratification' theory finds no support for the idea that states ratify human rights treaties in exchange of tangible rewards, such as international aid or trade agreements, or intangible rewards, such a reputational recognition. They acknowledge that there is a need for further research on how 'nonwestern' countries pursue international law and what their domestic considerations are.

2.2.1 *Causality between Human Rights Judgments and States' Behavior*

Establishing a causal link between human rights judgments and states behavior is another important aspect in compliance studies and the need for more studies on causal impact has been increasingly raised by scholars.[36] Although there is much scholarship on compliance and whether and when states comply with rules and norms of institutions that they choose to join by political scientists, there is still rather little research on the causal impact of international human rights institutions, agreements or judgments, particularly in relation to new democracies. Martin conducted a useful study on how various political scientists see compliance as a measure of outcome of commitments to international human rights law and institutions.[37] She identifies three categories of works on compliance by political science scholars by concluding that all of them however generally neglect to establish causality: the first one uses the language of compliance ending up to measure cooperation or domestic policy change; the second one combines compliance with cooperation; and the third category grounds its work on the legal concept of compliance developed by legal scholars and analyses the factors that lead to compliance.[38]

34 Grewal and Voeten (n 26).

35 Richard A. Nielsen and Beth A. Simmons, 'Rewards for Ratification: Payoffs for Participating in the Human Rights Regime?' (2015) International Studies Quarterly 59, 197–208.

36 Martin (n 6) 605–607; Bates (n 7).

37 Martin (n 6) 593.

38 Ibid 598.

Simmons finds that human rights agreements have a conditional impact on states' behaviour and that they have been instrumental in encouraging governments to improve their human rights records.[39] She argues that the causal impact is conditional on two domestic factors: mobilization of domestic groups and a relatively independent court system, particularly in the case of most civil rights.[40] In some instances she finds that the effects are most notable in democratic transitions. Vreeland, however, using a different measure of regime type, argues that, for example, ratification of the UN Convention Against Torture (CAT) by 'competitive dictatorships' may lead to further use of repressive measures or them more likely to use torture.[41] This begs for further research on when democratising states are more likely to improve their respect for human rights commitments and whether there is a causal link between its domestic policy decisions and actions for compliance. My in-depth national-level and case-level analysis of compliance in three specific domestic contexts offers new, additional insights into the dynamics of compliance and the causality between ECtHR judgments and the state behaviour. It does so not only with regard to material effect that is often easier to establish due to its deriving from the interpretation of the judgment findings, but also other, non-material types of impact that suggest some novel ways to look into the impact. Finally, my research offers contributions to the respective scholarship on how states on a spectrum of democratization varying from democratizing to increasingly authoritarian policies perceive compliance with ECtHR judgments where often the domestic political stakes are higher and where establishing causality is more challenging as a result. In the next section, I provide an overview of the existing implementation mechanism in the Convention system, before I move on to analyse how it applies in the challenging domestic contexts of the selected CoE member states.

2.3 Modalities of Implementation in the CoE System

The CoE implementation system is built on the underlying premise that all CoE member states have an unconditional obligation to abide by ECtHR judgments under Article 46 of the European Convention on Human Rights (ECHR). As the

39 Simmons (n 25).
40 Martin (n 6) 593.
41 James Raymond Vreeland, 'Political Institutions and Human Rights: Why Dictatorships Enter into the United Nations Convention against Torture', *International Organisation*, (2008) Vol. 62, No. 1, 65–101.

ECtHR's role in the implementation of its judgments is limited in that it has established that its judgments are essentially declaratory in nature leaving it to the respondent states to choose the means to discharge that obligation, the implementation supervision wheel is primarily in the hands of the Committee of Ministers (CM), the CoE's political body.[42] Exceptionally, where the ECtHR finds it necessary to indicate the type of measure, with a view to helping the respondent state to fulfill its obligations under Article 46 of the ECHR, it may indicate specific measures, leaving it to the supervision by the CM to ensure it is enforced.[43] Although the ECtHR remains reserved in exercising its remedial practice, it has been increasingly pragmatic and 'open to continued evolution', as suggested by Donald and Speck.[44]

The CM as the main supervisory body of the implementation of ECtHR judgments consists of government representatives of all 47 member states, i.e. ambassadors and other diplomats appointed to the CoE. Although formally the CM is composed of foreign ministers of each member state, in practice ministers delegate this role to their permanent representations in Strasbourg. The supervision of the implementation of ECtHR judgments, as one of the mandates of the CM, is normally carried out by Deputy Permanent Representatives of the member states. Under this mandate, the CM meets four times a year, usually for 2–3 days, in what are known as CM Human Rights Meetings to formally review member states' compliance with ECtHR judgments where it adopts formal decisions on the progress or the closure of a number of cases. Although the CM is tasked to supervise the implementation of all ECtHR judgments, technically, it examines the implementation of a number of cases at its quarterly meetings, varying between 25–30 cases selected for each meeting, known as the CM's 'indicative list'.[45] These meetings take place behind the closed doors, as a part of the peer review process, where only decisions adopted during the meetings and CM notes on cases (that do not include minutes of discussions) are made available to the public. As one of the interviewed CM delegates from a Western European country has put it, 'it is the confidentiality of these meetings that allows us to have genuine, open and often difficult

42 *Öcalan v. Turkey* [GC], appl. no. 46221/99, para 210, ECHR 2005-IV; *Scozzari and Giunta v. Italy* [GC], nos. 39221/98 and 41963/98, para 249, ECHR 2000-VIII.

43 *Broniowski v. Poland* [GC], no. 31443/96, § 194, ECHR 2004-V; *Assanidze v. Georgia* [GC], no. 71503/01, § 202, ECHR 2004-II.

44 Alice Donald, Anne-Katrin Speck, 'The European Court of Human Rights' Remedial Practice and its Impact on the Execution of Judgments' (2019), Volume 19, Issue 1, Human Rights Law Review 83–117.

45 The Committee of Ministers' Human Rights Meetings, available at https://www.coe.int/en/web/execution/committee-of-ministers-human-rights-meetings.

discussions on the progress, or rather the lack of progress in selected cases with respondent states'.[46] Criticism from the civil society on the need for more transparency of the process, however, has been continuously growing, questioning this necessity of confidentiality.[47] As Clara Sandoval, Philip Leach and Rachel Murray notes, 'interested (non-state) parties, such as litigants, victims, third party interveners, NHRIs or CSOs cannot assess their tenor or content', suggesting this to be the 'greatest deficiency as regards accessibility' to the supervision process.[48]

In its supervisory role, the CM is assisted by its Secretariat, the Department for Execution of Judgments of the European Court of Human Rights (DEJ) that consists of full time CoE staffers, primarily legal experts based in Strasbourg tasked exclusively with the implementation of ECtHR judgments. The DEJ ensures the smooth running of the CM's supervisory work and maintains the daily operations through regular communication with the national authorities, examination and publication of action plans and reports from the authorities and submissions from other interested actors, such as applicants, non-governmental organisations and national human rights institutions, and coordination and preparation of CM quarterly meetings, including drafting CM decisions. As Çali and Koch suggested, the DEJ is also the 'pivotal guardian against the politicisation of the monitoring of human rights compliance' referring to the political nature of the CM's peer review mechanism.[49] Although the supervision process should primarily be considered a legal one given the judicial nature of ECtHR judgments, the political composition of the CM may serve both ways in this process: it may lend the necessary political weight in cases requiring additional pressure but equally it may create limitations to effective scrutiny of one state by other member states.[50]

46 CM member state representative, SXB03, Strasbourg, 23 May 2017.

47 CSO representative, SXB10, London, 23 November 2016; CSO representative, GEO09, Tbilisi, online interview, 15 November 2016; Human rights lawyer and CSO representative, AZE02, online interview, 27 March 2018 and 13 July 2019; Clara Sandoval, Philip Leach and Rachel Murray, 'Monitoring, Cajoling and Promoting Dialogue: What Role for Supranational Human Rights Bodies in the Implementation of Individual Decisions?' (2020) Volume 12 Issue, Journal of Human Rights Practice.

48 Sandoval, Leach and Murray (n 47) [5.2].

49 Basak Çali, Anne Koch, 'Foxes Guarding the Foxes? The Peer Review of Human Rights Judgments by the Committee of Ministers of the Council of Europe' (2014) Volume 14, Issue 2, Human Rights Law Review 301–325 4.

50 Sandoval, Leach and Murray (n 47) [2.1].

2.3.1 *Scope and Procedure of Committee of Ministers Supervision*

The CM supervises the implementation of ECtHR judgments on merits and decisions on friendly settlements, but not decisions on unilateral declarations.[51] The CM Rules regulating supervision process require respondent member states to report to the CM on both individual and general measures that they are to take to fully implement ECtHR judgments.[52] *Individual measures* are aimed to ensure that the violations are ceased and that victims are fully remedied by ensuring their 'restitutio in integrum'. Such measures could include return of property, re-opening of civil or criminal proceedings, conducting effective investigation or release of an unlawfully detained person. *General measures* seek to prevent similar violations in the future and may include adopting new laws or amending existing ones, changing policies or judicial practice, improving material conditions such as prison conditions or provision of medical care in prisons.

Once a judgment or a decision becomes final (and is transferred to the CM for supervision of its implementation), the respondent Government is under an obligation to provide its action plan within six months setting out what steps it will take or has already taken to fully implement the judgment.[53] The Governments are then expected to continue cooperating with the DEJ by providing regular updates on the progress of the cases and respond to any questions or recommendations from the CM and the DEJ.[54] When a respondent Government considers all the measures taken, it is invited to provide an action report with a request to have a case closed as fully implemented. Implementation of a particular case is closed by the CM with its final resolution adopted at its quarterly meeting. All state action plans and reports, CM decisions and other submissions, such as those from the civil society and NHRIs are available on the HUDOC EXEC database administered by DEJ.

Since January 2011, the CM introduced a twin-track supervision system aimed at improving the efficiency and transparency of the process.[55] It provides

51 Rules of the Committee of Ministers for the supervision of the execution of judgments and of the terms of friendly settlements, adopted on 10 May 2006 at the 964th meeting of the Ministers' Deputies and amended on 18 January 2017 at the 1275th meeting of the Ministers' Deputies.

52 Ibid Rule 6.

53 DEJ Guide for the drafting of action plans and reports for the execution of judgments of the European Court of Human Rights, 16 July 2015.

54 Ibid.

55 Committee of Ministers Information document, Supervision of the execution of judgments and decisions of the European Court of Human Rights: implementation of the Interlaken Action Plan – Modalities for a twin-track supervision system, CM/Inf/DH(2010)37, 6 September 2010.

for classification of cases to be reviewed under either 'enhanced supervision', which concern cases in which the CM plays an active role and needs to give priority and which also entail a more intensive involvement of the DEJ, or 'standard supervision'.[56] It is usually cases under enhanced supervision that appear on the agenda of the CM quarterly Human Rights Meetings. The classification decision is taken at the first presentation of the case to the CM on the basis of advice by the DEJ and the criteria for allocating new cases to the enhanced supervision are the following:

- judgments requiring urgent individual measures;
- pilot judgments;
- judgments raising structural and/or complex problems as identified by the Court or by the CM;
- interstate cases.

All other cases shall be classified under the 'standard supervision' category and their supervision is largely carried out by the DEJ, with the CM's role being limited to 'verifying whether or not action plans or action reports have been presented by member states'.[57]

The type of supervision of a case may be changed by the CM upon request of a member state or the DEJ, and applicants, non-governmental organisations (NGOs) or NHRIs may also request the CM to examine a case under enhanced supervision in their written submissions if they believe the case would benefit from enhanced involvement of the CM and if the respondent state's actions are not sufficient or timely.[58] Similarly, a case under enhanced supervision may be transferred to standard supervision, usually initiated by a request of a member state, when the CM is satisfied with the implementation progress and no major obstacles to the implementation exist.[59]

Further to the supervision procedures, the CM classifies each case as 'leading', 'repetitive' or 'isolated'. The identification of the 'leading' cases is key to the supervision process as these are the cases revealing new and often structural and/or systemic problems that require general measures. Cases adopted by the ECtHR that address the same human rights issues after the leading cases are considered 'repetitive' and usually grouped together with the 'leading' cases for the review of implementation by the CM. 'Isolated' cases are those where

56 Ibid [6].

57 Ibid [12].

58 European Implementation Network Handbook for NGOs, injured parties and their legal advisers, Implementation of Judgments of the European Court of Human Rights, 2018, enriched in January 2020 6.

59 Ibid 6.

violations found appear to be related to specific circumstances of the individual case and do not usually require any general measures.[60]

2.3.2 *Involvement of other Actors in the CM Supervision Process*

Although the supervision process is primarily aimed at examining actions of respondent states by the CM and the DEJ in the form of inter-governmental engagement, a number of other actors can get involved in the process and play a significant role in contributing to the effectiveness of the supervision. Such actors include those directly affected by the cases and their implementation progress, such as injured parties and their legal representatives, as well as NGOs and NHRIs, and most recently, since January 2017, international organisations and other bodies such as the CoE Commissioner for Human Rights, who are entitled to provide their views on the state progress through 'alternative' reports, also known as 'Rule 9' submissions.[61] As the European Implementation Network (EIN), a Strasbourg-based NGO dedicated to supporting civil society's engagement in the implementation process, has put it, without the involvement of these actors, 'the CM faces the risk of hearing only the state's account concerning the implementation of judgments'.[62]

Written submissions under Rule 9 is the most formalized way for applicants, NGOs and other interested actors to contribute to the process. Under Rule 9.1 of the CM Rules, applicants and their legal representatives are entitled to submit communications to the CM with respect to the question of payment of just satisfaction and individual measures that concern their particular situation only. Rule 9.2 of the CM Rules allows interested NGOs and NHRIs to provide their input on the respondent state's actions and usually concern broader content, both relating to individual and general measures.[63] Such submissions may also entail recommendations to the CM and propose actions such as a swift examination of the case, change of the supervision procedure, putting the case on the CM quarterly meeting agenda and a debate on the case, among others. Under Rules 9.3 and 9.4, international organisations and the Commissioner for Human Rights of the CoE respectively can provide similar submissions, with the latter increasingly employing this avenue in the last year, along its so far more known contributions to the Court's examination of cases through third party interventions.[64]

60 Ibid 5.
61 CM Rules (n 51) Rule 9.
62 European Implementation Network Handbook (n 58) 8.
63 Ibid 9.
64 All Rule 9 submissions by the Commissioner for Human Rights are available at https://www.coe.int/en/web/commissioner/rule-9.

Further to formal written submissions, applicants and NGOs have been exploring other avenues to contribute to the supervision process, such as briefings to CM delegates on cases whose implementation is being examined by the CM as its quarterly meetings. Such briefings became regular since the establishment of the EIN, which serves as a bridge between the civil society in Europe and the Strasbourg processes. Although the increase in the involvement of the civil society in the supervision process is certainly observed in the last few years, the vast majority of leading cases pending implementation before the CM still remains unaddressed by the these human rights watchdogs.[65]

Other CoE bodies and mandates, such as the Committee on Legal Affairs and Human Rights of the Parliamentary Assembly of the Council of Europe (PACE) and its Sub-Committee on the Implementation of Judgments of the European Court of Human Rights, and the PACE Rapporteur on implementation of ECtHR judgments all have been increasingly involved with the question of the implementation of ECtHR judgments as the concerns over the poor implementation performance continue growing. The PACE, as the parliamentary body of the CoE, has been putting increasing efforts to promote the role of national parliaments in the domestic implementation process, as representatives of the public and the state institutions well placed to scrutinise the actions of the executive (which is normally in charge of implementation).[66] Such initiatives have been welcomed both with the CoE and the member states as part of the 'shared responsibility' objective aimed to improve the ECtHR implementation record.

It is in light of this existing literature on compliance with ECtHR judgments and the CoE implementation supervision structure that I analyse the behaviour of the three selected member states in the next three chapters.

---

65 Statistical data published by EIN at https://twitter.com/i/web/status/1350037528280109057; Sandoval, Leach and Murray (n 47) [5.2].

66 Alice Donald and Philip Leach, *Parliaments and the European Court of Human Rights* (OUP 2016); PACE Resolution 2178 (2017), The Implementation of judgments of the European Court of Human Rights, 29 June 2017.

CHAPTER 3

Azerbaijan

The New Achilles Heel of the Council of Europe?

This Chapter is dedicated to Azerbaijan's performance as a member state of the Council of Europe (CoE) in complying with European Court of Human Rights (ECtHR) judgments. In order to properly examine and explain Azerbaijan's behavior towards legally binding ECtHR judgments, it is important to first look into the wider political and legal context within which implementation takes place, and reflect on the historical processes that led to Azerbaijan's accession to the CoE, which I do in Section 3.1. Examination of Azerbaijan's compliance with ECtHR judgments in light of the country's accession commitments to CoE and prevailing motivations two decades ago offers a helpful insight into the progress made to date. I then discuss Azerbaijan's compliance with ECtHR judgments by looking into its domestic implementation system, types of human rights issues addressed by the ECtHR, reactions and steps taken by the authorities, and their interaction with the Committee of Ministers (CM), as well as other CoE bodies to that end (see 3.2.). I do so on the basis of the detailed analysis of action plans and reports submitted by Azerbaijan to the CM on individual cases or groups of cases, applicants' and NGOs submissions, and the CM responses to it, as well as the invaluable information received through over a dozen of interviews conducted with staff of various CoE bodies, CM delegates, a former Government official, human rights litigators, civil society representatives and applicants.[1] I finish this Chapter with some insights into processes that offer explanation to Azerbaijan's systemic failure to comply with ECtHR judgments, adequacy of the CM response to the deepening crisis, and finally discuss reasons for Azerbaijan's remaining in the CoE (see 3.2.3, 3.2.4 and 3.2.5).

1 In my professional capacity as a legal consultant with the European Human Rights Advocacy Centre (EHRAC), I acted as a legal representative in the cases of *Rasul Jafarov v Azerbaijan*, Appl. no. 69981/14 (ECtHR 17 March 2016) and *Aliyev v Azerbaijan*, Appl. nos. 68762/14 and 71200/14 (ECtHR 20 September 2018), both discussed in this book.

 | DOI:10.1163/9789004538214_004

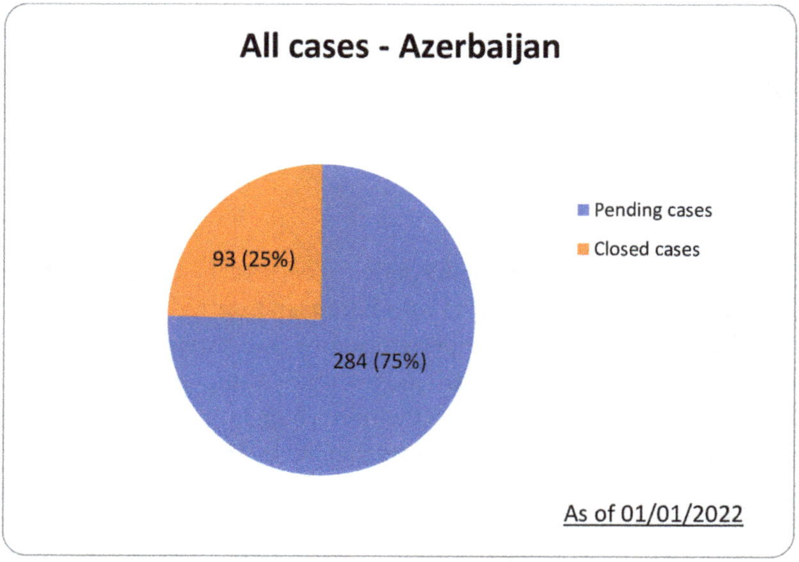

FIGURE 4 All ECtHR cases against Azerbaijan
SOURCE FOR DATA: HUDOC EXEC DATABASE

3.1 Azerbaijan and CoE

Azerbaijan, a country of 10 million lying at the very eastern border of the CoE, stands out for its regressively poor human rights compliance performance in the CoE. Almost two decades into its membership of the CoE 'family' since 2001, Azerbaijan's compliance with ECtHR judgments is the lowest among all 47 member states (Figure 1). As of 1 January 2022 (as my chosen end point of the research), 85% of its all 'leading' cases, i.e. revealing new structural and/or systemic human rights problems that require reforms, are still pending implementation indicating absence of timely and effective compliance with ECtHR judgments (Figure 4).[2]

2 Three closed cases include two friendly settlement cases and a case of failure to enforce a domestic court decision, which the CM described as not disclosing any systematic problems: CM Resolution CM/ResDH(2012)4 on the Execution of the judgment of the European Court of Human Rights in the case of Jafarli and Others against Azerbaijan, adopted on 8 March 2012 at the 1136th Meeting of the Ministers' Deputies; CM Resolution CM/ResDH(2019)70 on the Execution of the judgments of the European Court of Human Rights in the case of Akimova against Azerbaijan, adopted on 4 April 2019 at the 1343rd meeting of the Ministers' Deputies; CM Resolution CM/ResDH(2019)71 on the Execution of the judgment of the European Court of Human Rights in the case of Rahmanova against Azerbaijan, adopted on 4 April 2019 at the 1343rd meeting of the Ministers' Deputies.

Azerbaijan is among 10 member states with the highest number of cases pending implementation under 'enhanced supervision' procedure (1.1).[3] It is also the first and only CoE member state against which the infringement proceedings have been initiated by the CM requesting the ECtHR to assess if Azerbaijan failed to fulfill its obligation to comply with ECtHR judgments under Article 46(1) of the Convention.[4] As a representative of the Department for Execution of Judgments of the European Court of Human Rights (DEJ) has put it: 'it's like the CM sued Azerbaijan to the Court for its failings to comply with the ECtHR judgment when no other tools worked', signifying the political and symbolic importance of this step.[5] It resulted from Azerbaijan's 4-year failure to comply with the repeated CM calls to release the then imprisoned opposition politician and activist Ilgar Mammadov, following the Court's judgment finding that his arrest and pre-trial detention aimed 'to silence or punish the applicant for criticising the Government', in contradiction to the Convention's spirit.[6] On 29 May 2019, siding with the CM position, the ECtHR found that Azerbaijan had failed to comply with the judgment, limiting its ruling to the most urgent issue in the case: the release of applicant Mr Mammadov.[7] During the same years, in 2015–2020, the Court has also found Azerbaijan, unprecedentedly, failing to act in 'good faith' in nine more judgments relating to 13 individuals – human rights defenders, journalists, youth and political activists – finding a violation of Article 18 of the Convention, making Azerbaijan the absolute leader in such cases.[8] The ECtHR found that their arrest and detention

3 Supervision of the Execution of Judgments and Decisions of the European Court of Human Rights, 11th Annual Report of the Committee of Ministers (2017) 75; Supervision of the Execution of Judgments and Decisions of the European Court of Human Rights, 12th Annual Report of the Committee of Ministers (2018) 71, 89.

4 Interim Resolution of the Committee of Ministers on the execution of the judgment of the European Court of Human Rights in the case of *Ilgar Mammadov v Azerbaijan*, CM/ResDH(2017)429, 5 December 2017; Lize R. Glas, 'The Committee of Ministers goes nuclear: infringement proceedings against Azerbaijan in the case of Ilgar Mammadov' (The Strasbourg Observers, 20 December 2017), accessed 10 December 2019; Lucy Moxham, 'Implementation of ECHR judgments – have we reached a crisis point?' (UK Human Rights Blog, 7 July 2017), accessed 8 July 2019; Ramute Remezaite, 'Azerbaijan: Is it Time to Invoke Infringement Proceedings for Failing to Implement Judgments of the Strasbourg Court?' (EJIL:Talk! Blog of the European Journal of the International Law, 22 March 2017), accessed 8 July 2019.

5 DEJ official, SXB04, Strasbourg, 30 November 2016.

6 *Ilgar Mammadov v Azerbaijan*, appl. no. 15172/13 (ECtHR 22 May 2014).

7 *Ilgar Mammadov v Azerbaijan*, Appl. no. 15172/13 (ECtHR 29 May 2019).

8 *Rasul Jafarov v Azerbaijan*, Appl. no. 69981/14 (ECtHR 17 March 2016); *Anar Mammadli v Azerbaijan*, Appl. no. 47145/14 (ECtHR 19 April 2018); *Rashad Hasanov and Others v Azerbaijan*, Appl. nos. 48653/13 (ECtHR 7 June 2018); *Aliyev v Azerbaijan*, Appl. nos. 68762/

was for purposes other than those permitted by the Convention, aimed at preventing them from continuing their human rights work, journalistic activities and activism. These cases and the Court's findings are among the latest and perhaps most evident indications of the deepening crisis in Azerbaijan's failure to abide by its CoE commitments, and the growing institutional and political unease in Strasbourg, which I discuss at 3.2.3 below.

More generally, Azerbaijan's relationship with the CoE has become increasingly ambivalent, in the context of the growing authoritarian tendencies in Baku in the last few years. The Government's public position on the relations with the CoE appears to be equivocal: messages referring to Azerbaijan's willingness to cooperate with the CoE are often delivered in various CoE platforms, whereas the domestic public is largely conveyed contrasting messages, in Azerbaijani language, on the alleged 'anti-Azerbaijani' CoE stance, particularly following the CoE criticism on the country's poor human rights record. For example, in his speech at the Parliamentary Assembly of the Council of Europe (PACE) in June 2014, when Azerbaijan assumed its six-month Chairmanship of the CM, President Aliyev reiterated that '[m]embership of the Council of Europe was a conscious choice in 2001, and Azerbaijan is ready and willing to implement its commitments and obligations'.[9] At the end of the Chairmanship, Azerbaijan's Foreign Minister Elmar Mammadyarov reminded all PACE members of the importance of cooperation 'to help all our countries along the path to democracy and human rights'.[10] Around the same time, on 28 August 2014, in his speech to the youth in one of the regions of Azerbaijan, the President, referring to human rights defenders who actively advocate on the issue of political prisoners and other serious human rights issues in Azerbaijan in various international platforms (PACE in particular), warned that 'there are national traitors, who have sold their conscience to foreign anti-Azerbaijani circles, who try to break stability in Azerbaijan'.[11] In his article published on

14 and 71200/14 (ECtHR 20 September 2018); *Natig Jafarov v Azerbaijan*, Appl. no. 64581/16 (ECtHR 7 November 2019), *Ibrahimov and Mammadov v Azerbaijan*, Appl. No. 63571/16 (ECtHR 13 February 2020); *Khadija Ismayilova v Azerbaijan* (*No.2*), Appl. no. 30778/15 (ECtHR 27 February 2020); *Yunusova and Yunusov v Azerbaijan* (No. 2), Appl. No. 68817/14 (ECtHR 16 July 2020).

9 Speech of President Aliyev delivered in PACE ahead of Azerbaijan's Chairmanship on 24 June 2014, accessed 10 September 2017.

10 Speech of Azerbaijan's Foreign Minister Elmar Mammadyarov in PACE after the Chairmanship on 4 October 2014, accessed 10 September 2017.

11 'Ilham Aliyev: There are national traitors in country' (unofficial translation), 28 August 2018 available at http://www.azadliq.org/content/article/26557710.html, in English http://www.contact.az/docs/2014/Politics/083000088809en.htm#.VCNfkCuSy-V.

n 29 October 2015, the then Head of the Presidential Administration, Ramiz Mehtiyev, known as the second most influential state official after the President in the country, referred to the European institutions as using 'human rights as a method of political pressure on the sovereign state' and that the CoE and the ECtHR take part in the 'anti-Azerbaijani campaign'.[12] On 14 September 2015, during the parliamentary debate on the resolution of the European Parliament on Azerbaijan of 10 September 2015, critical of the human rights situation, several ruling party members suggested that Azerbaijan did not need to be a part of the European Union or the Council of Europe and that Azerbaijan entered into dialogue with them because it did not want to stay isolated.[13]

Such increasingly ambivalent public discourse of the authorities towards the CoE (and other European institutions), taken in combination with the deepening authoritarian policies towards its critics, is indicative of a much more complex story. Almost two decades into the CoE membership, Azerbaijan's political elite appears to be declaring its adherence to international obligations so long as it does not contradict its domestic politics, differently from its promises upon accession to the CoE (see 3.2.3 and 3.2.4). Throughout the years the country's leadership, geared by the country's President of 18 years and the ruling New Azerbaijan party that he chairs, developed an increasingly aggressive official anti-Western rhetoric, reminiscent of the Soviet era, which particularly intensified around the crackdown on civil society starting in 2013–2014. It officially denounced any criticism towards its wrongdoings and authoritarian policies as lie and bias, and aimed at slandering Azerbaijan picturing human rights defenders and other domestic critics as traitors and agents of the West.[14] As the ECtHR has now joined forces in exposing, through legally

12 Ramiz Mehdiyev, 'We can only be equal in our relations' 29 October 2015 (unofficial translation), available at https://www.amerikaninsesi.org/a/ramiz_mehdiyev/3027854.html.

13 Protocol of the parliamentary debate on adoption of resolution of the European Parliament on Azerbaijan of 10 September 2015, critical of the human rights situation, held on 14 September 2015 where several ruling party members stated Azerbaijan did not need to be a part of the European Union or the Council of Europe and that Azerbaijan entered into dialogue with them merely because it did not want to stay isolated when it achieved its independence, http://www.meclis.gov.az/?/az/stenoqram/387 accessed 23 September 2019 Information about parliamentary initiatives to follow the Russian example, in March 2016 and in January 2018, is available here https://basta2.com/az/2018/01/11/avropa-m%C9%99hk%C9%99m%C9%99sinin-q%C9%99rarlarinin-az%C9%99rbaycanda-icrasi-dayandirilacaq/.

14 George Mchedlishvili, 'Changing Perceptions of the West in the South Caucasus: Adoration No More' (Chatman House February 2016), accessed 29 July 2019 8; Therese Svensson and Julia Hon, 'Attitudes Toward the West in the South Caucasus' (Caucasus Analytical Digest, 15 February 2010) 14; Thomas de Waal, 'Azerbaijan Doesn't Want to be Western' (Foreign Affairs magazine, 26 September 2014); Richard D. Kauzlarich (former US ambassador to

binding judgments, some of the Government's ulterior purposes in limiting rights of its critics, it raises interesting but difficult questions as to the future relations of Azerbaijan with the ECtHR and the CoE.

3.1.1 *Azerbaijan's Accession to the CoE*

Azerbaijan's beginning with the CoE was rather promising. It joined the CoE in 2001 as one of the newly emerging countries with strong aspirations for democratisation, following the collapse of the Soviet Union.[15] It chose democratisation as the way forward from its years of Soviet occupation, with weak state structures and separation of power, further marked by heavy consequences of the ethnic and territorial conflict with Armenia over the Nagorno Karabakh region in 1988–1994. Azerbaijan's leadership at the time saw the CoE and the support from the West as a way to further strengthen its restored independence and statehood, and to find a peaceful solution to the conflict.[16] As the President Heydar Aliyev, father of the current President, stated in 2000:

> As an integral part of Europe, Azerbaijan shares European values and principles of pluralistic democracy, respect for human rights and basic freedoms, and supremacy of law. Azerbaijan considers these values as a major goal in its future development.
>
> We are confident that Azerbaijan's full membership of the Council of Europe will contribute to the process of democratisation in our country and will strengthen its positions to integrate Europe.
>
> I would like to assure you that Azerbaijan's accession to the Council of Europe will positively contribute to the negotiation process and to the establishment of stability in the region and it will promote political and economic progress in the South Caucasus as well as intensification of regional co-operation.[17]

Azerbaijan), 'The Heydar Aliyev Era Ends in Azerbaijan not with a Bang but a Whisper' (Brookings, 13 January 2015), accessed 15 July 2020; *Rasul Jafarov v Azerbaijan* (n 8) section D.

15 PACE report 'Azerbaijan's application for membership of the Council of Europe', Doc. 8748, prepared by the Political Affairs Committee and its rapporteur Mr Jacques Baumel (France, European Democratic Group), Appendix 7, 23 May 2000.

16 Former Government representative to CoE, AZE01, online interview, 14 August 2019.

17 Letter of the President of Azerbaijan to Lord Russell-Johnston, President of the Parliamentary Assembly of the Council of Europe, 25 March 2000, Appendix 7 of the PACE report 'Azerbaijan's application for membership of the Council of Europe', Doc. 8748, prepared by the Political Affairs Committee and its rapporteur Mr Jacques Baumel (France, European Democratic Group), Appendix 4, Address of President Heydar Aliyev, 23 May 2000.

As one interviewee, a former Azerbaijani diplomat to the CoE, put it in his balder explanation: 'we wanted to be a part of the European family and equally, we did not want to stay behind Georgia or particularly Armenia, with which we were at war, despite the very serious issues we had, which they did not have, such as the issue of political prisoners'.[18]

Azerbaijan's accession process was marked by its eagerly expressed commitments to all the conditions set by the CoE, including undergoing all the necessary reforms to ensure its compatibility with the Convention standards.[19] Although Azerbaijan's domestic political and legal framework, greatly influenced by the Soviet legacy, needed to be significantly reformed to meet the CoE standards, the CoE recognised the country's 'considerable progress towards the building of a democratic state in keeping with CoE's principles' and that it had 'substantially demonstrated its commitment to democracy and respect for human rights'.[20] Its weak separation of powers and lack of political pluralism, high levels of corruption, and the issue of political prisoners led to calls for substantial systemic changes to the system, to turn it into a democratic one, which, in turn, required significant political and capacity resources. The PACE considered that the country 'would progress more rapidly along the path of democratic reform as a full member of the Council of Europe' and that the membership would help to establish 'a climate of confidence in the region, thus contributing to a peaceful solution of the Nagorno-Karabakh conflict'.[21] The CoE, as it did with regard to other emerging states, endorsed its open door policy as a part of its strategy to spread the European values to the east and invited Azerbaijan to become a member of the Organisation ahead of the completion of all the necessary reforms.[22] [23] While recognising the existence of deeply rooted problems such as corruption and executive's influence on the judiciary, and the need to address the issue of political prisoners, which the CoE identified as particularly problematic during the negotiations, PACE concluded in 2000 that 'Azerbaijan has made considerable progress towards the

---

18 Interview (n 16).

19 PACE report on Azerbaijan's application (n 15).

20 Ibid [106].

21 Ibid [110].

22 Dean Spielmann, President of the European Court of Human Rights (2012–2015), 'Foreword', in Iulia Motoc and Ineta Ziemele (eds.), *The Impact of the ECHR in Democratic Change in Central and Eastern Europe* (CUP 2016), xxv); W. Sadurski, 'Partnering with Strasbourg: Constitutionalisation of the European Court of Human Rights, the Accession of Central and East European States to the Council of Europe, and the Idea of Pilot Judgments' (2009) Human Rights Law Review 397.

23 Former PACE Secretariat member, SXB08, Strasbourg, 2 December 2016.

building of a democratic state in keeping with Council of Europe principles' and that 'enormous changes' have been made, such as the abolition of death penalty and the strengthening of the judiciary.[24] The more tangible changes at the time, however, were limited to ensuring the necessary normative framework: through ratification of key CoE Conventions such as the ECHR and its Protocols, the European Convention for the Prevention of Torture and Inhuman or Degrading Treatment or Punishment and its protocols and the Framework Convention for the Protection of National Minorities, which became the integral part of the national legal system, as well as the adoption of national laws in line with these Conventions. Although these are undoubtedly significant steps, their adequate implementation in practice is the key indicator of genuine progress. Nevertheless, the PACE was satisfied to take the remaining commitments to solving some deep fundamental problems as promises to be delivered after Azerbaijan's accession: efforts to settle the conflict with Armenia by peaceful means only; to continue reforms aimed at strengthening separation of power, to solve the issue of political prisoners or fighting impunity of law enforcement agents.[25] As the former CoE senior official who has worked on the accession process of the new states post Cold War put it, 'legally speaking, the acceptance of Azerbaijan and other states may have been premature and not yet appropriate at the time, however, politically, these states acted as they were expected to act to join the club'.[26] All these deeply embedded issues, as the cases discussed in this Chapter show, remain all the more prevailing today, almost two decades after the accession. As the same official described it: 'You accept them but it may take a generation to put it right'.[27]

Independent Azerbaijan's leadership has since struggled to uphold its declarations, particularly with regard to adhering to free elections, one of the most fundamental features of democracy, with the country's political power held under tight grip of the Aliyev family for over two decades. Except for the first year of independence, the country's leadership was in the hands of Abulfaz Elchibey, elected in generally fair and free elections in 1992, who was however soon ousted from power through a military coup. The country's power was seized by Heydar Aliyev, the former leader of the Azerbaijan Communist Party and the leader of the KGB branch in Azerbaijan in 1993, who reportedly received 99 percent of votes in elections widely marred by election fraud.[28]

24 PACE report on Azerbaijan's application (n 15) [106–107].
25 Ibid [13].
26 Former PACE Secretariat member, SXB08, Strasbourg, 2 December 2016.
27 Ibid.
28 Freedom House, Freedom in the World 2001, Azerbaijan, accessed 20 July 2020.

A new 1995 Constitution has further cemented a strong presidential system, setting a legal and institutional framework for President's institute, as the head of the executive power, with only nominal independence of the judiciary or the legislative power. Aliyev's re-election in 1998, which featured serious irregularities in vote-counting, and the election of his son Ilham Aliyev, the incumbent president, in 2003, has allowed the Aliyev family to maintain their authoritarian rule in the country. Azerbaijan's first post-Soviet parliamentary elections in 1995, described as not free and unfair by independent observers, secured a majority of seats for the Yeni Azerbaijan Party, which has remained the ruling party since then, chaired by Ilham Aliyev to date.[29] All parliamentary elections ahead of the CoE accession in 2001, including those held in 2000, have seen the opposition candidates being barred from running in the elections, the stuffing of ballot boxes and other instances of election fraud, cited by international observers.[30] This led to the long-term ruling of the Aliyevs with strong presidential powers and little if any effective political leverage of the opposition in the national parliament Milli Majlis. Although Azerbaijan initially seemed to embrace the CoE assistance in reforming its electoral regulation through a referendum on the amendments to the Constitution in 2002, it did not lead to 'freer and fairer electoral system' and no free and fair elections have been held to date, according to international and domestic observers.[31] Almost two decades later, at least 23 ECtHR judgments, known as *Namat Aliyev* group of cases, addressing the systemic issues hindering free and fair parliamentary elections, such as arbitrariness of actions of electoral commissions and domestic courts, including the Constitutional Court, in Azerbaijan are pending implementation since 2010.[32] In its December 2019, the CM, referring to 'the complexity of issues raised' and the 'fundamental nature of the rights at issue', called upon the Government 'rapidly to enhance the ongoing bilateral

---

29 Freedom House, Freedom in the World 2002, Azerbaijan, accessed 20 July 2020.

30 Ibid.

31 Freedom House, Nations in Transit 2002, Azerbaijan, accessed 20 July 2020 OSCE/ODIHR Election Observation Mission Final Report of 11 February 2006 on parliamentary election held on 6 November 2005, accessed 20 July 2020; OSCE/ODIHR Election Observation Mission Final Report of 25 January 2011 on early parliamentary election held on 7 November 2010, accessed 20 July 2020; OSCE/ODIHR Election Observation Mission Final Report of 18 July 2018 on early parliamentary election held on 11 April 2018, accessed 20 July 2020.

32 *Namat Aliyev v Azerbaijan*, Appl. No. 18705/06, (ECtHR 8 July 2010) and 22 repetitive cases, available on HUDOC EXEC, accessed 14 November 2019.

contacts' with Strasbourg, which is suggestive of absence of substantive progress in this field to date.[33]

The Aliyevs also led Azerbaijan's accession process to the CoE. While the father, Heydar Aliyev, was the lead negotiator in Azerbaijan's accession process with the CoE, his son, the incumbent President, served as the chairman of the first Azerbaijani delegation to the PACE until his election as President in 2003. This may be explained by their eagerness to ensure that ruling power's interests abroad were in line with their domestic policies, and were defended adequately, but may also signify the importance and prioritisation of Azerbaijan's successful accession to the CoE for the ruling elite.[34]

Gradual evaporation of Baku's declared enthusiasm for the CoE instigated reforms is also marked by other fundamental issues identified by the CoE upon accession, such as the question of political prisoners, executive's influence over judiciary or corruption. These issues remain prevalent today, and are being continuously addressed by various CoE bodies. For example, during the Chairmanship of the CM in 2014, President Aliyev reiterated their readiness to implement CoE commitments just one month before the unprecedented civil society crackdown, which led to imprisonment of key human rights defenders and de facto closure of leading human rights organisations in Baku.[35] During the same speech, the President announced reforms aimed at modernising the country with a particular focus on fighting corruption in Azerbaijan, ranked among the lowest in the global Corruption Perception Index of Transparency International (152 out of 180).[36] This came at the time when the 'caviar diplomacy' scandal in Strasbourg concerning allegations of corruption and bribing by the Azerbaijani officials in PACE to secure favourable votes turned into the first ever CoE investigation into corruption allegations within PACE in 2018.[37] In its 219-page report, the Independent Investigation Body established by PACE concluded that it found strong grounds to believe that a number of PACE members had engaged in activities of corruptive nature, some of which were aimed at securing politically favorable decisions on highly sensitive issues to

33 CM decision on the *Namat Aliyev* group of cases (Appl. No. 18705/06), adopted during its 1362th DH meeting on 3–5 December 2019.

34 Freedom House, Nations in Transit 2003, Azerbaijan, accessed 20 July 2020; Former PACE Secretariat member, SXB08, Strasbourg, 2 December 2016; Human rights lawyer and CSO representative, AZE02, online interview, 27 March 2018.

35 Speech of President Aliyev (n 11).

36 Transparency International, Anti-Corruption Helpdesk, 'Azerbaijan: Overview of Corruption and Anti-corruption' 2017, accessed 20 July 2020 3.

37 European Stability Initiative, Caviar Diplomacy. 'How Azerbaijan silenced the Council of Europe', Part 1, accessed 20 July 2020.

Azerbaijan, such as the issue of political prisoners.[38] [39] Such unprecedented findings are a clear indication of Azerbaijan's contempt of the organization, yet still aiming to appear as a CoE values respecting state in the CoE eyes.

Another recent example is the ECtHR's 'Article 18' judgments, which did not only offer, for the first time in the history of Azerbaijan-CoE saga of political prisoners, judicial scrutiny of this issue, but also reinforced PACE's political efforts to address this issue. Following the failure of her predecessor Mr Christoph Strasser (German MP), the then PACE rapporteur on political prisoners in Azerbaijan, to have the PACE vote in favour of the resolution on political prisoners in Azerbaijan in 2013, as a result of Azerbaijan's successful 'caviar diplomacy', allowing the defeat of the PACE voting, the newly appointed rapporteur Ms Thorhildur Sunna Ævarsdottir (Icelandic MP) in 2019 brought this issue back to the PACE for a debate.[40] She relied entirely on ECtHR findings of Article 18 violations to reinforce her position on the existence of political prisoners and de-politicise the process that her predecessor struggled to achieve:[41]

> In this report, I do not present my own list of presumed political prisoners. I have chosen this approach because I have one great advantage over my predecessors as rapporteur: I can rely on the authoritative, binding judgments of the European Court of Human Rights to establish the facts of the situation – which, as I have already observed, can leave no doubt that the phenomenon of political prisoners in Azerbaijan is real.

Against such deeply compromised context, it is inevitable to question the PACE decision of 2001 to invite Azerbaijan to join the CoE in light of all the existing systemic issues it was aware of. Although it may be safe to conclude, today, that Azerbaijan was not ready to commit to the CoE standards at the time, and

38 Report of the Independent Investigation Body into allegations of corruption within the Parliamentary Assembly, 15 April 2018, Council of Europe, accessed 20 July 2020, 144, 147.

39 PACE report on Azerbaijan's application (n 119), para 13(iv)(b); European Stability Initiative, 'Showdown in Strasbourg the Political Prisoner Debate in October 2012', February 2013, accessed 20 July 2020; PACE draft Resolution No 13011 'The definition of political prisoner', proposed by rapporteur Mr Christoph Strasser, Committee on Legal Affairs and Human Rights, 5 September 2012, accessed 20 July 2020.

40 'PACE votes to reject draft resolution on political prisoners in Azerbaijan', PACE News, 23 January 2013, accessed 20 July 2020; European Stability Initiative, The European Swamp (Caviar Diplomacy Part 2) – Prosecutors, corruption and the Council of Europe, 17 December 2016, accessed 20 July 2020.

41 PACE Committee on Legal Affairs and Human Rights, Reported cases of political prisoners in Azerbaijan Report, Rapporteur Ms Thorhildur Sunna ÆVARSDÓTTIR, Iceland, Socialists, Democrats and Greens Group, adopted on 10 December 2019.

that the invitation was likely too advance, the PACE decision can be justified in light of the overall pro-democratic atmosphere at the time and Azerbaijan's strongly worded promises to deliver indicating its willingness and good faith to become a part of the 'European family' it aspired to become. As, two decades later, Azerbaijan's ruling power appears to be engaging with the CoE in its own terms, demonstrating no substantive tangible changes to the long identified issues on the ground, the CoE is once again faced with the same question regarding Azerbaijan, as a full member state this time: is Azerbaijan willing and able to comply with CoE standards? To answer this question, it is important to examine Azerbaijan's compliance with ECtHR judgments as one of the core CoE mechanisms established to assist the member states in embedding CoE standards and principles in their domestic systems. As the former Judge from Azerbaijan in the ECtHR, Khanlar Hajiyev, wrote in 2016, the protection of human rights will depend on 'how successfully the case law of the European Court will be integrated into legal and judicial culture in Azerbaijan'.[42] The below sections offer closer insights into this issue.

3.2 Azerbaijan's Compliance with ECtHR Judgments

In this Section, I analyse Azerbaijan's compliance with its ECtHR judgments and discuss factors aimed to offer explanation to its behavior. As the implementation always takes place in the country's domestic legal, political and social context, I examine both the institutional framework for implementation and the individual cases related context. I begin by offering some insights into the domestic implementation system and its effectiveness in facilitating implementation as the platform aimed to enable this process (see 3.2.2). In Section 3.2.3, I analyse compliance with individual ECtHR judgments, or groups of judgments by reviewing action plans and reports as official accounts of its progress in complying with the judgments. I assess such information against the submissions by applicants and the civil society, also known as 'alternative reports', and the CM responses to it in particular cases. Finally, I position the acclaimed progress of these cases against the wider situation relating to a particular human rights issue identified by the Court in the country (see 3.2.3.2).

My analysis predominantly focuses on leading cases, including those already closed by the CM as 'complied with', but also repetitive cases when they

42 Khanlar Hajiyev, 'Azerbaijan' in I. Motoc & I. Ziemele (Eds.), *The Impact of the ECHR on Democratic Change in Central and Eastern Europe: Judicial Perspectives* (CUP 2016) 79.

concern important individual measures or when the respective ECtHR judgments include other significant findings (see 1.3). I discuss Azerbaijan's compliance with ECtHR judgments both in terms of its substantive progress on the national level, as well as the procedural aspect relating to Azerbaijan's engagement with the Strasbourg supervision processes. This in-depth analysis allows for some useful insights into the 'internal' compliance processes, beyond the official statistics, that offer possible explanations to Azerbaijan's behaviour.

3.2.1 *Azerbaijan and the Court*

Since the Convention entered into force for Azerbaijan on 15 April 2002, the ECtHR delivered more than 250 judgments against Azerbaijan, with the first judgment adopted in February 2007.[43] In 96% of the judgments, the ECtHR found at least one violation of the Convention varying from fundamental rights such as the right to life and prohibition of torture to freedom of association and assembly to a right to free elections to a right to fair trial (Figure 5).[44] Since 2018, Azerbaijan was among ten member states against which almost 85% of all pending cases had been brought to the ECtHR, totaling approx. 3% applications pending before the Court each year.[45] The number of cases brought to the ECtHR against Azerbaijan has been consistently growing since its accession to the CoE, suggesting the ECtHR's growing popularity and significance in the country.[46] Although there appear to be no public opinion polls on the perceptions of the CoE and the ECtHR specifically, the latter is highly regarded among the interviewed civil society groups litigating cases before the ECtHR and victims of human rights violations, often referred to by them as the 'only independent effective judicial mechanism' to seek for redress for human rights abuses.[47] They suggested that the ECtHR's public profile particularly grew in the recent years, since 2014, during the crackdown on the civil society, religious activists, political opposition and independent lawyers who saw the ECtHR as the recourse for justice as the national judiciary failed to effectively address the authorities' use of the domestic criminal justice system against

43 ECtHR Overview 1959–2021, European Court of Human Rights, 8.

44 Ibid.

45 ECHR Analysis of Statistics 2018, published in January 2019, accessed 20 July 2020 8; ECHR Analysis of Statistics 2021, published in January 2022, accessed 1 September 2021, 8.

46 Compare 2100 applications in 2021 and 2050 applications in 2018 to 1256 in 2010, and 43 in 2001, see ECtHR annual reports of 2021, 2018, 2010 and 2001.

47 Human rights lawyer and CSO representative, AZE02, online interview, 27 March 2018 and 13 July 2019; Human rights lawyer, AZE03, Tbilisi, 11 March 2018; Applicant and CSO representative, AZE06, Brussels, 12 December 2018; Applicant, AZE07, online interview, 17 September 2019.

the critics and to offer any effective redress.[48] Differently from the CoE political bodies, whose response to the crackdown amidst Azerbaijan's chairmanship of the Committee of Ministers in 2014 has disappointed and disillusioned some of the interviewed domestic human rights groups, the ECtHR appears to maintain its high authority among those groups as the institution able to offer independent and authoritative legal assessment of Azerbaijan's actions in light of its international human rights obligations and offer remedies, even if limited, to the victims. As one of the interviewed human rights lawyers from Azerbaijan described it:

> The European Court was the only mechanism that allowed us to establish the fact of persecution of the civil society – and the existence of political prisoners more generally – and to refute the Government's official narrative to picture its critics as criminals, and the continuing denial of existence of political prisoners in the country.[49]

Strong positive perception of the ECtHR as an authoritative judicial body offering effective legal recourse to establishment of truth, as part of justice, for victims of human rights violations was often named by interviewees as one significant factor justifying Azerbaijan's remaining in the CoE in the growing debates in Strasbourg, among academia and the civil society on the country's crossing of the CoE's red line in the context of its emerging authoritarian tendencies in the recent years (discussed further at 3.2.5).[50]

Statistically, Azerbaijan stands out for its lowest record, in percentage terms, among all CoE member states of 'closed' cases as the measurement of full compliance by the CM (Figure 1). As of 1 January 2022, over 370 cases against Azerbaijan had been transferred to the CM for supervision, of which over 280 were pending implementation and only over 20% of cases have been closed since the first judgment against Azerbaijan was adopted in February 2007 (Figure 4). The 2018–2021 has seen an increase of closed cases from 3% to 23% due to the CM's newly introduced 'partial closure' procedure allowing it

48 Ibid.

49 Human rights lawyer and CSO representative, AZE02, online interview, 13 July 2019.

50 Former Government representative to CoE, AZE01, online interview, 14 August 2019; Human rights lawyer and CSO representative, AZE02, online interview, 27 March 2018; Applicant and CSO representative, AZE06, Brussels, 12 December 2018; Representative of Office of the CoE Commissioner for Human Rights, SXB09, Strasbourg, 4 April 2019; CM member state representative, SXB02, Strasbourg, 23 May 2017 CM member state representative, SXB03, Strasbourg, 23 May 2017.

FIGURE 5 Violations found in cases v Azerbaijan
SOURCE FOR DATA: HUDOC DATABASE, AS OF 1 JANUARY 2022

to close cases where individual measures, such as payment of compensation, have been taken – with general measures remaining pending.[51] The number of Azerbaijani cases pending implementation for more than five years has been steadily growing in the last years, with a sharp 50% increase in 2018, totaling to 74% of all cases pending full implementation.[52] I argue however that the best indicator of tangible progress in compliance lies in the statistics on leading cases as they reveal key systemic and/or structural issues requiring substantive reforms in the domestic system (Figure 6). If leading cases are not closed, this suggests that underlying human rights problems behind identified violations

51 Supervision of the Execution of Judgments and Decisions of the European Court of Human Rights, 12th Annual Report of the Committee of Ministers (2018) 64; HUDOC EXEC database 'closed cases' against Azerbaijan as of 3 January 2018, accessed 3 January 2018; George Stafford, 'The Implementation of Judgments of the European Court of Human Rights: Worse Than You Think – Part 1: Grade Inflation' (EJIL:Talk! 7 October 2019), accessed 10 December 2019.

52 CM Annual Report 2018 (n 3) 72 (40 out of 54 cases were pending implementation for more than five years).

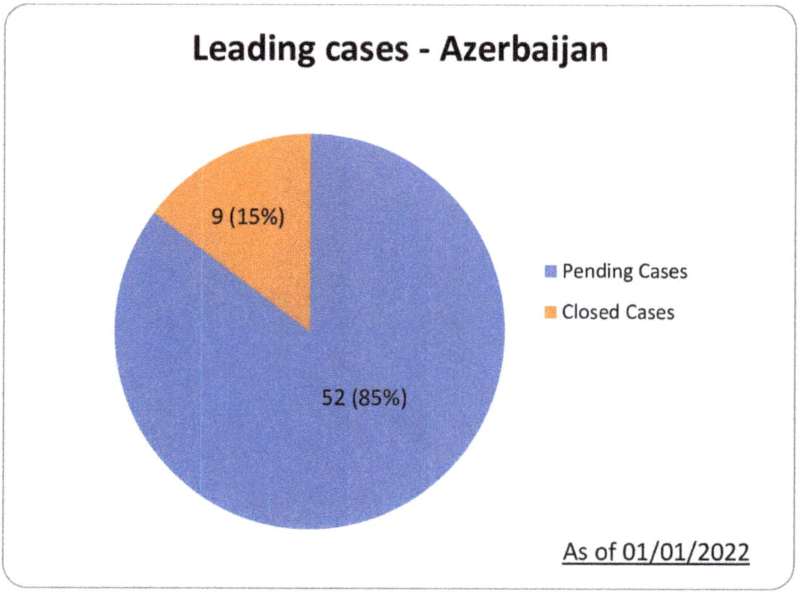

FIGURE 6 Leading cases v Azerbaijan
SOURCE FOR DATA: HUDOC EXEC DATABASE

are not dealt with by the respondent state: 85% of Azerbaijan's leading cases remain pending as of 1 January 2022, with nearly 60% of such cases awaiting implementation for more than 10 years (Figure 6).[53] Azerbaijan's leading cases concern fundamental issues such as unlawful actions of the security forces and ineffective investigations into death and physical use of force, including in custody the lawfulness of detention on remand, protection against abuse of power and arbitrary application of criminal laws, the fairness of judicial proceedings, freedom of expression, freedom of assembly and association, protection of property rights, including in the conflict context and electoral rights.[54]

53 HUDOC EXEC database, accessed 1 January 2022.

54 Country factsheet on Azerbaijan prepared by the Department for the Execution of Judgments of the European Court of Human Rights, accessed 1 January 2022 In addition to th five groups of cases, *Mikayil Mammadov, Muradova and Mammadov* (*Jalaloglu*) group of cases, *Ilgar Mammadov* group of cases, *Mahmudov and Agazade* group of cases, *Ramazanova* group of cases, and Sargsyan case, examined in detail, there are also cases raising issues of the fairness of judicial proceedings, such as the *Huseyn and Others* group (Appl. no. 35485/05, 26 October 2011) and the *Insanov* case (Appl. no. 16133/08, 14 June 2013); freedom of assembly in the *Gafgaz Mammadov* group of cases (Appl. no. 60259/11 14 March 2016), protection of property rights in the *Mirzayev* group of cases (Appl. No.

40% of the leading cases against Azerbaijan are deemed by the CM to require 'enhanced supervision', in effect meaning closer and more frequent supervision of the Government's actions by the CM and DEJ.[55] To put it in a broader ECtHR statistical perspective, of the approximately 1,300 leading cases pending implementation in January 2022, some 300 (around 28% of all pending leading cases) were subject to enhanced supervision.[56]

Both the respective staggering statistical numbers and the level of diversity of significant systemic human rights issues in the domestic system revealed by ECtHR judgments no doubt signify a deeply problematic picture of compliance for Azerbaijan. It does not only serve as a clear indication of the authorities' systemic failure to comply with ECtHR judgments (and its unconditional legal obligation to do so) but also fundamentally questions the country's ability and willingness to abide by these commitments. In the proceeding sections I further examine this issue.

3.2.2 *Domestic Implementation System: One Man's Land*

As implementation takes place at home, in the domestic systems, setting up domestic mechanisms or procedures has been recognised as an important step for the timely and effective implementation of ECtHR judgments, as a means of institutionalizing and enhancing domestic efforts to that end.[57] This approach is well reflected in the managerial theory of compliance, which focuses on the capacity of the authorities to effectively comply with ECtHR judgments, along existence of political will.[58] I suggest that the existence of domestic structures is particularly relevant in domestic contexts like Azerbaijan where there is no strong political culture of receptiveness of human rights obligations and international human rights institutions, and state organisation is reliant on one leading political power. Such structures would allow for better institutionalization of implementation processes and would potentially contribute to the depolitisation of ECtHR cases and their implementation, which often challenge domestic political interests of the ruling power.

50187/06 3 March 2010) and electoral rights in the *Namat Aliyev* group of cases (Appl. No. 18705/06 8 July 2010).

55 HUDOC EXEC database, last accessed 1 January 2022.

56 Ibid.

57 Brussels Declaration on the 'Implementation of the European Convention on Human Rights, our shared responsibility' (Committee of Ministers, 27 March 2015); Rachel Murray and Christian De Vos, 'Behind the State: Domestic Mechanisms and Procedures for the Implementation of Human Rights Judgments and Decisions' (2020), Volume 12 Issue 1, Journal of Human Rights Practice, 1–26.

58 Open Society Justice Initiative, *From Rights to Remedies. Structures and Strategies for Implementing International Human Rights Decisions* (2013) 15.

In Azerbaijan, the Office of the Government Agent (OGA) to the ECtHR is tasked to 'coordinate' the implementation work on the domestic level, along its role of representing the Government in proceedings before the ECtHR.[59] The Presidential Decree establishing this role does not set out any further regulations on this role or how the coordination process would be organised. Only other reference to the process of implementation of ECtHR judgments was made in the 2011 National Human Rights Program, approved by the President, stipulating which national institutions shall be involved in the implementation of this particular commitment, in general terms, without specifying their mandates: 'Cabinet of Ministers of the Republic of Azerbaijan, Administration of the President of the Republic of Azerbaijan, Milli Mejlis of the Republic of Azerbaijan, Ministries of Justice and Foreign Affairs of the Republic of Azerbaijan, Scientific Research Institute for Human Rights of the Azerbaijan National Academy of Sciences'.[60] It further stated that the Government Agent *may* establish working groups and invite relevant experts, which essentially grants the Agent's Office a unique hierarchical institutional standing over the implementation process. Against this limited normative regulation, my below findings into the domestic implementation system of Azerbaijan are informed by the interviews and documentary research.

3.2.2.1 Dual Role of the Agent's Office

OGA's dual role of, firstly, representing the Government's interests during the Court proceedings and, secondly, coordinating the implementation process of the Court's judgments against Azerbaijan raises some questions in light of the exclusive prerogative of the OGA to initiate the implementation process without any formal procedures in place. Such dual role designated to OGAs is common among many national systems of the CoE member states and its effectiveness highly depends on the level of political standing of the Agent and resources allocated to perform these functions.[61] Its standing will determine how much influence it will have over responsible domestic institutions within whose competence issues identified in ECtHR judgments fall in order to ensure adequate response to ECtHR judgments. I argue that it is particularly relevant where judgments reveal politically sensitive human rights issues,

59 Presidential decree on Plenipotentiary of the Republic of Azerbaijan to the European Court of Human Rights, No. 3, 8 November 2003.

60 National Program for Action to Raise Effectiveness of the Protection of Human Rights and Freedoms in the Republic of Azerbaijan, 27 December 2011 [1.2].

61 Open Society Justice Initiative report (n 58) 33, 35.

which may lead to resistance of certain national authorities and political powers to engage in genuine reforms.

In Azerbaijan, the OGA forms a part of the Presidential Administration, and the Agent is appointed by the President, which holds superior executive power in the country, presupposing strong political standing for the Agent over coordination of implementation of ECtHR judgments. In light of the hostile domestic political climate towards human rights, discussed in Section 3.1 above, his standing however shall be shaped, in each case, by the Presidential Office's approach towards reforms needed to comply with those judgments. In other words, although the OGA's formal institutional standing is the highest it could have in the national political and institutional system, the ability to exert it on other state bodies shall be predetermined by the leadership of the Presidential Administration. In absence of sufficient political willingness or in a case of active resistance by the Presidential Administration to comply with a particular judgment, it is highly questionable if the Government Agent would be in a position to do so. The holding of the Government Agent's role by the same person since the first appointment to this position in 2003 by the President for over sixteen years further presupposes the loyalty to the Presidential Administration.[62]

As the majority of interviewed human rights lawyers and applicants have noted, such a standing is largely dependent on the nature of human rights issues raised by the judgments and the domestic problems that they expose.[63] One of them noted: 'Although no information is available to the public on how implementation [of ECtHR judgments] is organised [by OGA], we as litigators and NGOs know very well that all decisions come from the Presidential Administration'.[64] Such insight shall be seen in light of the self-evident statistics on cases revealing structural systemic problems, as well as their sensitivity in the political domestic context. As an example, many interviewed lawyers referred to the failure of the authorities to pay full and timely just satisfaction (i.e. compensation ordered by the Court) in cases finding violations of rights of human rights defenders, youth activists and political opposition in recent

62 Presidential decree on the appointment of Chingiz Askerov to the position of the Government Agent before the European Court of Human Rights, No. 34, 8 December 2003.

63 Human rights lawyer and CSO representative, AZE02, online interview, 13 July 2019; Human rights lawyer, AZE03, Tbilisi, 11 March 2018; Human rights lawyer, AZE04, Tbilisi, 11 March 2018; Human rights lawyer and CSO representative, AZE05, online interview, 16 March 2018.

64 Human rights lawyer and CSO representative, AZE02, online interview, 27 March 2018.

years.[65] They suggested this indicates the selective approach of the Presidential Administration towards paying just satisfaction to certain applicants in ECtHR judgments politically unfavored by the authorities, such as human rights defenders, as such payments is very straightforward procedure that does not require any complex or time consuming efforts and Azerbaijan, as a rule, has been complying with this obligation until then.[66] For example, human rights defenders Intigam Aliyev and Rasul Jafarov whose detention in 2014 was found to be aimed to punish them for their human rights work by the ECtHR reported to the CM that their compensations were not paid in full three years after the ECtHR ordered the payments to the Government.[67] The authorities explained it to the DEJ to be related to budgetary limitations, however, the numerical perspective questions this argument. According to the official state budget of 2019 and 2018, 4,861,298 AZN (approx. 2,57 million EUR) and 2,006,400 AZN (approx. 1,07 million EUR) were allocated to the Presidential Administration to cover expenditures for defending the state interests before the ECtHR and for the execution of the ECtHR judgments in 2019, to be compared against sums of just satisfaction awarded by the ECtHR, equalling to 817,451 EUR in 2017 and 186,972 EUR in 2018.[68] In many of these 'Article 18' cases, partial payments were made to applicants on ad hoc basis (both in terms of amounts and time-frame), with applicants often having to chase the OGA about the payments by email or by phone, as there is no existing practice of any formal notifications on payments made by OGA to applicants.[69] As for most CoE member states, payment of just satisfaction is the remedy with the highest and most straight-forward compliance rate, such practice by the Azerbaijani Government further

65 Q&A on the European Court of Human Rights award of 'just satisfaction' (ECtHR Press Service 26 March 2019), March 2020.

66 Applicant's submission under Rule 9.1 of the Rules of the Committee of Ministers for the Supervision of Execution of Judgments in the case of *Aliyev v Azerbaijan*, Appl. nos. 68762/14 and 71200/14, 14 November 2019; Human rights lawyer and CSO representative, AZE02, online interview, 13 July 2019; Human rights lawyer, AZE03, Tbilisi, 11 March 2018; Human rights lawyer and CSO representative, AZE05, online interview, 16 March 2018; Applicant, AZE07, online interview, 17 September 2019; Applicant, AZE08, email communication, 26 February 2020.

67 Communication from the applicant's representatives (01/09/2017) in the case of *Rasul Jafarov v. Azerbaijan* (Application No. 69981/14); Communication from the applicant's representatives (19/09/2019) in the case of *Aliyev v. Azerbaijan* (Application No. 68762/14).

68 State budget of the Republic of Azerbaijan for 2019, budget line 1.14.3.3.1, accessed 20 March 2020 State budget of the Republic of Azerbaijan for 2018, budget line 1.14.3.3.1, accessed 20 March 2020; CM Annual Report 2018 (n 3) 76.

69 Interviews (n 66).

indicates its failure to abide by the implementation obligations in absence of clear procedures (see also 7.1).

Another example of the consequences of selective discretionary powers in absence of clear procedures relates to re-opening of domestic court proceedings on the basis of ECtHR judgments. Although the domestic laws provide that ECtHR judgments shall serve as a basis for consideration of re-opening of domestic proceedings by the Supreme Court (such as those e.g. finding fair trial violations), it does not establish sufficiently clear procedure for referral of judgments to the Supreme Court, which in practice leads to ambiguous interpretations and inconsistent and protracted application of these laws.[70] The relevant provisions stipulate that the Supreme Court shall review the cases within 3 months of referral of ECtHR judgments, failing to detail how such referral are to be ensured. As a result, several interviewed lawyers referred to instances of Supreme Court informing them that ECtHR judgments of their respective clients have not been referred to it yet.[71] As the law does not provide for any clearly established right and procedure for applicants to inquire about the decisions of the Supreme Court or activate this procedure, in practice it is left to the discretion of the authorities an the OGA in particular as the 'recipient' of final ECtHR judgments from the Court. For example, in the selected *Ilgar Mammadov* group of case, comprising cases of several applicants, Government critics, whose arrest and detention were found unlawful and carried in abuse of power by the ECtHR, the Government reported to the CM that all the judgments in this group were referred to the Supreme Court for re-examination on 12 September 2019, more than five years after the adoption of the first judgment in this group.[72] Although the Supreme Court is obliged, under the domestic law, to examine such cases within three months, there have been no developments until April 2020, when it quashed the conviction of two applicants in the group, Rasul Jafarov and Ilgar Mammadov, but not of the remaining applicants, without any explanation of such differentiation of cases.[73] In another case, the case of imprisoned journalist Eynulla Fatullayev, the Supreme Court

70 Criminal Procedural Code of the Republic of Azerbaijan 14 July 2000 (Articles 455–456); Civil Procedural Code of the Republic of Azerbaijan 28 December 1999 (Articles 431.1–431.3).

71 Human rights lawyer and CSO representative, AZE02, online interview, 27 March 2018 and 13 July 2019; Human rights lawyer, AZE03, Tbilisi, 11 March 2018; Human rights lawyer, AZE04, Tbilisi, 11 March 2018.

72 Communication from Azerbaijan concerning the *Ilgar Mammadov* group of cases v. Azerbaijan (Application No. 15172/13), Action plan of 20 September 2019.

73 Action report from Azerbaijan concerning cases of *Ilgar Mammadov v Azerbaijan* (Appl. No. 15172/13) and *Rasul Jafarov v Azerbaijan* (Appl. No. 69981/14), 23 April 2020.

quashed his conviction following the ECtHR judgment, however, new – drug related- charges were brought against him while in detention, around the same time, which kept him in detention until he was released under the presidential pardon.[74] This was also the case with the imprisoned former Minister of Health Care Ali Insanov, in which the ECtHR found in violation of fair trial, when the Government reported to the CM ten months later that the Supreme Court quashed its earlier decision and reopened the criminal proceedings by returning the case for a new examination to the appellate court.[75] The Appeal Court and the Supreme Court however upheld his conviction after the alleged rectifications of the shortcomings in the earlier trial, which Mr Insanov contested as remaining unfair.[76] In the case of two applicant NGOs in the selected group of *Ramazanova and Others*, the Azerbaijan Lawyers Forum, and Tebieti Mühafize Cemiyyeti and Israfilov, whose denied state registration and dissolution respectively by the Ministry of Justice was found in violation of their right to freedom of association, the Supreme Court reopened the cases seven months after the judgments became final and quashed its original decisions and referred cases to the Appeal Court for reconsideration.[77] These few cases, on the re-opening of which the Government reported to the CM in its communications, and absence of any public information on all re-examined cases by the Supreme Court, suggest very inconsistent and rare practice of the application of these provisions. Given that a right to fair trial and a right to liberty and security are the two most commonly found violations by the Court in cases against Azerbaijan (38% and 36% of all cases respectively), as well as cases relating to ineffective investigations into actions of law enforcement agents or ill-treatment and torture allegations by individuals in police custody or prisons (23%) (see Figure 5), all of which would be eligible for re-examination by the Supreme Court post ECtHR judgments, more than half of all successful complainants before ECtHR are denied access to a potentially effective domestic

74 Communication from Azerbaijan to the Committee of Ministers in the case of *Fatullayev v Azerbaijan* (Application No. 40984/07), 26 May 2011.

75 Communication from the authorities to the Committee of Ministers in the case of *Insanov against Azerbaijan* (Application No. 1613/08), 12 February 2016.

76 Communication from the applicant to the Committee of Ministers in the case of *Insanov against Azerbaijan* (Application No. 1613/08), 22 May 2015.

77 HUDOC EXEC database on *Ramazanova and Others v Azerbaijan*, section 'Status of Execution', accessed 12 December 2019; Human rights lawyer and CSO representative, AZE02, online interview, 27 March 2018.

remedy – the likelihood of which may be increased with clear procedures for the application of such remedy in place.[78]

Although the OGA is not responsible for implementation of judgments, its coordinator role serves as the very starting point of the process, which may delay or even stall the implementation process without having responsible ministries or other state agencies involved. The Presidential Administration's position on the judgments, at the very outset, sets the ground for the Agent's 'coordinator' role, particularly in relation to highly adverse cases where, at the litigation phase, the Government Agent, representing the Government's position, has refuted applicants' allegations or even denied their existence.[79]

3.2.2.2 Allocation of Resources

As for the issue of resources, which further predetermines the OGA standing in its 'coordinator' role, apart from the above mentioned state budgetary allocations to cover expenditures relating to the representation of the state interests before the ECtHR and the implementation of its judgments, no information is available to public as to what other resources, such as human resources, are allocated to ensure effective functioning of the OGA. No information is provided on the composition of the OGA on the website of the Presidential Administration. The interviewed lawyers and applicants all referred to two members of the personnel who they were aware of from their experience: the Government Agent and one more person in the OGA office as the contact point for inquiries on payments of just satisfaction.[80] On the face of the available information and the number of cases in communication by the Court (e.g. over 300 cases as of 1 January 2020) or pending implementation before the CM, the OGA is under-resourced to effectively pursue its dual role.

78 *Insanov* case (Appl. no. 16133/08 14 June 2013), *Huseyn and Others* group (Appl. no. 35485/05 26 October 2011), *Jannatov* case (App. No. 32132/07 31 October 2014), *Layijov* case (Appl. no. 22062/07 10 July 2014), *Humadov* group (Appl. no. 13652/06 3 March 2010) *Tarverdiyev* group (Appl. no. 33343/03, 26 October 2007), *Ilgar Mammadov* group of cases (Appl. no. 15172/13, 22 May 2014); *Gafgaz Mammadov* group of cases (Appl. no. 60259/11, 14 March 2016).

79 See, for example, ECtHR judgments in the *Ilgar Mammadov* group of cases finding violations of Article 18 of ECHR: *Ilgar Mammadov* (n 110) [82, 135, 136]; *Rasul Jafarov* (n 112) [97, 98, 151]; *Aliyev* (n 112) [149, 150, 195].

80 Human rights lawyer and CSO representative, AZE02, online interview, 27 March 2018 and 13 July 2019; Human rights lawyer, AZE03, Tbilisi, 11 March 2018; Human rights lawyer, AZE04, Tbilisi, 11 March 2018; Human rights lawyer and CSO representative, AZE05, online interview, 16 March 2018; Applicant and CSO representative, AZE06, Brussels, 12 December 2018; Applicant, AZE07, online interview, 17 September 2019; Applicant, AZE08, email communication, 13 September 2019 and 26 February 2020.

3.2.2.3 Absence of Formal Procedures for Coordination and Involvement in the Process

Apart from the role of OGA, there are no clear normative procedures set in place to establish a framework for coordination of the implementation work of ECtHR judgments, leaving it entirely to the discretion of the OGA to initiate the process and define its parameters. Absence of any formalised domestic infrastructure makes it very difficult if not impossible for other relevant domestic institutions to get involved or suggest certain actions, unless instructed by the OGA. From the very limited information available to the public and information obtained through interviews, it appears that no other state institution has sufficient standing, or information, to initiate reforms stemming from the implementation process.[81] As one of the interviewed lawyer noted: 'one of the main problems is the lack of clear involvement of other state actors, which is not possible in what appears to be a hierarchical top-down system ran by the Government Agent'.[82]

The Government Agent is also the key national focal point for the Strasbourg institutions involved in the supervision process, in line with the CM recommendation of 2008 for each state to appoint a national coordinator.[83] It is the Government Agent who usually attends the quarterly CM meetings on the implementation of ECtHR judgments in Strasbourg and communicates with the DEJ on the more technical work related to implementation, with little involvement of the Strasbourg based Azerbaijani delegation, representing the Ministry of Foreign Affairs.[84] The interviewed former representative of the Government to the CoE, delegated by the Ministry of Foreign Affairs, suggested that the direct communication on implementation of ECtHR judgments between Baku and Strasbourg may be indicative of the Presidential Administration's intention to maintain control over the state's engagement with the CM and the DEJ, directed by the Presidential Administration, further enhancing the monopoly held by the OGA over this process.[85]

81 Human rights lawyer and CSO representative, AZE02, online interview, 27 March 2018; Human rights lawyer, AZE04, Tbilisi, 11 March 2018; Human rights lawyer and CSO representative, AZE05, online interview, 16 March 2018. The Government Agent did not respond to two requests for an interview.

82 Human rights lawyer, AZE04, Tbilisi, 11 March 2018.

83 CM/Rec(2008)2 on efficient domestic capacity for rapid execution of judgments of the European Court of Human Rights, adopted by the Committee of Ministers on 6 February 2008 at the 1017th meeting of the Ministers' Deputies.

84 Presidential Decree of 8 December 2013 No 34, accessed 20 March 2020 CM member state representative, SXB01, Strasbourg, 23 May 2017; CM member state representative, SXB02, Strasbourg, 23 May 2017.

85 Former Government representative to CoE, AZE01, online interview, 14 August 2019.

As for the involvement of other, non-executive state actors in the implementation process, such as the national parliament with its legislative and oversight roles, Azerbaijan's parliament, Milli Meclis, has no formal role in the implementation process or is in any other way involved. In its legislative role, which may be relevant in adopting new or amending existing laws as part of general measures, Milli Meclis is dependent on the legislative initiatives taken by the executive, particularly the ministries responsible for justice and interior sectors. For example, in one of the closely supervised and actively debated group of cases by the CM, *Mahmudov and Agazade* group, decriminalization of defamation was the key measure that the Government has committed to undertake.[86] The Government has initially seemed to engage with the process, including by seeking expert advice from the Venice Commission, which, however, eventually led to no tangible progress and the draft amendments have never reached the parliament for its debate and adoption.[87]

Milli Meclis does not conduct any oversight over the executive's work to comply with ECtHR judgments. The Government does not account in any formal way to the parliament for its respective work as no such reporting mechanisms are put in place in the domestic system, enabling the parliament to scrutinize the executive's compliance with ECtHR judgments. Another significant constraint to the parliament's ability to independently scrutinize the work lies in its political composition. The vast majority of parliamentary seats are held by the New Azerbaijan Party, chaired by the President, since the independence of Azerbaijan from the Soviet Union, through highly compromised elections, effectively making Azerbaijan a one party dominant state (see introductory part at 3.1). Such composition makes the parliament's ability to effectively scrutinize the executive's actions very unlikely even if a formal mechanism for such review would be put in place. Two main opposition parties, Musavat Party and Popular Front Party, lost their seats since 2010 elections and did not manage to regain it to date, making Milli Meclis an opposition-free parliament.[88] The adoption of increasingly advocated formal procedures to have national parliaments involved in the implementation process would

86 Communication from Azerbaijan concerning the *Mahmudov and Agazade* group of cases against Azerbaijan (Appl. no. 35877/04), Action plan, 26 February 2014.

87 Reply from Azerbaijan to the questions pursuant to the decision adopted at the 1250th meeting (DH) in the *Mahmudov and Agazade* group of cases v. Azerbaijan (Appl. no. 35877/04) (in reply to document DH-DD(2016)343), 20 April 2016; Opinion on the Legislation pertaining to the Protection against Defamation of the Republic of Azerbaijan, adopted by the Venice Commission, at its 96th Plenary Session, (Venice, 11–12 October 2013).

88 OSCE/ODIHR Election Observation Mission Final Report, Parliamentary elections, Republic of Azerbaijan, 7 November 2010 28.

undoubtedly serve as a first step towards enabling individual members of the parliament to question the status quo or to increase the very limited transparency, however, more substantial domestic political reforms challenging the existing concentration of power. The first ever early dissolution of the parliament by the President in December 2019, which followed the dismissal of the long-term Head of Presidential Administration and several ministers, for the alleged need for modernization, surprising many domestic and international actors, had created some hopes for reforms, however, the early parliamentary elections in February 2020 did not result in any significant changes.[89] It secured strong majority of seats to the ruling party of the President, offering no prospects to the unprecedented number of independent candidates from the civil society in these elections, described by the OSCE ODIHR Election Monitoring Mission as preventing 'genuine competition' due to the 'restrictive legislation and political environment'.[90]

3.2.2.4 Absence of Information and Public Scrutiny

No information is available to the public on the authorities' implementation work or any progress made on any of the cases. This process takes place behind closed doors and no details, including decisions made or budget expenses required, are disclosed publicly, preventing the applicants, the civil society or the media from exercising any effective oversight over the actions of the executive or to contribute to the process.[91] There is no dedicated website page or any other public information platform available on the implementation of ECtHR judgments – neither on ECtHR judgments adopted against Azerbaijan, nor on the actions taken by the Government. All interviewed domestic litigators, lawyers and NGOs noted that Government submissions to the CM, as a part of the supervision process, or any other related information on the CM website is their main source of information as to what steps are being taken is being done in their own or other cases.[92] As a representative of one NGO

89 Tom de Waal, 'Is Change Afoot in Azerbaijan?' (Carnegie Europe, 5 November 2019), accessed 12 December 2019.

90 OSCE ODIHR International Election Observation Mission Statement of Preliminary Findings and Conclusions, Republic of Azerbaijan-Early Parliamentary Elections, 9 February 2020 1.

91 Human rights lawyer and CSO representative, AZE02, online interview, 27 March 2018; Human rights lawyer, AZE03, Tbilisi, 11 March 2018; Human rights lawyer, AZE04, Tbilisi, 11 March 2018; Applicant, AZE07, online interview, 17 September 2019.

92 Human rights lawyer and CSO representative, AZE02, online interview, 27 March 2018; Human rights lawyer, AZE03, Tbilisi, 11 March 2018; Human rights lawyer, AZE04, Tbilisi, 11 March 2018; Human rights lawyer and CSO representative, AZE05, online interview, 16 March 2018; Applicant and CSO representative, AZE06, Brussels, 12 December 2018;

who would be willing to engage in the implementation process noted: 'Our Strasbourg colleagues certainly know more of our Government's actions on implementation than we do, based here in the capital Baku'.[93] As those submissions are provided in English, the domestic actors' access to such information is often dependent on their ability to read in English, which I identified as one of the key constraints for effective involvement of the Azerbaijani non-state actors in the process. Not all ECtHR judgments against Azerbaijan are available in Azerbaijani and there is no consolidated platform where the translations or any analysis or structured listing of the judgments would be available and easily accessible to the public: some of the translated judgments (both against Azerbaijan and other CoE Member States) are placed on the websites of the Judicial Council (last updated in 2008) and the Supreme Court without any indication as to why those judgments were selected to be translated into Azerbaijani.[94]

The interviewed NGO representatives and lawyers reported that, in their experience, no public debates or consultations, such as working groups on certain reforms, have ever been held on the adoption of any legislative reforms or policies stemming from ECtHR judgments under the auspices of the Government Agent operating under the tightly concentrated power of the Presidential Administration.[95] The civil society's involvement in the domestic process is therefore non-existent and there are no formal procedures for them to be involved. As one of the interviewed NGO representatives highlighted: 'not only that we are excluded from this process, but in some instances, we are also subjected to retaliatory measures for engaging directly with the DEJ and CM, by submitting our reports contradicting the Government's position in its action plans'.[96] Such isolation of the civil society by the authorities is not unique to the process of implementation of judgments and appears to be reflective of the wider hostile approach towards the civil society and the absence of any

Applicant, AZE07, online interview, 17 September 2019; Applicant, AZE08, email communication, 13 September 2019.

93 Human rights lawyer and CSO representative, AZE02, online interview, 27 March 2018.

94 Websites of the Judicial Council http://www.judicialcouncil.gov.az/bey_akt.php and the Supreme Court http://supremecourt.gov.az/category/view/84, accessed 12 November 2019.

95 Human rights lawyer and CSO representative, AZE02, online interview, 27 March 2018; Human rights lawyer, AZE03, Tbilisi, 11 March 2018; Human rights lawyer, AZE04, Tbilisi, 11 March 2018; Human rights lawyer and CSO representative, AZE05, online interview, 16 March 2018; Applicant and CSO representative, AZE06, Brussels, 12 December 2018; Applicant, AZE07, online interview, 17 September 2019; Applicant, AZE08, email communication, 13 September 2019.

96 Human rights lawyer and CSO representative, AZE02, online interview, 27 March 2018.

inclusive practices in matters of public interest.[97] The CM supervision process is therefore the only way for Azerbaijani civil society groups, and often for individual applicants, to engage with the authorities on the implementation of ECtHR judgments.

In light of the growing consensus in the CoE for the creation of strong and inclusive domestic mechanisms and increased domestic capacity to comply with ECtHR judgments, as a part of addressing the deepening implementation challenges and strengthening the supervision system in the CoE, Azerbaijan appears to have done little if anything to comply with the call for 'shared responsibility' for ECtHR judgments, referred to in the CM Brussels Declaration.[98] The current domestic implementation process is defined by huge concentration of power in the hands of the Presidential Administration that holds the highest executive power, the absence of any checks and balances through the national parliament or public consultations, no coordinated procedures to facilitate implementation, and lack of transparency of the work of the responsible institutions – failing to meet the majority of the recommendations by the CM and PACE in that regard, jointly agreed by representatives of the same member states, including Azerbaijan. The current system appears to be operating on foundations of discretion, hierarchy and concentration of power and fails to abide by the principles of transparency, inclusiveness and accountability, as elements of a democratic state. In such a context, where implementation is largely and primarily dependent on the political will, consolidated in the hands of one institution, clear formalised procedures for implementation defining ways and roles for other domestic actors would be of particular importance. Such clear domestic infrastructure would not only strengthen state's capacities for compliance but would also likely serve as a platform to facilitate more socialization of state institutions with the international human rights obligations. These empirical data based findings strongly support the foundations of the constructivism theory that states would better comply with their obligations through their exposure to and interaction with human rights norms and institutions.

3.2.3 *Systematic Failure of 'Good Faith' Engagement with the CM*

My qualitative study finds that Azerbaijan's engagement with the Strasbourg supervision process on the implementation of ECtHR judgments is sporadic, selective, process-oriented, and largely reactive to the CM's consistent pressure.

97 Interviews (n 95).
98 Brussels Declaration (n 57).

There is a widespread pattern of failure to consistently comply with the existing CM procedures requiring timely action plans and reports, and where it does, it frequently reports on actions, which appear to superficially advance implementation but fails to demonstrate substantive progress in practice. Frustration over such willful reluctance has been shared by all interviewed CM delegates from Western European countries who have been actively involved in the CM supervision process. As one of them has described it in 2017:[99]

> In three years of mine, there have been very few instances where some substantial information was provided [by Azerbaijan]. There is no discussion on execution of the judgments, no substantive engagement. The Government Agent speaks but he does not provide any information, he sometimes just reads out the answer, but does not engage in any discussion with us.

The analysis of all the available information on Azerbaijani cases on the CM HUDOC EXEC database shows that the authorities frequently disregard the general CM supervision rules requiring to provide regular action plans and reports, and specific CM calls for progress, particularly in cases exposing deep structural and systemic human rights issues and failings of the domestic system. A pattern of selective engagement with the CM is observed across majority of cases, where the Government provides information of its choice as an update on the cases but fails to effectively engage with specific requests or inquiries from the CM. By way of example, in the *Muradova, Mammadov (Jajaloglu) and Mikayil Mammadov* group of cases, one of the five groups of cases which I analysed in greater detail, consisting of 20 cases revealing lack of effective investigations into death or ill-treatment allegedly imputable to law enforcement agents (with the first judgment delivered by the ECtHR in 2007), the Government provided its first action plan/update 11 years later, in January 2018.[100] As only four applicants out of 20 submitted their written positions regarding implementation to the CM once during all this period, and only one Azerbaijani NGO submitted its 'Rule 9' report focusing on violence against peaceful protesters in the *Muradova* group in 2013 in particular, the CM was left without any information on any progress on this extensive group addressing

99 CM member state representative, SXB01, Strasbourg, 23 May 2017.

100 Communication from the authorities (updated information) (20/02/2018) concerning the cases of. *Muradova, Mammadov (Jalaloglu) and Mikayil Mammadov v Azerbaijan* (Appl. nos. 22684/05, 34445/04, 4762/05).

grave human rights violations for this lengthy period of time.[101] The submission of the action plan appears to have been triggered by the CM decision of September 2017 expressing concern that no information had been provided on the group of cases since 2010 and urging the Government to inform the CM about any progress.[102] Although the Government responded to the CM's call to provide an update, the submitted action plan failed to address the essential individual measures in such cases, such as the progress of investigations, if any, into the very serious allegations against law enforcement agents. It disregarded the CM's questions and provided no requested information to date. Instead, it provided information of its own choice as to what was deemed as progress. It informed the CM about the adoption of two executive orders: the Presidential Order of 11 February 2017 instructing the Ministry of Justice to 'strengthen control of detention conditions of convicts and arrested persons, their food supply, medical and welfare support'; and a joint Order of the Minister of Justice and the Prosecutor General on 'additional measures to secure the rights of those arrested and detained', such as that 'the United Nations and the Council of Europe Conventions against torture and other cruel, inhuman or degrading treatment or punishment and protocols thereto shall be brought to the personnel's attention and education of the said legal acts continued during professional training'. Although the adopted orders may be seen as a relevant step towards ensuring effective general measures aimed at creating adequate legislative framework for ensuring prevention of similar violations, its actual effectiveness lies in implementation in practice that would lead to prevention of similar cases – none of which the Government addressed as of January 2022 as the end date of this research. The observed pattern also suggests that the Government appears to have deliberately chosen to not engage with the CM on examining the progress of the individual measures that would offer remedies to applicants who complained of very serious violations, including death in custody, over a decade ago – an essential part of compliance with ECtHR judgments. The Government's further disregard of the CM's subsequent decision of March 2018, following the Government's respective report, reiterating its call for updates on the state's duty to conduct effective investigations – and of its duty to provide timely reports to the CM on complying with the ECtHR judgments – without any further updates is suggestive of the Government's

101 HUDOC EXEC database, *Muradova, Mammadov (Jalaloglu) and Mikayil Mammadov v Azerbaijan* (Appl. nos. 22684/05, 34445/04, 4762/05) accessed 1 June 2020.

102 CM decision on the cases of *Muradova, Mammadov (Jalaloglu) and Mikayil Mammadov v Azerbaijan* (Appl. no. 22684/05, 34445/04, 4762/05), adopted at the 1294th meeting, 19–21 September 2017.

selective policy towards its compliance obligations, which is also observed in other examined cases (as discussed below).[103] As one of the interviewed human rights lawyers explained it:

> Such serious allegations in closed institutions, which remain a big problem today, imply responsibility of the law enforcement structures and the authorities deliberately choose to not engage with it in Strasbourg. There is no political will in the domestic system to systematically address this widespread problem and the Strasbourg process would only expose this.[104]

Numerous reports of interviewed civil society representatives indicate that ill-treatment in custody and impunity remain one of the most widespread human rights concerns, and the findings of the European Committee for Prevention of Torture (CPT) from 2004–2017 that 'torture and other forms of physical ill-treatment by the police and other law enforcement agencies, corruption in the whole law enforcement system and impunity remain systemic and endemic' further reinforce this finding.[105]

Similar patterns are observed in other groups of cases revealing systemic structural issues, such as arbitrary interferences with freedom of assembly, protection of property or serious failings of the domestic courts to ensure fair trial in criminal proceedings. In the *Gafgaz Mammadov* group of cases relating to 21 cases of arbitrary and unlawful detention of peaceful protesters, no information whatsoever was provided by the authorities to the CM since 2016 on either individual or general measures despite the CM's repeated calls in its three consecutive decisions in June 2017, December 2017 and June 2018 and March 2021 for an action plan.[106] In February 2021, the Government only provided a brief action report informing about the payments of compensation to most of the applicants and the automatic erasure of administrative convictions after a certain period of time, specifying any general measures to be taken. With only

103 CM decision on the cases of *Muradova, Mammadov (Jalaloglu) and Mikayil Mammadov v Azerbaijan* (Appl. no. 22684/05, 34445/04, 4762/05), adopted at the 1310th meeting, 13–15 March 2018.

104 Human rights lawyer, AZE04, Tbilisi, 11 March 2018.

105 Human rights lawyer and CSO representative, AZE02, online interview, 13 July 2019; Human rights lawyer, AZE03, Tbilisi, 11 March 2018; CoE News, 'Azerbaijan: torture, impunity and corruption highlighted in new anti-torture committee publications', 18 July 2018, accessed 20 June 2019.

106 HUDOC EXEC database, *Gafgaz Mammadov* group of cases, Appl. no. 60259/11, 15 October 2015 accessed 1 January 2022.

two submissions from two applicants in 2019 and one in February 2021, and no NGO submissions, the CM is again left in an information vacuum during all this period, continuing to remind the authorities of their obligations to cooperate and report on the progress.[107] In a number of groups of cases relating to failings to ensure fair trial guarantees in criminal proceedings, as the most common violation found by the Court in cases against Azerbaijan, no action plans or reports have been provided on the Government's plans to address this systemic issue through general measures.[108] In the case of *Sargsyan v Azerbaijan* of 2015 that I selected for my in-depth analysis and which concerns violations of property rights of displaced people as a result of the Nagorno Karabakh conflict, the Government initially attempted to convince the CM that no additional measures were necessary as the system was place, and later discontinued any dialogue with the CM.[109] In this case, the ECtHR referred to a specific remedy by ordering the Government (as well as to the Armenian Government's in its twin judgment *Chiragov and Others v Armenia*) to establish a property claims mechanism, highlighting at least a thousand similar cases pending before the ECtHR, thus excluding the risk of disagreement on the necessary measures. After two years of silence, in March 2017, the Government informed the CM in its brief report that such a mechanism already exists in Azerbaijan, without any further information as to how it would be applied to this particular situation.[110] It disregarded the CM's subsequent call in March 2017 to engage on a more constructive level and provide information on the mandate of the existing mechanism and the accessibility for persons in the applicant's position, i.e. ethnic Armenians,[111] nor did it respond in any way to the November 2016 submission by an NGO setting out the relevant international standards for the establishment of an adequate property rights mechanism.[112] In the same report of March 2017, the Government also noted that 'the main responsibility in this case belongs to the Republic of Armenia', implying Armenia's status as

107 Ibid.

108 HUDOC EXEC database, *Huseyn and Others* group of cases, Appl. no. 35485/05, 26 July 2011 accessed 1 August 2019.

109 *Sargsyan v. Azerbaijan*, App. no. 40167/06 (ECtHR 15 June 2015); *Chiragov and Others v. Armenia*, App. no. 13216/05 (ECtHR 15 June 2015).

110 Government action plan in the case of *Sargsyan v Azerbaijan* (Appl. no. 40167/06), 6 March 2017.

111 CM decision in the case of *Sargsyan v Azerbaijan* (Appl. no. 40167/06), adopted during its 1280th meeting on 7–10 March 2017.

112 Communication from an NGO (EHRAC) (02/11/2016) in the cases of *Chiragov and Others v Armenia* (Application No. 13216/05) and *Sargsyan v Azerbaijan* (Application No. 40167/06).

the occupying power of the disputed territories, which offers some explanation to the Government's level of (un)willingness to commit to its obligation to ensure substantive legal remedies to victims outside of the politicized framework of this protracted conflict, articulated in the ECtHR judgment.

The CM's limited protracted and inconsistent engagement with the Azerbaijani authorities on these cases raising deep systemic domestic problems and pending implementation for lengthy periods of time, in absence of very limited involvement of the applicants and the civil society, and no involvement of the national human rights institutions, suggest two findings. Firstly, the Azerbaijani authorities fail to abide by the existing CM rules to report on the implementation progress in a consistent and substantive manner, and secondly, the lack of timely and adequate response from the CM or any consequences allow the authorities to get away with their failure to engage with the CM and their legal obligations. I further analyse what determines such behaviour of the Azerbaijani authorities.

3.2.3.1 Triggers for Government's Engagement with the CM Supervision Process

Blatant above discussed failings of the Government to abide by the CM procedures and engage in a constructive dialogue are particularly noticeable in leading cases examined under *standard* supervision, where the CM's explicit involvement is absent or very limited, e.g. where there are no official CM decisions with specific recommendations or timeframes indicated. In at least 60% of such cases, *no* information has been provided by the Azerbaijani authorities to the CM as of 1 January 2022 and the information on the remaining cases is limited to brief updates on individual measures such as payments of compensation. Action plans and reports on general measures remain awaited by the CM in the vast majority of such cases, and those reported to the CM often refer to measures such as translation and dissemination of judgments among domestic actors. Although these are important steps towards full implementation, they are the very first steps in setting the ground for implementation, and difficult to measure in terms of its practical impact in putting an end to similar violations in the future.

For example, in one group of cases, the *Huseyn and Others* group, examined under standard supervision, involving 13 applicants who the ECtHR found being denied fair trial, no action plans or reports have been provided since 2011;[113] In the selected *Ramazanova* group of cases, involving cases from

113 HUDOC EXEC database, *Huseyn and Others* group of cases, appl. no. 35485/05, 26 July 2011 accessed 1 January 2022.

2007 onwards relating to the failure of the Ministry of Justice to register non-governmental organisations, and its decision to dissolve one organisation, an issue that remains central in the country, in the context of the growing repression of the civil society in the recent years, no action plan or report has been provided by the Government the September 2022 meeting of the CM when it informed about the developments regarding individual measures.[114] It limited its updates to the CM to information on payment of compensation and re-registration of the applicant NGOs in this group of cases except for the organisation of the renowned Government critic and human rights lawyer Intigam Aliyev (who is also one of the applicants in the *Ilgar Mammadov* group of cases concerning Article 18 violations of rights of Government's critics). In relation to his case specifically, the authorities informed the CM that Mr Aliyev failed to submit the necessary documents for the re-examination of the application, something that he had denied being informed about.[115]

Cases under 'standard supervision', as a rule, imply that the implementation process is undergoing smoothly and there is no need for the CM's active involvement along the technical communication between the respondent Government and the CM Secretariat (see 2.3.1). In that case, the Government is not challenged for failing to report on the sufficient or any progress by any additional triggers, such as CM decisions and reviews at its quarterly human rights meetings. In many of these cases, protracted periods of time are observed between developments reported by the Government, if any, and further follow up, such as official requests for further updates, by the CM or its Secretariat, in the case of which the Government does not abide by its obligation to provide updates in its own initiative.

As the analysis suggest, the Government's official engagement with the CM, quantitatively, is significantly more frequent in cases examined under enhanced supervision. The identified patterns of engagement indicate that this is largely due to the regular and, in some instances, persistent 'chasing policy' of the CM, along the regular communication maintained by the DEJ with the Government of Azerbaijan, serving as additional pressure. The CM classification of cases under enhanced supervision, as a rule, leads to closer and more regular scrutiny both by the DEJ and CM, resulting in formal CM decisions indicating what further steps are expected from the respondent state (see 2.3.1).

114 HUDOC EXEC database, *Ramazanova and Others v Azerbaijan*, Appl. No. 44363/05, 1 February 2007 accessed 1 January 2022.

115 HUDOC EXEC database, *Aliyev and Others v Azerbaijan*, 28736/05, judgment of 18 December 2008 accessed 1 January 2022; Human rights lawyer and CSO representative, AZE02, online interview, 27 March 2018 and 13 July 2019.

The vast majority of leading cases against Azerbaijan under enhanced supervision have been on the agenda of the CM quarterly human rights meetings 102 times since the CM human rights meeting in March 2011 (as of which the CM publishes lists of debated cases that include Azerbaijani cases),[116] with at least 3 Azerbaijani cases per meeting on average.[117] At least one Azerbaijani leading case has been examined in the vast majority of CM quarterly meetings, and the remaining 20 pending cases under standard supervision have been reviewed 28 times during the same period of time. As the interviewed DEJ representative explained,

'When we think that the process needs support or criticism [from CM delegations], we will put it on the agenda for the CM to provide its support to the execution process by support or encouragement, criticism or threats, and this is when the [respondent] states do not make constructive proposals. If the states are in agreement that reforms are needed and accept our support, why debate them with all country delegations?'[118]

In the majority of the 14 leading cases under enhanced supervision, the Government provided action plans or reports, or other official written communications to the DEJ, predominantly in response to either the CM calls or applicants' or NGOs' submissions criticising the Government's actions or inaction. This is particularly noticeable in two groups of cases where the formal CM involvement has been most frequent among all Azerbaijani cases to date, the implementation process of both of which I selected for my analysis: the *Mahmudov and Agazade* group, involving three applicants journalists, relating to their imprisonment for articles critical of the authorities under criminal defamation laws, and the *Ilgar Mammadov* case (later formed as the *Ilgar Mammadov* group following the adoption of other similar cases), disclosing arbitrary nature of arrest and detention of the Government critics, aimed to punish them for their activism and human rights work ('Article 18' cases). Azerbaijan's actions relating to implementation of these two groups have been closely and regularly scrutinised by the CM since the transfer of the respective judgments for its supervision, differently from the majority of other leading cases and all cases under standard supervision. The CM adopted 21 decisions and four interim resolutions in relation to the *Mamhudov and Agazade* group during the period of December 2011 and June 2018, followed by three action plans and reports and 13 'Government communications'; and 16 CM decisions

116 CM lists of cases available here https://www.coe.int/en/web/execution/committee-of-ministers-human-rights-meetings accessed 10 December 2021.

117 Ibid.

118 DEJ official, SXB04, Strasbourg, 30 November 2016.

and five interim resolutions in the case of Ilgar Mammadov during December 2014-December 2017 (followed by further decisions on the case as part of the group of cases in the following years), with two action plans and 11 'Government communications' from the authorities.[119]

Both groups of cases have been regularly included on the agenda of the CM's human rights meetings, leading to debates on these cases by the CM delegations, dedicated for the implementation of ECtHR judgments – with the case of Ilgar Mammadov also being debated at every regular CM meeting, beyond human rights meetings, since June 2016 as a matter of exerting pressure on Azerbaijan until it complies with the CM calls to release Mr Mammadov.[120] To compare, in cases where the CM attention was rather protracted, such as, for example, in the *Mirzayev* group of cases concerning non-enforcement of final domestic court decisions, with CM decisions adopted in 2011, 2012 and 2019, the Government's engagement was limited to two submissions in 2011 and 2019, and similar patterns are observed in many other leading cases under enhanced supervision discussed in the introduction of Section 3.2.3 (see, for example, *Muradova, Mammadov (Jalaloglu) and Mikayil* group of cases).[121]

In both groups, the applicants' and human rights organisations' active use of their right to submit alternative 'Rule 9' reports assessing the Government's actions/inaction and proposing recommendations as to what steps need to be taken indicates further 'activation' of the Government's engagement with the Strasbourg supervision process. In the case of *Mahmudov and Agazade* group, two submissions by the applicants and 10 submissions by human rights organisations were prepared, including a joint submission of 32 NGOs calling for immediate release of one of the applicants, journalist Eynulla Fatullayev, as ordered by the ECtHR in its judgment.[122] In the case of Ilgar Mammadov, 25 submissions were provided by the applicant and two by NGOs.[123] Out of six instances when the Government of Azerbaijan used its right to respond to

---

119 HUDOC EXEC database, *Mahmudov and Agazade v Azerbaijan*, appl. no. 35877/04, 18 December 2008, and *Fatullayev v Azerbaijan*, appl. no. 40984/07, 4 October 2010, reviewed as *Mahmudov and Agazade* group of cases, last opened on 1 August 2019; *Ilgar Mammadov v Azerbaijan*, appl. no. 15172/13, 22 May 2014, reviewed as part of *Ilgar Mammadov* group.

120 Interim Resolution CM/ResDH(2016)144 on the execution of the judgment of the European Court of Human Rights in the case of *Ilgar Mammadov against Azerbaijan*, adopted by the Committee of Ministers on 8 June 2016 at the 1259th meeting of the Ministers' Deputies.

121 HUDOC EXEC database, last accessed on 1 December 2021.

122 HUDOC EXEC database, *Mahmudov and Agazade* group v Azerbaijan, NGO submissions and Applicant communications under section 'Related' accessed 16 October 2019.

123 HUDOC EXEC database, *Ilgar Mammadov* v Azerbaijan, NGO submissions and Applicant communications under section 'Related' accessed 16 October 2019.

applicants' or NGO submissions, 50% of such replies related to the two respective groups of cases: it responded to an NGO submission in the *Mahmudov and Agazade* group in November 2016 and to two submissions of Ilgar Mammadov in March 2016 and March 2017.[124] Although it is not clear what triggered the Government's response to these particular submissions (8% of all submissions in both groups of cases) and not the others, it engaged the Government with the process, which otherwise was a non-existent possibility for civil society actors on the domestic level at that time.

This quantitative analysis suggests the significance of consistent CM involvement with the process to the Government's responsiveness and engagement with the supervision process. A more fundamental question however is how effective such enhanced engagement is in bringing real change to the situation on the domestic level. Although the regular CM involvement helps ensure more frequent engagement from the Government, the analysis of the *content* of the Government's submissions in such cases, however, suggests that closer CM's scrutiny does not guarantee a constructive and content oriented engagement, which would ultimately lead to substantive changes on the ground. The Government's responses largely include what appears to be selective and less politically sensitive or otherwise domestically challenging information, failing to substantially address the CM's specific calls on the identified complex and structural issues, or urgent individual measures. For example, in the above mentioned *Muradova, Mammadov (Jajajoglu) and Mikayil* group of cases, when asked about the investigation of death and ill-treatment allegations in 20 individual cases, the Government limited its brief response to information on the adoption of two orders, disregarding the specific questions of the CM.[125] In the *Mahmudov and Agazade* group of cases, addressing serious systemic issues such as arbitrary application of criminal laws and lack of independence of judiciary, the authorities primarily focused on trainings delivered to judges and prosecutors, and their visits to Strasbourg, conferences held on related topics, and the existence of the long term CoE Action Plan for Azerbaijan

---

124 Communication from a NGO (Amnesty International) (28/11/2016) and reply from the authorities (30/11/2016) in the case of *Mahmudov and Agazade against Azerbaijan* (Appl. no. 35877/04); Communication from the authorities (07/03/2016) in reply to the communication of the applicant's representative of 02/03/2016 in the case of *Ilgar Mammadov against Azerbaijan* (Appl. no. 15172/13); Communication from the authorities (06/03/2017) in reply to the communication of the applicant's representative (DH-DD(2017)258) in the case of *Ilgar Mammadov v. Azerbaijan* (Appl. no. 15172/13).

125 Action Plan (Update to the information on execution of the Court's judgments) in *Muradova (no. 22684/05), Mammadov (Jalaloglu) (no. 34445/04) and Mikayil Mammadov groups (no. 4762/05) v. Azerbaijan*, 20 February 2018.

aimed to address a number of identified problems, none of which allow the CM to assess their effectiveness in eliminating the identified problems and the progress made so far.[126] The same approach is observed in the Government's replies to NGO or applicant submissions where it baldly refuted the information provided as having 'nothing to do with the subject' of the case[127] or is 'unsubstantiated and of speculator character'.[128]

Among the five selected groups of cases, some positive developments are however observed with regard to individual measures taken in relation to some of the applicants in the *Ilgar Mammadov* group of cases, which address highly politically sensitive issues, raising questions of what triggers such developments. In April 2020, after several years of no progress in cases following ECtHR judgments in 2014 and 2015, two of the applicants, Ilgar Mammadov and Rasul Jafarov, had their convictions quashed by the Supreme Court on the basis of ECtHR judgments.[129] A number of contributing factors shall be considered here, including a very regular and frequent scrutiny of the CM and other CoE bodies of the case of Ilgar Mammadov, including the successful use of infringement proceedings under Article 46(4) of the ECHR, followed by Mammadov's release in August 2018 (see 1.1). It is suggested that such enhanced systemic pressure on the Government from multiple actors, the CM, the ECtHR with its increasing number of legally binding 'Article 18' judgments, supported by the active involvement of the applicants contributed to the Government's delivering of compliance, even if partially, as the remaining applicants await their acquittal.

3.2.3.2 What Systemic Change on the Ground?

One fundamental indicator of any tangible progress made in addressing the systemic structural problems by the authorities is their assessment in the context

126 HUDOC EXEC database, *Mahmudov and Agazade v Azerbaijan*, Appl. no. 35877/04, 18 December 2008, and *Fatullayev v Azerbaijan*, Appl. no. 40984/07, 4 October 2010, reviewed as *Mahmudov and Agazade* group of cases accessed 1 August 2019.

127 (n 228); Communication from the authorities (07/03/2016) in reply to the communication of the applicant's representative of 02/03/2016 in the case of *Ilgar Mammadov against Azerbaijan* (Appl. no. 15172/13); Communication from the authorities (06/03/2017) in reply to the communication of the applicant's representative (DH-DD(2017)258) in the case of *Ilgar Mammadov v. Azerbaijan* (Appl. no. 15172/13).

128 Communication from 7 NGOs (05/09/2014) in the *Ramazanova and others* group of cases and *Tebieti Mühafize Cemiyyeti and Israfilov against Azerbaijan* (Appl. no. 44363/02 and 37083/03) and reply from the authorities (17/09/2014).

129 Action report from Azerbaijan concerning cases of *Ilgar Mammadov v Azerbaijan* (Appl. No. 15172/13) and *Rasul Jafarov v Azerbaijan* (Appl. No. 69981/14), 23 April 2020.

of the current situation of the respective human rights issue in the country. The detailed analysis of the lifespan of implementation of the five selected groups of cases well demonstrates that such pressure-rather-then-dialogue based supervision process does not guarantee full and timely implementation of ECtHR judgments, and such increased socialisation with the process is not sufficient to bring about change in absence of any political will domestically.

In the five analysed groups of cases, all exposing issues of systemic structural nature, varying in the nature of human rights issues, measures needed to address the violations, the type of supervision and levels of involvement by the CM, length of time it has been pending implementation, no substantive change has been observed, particularly in terms of general measures. Although the adoption of individual measures offering some remedy to applicants is undoubtedly significant, the true indication of the state's willingness to fully comply with ECtHR judgments lies in the effectiveness of its actions taken to address the very core of the systemic problem, as identified by the ECtHR.

In the *Mahmudov and Agazade* group of cases, which concern measures relating to decriminalization of defamation and the need to put an end to arbitrary application of criminal legislation to limit freedom of expression, aimed to prevent further prosecution of journalists and bloggers for their criticism, no such progress has been observed to date. Although the Government has initially engaged in the process of decriminalizing defamation, it later ceased this process, maintaining defamation criminalized to date, and cases of arbitrary application of criminal laws continue to be reported. As noted by various international and domestic human rights organisations and institutions, including the Commissioner for Human Rights of the COE, who noted in December 2019 that 'journalists and social media activists, who had expressed dissent or criticism of the authorities, are detained or imprisoned in Azerbaijan on a variety of charges', signaling the authorities' failure or willingness to put an end to this systemic problem.[130] Critical media continues being under severe repression, including through criminal charges and other means of pressure such as travel bans against journalists or arbitrary blocking of critical news websites, which offers no indication of progress in putting an end to persecution of critical journalists.[131]

130 Commissioner for Human Rights report following her visit to Azerbaijan from 8 to 12 July 2019, 11 December 2019, CommDH(2019)27, accessed 20 March 2020, 8; Human Rights Watch World Report 2020: Azerbaijan, accessed 20 March 2020; A Unified List of Political Prisoners in Azerbaijan, prepared by Azerbaijani human rights groups, 3 September 2019, accessed 20 March 2020.

131 Human Rights Watch World Report 2020, Azerbaijan; Reporters Without Borders, Azerbaijan profile page, accessed 22 August 2020.

In the *Muradova, Mammadov (Jalaloglu) and Mikayil* group of cases, relating to ill-treatment allegations by police and other law enforcement agents, and failure to effectively investigate, no progress has been reported by the authorities, except for the adoption of two executive acts, discussed above. Furthermore, in 2018, the CPT described the situation publicly as 'remain[ing] systemic and endemic' further suggesting no tangible progress made since its first report in 2004 or first ECtHR judgment in 2007. All interviewed human rights lawyers and civil society representatives named ill-treatment and torture by law enforcement agents as the most egregious human rights issue, which they struggle to address due no access to closed institutions and prevailing impunity and 'protectionism' among relevant state bodies.[132] Further to that, interviewed human rights lawyers raised their concerns about being subjected to retaliations for publicly exposing such cases reported by their clients in detention as the only 'whistleblowers' on this issue.[133]

The *Ilgar Mammadov* group of cases represents a new category of cases in the Court's jurisprudence dealing with *bad faith* in the Government's actions in limiting human rights of its critics. This group does not only identify the violations in the Government's actions but also exposes the ulterior purpose behind such actions signaling its intentional abuse of power to limit individual Convention rights, and Azerbaijan's growing authoritarian tendencies. Such failings are further accompanied by the judiciary's failure to ensure effective judicial oversight over such limitations, signaling its inability to stand against authoritarian policies of the executive and the low likelihood of expected reforms in the 'bad faith' context. The low prospects of timely and relevant progress is further illustrated by the Government's persistent refusal for four years in 2014–2018 to comply with the CM call to release one of the applicants in this group, *Ilgar Mammadov*, baldly denying any bad faith behind his arrest and detention despite the Court's findings. These cases disclose fundamental deficiencies in the national system and state organisation, which require deep structural reforms reorganizing the current domestic political status quo and

132 Human rights lawyer and CSO representative, AZE02, online interview, 27 March 2018; Human rights lawyer, AZE03, Tbilisi, 11 March 2018; Human rights lawyer, AZE04, Tbilisi, 11 March 2018; Human rights lawyer and CSO representative, AZE05, online interview, 16 March 2018; Applicant and CSO representative, AZE06, Brussels, 12 December 2018; Applicant, AZE07, online interview, 17 September 2019; Applicant, AZE08, email communication, 13 September 2019.

133 Human rights lawyer and CSO representative, AZE02, online interview, 27 March 2018; Human rights lawyer, AZE04, Tbilisi, 11 March 2018.

the prevailing attitudes among state officials towards the concept of public criticism and accountability.

The *Ramazanova and Others* group of cases of 2008–2010 relate to issues that re-emerged during the so called 'unprecedented civil society crackdown' in 2014 leading to criminal prosecution of leading human rights defenders and NGOs for alleged failure to comply with NGO laws, including a requirement for NGOs to acquire state registration and register their grants. The alleged failure to register NGOs with the Ministry of Justice was used as one of the pretexts, along the alleged failure to register grants with the same Ministry, to prosecute NGO leaders in 2014 under charges of illegal entrepreneurship, tax evasion, abuse of power and other charges. In its 'Article 18' judgments relating to prosecuted human rights defenders (see *Rasul Jafarov, Aliyev, Mammadli*), the ECtHR relied on the 'general context' referring to the legislative environment regarding the operation of NGOs as 'increasingly harsh and restrictive', applied in 'intransigent and arbitrary manner', which drove a number of NGOs to operate on the fringes of the law' (*Rasul Jafarov*, para 120). Such findings, taken together with the civil society reports of their inability to continue their activities as NGOs, indicate not only the Government's unwillingness to improve the legislative and policy environment for NGOs but also exposes its intentional ulterior purpose to eliminate the civic space, which makes the prospects of timely and effective implementation less likely.

The Government's failure to take adequate actions in the *Sargsyan* case is illustrated by its disregard of the CM calls to engage in a dialogue to discuss the proposed measures and the further steps, including those proposed by NGOs in their submissions in this cases, as well as by its unwillingess to frame its obligation to comply with this ECtHR judgment outside the wider political context of the conflict and its hostile relations with the Armenian Government. Its initial report on the existing compensation mechanism without any further engagement with the CM appears to be the Government's attempt to offer a quick solution to compliance, however, as later appeared, falling short of genuine intent to seek for ways to comply with the very specific remedy indicated by the ECtHR. Such behavior is reminiscent of the Government's wider failure to meet its CoE accession commitment to seek for a peaceful solution to the conflict, which this judgment offers to facilitate to some extent. Although the judgments deal with the aftermath of the conflict, i.e. rights of displaced individuals, they carry a strong potential in breaking the deadlock of political negotiations in the frozen conflict that has been pending for over two decades without any tangible results, if used willfully and determinedly, particularly given the ECtHR's strong stance that the ongoing negotiations did not release the states from their duty to take other measures.[134]

All five groups of cases feature similar patterns of the State's 'forced dialogue' with the Strasbourg process contingent on the level of CM's efforts to engage with Azerbaijan on particular cases or groups of cases. Although legally binding, the unconditional Convention obligation to comply with ECtHR judgments does not carry sufficient primacy for the Government to engage effectively in the implementation process on its own initiative and in good will. It is in cases of a systemic follow up both by the CM and its Secretariat where the Government's enhanced engagement is observed. This socialization process however does not sufficiently catalyse the domestic decision makers for positive change and is not a guarantor of positive tangible systemic results. The analysed cases exemplify the Government's policy to unilaterally decide on the substance of the actions to be reported to the CM as progress, in disregard of the CM's calls for dialogue on their effectiveness and/or sufficiency. The diverse nature of the human rights issues in these selected examples suggests that the Government's response to these judgments and CM's pressure is less dependent on the type of human rights issue as a potentially sensitive one to the domestic authorities as it is affected by the *systemic* nature of the identified problems, exposing deep structural deficiencies of the domestic system and state organisation. A strong pattern of failure to effectively engage with the supervision process in the vast majority of leading cases is predetermined by the wider political and legal domestic system, organised on the basis of power grips by the executive and political interests, falling short of human rights conducive culture and adequate checks and balances. As Grewal and Voeten suggested in 2015, democratizing states resisting compliance with ECtHR judgments become slower in complying with their obligations due to lack of institutional mechanisms that would step in to correct such failings.[135] When the very state fundamentals are built on and maintained by the authoritarian ideology lacking respect for and recognition of individual rights and freedoms, socialisation with the Strasbourg process can lead to some ad hoc positive developments individual cases, however, not sufficient to break through the

134 Philip Leach, 'Thawing the Frozen Conflict? The European Court's Nagorno-Karabakh Judgments' (EJIL: TALK! 6 July 2015), accessed 20 March 2020; Ramute Remezaite, 'Introductory Note to *Chiragov and Others v Armenia* and *Sargsyan v Azerbaijan* (EUR. CT.H.R.)' International Legal Materials (American Society of International Law 57(3) June 2018) 405–436.

135 Sharanbir Grewal and Erik Voeten, 'Are New Democracies Better Human Rights Compliers?' (2012) SSRN e-Library, accessed on 3 July 2016, 25.

wall of systemic structural problems exposing the weaknesses of the very foundations of the state. In the following section, I discuss some of the factors that offer explanation to Azerbaijan's poor engagement with the supervision process and compliance with ECtHR judgments.

3.2.4 *Explaining Azerbaijan's Absence of Good Faith*

The CoE system has long operated on the assumption that its member states act in good faith when addressing their human rights violations.[136] In the case of Azerbaijan, as discussed above, the CoE's reliance on the state's willingness to become a democratic European state stemmed from the Government's strong repeated assurances that they were *willing* and *able* to abide by the CoE standards, regardless of absence of sufficient political pluralism and entrenched democratic guarantees. Almost two decades later, however, the democratic, human rights and rule of law records do not only not suggest any incremental improvement but are symptomatic of growing authoritarian tendencies. Against this context, I argue that the implementation process of individual human rights judgments does not take place in isolation from the wider political and social context in the country, and is largely driven by the domestic political realities. As Alice Donald and Anne-Katrin Speck argued in her article on the dynamics of domestic human rights implementation, implementation needs to be understood in the context of pre-existing conditions, which may shape perceptions of what remedies are practically feasible and politically attainable.[137] I therefore suggest that there is a direct correlation between absence of strong foundations for respect for democracy, rule of law and human rights or willingness to create them in Azerbaijan, and its systemic failure to comply with ECtHR judgments. My findings offer several conclusions in that regard.

Firstly, there is no sufficient overall domestic political support to comply with ECtHR judgments and engage in substantive reforms stemming from those judgments stemming from the absence of a strong domestic human rights agenda. The Government has continuously claimed its readiness to comply with ECtHR judgments (and wider CoE commitments), however, its actions suggest the opposite. Although ECtHR judgments can serve as one of

136 Başak Çalı, 'Coping with Crisis: Whither the Variable Geometry in the Jurisprudence of the European Court of Human Rights' (22 February 2018) Vol. 35, No. 2 Wisconsin International Law Journal 36, accessed 27 February 2019.

137 Alice Donald and Anne-Katrin Speck, 'The Dynamics of Domestic Human Rights Implementation: Lessons from Qualitative Research in Europe' (2020), Volume 12 Issue 1, Journal of Human Rights Practice 1–23, 1–2, 7.

the CoE support mechanisms offered to member states to help identify and address its systemic human rights problems, which often, justifiably, require extensive time resources and efforts, I suggest that the ECtHR findings of state's acting in 'bad faith', which the Court recognized as s a systemic structural problem, and the systemic failure to engage with the Strasbourg processes is a turning point in this approach vis-a-vis Azerbaijan. The establishment by the ECtHR, in a legal authoritative way, of the authorities' abuse of power to limit individual rights in a systemic way, and the domestic courts' consistent failure to offer effective judicial review, is indicative of their wider approach towards the unwillingness to establish a human rights conducive culture with the support of ECtHR judgments. With these judgments, exposing politically motivated prosecutions, the ECtHR did not only rule on the violations of rights of affected individuals but also unveiled the repressive domestic politics, disclosing structural deficiencies of the domestic system and making it increasingly difficult for the Government to defy its repressive policies.[138] In *Aliyev*, the Court established a 'troubling pattern' of such behavior in prosecuting human rights defenders and civil society activists, and called for measures to eradicate it (paras 223, 226). In *Natig Jafarov*, the Court referred to such prosecutions as effecting 'the very essence of democracy', in which 'individual freedom may only be limited in the general interest (para 69). These cases are particularly illustrative of the pre-existing context, which predetermines the authorities' general approach towards CoE's promoted principles where it does not only fail to protect them but also intentionally abuse them for its own domestic political gains, superseding its international human rights obligations. This approach is well reflected in the President Aliyev's reactionary comment to the PACE resolution on political prisoners in Azerbaijan adopted in January 2020, which relied extensively on ECtHR's respective judgments and called for their full implementation:

> This organization, unfortunately, does not have any authority today. Its decisions are absolutely irrelevant for us. The latest resolution adopted in connection with Azerbaijan has no meaning for us; for us, it has no more value than a piece of paper. We do not accept any of the far-fetched accusations contained in it and will not fulfil any of their "requirements".[139]

---

138 See e.g. Reply of the authorities of 17 September 2014 to the communication from 7 NGOs in the *Ramazanova and Others* group of cases of 5 September 2014.

139 APA News, 'President Ilham Aliyev receives Turkish Foreign Minister Mevlut Cavusoglu', 6 February 2020, accessed 5 March 2020.

I further suggest that the domestic context is particularly relevant in cases where ECtHR judgments trigger the exposure of deep political and structural sensitivities in the domestic state system and the existing culture of strong consolidated executive power structures. The high likelihood of such scenarios in Azerbaijani cases is predetermined by the fact that the vast majority of ECtHR judgments, also known as 'leading cases', reveal deeply rooted structural problems in the domestic system, and are therefore politically sensitive to implement as they often challenge the very organization of the state (varying from the issue of political prisoners to lack of independence of judiciary to absence of fair and free elections). Strong reluctance of the long term ruling elite to change the existing status quo offers no 'easy' way to implement the judgments without deconstructing the exposed deficiencies of the domestic system. As a way of example, supporting this hypothesis, the likelihood to see any substantial progress in the *Nemat Aliyev* group of cases calling for fundamental reforms in the electoral system and the application of the laws to ensure free and fair elections is highly questionable in light of the decades long ruling elite's grip to maintain its consolidated state power. Creating favourable environment for the civil society conducive to their effective operation, as part of the selected *Ramazanova and Others* group and the *Ilgar Mammadov* group, would run against the very intention of the authorities to limit the civic space and in that way control and suppress public criticism on their policies. The measures required in the *Muradova, Mammadov (Jalaloglu) and Mikayil* group would involve effective investigation and prosecution of responsible law enforcement agents, and substantial reforming of the whole law enforcement mechanism, where torture, corruption and impunity remains 'systemic and endemic', as concluded by the CPT.[140] The *Sargsyan* case exposes conflict affected domestic sensitivities involving rewarding compensations to Armenian victims of property rights violations in politically hostile 'enemy' state in the context of years long failure to demonstrate genuine willingness to reach a peaceful solution to the conflict.[141] None of these cases offer an easy way out for the authorities to ensure both full and effective compliance with these judgments and maintaining of strong authoritarian power grip and domestic political interests of the ruling regime.

The research findings further suggest that high political sensitivity around one case, or group of cases, is likely to significantly affect the Government's overall engagement with the CM process in other cases, perceived by the

140 CoE News on torture and impunity in Azerbaijan (n 105).
141 Leach, Remezaite (n 134).

Government as a politicized process against he country. A good illustration of this phenomenon was the case of Ilgar Mammadov and the political turmoil that its implementation question has led as it brought back the issue of political prisoners in Azerbaijan to the CoE table. The CM, which had repeatedly called for Mr Mammadov's release, following the ECtHR judgment of May 2014, from December 2014 to December 2017 and eventually triggered the infringement proceedings on 5 December 2017, during which he was eventually released, has faced increasing difficulties to engage with Azerbaijan not only in this case but also in other cases. As described by the interviewed DEJ representative in 2017:

> They are the only country among all 47 [member states] where when you have them on the agenda, no new information in provided. Full stop. There is a complete lack of engagement with the process.[142]

The persistent refusal of the Government to respond to the CM repeated calls to release Mr Mammadov as the then potentially main political rival to the incumbent President in the presidential elections in October 2013, as part of the implementation of ECtHR judgment has led to gradual disengagement of the Government from the CM process, which appeared to have also affected Azerbaijan's engagement in other cases. As the DEJ representative described it at the time, 'there are major communication problems and this means we are in a very difficult situation with Azerbaijan to find a way out from the current deadlock'.[143] His offered explanation referred to 'the nature of the problem as the Court struck down on several fundamental problems such as arbitrary application of criminal laws, and for the authorities it is more important to show the power than to respect the Convention'.[144] This suggests that the higher the political sensitivity of the consolidated political power is to the required measures, the less likely that the domestic interests will eventually yield to the legal authority of ECtHR judgments and the interpretation of the measures needed by the CM as a political body through its peer-review system. This approach of disregard and bald disagreement has been reiterated by President Aliyev as the highest political power in the country in his response to the earlier quoted PACE report on political prisoners in Azerbaijan:

> They try to describe Azerbaijan only in black colors and again, relying on unfounded and falsified data, publish reports and adopt resolutions.

142 CM member state representative, SXB03, Strasbourg, 23 May 2017.
143 DEJ official, SXB04, Strasbourg, 30 November 2016.
144 Ibid.

> There are allegedly political prisoners here and democratic process is supposedly obstructed in Azerbaijan. All this is a lie, there are no political prisoners in Azerbaijan – we know this well.[145]

Similar approaches, although not as bald and explicit, were observed just before the arrests during the 2014 crackdown, that led to the ECtHR's 'Article 18' judgments when the President of Azerbaijan, during his inaugural speech f Azerbaijan's Chairmanship at the CM in PACE in June 2014, reiterated his readiness 'to confront double standards' vis a vis Azerbaijan, implying that the increased focus on Azerbaijan and the issue of political prisoners, including Mr Mammadov's release is unjustified and politically biased.[146] He baldly reiterated that 'Azerbaijan is ready and willing to implement its commitments and obligations' just two months before the arrests of civil society leaders that led to their criminal prosecution in the midst of Azerbaijan's CM chairmanship.[147] Such consistent dismissal of the ECtHR and the CM positions, although at times combined with information provided to the CM as referring to some progress, does not offer any guarantees of genuine readiness of the domestic system to enter into constructive dialogue with the aim to comply with ECtHR judgments. In light of the consolidation of domestic political power in the President's hands, the likelihood of overturning such an approach by any other state institutions, including the judiciary, is very low if not non-existent.

In light of Azerbaijan's generally low engagement with the CM supervision process, discussed in Section 3.2.3, the growing disengagement is well illustrated through cases where some communication was observed around the time of the CM's intensifying focus on highly sensitive cases such as Mr Mammadov's release or other cases of politically motivated prosecution. This is particularly noticeable in the *Mahmudov and Agazade* group of cases, where considerable substantive engagement was initially observed in in the first two years of the implementation. Around 2012–2013, as part of the implementation of this group, the authorities reported to the CM their preparation for reforms to amend the legislation on criminal defamation to be in line with the Convention norms and sought for assistance from the Venice Commission to that end. It provided updates to the CM on a frequent basis in light with what

145 APA News (n 139).

146 President Aliyev speech in PACE (n 9).

147 PACE Resolution 2185 (2017) 'Azerbaijan's Chairmanship of the Council of Europe: what follow-up on respect for human rights? (11 October 2017).

was expected to be done in this group of cases.[148] As one of the interviewed CM delegates has put it, 'at some point there was some more proper discussion on the *Mahmudov and Agazade* group and the necessary law amendments but that … stopped and suddenly there was no engagement with them anymore'.[149] The CM attempted to address this shift in its decisions on this group of cases: since June 2015, the CM has repeatedly 'deplored the absence of any information', insisted on 'the necessity to strengthen without any delay the dialogue with all relevant bodies/institutions of the Council of Europe', reminded of 'the importance of the dialogue', and continued 'stressing anew the importance of finding solutions to the problems' at every quarterly meeting except for one until June 2018.[150] These efforts however did not generate *any* domestic response, leading this group to further standstill.

Such a notable shift in the domestic strategy towards implementation signifies a strong likelihood of the Government's decision to cut its engagement with the Strasbourg process as a result of the growing tensions around the high political sensitivity of 'Article 18' cases, nine of such cases as of July 2020, and the issue of release of Mr Mammadov in particular, with the increasing pressure from the CM and various other CoE bodies. The highly politicised approach to certain salient human rights judgments and the overall supervision system by the country's leadership suggests that while often presented as a seemingly technical exercise, implementation is fundamentally seen as a political process where domestic interests shall be considered before the primacy of ECtHR judgments and the overall unconditional obligation to comply with ECtHR judgments under Article 46(1) of the Convention. The very disagreement on the interpretation of necessary measures stemming from ECtHR judgments that establishes fundamental deficiencies of the domestic system and the continuing systemic failure to effectively engage with the Strasbourg process is indicative of the authorities' inability to effectively domesticate the Convention standards two decades after the accession to the CoE when it runs contrary to the very organisation and structure of the state and the domestic political costs are too high. It also raises questions as to the ability and existing constraints of the Strasbourg supervision system to ensure compliance of ECtHR judgments in such circumstances.

---

148 HUDOC EXEC database, *Mahmudov and Agazade* group of cases, Government Communications examined during CM meetings on 4–6 December 2012, 4–6 June 2013 and 3–5 December 2013, accessed 29 March 2020.

149 CM member state representative, SXB01, Strasbourg, 23 May 2017.

150 HUDOC EXEC, *Mahmudov and Agazade v Azerbaijan*, CM decisions, accessed 27 December 2021.

3.2.5 *Adequacy of the Response of the CM and the CoE to Azerbaijan's Acting in Bad Faith*

Azerbaijan's lowest implementation rank among all CoE member states and the deepening communication crisis between Baku and Strasbourg inevitably pose questions as to effectiveness of the response to the situation from the CM and DEJ, as well as other CoE bodies involved in the implementation of ECtHR judgments. As Çali and Koch suggest, the CM peer-review mechanism, supported by the DEJ as its expert Secretariat, offers a combination of both the authoritative legal expert review and political facilitation, which may help counter-balance the pitfalls of politicisation of the process.[151] I argue that although the CM and other CoE bodies demonstrated strong and at times unprecedented incentives to address non-implementation of some of the most salient human rights judgments against Azerbaijan, the response lacked sufficient robustness and coordination of the employed methods. As a result, it failed to maintain a uniform principled position to Azerbaijan's deepening disregard to its Convention obligations. I further suggest that the CoE supervision system may not have sufficient authority and political determination to address the failure of such serious non-compliers as Azerbaijan to deal with systemic structural human rights issues unless it ensured a fair balance of facilitative and coercive measures in responding to this challenge.

The CM, as the supervisory body for compliance with ECtHR judgments, has increasingly scrutinized a number of leading Azerbaijani cases through its various procedures in the last years. CM's enhanced involvement, along the standard DEJ-coordinated procedures, is driven by Azerbaijan's being among 10 member states with the highest number of cases under 'enhanced supervision' procedure. The interviewed DEJ representative suggested this was largely influenced by the exposure of the structural flaws of the domestic system in many judgments:

> Azerbaijan has encountered much more head on structural fundamental deficiencies of its state organisation. No country has as many decisions from the Court finding that the decisions of the domestic courts or prosecutors are arbitrary and purposely misuse the criminal legislation to limit freedom of expression. This, of course, has led to [a] more serious approach vis a vis Azerbaijan calling for greater independence of judiciary, challenging, to some extent, the President's ability to ensure it as he

151 Basak Çali, Anne Koch, 'Foxes Guarding the Foxes? The Peer Review of Human Rights Judgments by the Committee of Ministers of the Council of Europe' (2014) Volume 14, Issue 2, Human Rights Law Review 301–325 22.

> is the guarantor of independent judiciary under the Constitution. So it is much more head on fight with its state organisation.[152]

The sheer variety of tactics employed by the CM and the DEJ to engage with Azerbaijan on the substance, in response to its persistent failures to respond to Strasbourg calls, compared to other CoE member states, is indicative of their enhanced efforts to address the situation. Apart from standard requirements to the Government to provide regular action plans and action reports, Azerbaijani cases have been put on the agenda of the CM human rights meetings on numerous occasions, and in a consistent manner, as discussed in Section 3.2.3.1 and a large proportion of them put for a 'debate' by the CM at its quarterly human rights meetings exclusively held for implementation matters. Debates on particular cases do not only lead to formal CM decisions with specific recommendations to respondent states but also expose the particular delegation in front of all the CM members to account for insufficient steps taken or the disregard of CM recommendations, ensuring more intense scrutiny of the respective cases. It allows CM members to scrutinize the (non) implementation of a particular case in real time, with an Azerbaijani representative in the CM meeting room, as opposed to otherwise more formal written communication between the Government and the DEJ. It may also serve as an additional incentive on the respondent state to present its position on the progress of a particular case in a timely and adequate way when it is to be formally reviewed by a forum of 46 other delegations – and has been proven to be effective in that regard in the case of Azerbaijan, as discussed in the preceding section. One of the interviewed DEJ representatives reiterated that they would decide to put a case for a debate when 'the states do not make constructive proposals' for their actions to comply with judgments and do not engage in the usual 'order of business'.[153]

Failing to secure any constructive progress from enhanced communication, and, in some instances, faced with bald disregard of CM's calls for updates in the examined cases, through their usual supervision procedures, the CM and DEJ employed other, less conventional supervision methods to respond to the information vacuum and to advance the process with Azerbaijan in some of the closely scrutinized cases. For example, in the *Mahmudov and Agazade* group of cases, relating to criminal prosecution of journalists, the DEJ sent Azerbaijan a detailed case specific list of questions in June 2014 and, similarly,

152 DEJ official, SXB04, Strasbourg, 30 November 2016.
153 DEJ official, SXB04, Strasbourg, 30 November 2016.

extended an invitation to the CM delegations to pose specific questions to Azerbaijan in writing, which they did in their decision in March 2016, in the hope of exerting influence on Azerbaijan to provide specific substantive information on the progress of the cases.[154] Such a move, taken only once in relation to Azerbaijan, and not ever taken in any Georgian or Armenian cases that I have analysed for this research, provided for an additional opportunity for individual CM delegations to place more direct scrutiny on this particular group directly with the Government of Azerbaijan. Although the Government of Azerbaijan submitted its answers to the questions, it primarily focused on trainings provided to various relevant state institutions and bodies, which the CM found as failing to 'relieve concerns' and insisted on 'the necessity to strengthen without further delay the dialogue', in its fourth interim resolution in this group of cases.[155] The CM adopts interim resolutions, as opposed to its decisions, as a means of, e.g. expressing concern or putting increased pressure on a state to provide information on progress achieved as a weightier procedural instrument, which in this case further signifies the growing concern over the Government's inaction.[156] Around the same time, two of the interviewed CM delegates also recalled their attempts to hold informal individual dialogues with the Azerbaijani delegation to discuss the necessary reforms, with the aim to 'build trust' in their support to Azerbaijan in this process, but regretted that they 'did not succeed' as Azerbaijan was not willing to engage in any substantive discussions formally or informally.[157]

In other cases, the CM attempted to address the growing resistance and disregard of Azerbaijan to comply with suggested measures were complemented by the various steps taken by other CoE bodies, indicating evidence of cumulative efforts of the CoE to ensure compliance. In the case of *Ilgar Mammadov*, for example, in light of the communication deadlock and the failure of Azerbaijan to comply with the CM's repeated calls to release Mr Mammadov

154 CM decisions on the *Mahmudov and Agazade* group of cases, adopted at its 1201st meeting on 5 June 2014 and at its 1250th meeting on 8–10 March 2016.

155 Reply from Azerbaijan to the questions pursuant to the decision adopted at the 1250th meeting (DH) in the *Mahmudov and Agazade group of cases v. Azerbaijan* (Appl. no. 35877/04), 20 April 2016; CM Interim Resolution CM/ResDH(2016)145 on the execution of the judgments of the European Court of Human Rights in the cases of *Mahmudov and Agazade against Azerbaijan* and *Fatullayev against Azerbaijan*, adopted by the Committee of Ministers on 8 June 2016 at the 1259th meeting of Ministers' Deputies.

156 European Implementation Network Handbook for NGOs, injured parties and their legal advisers, Implementation of Judgments of the European Court of Human Rights, 2018, enriched in January 2020 12.

157 CM member state representative, SXB01, Strasbourg, 23 May 2017.

from prison, the efforts taken to secure implementation were extended beyond the CM realm, by invoking other CoE mechanisms such as the official human rights inquiry under Article 52 of the Convention into 'Azerbaijan's implementation of the European Convention of Human Rights' launched by the Secretary General of the CoE.[158] In his official statement, Secretary General Thorbjørn Jagland noted that 'judgments from the European Court of Human Rights have highlighted an arbitrary application of the law in Azerbaijan, notably in order to silence critical voices and limit freedom of speech' expressing concern on 'the lack of positive steps to address the situation', on the basis of which he launched his first ever inquiry. His particular focus on the case of Mr Mammadov, which he described as a case 'when individuals are deprived of their liberty due to an abuse of power by a country's legal authorities' suggests that the inquiry was launched to complement the efforts of the CM to secure compliance with the respective ECtHR judgment, generating additional pressure on the authorities to engage and explain how it complies with this and other ECtHR judgments.

This tool however appeared to be of limited effectiveness as it did not entail any formal procedures or enforcement mechanism, and is primarily of a diplomatic nature, largely dependent on the authorities' good will to engage. In this particular case, it took 13 months from the official decision of the Secretary General until his representative travelled to Baku in January 2017 to meet the authorities and discuss the issues of concern, including the release of Mr Mammadov.[159] Following the visit, the Government noted, in their action plan submitted to the CM a month later, that the authorities 'confirmed their readiness to examine all avenues suggested by the mission to further execute the Court's judgment', however failing to commit to more specific plans or timeframes, or stipulate what their readiness entailed in light of the ECtHR findings, i.e. if this involved the release of Mr Mammadov.[160] In the same action plan, it once again reiterated the adoption of the Presidential Order of 10 February 2017, on the liberalisation of the penal policy, which it has also referred to in the *Mahmudov and Agazade* group of cases, without any further engagement with the specific repeated calls from the CM relating to the release

158 CoE News, 'Azerbaijan human rights inquiry', Secretary General, Strasbourg, 16 December 2015, accessed 27 March 2019.

159 PACE Committee on Legal Affairs and Human Rights, The Implementation of Judgments of the European Court of Human Rights, Rapporteur Mr Pierre-Yves Le Borgn, 12 June 2017 [27], accessed 18 September 2019.

160 Communication from Azerbaijan concerning the case of *Ilgar Mammadov v. Azerbaijan* (Appl. no. 15172/13), 14 February 2017.

of Mr Mammadov or any other specific measures.[161] Although this rarely used 'Article 52' procedure triggered the Government's response, through a new action plan to the CM, substantively, it did not advance the progress of the case with any practical tangible steps as the Government continued resorting to its tactics to reiterate its wider commitments without taking any tangible specific measures.

Following three years of repeated calls by the CM for the release of Mr Mammadov and its other attempts to ensure compliance with its calls, as Mr Mammadov continued languishing in prison, the CM eventually reached a decision in December 2017 to initiate infringement proceedings against Azerbaijan in the case of Mr Mammadov that some of the CM delegations have seen as the 'last resort' measure.[162] The CM's request to the Court to rule if Azerbaijan had failed in its obligation under Article 46(1) of the Convention to comply with the judgment in this particular case, on behalf of 46 member states, and its perception as a last resort measure is indicative of the CM's reaching a position that it has exhausted all available diplomatic political means in its possession to ensure compliance in this particular case, to no avail. The CM's return of the case back to the Court as a judicial institution for its legal interpretation on Azerbaijan's adherence to its Article 46(1) obligations signifies the CM's resort to measures seeking for a legally binding framework from the Court to ensure compliance with the judgment that is no longer a matter of negotiations between the respondent state and Strasbourg but a legally binding decision. Although Mr Mammadov was conditionally released by Baku Appeal Court in August 2018, nine months before the Court ruled on the infringement proceedings, no explicit references to the ongoing proceedings before the ECtHR were made by the domestic courts that would indicate any direct causal link, with the authorities arguing in the infringement proceedings that it did not fail to comply with the ECtHR judgment by refusing to release Mr Mammadov. It is suggested that it was the highly political salience of this judgment and the unprecedented focus on this case that predetermined the persistent position of the Government insisting that it did not fail in its obligation to comply by refusing to release Mr Mammadov as part of the implementation process while in effect taking steps in line with the CM calls.[163] Only in April 2020,

161 CM decision in the case of *Ilgar Mammadov*, adopted at its 1280th meeting in March 2017.

162 Interim Resolution of the Committee of Ministers on the execution of the judgment of the European Court of Human Rights *Ilgar Mammadov v Azerbaijan*, CM/ResDH(2017)429, 5 December 2017; CM member state representative, SXB02, Strasbourg, 23 May 2017; CM member state representative, SXB03, Strasbourg, 23 May 2017.

163 *Ilgar Mammadov v Azerbaijan*, Appl. no. 15172/13 (ECtHR 29 May 2019) [126–132], Annex to the judgment, [8–10, 23].

the Supreme Court has eventually adopted a decision to quash the conviction of Mr Mammadov and fully remedy him for the violations, which has likely been influenced by the mounting pressure on the authorities in this case (see 3.2.3.1).

In this context of the mounting tensions between Azerbaijan and the CM, and the growing number of new cases raising the issue of the 'bad faith' in the authorities' actions being sent to the Court in the midst of the systemic criminal prosecution of civil society members in 2014–2015, a number of CoE bodies explored various other methods to respond to the deepening crisis vis-à-vis Azerbaijan, including in relation to implementation of ECtHR judgments. During the escalation of the crackdown on the civil society, the Commissioner for Human Rights Nils Muižnieks did not only resort to its more conventional work methods, such as public statements, calling Azerbaijan 'an area of darkness', but also intervened as a third party in a number of cases of persecuted human rights defenders, journalists and lawyers to assist the Court with adequately addressing the situation on the ground – which he described as 'an illustration of a serious and systemic human rights problem in Azerbaijan, where critical voices are often subject to reprisals and judicially harassed'.[164] The ECtHR relied extensively on the Commissioner's interventions, as well as the various opinions of the Venice Commission on the laws regulating NGO activity in Azerbaijan, in its judgments of the above applicants establishing the illegality of the authorities' actions and the ulterior purpose behind such actions in a violation of Article 18 of the Convention.[165] The Commissioner sought to assist the Court with his third party interventions as 'an additional tool at the Commissioner's disposal ... to provide objective and impartial information to the Court ...', which he has done systematically in the majority of human rights defenders' cases against Azerbaijan, serving as a successful model of cooperation of the CoE bodies on the same matter through their respective mandates.[166]

Amplification of these efforts in turn generated further engagement of CoE bodies calling for action upon Azerbaijan on the same issues. The ECtHR judgments against Azerbaijan exposing systemic use of arbitrary deprivation of

164 CoE News, 'Commissioner Muižnieks intervenes before the European Court of Human Rights on the case of Intigam Aliyev' (18 March 2015), accessed 28 March 2019; CoE Commissioner opinion article, 'Azerbaijan: an area of darkness' (28 October 2015), accessed 28 March 2019.

165 *Rasul Jafarov* [120]; *Aliyev* [223] (n 8).

166 CoE News, 'Commissioner Muižnieks intervenes in cases concerning Azerbaijan before the European Court of Human Rights', 24 February 2015.

liberty against critics by the authorities acting in abuse of their power formed the basis for the report of the renewed PACE rapporteur mandate on political prisoners in Azerbaijan, in effect enabling the PACE to establish the existence of political prisoners in Azerbaijan, which the Azerbaijani Government and the delegation to the PACE refuted as the politicised 'double standard' process against the country.[167] In her report of December 2019, the PACE rapporteur, Icelandic MP Ms Thorhildur Sunna Ævarsdottir, referred to the respective ECtHR judgments as a strong advantage in addressing this highly sensitive and important issue in Azerbaijan in the context of its compliance with its CoE membership commitments.[168] The rapporteur's report further endorsed the CM efforts to ensure compliance in the *Ilgar Mammadov* group and other cases by calling upon the Azerbaijani authorities to '[t]ake promptly every possible step towards full implementation of the judgments of the European Court of Human Rights'.[169] This report follows earlier attempts of PACE to endorse the CM work to ensure swift implementation of ECtHR judgments in the earlier reviews of Azerbaijan's commitments through the PACE monitoring procedures. In its report in 2017, reflecting on the deepening communication crisis, the PACE called upon Azerbaijan to 'cooperate more closely' with the CM and the DEJ in complying with the judgments, including 'the cases of the so-called "political prisoners"/"prisoners of conscience"'.[170] Relying on the CM's identification of several systemic, structural issues in a number of leading cases against Azerbaijan, such as the lack of independence of judiciary or arbitrary use of criminal laws, the PACE urged Azerbaijan to take 'much more effective measures', thus indicating the deepening concern over Azerbaijan's failure to comply with ECtHR judgments.[171]

Such diverse efforts by the CM, DEJ and several other CoE bodies to engage with Azerbaijan's poor compliance with some of the most salient ECtHR judgments well illustrate their cumulative attempts to address the deepening concern and serves as a good example of their ability to reinforce each other's actions to scrutinise Azerbaijan's performance on particular cases or issues. The consistent pressure from the CoE on the issue of arbitrary arrests and

167 PACE Committee on Legal Affairs and Human Rights, Reported cases of political prisoners in Azerbaijan, Rapporteur Ms Thorhildur Sunna ÆVARSDÓTTIR, Iceland, Socialists, Democrats and Greens Group, No. 15020 (10 December 2019), accessed 28 March 2019.

168 Ibid [54].

169 Ibid [11.4].

170 PACE Committee on the Honouring of Obligations and Commitments by Member States of the Council of Europe (Monitoring Committee), Report No. 14403 on the functioning of democratic institutions in Azerbaijan 25 September 2017, accessed 28 March 2019.

171 Ibid [4, 6].

political prisoners suggests its mounting willingness to employ the various methods and procedures to respond to Azerbaijan's growing failure to effectively engage with the Strasbourg implementation process. Such response is in line with this study's findings showing a clear tendency for the Azerbaijani authorities to engage better in cases where there is enhanced persistent attention from the CM and other bodies. The findings of my research, however, also offer conclusions that such enhanced focus does not guarantee timely tangible results, which raises the question of adequacy and efficiency of such efforts.

Effective state's socialisation with international human rights judgments is in its nature based on dialogue and cooperation, with domestic mechanisms playing the primary role in compliance, where the monitoring mechanisms, as suggested by several scholars, have positive facilitative effects on compliance outcomes.[172] Azerbaijan's example with regard to the discussed cases brings challenges to this concept in that the state as a party to the dialogue is showing signs of mounting unwillingness to engage in any genuine discourse with the Strasbourg process aimed to assist it in complying with respective judgments. In such circumstances, particularly where persistent urging and pressure proves to be an efficient mean for communication, in absence of wilful engagement, the carrot and stick approach becomes more relevant, in light of which I assess the CM's and the wider CoE efforts. The growing number of cumulative and diverse attempts is observed, primarily in the various forms of repeated regular calls for action as a form of pressure for further progress. Apart from some limited specific individual measures, however, such efforts led to no real tangible reforms aimed to address the deeply structural systemic human rights issues. I suggest three factors affected this outcome.

Firstly, although the CM and other bodies have taken increasingly firm steps to exert pressure on Azerbaijan for its failings, the impact of some of these actions would have likely benefited from greater robustness in maintaining constant pressure on the authorities to deliver the results. For example, more than three years of calls by the CM for release of Mr Mammadov and the continuing calls of the CM to acquit other applicants in the same group of cases for a protracted period, without any clear references to possible consequences of failure to comply, or the prolonged process of 13 months until an official human rights inquiry visit to Baku was held under Article 52 of the Convention by the office of the Secretary General, which has put other efforts 'on hold'

172 Çali and Koch, Donnelly, 'International Human Rights: A Regime Analysis' (1986) 40 International Organization 599.

for that period of time, may have incentivised the Azerbaijani authorities for swifter reactions if generated in a rigorous manner.

Secondly, as the growth in accumulation of the actions of the various bodies is significant, the inconsistency of actions among some of the institutions has likely diminished the firmness of the actions in the eyes of the authorities as to their tolerance to Azerbaijan's failures. For example, as the infringement proceedings were pending before the Court, as a clear signal to a firmer stance of the CM towards Azerbaijan's inaction, around the same time, in 2018, the CoE renewed its financial and programmatic support to Azerbaijan with the aim to help address some of the structural issues exposed through the ECtHR judgments through the multi-year high-budget CoE-Azerbaijan Action Plan 2018–2021, resorting to its 'open door' policy to offer further support to the member state to meet the Convention standards.[173] Although such support can be very beneficial if received adequately and with genuine eagerness, it appeared to further enable Azerbaijani authorities to demonstrate the implementation process as *ongoing* to the CoE counterparts in that the activities, as part of the Action Plan, are underway, as part of implementation of some of the judgments.[174] Two decades of such significant financial and programmatic support with little tangible structural change on the ground, and the re-emerging authoritarian tendencies on the systemic level call for re-assessment of the effectiveness of such policies by the CoE.

Thirdly, and relatedly, the Azerbaijani authorities were subjected to no coercive measures, in that they would have some material consequences on the state, or a realistic threat of any such measures by the CoE as a serious non-complier, which the CoE has in its possession and which may incentivize Azerbaijan to reconsider its approach towards its Convention obligations. The sticks approach is also ripe for testing in that Azerbaijan has effectively faced no accountability for numerous egregious violations in the context of the deepening authoritarian domestic tendencies and the blatant disregard of its obligations to effectively remedy them. One such measure could be the suspension of the programmatic financial funding to the state run programmes by the CoE or the suspension of Azerbaijan's voting rights in the CoE bodies, such as PACE or the CM. The misbalance in the CoE's 'sticks and carrots' approach does not only allow such non-compliers as Azerbaijan to continue their behaviour 'business as usual' but also seriously challenges the CoE ability to address

173 Council of Europe Action Plan for Azerbaijan 2018–2021 (11 September 2018), accessed 28 March 2019.

174 Communication from Azerbaijan concerning the *Ilgar Mammadov* group of cases v. Azerbaijan (Appl. no. 15172/13), Government Action Plan of 20 September 2019, 9.

such systemic disregard of obligations by a member state two decades later, during which the re-emergence of authoritarian methods has been increasingly exposed. As the absolute nature of the legal obligation to comply with ECtHR judgments is spelled out in a very explicit manner in Article 46 of the Convention, the evident continuing failure to engage on substance with the CM supervision process and the absolute statistical numbers of Azerbaijan's 85% of leading cases remaining pending, with over 50% of such cases awaiting implementation for more than 10 years, undoubtedly suggest the need for a more coercive response to the situation.

Finally, it is worth reiterating the earlier findings that the vast majority of cases against Azerbaijan, which are not subjected to such enhanced scrutiny by the CM and other CoE bodies as described above, effectively go largely unaddressed by the authorities with no tangible progress reported, particularly those pending implementation under 'standard supervision'. Although the limited resources of the CM and DEJ are significant factors to be taken into consideration, the deepening implementation crisis calls for reconsideration of the Strasbourg's peer-review priorities with regard to Azerbaijani cases.[175] It should review its employed ways to enhance its focus on the vast number of cases currently pending 'dilatory' implementation where in effect no progress has been reported for protracted periods of time. This is particularly relevant to those cases that remain highly relevant to today's human rights realities on the ground, such issues of widespread ill-treatment and torture in detention, systemic failure to ensure fair trial in criminal proceedings or overly restrictive legislation effectively disabling NGO work and the exercise of freedom of association.

3.2.6 *Why Does Azerbaijan Remain in the CoE?*

In light of the above conclusions offered by the findings of my study, I will conclude this Chapter by discussing why Azerbaijan remains a part of the CoE as its Convention obligations appear to increasingly contradict its domestic interests and priorities, and its leadership calls the growing criticism and attention to Azerbaijan as the CoE policy of 'double standards'. Equally, this raises the question of Azerbaijan's crossing of the red line of the CoE in light of its systemic and abusive failure to act in line with its Convention obligations.

In its interview in February 2020, commenting on the PACE resolution on political prisoners in Azerbaijan, prepared on the basis of findings of a number

175 Alice Donald, Debra Long, and Anne-Katrin Speck, 'Identifying and Assessing the Implementation of Human Rights Decisions' (2020), Volume 12 Issue 1, Journal of Human Rights Practice, 1–24 [2.1].

of ECtHR judgments, President Aliyev set out his approach to the criticism from the CoE:

> This organization, unfortunately, does not have any authority today. Its decisions are absolutely irrelevant for us. The latest resolution adopted in connection with Azerbaijan has no meaning for us; for us, it has no more value than a piece of paper. We do not accept any of the far-fetched accusations contained in it and will not fulfil any of their "requirements."[176]

Despite Baku's growing hostility towards the CoE as 'having no authority' and explicit affirmations that it will not comply with its calls, the country remains in the Organisation and continues engaging with its various platforms, even if to a limited extent. If the ruling power finds the CoE approach towards Azerbaijan as aimed against the state of Azerbaijan, what value does remaining in the CoE carry for Azerbaijan and are there any incentives to continue doing so? I discuss this increasingly viable question in the CoE context in light of the existing compliance theories on state engagement with international tribunals and apply it to the Azerbaijani context. This issue has been increasingly discussed by the academia, civil society and the Strasbourg officials in the context of Russia's growing intransigence towards ECtHR judgments and its strong geopolitical status but much less so in relation to Azerbaijan – which at times sends much balder messages discrediting the CoE making this question even more pertinent.[177]

Azerbaijan's official position for accessing the CoE, discussed in Section 3.1, relied on its determination to become a European state sharing the values of 'pluralistic democracy, respect for human rights and basic freedoms', which it considered to be 'a major goal in its future development'.[178] Although such affirmations were common among newly emerging states in the post Cold War Europe, domestically, the level of understanding among state institutions and political powers on what adhering to 'European values' would entail in

176 APA News on President Aliyev speech (n 139).

177 Philip Leach and Alice Donald, 'Russia Defies Strasbourg: Is Contagion Spreading?' (*EJIL:Talk! Blog of the European Journal of International Law*, 19 December 2015) accessed 9 September 2018; Bill Bowring, 'Russia and the Council of Europe: An Incompatible Ideology, and a Transplanted Legal Regime?' (September 1, 2018) P. Sean Morris (ed) Russian Discourses on International Law: Sociological and Philosophical Phenomenon (Abingdon, Routledge: 2018) 133–157; Netherlands Helsinki Committee, 'Russia's Departure from the Council of Europe Should Be Avoided' (5 December 2018), accessed 23 March 2019.

178 Address of Azerbaijan's President Heydar Aliyev to PACE 2000 (n 17).

practice was questionable. As one senior official of the CoE who participated in the compatibility assessment of the new member states in late 1990s has put it, 'we knew they were not ready and that it would take time to make progress but these were exciting times in Europe and it was a political decision of the member states to accept them'.[179] Along the objective to become a 'European family', he emphasized the motivation of equal significance 'to not stay behind Armenia and Georgia' despite 'the very different situation in Azerbaijan, such as the issue of political prisoners' and to 'advance the issue of Armenian occupation of the Nagorno Karabakh'.[180] Several interviewed human rights lawyers offered their explanations to the then understanding of the European values referring to it as the geopolitical association with the 'club of Western democracies' implying the growth of the international credibility of the country in the European arena. As one of them explained: 'even today, two decades later, our officials and even the society struggle to get to grips with such concepts, well embedded in Western Europe, as inclusiveness, tolerance and equality. Back then, upon accession, there was no understanding on what it actually entails and now there is no genuine willingness to accept them as they often contradict with our 'traditional values''.[181] Being a part of the international community was also perceived in Baku as a way to build the international image and the recognition by other states, including through the 'caviar diplomacy' aimed to subvert the CoE procedures, and benefit from international cooperation and other partnerships, such as the European Union or the international financial institutions.[182] Lastly, the CoE provides Azerbaijan with an engaging platform to raise the issue of the occupied Nagorno Karabakh territories, which it has extensively explored and continues exploring in various CoE forums.[183]

As I discuss in Chapter 2, the prevailing *constructivism* and *rational choice* compliance theories suggest that international law socializes states by their exposure to and interaction with human rights norms and institutions, but that states do so motivated by material incentives such as self-interests of governments.[184] As the *constructivism* theory finds very little support in Azerbaijan's

179 Former PACE Secretariat member, SXB08, Strasbourg, 2 December 2016.

180 Ibid.

181 Human rights lawyer, AZE03, Tbilisi, 11 March 2018.

182 Former Government representative to CoE, AZE01, online interview, 14 August 2019; Human rights lawyer and CSO representative, AZE02, online interview, 27 March 2018.

183 Among others, see the speech of Mr Samad Sayidov, Representative of the Azerbaijani Delegation to PACE on 26 April 2018, accessed 23 March 2019.

184 Ryan Goodman and Derek Jinks, *Socializing States: Promoting Human Rights Through International Law* (OUP 2013); Jutta Brunee and Stephen J. Toope, Legitimacy and Legality in International Law: An Interactional Account (CUP 2010) AJIL; Jack L. Goldsmith and

behavior in terms of its compliance with ECtHR judgments as a state that continues featuring authoritarian tendencies two decades after accessing the CoE, I focus largely on the *rational choice* theory in explaining Azerbaijan's approach to the CoE. I suggest that Azerbaijan's incentives to remain in the CoE may be gradually diminishing in light of the increasingly contentious relationship with the CoE as the Government fails to find any incentives in complying with ECtHR judgments when navigating its domestic interests. Relying on one of the competing explanations for compliance, or noncompliance with international law offered by Hillebrecht, focusing on the endogenous nature of international law, I further argue that Azerbaijan still gains more than it has to lose by remaining in the CoE, particularly the endorsement of its international reputation as a member state of the regional human rights organization, and the related political and financial gains.[185] As a part of this explanation, Hillebrecht argues that states with poor human rights record have little to lose but much to gain, such as possible foreign aid, international legitimacy and reduction in international meddling in domestic affairs even when they know that their international obligations will not be enforced. Her two other explanations, coercion and enforcement, find little support in Azerbaijan's case as a poor human rights complier as neither the other member states, nor the institution itself demonstrated sufficient authority and/or capacities to 'coerce' Azerbaijan to enforcing ECtHR judgments or 'punish' it for its continuing failings.[186] The shift in the CoE approach towards responding to the Government's systemic failures may however lead to higher domestic stakes and change the dynamics in the relationship that would likely allow the 'socialisation' role of the CoE an opportunity to (re)gain its momentum. As one of the senior CoE officials suggested, 'although some stronger steps such as infringement proceedings have been taken by the CoE to respond to the crisis with Azerbaijan, the ruling power has not yet faced any realistic threats of having its membership at stake for its disengagement and systemic failure to comply'.[187] In absence of any effective political and institutional checks over the executive's failings from other domestic actors, such as the judiciary, the legislature or the civil society, adequate constraints put on the Government by the CoE in response to its systemic refusals to abide by the ECtHR judgments would likely

---

Eric A. Posner, *The Limits of International Law*, (OUP 2005); Andrew T. Guzman, *How International Law Works: A Rational Choice Theory* (OUP 2010).

185 Courtney Hillebrecht, Domestic Politics and International Human Rights Tribunals: The Problem of Compliance. New York: Cambridge University Press, 2014 33.

186 Ibid 34–36.

187 Former PACE Secretariat member, SXB08, Strasbourg, 2 December 2016.

serve as an incentive for the authorities to reconsider its actions, when faced with a real threat to lose its political, reputational and financial gains that it has been enjoying for almost two decades. The CoE, however, to the dismay of the protection of the European values, has not yet found sufficient determination to adequately respond to the member state that has undoubtedly crossed the red line of the Convention on numerous occasions and continues doing so, facing no constraints for such behaviour.

3.3 Conclusion

Almost two decades into the CoE membership, Azerbaijan became perhaps the most primary test case for the 'open door' policy of the CoE, which embraced the incrementalist approach in early 2000s in accepting newly emerged states that still had a long way to go to effectively domesticate the CoE standards at home. Despite its strongly affirmed adherence to democratic ideals upon accession to the CoE, today Azerbaijan does not only 'lead' as the worst non-complier with ECtHR judgments; the basic fundamental values that Azerbaijan has committed to addressing for its advance accession to the CoE, such as free and fair elections, free media, free speech without repercussions, zero corruption remain at great peril, many of which the ECtHR continues addressing through its judgments. The extraordinary number of the usually rare 'Article 18' cases exposing the bad faith of the authorities in limiting the Convention rights in particular is a strong attestation to the state's failure of tangible progress and to the shift from its approach of being a democratising state, willing to live up to the CoE values and to act in good faith, to a state with strong authoritarian tendencies, no longer acting in the Convention's spirit.

Azerbaijan's low compliance record and minimal substantive engagement with the Strasbourg processes in the context of the worsening human rights situation in the country is no longer only a testament to the complex human rights issues it brought with it as a new aspiring democracy, which the CoE was willing to accept and tolerate, but also portrays the recurring and systemic unwillingness of Azerbaijan to adhere to the Convention values. As the analysis of the implementation processes of the selected number of ECtHR judgments suggests, the judgments appear to merely reflect the dire human rights situation rather than serve as catalysts for structural systemic domestic change. The Court's findings of violations of Article 18 of the Convention also serve as a significant legal recognition of the state's abuse of power acting in 'bad faith', which the Government of Azerbaijan has persistently denied to

CoE.[188] These staggering testimonies of Azerbaijan's systematic failure to genuinely engage with the Convention system have posed some difficult questions as to the adequacy of the CoE system's response to growing authoritarian tendencies in Azerbaijan.

The research findings inform that Azerbaijan fails to systematically engage with the standard Strasbourg monitoring processes in vast majority of pending cases unless there is an enhanced attention by the CM and DEJ, which generates communication. This however does not guarantee any tangible systemic changes on the ground and is limited to adoption of individual measures remedying individual applicants. This is explained by absence of a strong domestic human rights agenda that ECtHR judgments would help the Government to advance, strong consolidated executive power and political interests non-conducive to human rights and democratic values, absence of domestic checks and balances to challenge the executive's non-compliance and shortage of clear coercive measures from the CoE sending a message that such systemic non-compliance has adequate cost. In states with strong totalitarian legacies like Azerbaijan, where ECtHR judgments addressing deep-rooted complexities of human rights issues strike to the core of the system's structural fundamental deficiencies, which the long-term consolidated political power aims to maintain, the ECtHR is no longer seen as a progress supporting institution but as one that potentially undermines the very functioning of the state organisation.

188 Speech of Mr Samad Sayidov, Representative of the Azerbaijani Delegation to PACE [1:20:09] (n 183); European Stability Initiative report (n 39).

CHAPTER 4

Armenia's Compliance with Judgments of the European Court of Human Rights

A Litmus Test for the CoE?

This Chapter discusses Armenia's compliance with ECtHR judgments in its domestic context. In contrast to Azerbaijan, the analysis of Armenia's compliance performance allows for some more positive findings, however, some significant concerns rise too. Section 4.1 starts by setting out the wider political and legal context within which Armenia joined the Council of Europe (CoE) in 2001 and which sets the ground for the implementation of judgments of the European Court of Human Rights (ECtHR) since the first judgment adopted against Armenia in 2007. In Section 4.2, I discuss Armenia's compliance performance by overviewing the effectiveness of its domestic implementation system as an institutional framework and by examining the implementation process and the outcomes of specific ECtHR judgments. I do so on the basis of the detailed analysis of both the official material provided by the Armenian authorities and applicants to the Committee of Ministers (CM), and the CM's official responses, available on the HUDOC EXEC database, as well as those of other CoE bodies where relevant, and the information obtained during a dozen interviews and written communications with the Armenian authorities, CM delegates and the staff of the Department for Execution of Judgments of the European Court of Human Rights (DEJ), human rights litigators and civil society representatives (see 1.3.2). I finish with Section 4.3 by offering some insights into factors that affect timely and efficient implementation process in Armenia, as well as good practice examples of the Strasbourg and domestic actors enhancing State's compliance with its Convention obligations. Section 4.4 concludes this Chapter.

4.1 Armenia and CoE: Historical and Contextual Setting

Among all three researched countries, Armenia appears least frequently on the agendas of the various CoE bodies, and, perhaps relatedly, is the least researched with regard to its compliance with CoE commitments, including

 | DOI:10.1163/9789004538214_005

ECtHR judgments.[1] Among the CoE member states, statistically, it falls within the medium of the performance scale, displaying no extreme highs or lows in its compliance performance record. As one of the interviewed CM representatives from a Western European country put it: 'We almost never hear about Armenian cases at the CM, which must mean Armenia is not doing bad'.[2] In the wider CoE political and social context, Armenia is largely known for its continuing conflict with Azerbaijan over Nagorno Karabakh, since 1988, the solution to which and the continuing consequences of which the CoE has been determined to mediate since the two states' accession.[3] It is also known for its strong political and economic ties with Russia, at least until its 2018 peaceful Velvet Revolution, which led to the removal of the long-term political elites from power, creating space for a more accountable and representative Armenia.[4] As a small landlocked former Soviet Union state with a population of nearly 3 million, without any rich natural resources or access to sea that would allow enhance its economic independence, Armenia is often seen as a state displaying a mixture of features of democratic and authoritarian systems, and is highly dependent on foreign investment and other international support.[5]

Armenia applied to join the CoE in 1996 as part of its plan for democratisation and forming closer ties with Europe, and was accepted to the CoE on 25 January 2001, the same day as Azerbaijan. As the interviewed representative of the Armenian delegation to the CM described it, 'we needed the CoE as a credible organisation to accompany us during the democratisation period and help address the existing democratic deficiency through its standard setting, monitoring and cooperation activities'.[6] As the CM as the highest political body of the CoE declared in 1996, a few months after Armenia submitted its application, it was ready 'to facilitate and expedite as far as possible Armenia's

1 Alvina Gyulumyan and Davit Melkonyan, 'The supremacy of the European Convention on Human Rights: Armenia's path', edited by Iulia Motoc and Ineta Ziemele, *The Impact of the ECHR on Democratic Change in Central and Eastern Europe, Judicial Perspectives*, (CUP 2016); Helsinki Citizens' Assembly Vanadzor, Situation of Execution of European Court of Human Rights Judgments by Republic of Armenia, Study (2007–2015), Vanadzor 2016.

2 CM member state representative, SXB01, Strasbourg, 23 May 2017.

3 PACE Opinion 221 (2000), Armenia's application for membership of the Council of Europe, 28 June 2000 [8].

4 Anna Ohanyan, 'Armenia's Democratic Dreams' (Foreign Policy 7 November 2018), accessed 23 March 2020; Andrei Beketov, 'Nikol Pashinyan: Armenia will not be authoritarian' (Euronews 8 March 2019), 23 March 2020.

5 Freedom House, Freedom in the World 2017, Armenia, accessed 23 March 2020.

6 Governmental Official, ARM01, Strasbourg, 23 May 2017.

transition to democracy with a view to its rapid accession to the Council of Europe'.[7] Along the democratisation path for Armenia, the Parliamentary Assembly of the Council of Europe (PACE) has also expressed its belief that the accession of both Armenia and Azerbaijan could help 'establish the climate of trust necessary for a solution to the conflict in Nagorno-Karabakh', which was among the key factors for the CoE to accept both countries at the same time.[8] [9] Similarly to the cases of Azerbaijan and Georgia, the CoE relied on its open door policy to accept Armenia as a member, however, recognising that Armenia's 'current democratisation is not yet complete'.[10] The PACE report of eminent lawyers on the conformity of the Armenian legal system with the standards of the CoE in 2000 concluded as follows:[11]

> Some fear that Armenian membership of the Council of Europe will obscure realities and bestow a certificate of good conduct in the human rights field upon this State, while others consider that it might provide assistance and the requisite support along the road to democracy.
>
> Armenia is on the right road towards democracy, but only after completion of the reform of the judicial system ... will we be able to say that Armenia's domestic legal system is compatible with the Council of Europe's standards in the human rights field.

The CoE's awareness of the necessary reforms still to be made by Armenia upon its admission to the CoE is a strong testimony to the political determination of the European political leaders that 'a new iron curtain should not be drawn behind these states as this would run the risk of preventing the spread of the Council of Europe's basic values to other countries', with reference to the three South Caucasus states.[12] This policy of openness and inclusiveness, based on the emerging states' trust and commitment to deliver, has set the basis for their democratisation path as a way to test their commitment and genuineness.

As a general framework, the CoE accession conditions for Armenia were based on its ability to implement the principles of pluralist parliamentary

7 CM Resolution (96) 21 on Armenia, Request for an opinion from the Committee of Ministers to the Assembly, Accession of Armenia to the Council of Europe, adopted by the Committee of Ministers on 15 May 1996 at the 566th meeting of the Ministers' Deputies.

8 PACE Opinion 221 (2000) (n 3) [8].

9 Report of PACE Political Affairs Committee, Doc. 8747, Armenia's application for membership of the Council of Europe, 23 May 2000 [62–63, 70].

10 Ibid Appendix 1 [5].

11 Ibid Appendix 1 [5–6].

12 PACE Recommendation 1247 (1994) on Enlargement of the Council of Europe [8].

democracy, respect for human rights and the rule of law.[13] The CM stipulated that Armenia's legislative and judicial system had to be brought in line with the principles of the rule of law as a precondition for its membership.[14] As a part of it, the PACE, following its compatibility study of Armenia with CoE standards, has further stipulated Armenia's undertakings to ratify a number of CoE treaties. It included the European Convention on Human Rights (ECHR), its Protocols and the compulsory jurisdiction of the ECtHR, the European Convention for the Prevention of Torture and Inhuman or Degrading Treatment or Punishment and its protocols, the European Social Charter and others. The undertakings also included pursuing efforts to solve the conflict with Azerbaijan in peaceful manner only; to adopt a number of laws to comply with the CoE standards, such as laws amending the Criminal Code to abolish death penalty and decriminalise consensual homosexual relationships between adults, a law on civil service, new laws on media, political parties, non-governmental organisations, a law on ombudsman, and a law reforming the responsibility and demilitarisation of the prison system, among others.[15] It paid particular attention to the necessary reforms of the judicial system to ensure its full independence, guarantee full practice of other 'non-traditional' religions without any discrimination and ensure that conscientious objectors have access to alternative service, and that all imprisoned persons on such grounds at the time are pardoned. Armenia has also committed to institute, without delay, a follow-up procedure to complaints received on alleged ill-treatment in police custody, pre-trial detention centres, prisons and the army. Finally, Armenia explicitly committed to cooperate with the CoE in achieving these objectives and in ensuring its full compliance with the CoE standards. Notably, many of these issues have been addressed by ECtHR in its judgments, the implementation of which I discuss in this Chapter.

Similarly to Azerbaijan and Georgia, at the time of the accession negotiations, Armenia's domestic state organization has been grappling with the deeply entrenched Soviet legacy in its political and legal systems on one side, and Armenia's newly proclaimed pro-European democratization ideals on the other side. Its post-independence, pre-accession political landscape was marked by numerous irregularities identified by independent international observers in its first parliamentary elections in 1995 and 1999, and presidential elections in 1996 and 1998, causing concern over its fairness and questioning

13 CM Resolution (96) 21 on Armenia's accession to the CoE (n 7).
14 Ibid.
15 PACE Opinion 221 (2000) on Armenia (n 3) [13.2, 13.3].

the results.[16] The 1999 parliamentary elections have seen the emergence of the new "Unity" group, made up of the Armenian Republican Party and the Armenian People's Party as the main political force of conservative political leaning in the Parliament. The volatile political environment was further shaken by the criminal operation in the Armenian Parliament on 27 October 1999, which led to the killing of the then Prime Minister Vazgen Sarkissian, the Speaker of the Parliament Karen Demirchian and six other leading political figures, resulting in the loss of leadership of two new major political formations in the country, which however did not endanger their remaining in power.[17] The post CoE membership 2003 presidential and parliamentary elections saw shortages of democratic standards and significant amounts of electoral fraud, and the Republic Party of Armenia retained its monopoly by having President Robert Kocharian in office and by retaining parliamentary majority in the parliament.[18] The 2007 parliamentary elections and 2008 presidential elections, continuing to display some deficiencies of democratic election standards despite some improvements, secured the President's post to the Republican Party's Serzh Sargsyan who maintained the post, and the parliamentary majority for his party, until the 2018 Velvet Revolution.[19] The 2008 presidential elections saw several days of peaceful protests in capital Yerevan organized by supporters of the unsuccessful presidential candidate Levon Ter Pterosyan, which led to police and army units forcibly dispersing the crowds and resulted in 10 killed protesters, also known as the 'March 1' events.[20] As human rights groups express concern that no effective domestic full investigation into deaths of the protesters and the police and army actions have been conducted for over a decade, the ECtHR is to review the state's actions as the complaints have

16 Report of PACE Political Affairs Committee on Armenia (2000) (n 9) [26–30].

17 Ibid [17–18]; Washington Post, 'Gunmen Take Over Armenian Parliament; Premier Killed' (27 October 1999), accessed 29 March 2020; Radio Free Europe/Free Liberty, 'Ten Years Later, Deadly Shooting In Armenian Parliament Still Echoes' (27 October 2009), accessed 29 March 2020.

18 Freedom House, Nations in Transit, Armenia, 2004, accessed 29 March 2020; OSCE ODIHR Final Report on presidential election in Armenia on 19 February and 5 March 2003 (28 April 2003) 1; OSCE ODIHR Final Report on parliamentary elections in Armenia on 19 February 2008 (30 May 2008) 1.

19 OSCE ODIHR Final Report on presidential election in Armenia on 19 February 2008 (30 May 2008) 1; OSCE ODIHR Final Report on parliamentary elections in Armenia on 12 May 2007 (10 September 2007) 1.

20 Human Rights Watch report 'Democracy on Rocky Ground, Armenia's Disputed 2008 Presidential Election, Post-Election Violence, and the One-Sided Pursuit of Accountability' (25 February 2009), accessed 29 March 2020.

been brought by the families of the deceased.[21] Up until the Velvet Revolution in 2018, Armenia's political climate has been described as characteristic of 'soft' authoritarian tendencies, with low public trust and influence, weak opposition and compromised separation of powers.[22] It remains to be seen if the post Velvet Revolution Government will demonstrate sufficient political power and interest to succeed in addressing these challenges.[23]

Apart from the volatile political pluralism, Armenia's legal system and the rule of law featured a number of vulnerabilities characteristic of the newly emerged post-Soviet states. It lacked sufficient legal framework and its proper implementation to ensure the judiciary's independence from the executive and the prosecution, as well as wider problem of implementation of domestic legislation, which the authorities admitted at the time, justifying it with the need for change of attitudes in the domestic system.[24] As the interviewed representative of the Armenian Government to the CoE described it, 'the problems that we have are the ones common for countries in transition and reforms are always unpopular, and changing practice takes time and resources'.[25] Other issues related to reports of torture and homicide of conscripts in the Armenian army, and a climate of impunity with no or insufficient investigations, and the need for a substantial prison reform, with regard to which the Armenian authorities expressed their willingness to be addressed with the support of the CoE.[26] Amidst of all these commitments taken by Armenia, international organisations and human rights groups alerted on the slow observance of these commitments by Armenia in the first decade of Armenia's membership. They continued reporting widespread practices of torture and ill-treatment in the army and police custody, failure to address violations of prisoners' rights, lack of effective compensation to victims of torture and ill-treatment by state officials, continuing imprisonment of conscientious objectors in violation of Armenia's commitment to adopt a law on alternative service, and the wider already reported problems in the army.[27] Systemic corruption among the

21 European Human Rights Advocacy Centre, 'Ten years on, families of those killed during 1 March protests in Yerevan need answers' (1 March 2018), accessed 29 March 2020.

22 Freedom House, Freedom in the World 2017, Armenia, accessed 29 March 2020 Washington Post, 'Armenian protesters brought down a prime minister. Here's why they are in the streets' (20 April 2018), accessed 29 March 2020.

23 Foreign Policy, 'Armenia's Democratic Dreams' (n 4).

24 Report of PACE Political Affairs Committee on Armenia's application (2000) (n 9) [74–75].

25 Governmental Official, ARM01, Strasbourg, 23 May 2017.

26 Report of PACE Political Affairs Committee on Armenia's application (2000) (n 9) [83–85, 887].

27 Report of the UN Committee Against Torture, Twenty-fifth session (13–24 November 2000) and Twenty-sixth session (30 April – 18 May 2001), New York 2001, [33–39];

authorities, weak rule of law and the volatile judicial independence, leading to low public trust, remained among issues of concern, which put Armenia into the category of a 'partly free' country since its independence to date.[28] Many of these issues remained on the agenda of the international organisations and human rights groups for proceeding years, including the ECtHR, some of the judgments of which addressing these matters I analyse in this Chapter.[29]

4.1.1 *Armenia and the ECtHR*

In Armenia, as the results of the interviews suggest, the ECtHR is perceived with highest authority among various domestic actors. As the representative of the Armenian delegation to the CM described it, 'the Court always comes as the jewelry of the crown to our minds and it is highly valued in Armenia'.[30] Many interviewed domestic actors described it as 'the mechanism to go to' when justice for human rights violations is not possible in the domestic courts and is an effective way to set the legal ground for the necessary reforms and maintain a dialogue with the domestic authorities.[31] Interviewed lawyers and civil society representatives also linked the high respect for the ECtHR to the very low public trust in the Armenian judiciary and its questioned ability to adjudicate cases relating to individual rights and freedoms on the basis of the European standards.[32]

The ECtHR's popularity is also evidenced by the growing numbers of applications to the Court by applicants from Armenia, totaling to 1,900 applications in 2019, constituting 3,4% of all pending applications before the ECtHR, that rose

Human Rights Watch World report 2002, Armenia, accessed 20 March 2020; Freedom House Freedom in the World Report 2007, Armenia country report 50–51, accessed 29 March 2020.

28 Freedom in the World rankings 2019, Armenia, accessed 29 March 2020.

29 UN CAT News, 'UN Committee against Torture to review Armenia' (17 November 2016), accessed 30 March 2020; UN CAT Concluding Observations on the fourth periodic report of Armenia, CAT/C/ARM/CO/4, 26 January 2016; Human Rights Watch World report 2015: Armenia, Events of 2014, accessed 29 March 2020; Freedom House, Freedom in the World 2018, Armenia (28 May 2018), accessed 30 March 2020.

30 Governmental Official, ARM01, Strasbourg, 23 May 2017.

31 Lawyer, ARM07, Yerevan, 28 April 2017; Lawyer, ARM08, online interview, 13 June 2017; CSO representative, ARM09, Yerevan, 28 April 2017; CSO representative, ARM10, Yerevan, 27 April 2017; CSO representative, ARM11, Yerevan, 27 April 2017.

32 Lawyer, ARM05, Yerevan, 28 April 2017; Lawyer, ARM06, Yerevan, 28 April 2017; Lawyer, ARM07, Yerevan, 28 April 2017; Lawyer, ARM08, online interview, 13 June 2017; Report of PACE Political Affairs Committee on Armenia's application (n 301) [74–75].

from 7 in 2001, 21 in 2002 and 923 in 2010.[33] As of 31 December 2021, the ECtHR found at least one violation in 93% of all cases in which it delivered judgments against Armenia.[34] The ECtHR adopted its first judgment against Armenia in January 2007, finding it in violation of the applicant's right to freedom of assembly for failing to adopt a law that would clearly set out the limitations of this right.[35] Referring to Armenia's transitional period post independence, the Court ruled that 'it may take some time for a country to establish its legislative framework in a transition period, but it cannot accept the delay of almost thirteen years to be justifiable, especially when such a fundamental right as freedom of peaceful assembly is at stake', addressing one of the outstanding issues flagged by the CoE during Armenia's accession process.[36] Since then, over the period of fifteen years, as of 1 January 2022, 150 ECtHR judgments against Armenia have been transferred to the CM for implementation, with 110 of them already closed by the CM as implemented (Figure 7).[37] Among all the judgments, 66 of them are categorised by the CM as 'leading cases' identifying structural systemic issues in the domestic system (Figure 8). As of 1 January 2022, around 50% (23) of all the leading cases remained pending implementation, with five of them, or 21% of all pending leading Armenian cases, being supervised under the 'enhanced procedure', requiring closer and more frequent follow up by the CM and DEJ. Among these five groups of cases, three of them, relating to actions of security forces and effective investigations, medical care in prisons, and protection of home and property of displaced persons have been pending implementation for more than five years.[38, 39]

In its judgments against Armenia, the ECtHR has addressed a wide variety of systemic issues, such as allegations of ill-treatment and torture by security forces and the effectiveness of investigations, death of military conscripts, detention conditions and medical care in prisons, lawfulness of detention, fair trial, freedom of religion (conscientious objectors), freedoms of expression and assembly, electoral rights and the effectiveness of domestic remedies,

33 European Court of Human Rights Annual Report 2018 169; European Court of Human Rights Annual Report 2002 102; European Court of Human Rights Annual Report 2010 148, European Court of Human Rights Annual Report 2019 132, accessed 30 March 2020.

34 ECHR Overview of 1959–2021 8, accessed 15 December 2021.

35 *Mkrtchyan v Armenia*, Appl. no. 6562/03 (ECtHR 11 January 2007).

36 Ibid [43].

37 HUDOC EXEC database, accessed 1 January 2022.

38 Supervision of the Execution of Judgments and Decisions of the European Court of Human Rights, 13th Annual Report of the Committee of Ministers (2019) 73.

39 Armenia Country Factsheet, published and last updated by the Department for Execution of Judgments of the European Court of Human Rights, updated on 15 March 2021.

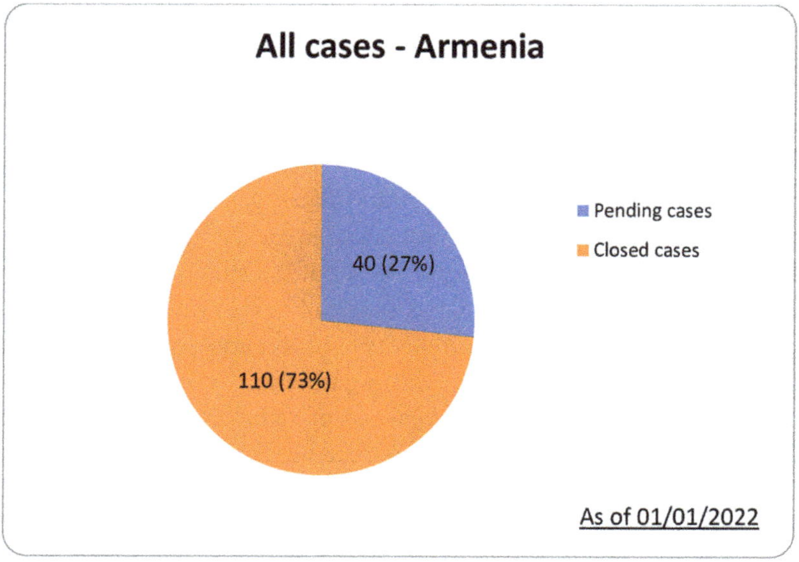

FIGURE 7 All ECtHR cases against Armenia before the CM
SOURCE: HUDOC EXEC DATABASE, AS OF 1 JANUARY 2022

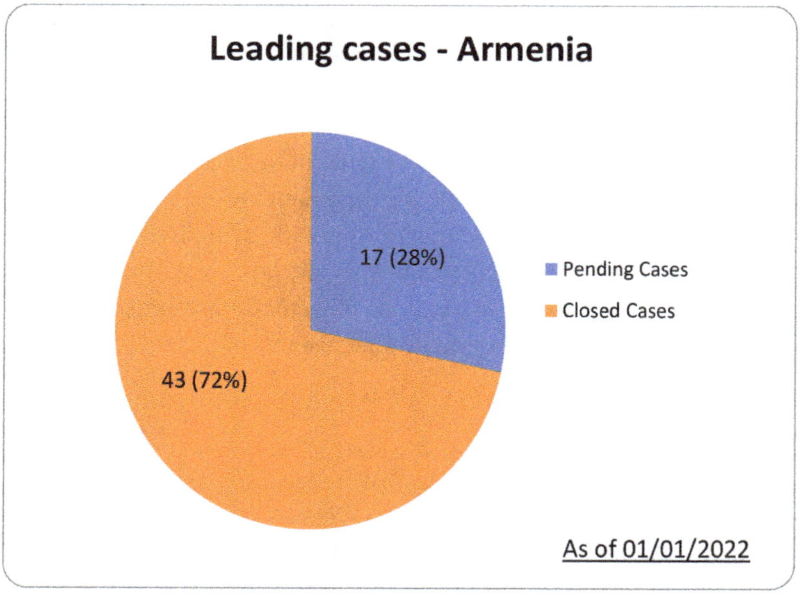

FIGURE 8 All leading cases against Armenia
SOURCE: HUDOC EXEC DATABASE, AS OF 1 JANUARY 2022

among others (Figure 9). The five pending groups of leading cases under enhanced supervision relate to violations that arose in the context of the dispersal by the authorities of the wide-scale opposition protests against the outcome of the 2008 presidential elections (*Mushegh Saghatelyan* group), actions of security forces relating to allegations of ill-treatment in custody (*Virabyan* group) and absence of effective investigations into the death of a military conscript based in Nagorno-Karabakh (*Muradyan* case), medical care in prisons (*Ashot Harutyunyan* group), and protection of property and home in the context of the Nagorno Karabakh conflict (*Chiragov and Others*).[40] Among those closed by the CM as cases in which key reforms have been adopted are cases relating to enforcement of domestic judicial decisions (*Khachatryan* case), conditions of detention (*Kirakosyan* case), access to a court and fair trial (*Piruzyan* case, *Melikyan* case, *Shamonyan* case), alternative service for conscientious objectors (*Bayatyan* case) and others.[41] As many of the issues in all these cases were identified as to be addressed during Armenia's accession process to the CoE, the analysis of the implementation of the selected five ECtHR judgments, or groups of judgments, offer some insights into the ECtHR's contribution to Armenia's progress in complying with the judgments but also in strengthening its respect for rule of law, human rights and democratic values as CoE commitments. The five groups of cases that I analyse in this Chapter are the *Ashot Harutyunyan* group, *Bayatyan* group, *Chiragov and Others* case, *Mkrtchyan* case, and *Virabyan* group (see 1.3.1).

4.2 Armenia's Compliance with ECtHR Judgments

4.2.1 *Domestic Implementation System*

In this Section I review Armenia's domestic implementation system and its ability to enable timely and full compliance with ECtHR judgments. Armenia's domestic institutional setting for implementation of ECtHR judgments has been substantially reformed following the change of power resulting from the Velvet Revolution in 2018. With this reform, on the basis of a newly adopted 2019 Law on the Representative of the Republic of Armenia before the European Court of Human Rights, the mandate of a coordinating institution has been transferred from the Ministry of Justice to the Office of the Prime Minister as the new Government Agent Office (GA Office).[42] The mandate

40 Ibid.

41 Ibid.

42 Law on the Representative of the Republic of Armenia before the European Court of Human Rights, 10 July 2019, signed by the President on 23 July 2019, HO-141-N.

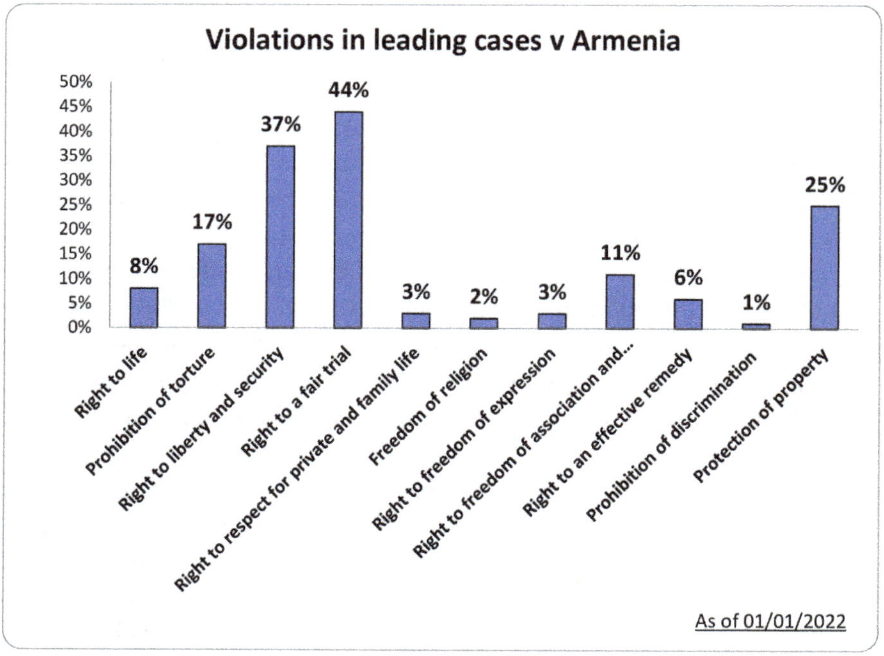

FIGURE 9 Violations in cases against Armenia
SOURCE: HUDOC DATABASE, AS OF 1 JANUARY 2022

given to the Ministry of Justice in 2003, after Armenia joined the CoE, and regulated by the Government Decree has now been established by a law adopted by the parliament, aimed to ensure 'comprehensive regulation' of this mandate.[43] According to the new mandate, such reform was aimed to ensure that domestic 'institutional capacities for implementation of ECtHR judgments are enhanced' and that a 'stronger mechanism' is put in place on the domestic level.[44] The new mandate appears to communicate a more open approach towards seeing implementation as a domestic project of cooperation, with the new GA Office having a coordinating role in the process. As the representative of the new GA Office noted in that regard, 'Execution of judgments is a comprehensive and inclusive process. A single body … is not and cannot be in the capacity or position to decide on matters of execution without considering the respective issues with relevant State stakeholders'.[45] Such public stance is a welcome start for a mandate that aims to improve the state's institutional

43 Government Official, ARM02, email communication, 12 May 2020.
44 Ibid.
45 Ibid.

capacities, in line with the CM 2008 Recommendation on efficient domestic capacity for rapid execution of judgments, and it remains to be seen how it materialises in practice.[46] In this newly organised institutional setting, the Ministry of Justice is assigned a crucial role as one of the main implementation partners on the domestic level, with coordination being carried by the Prime Minister's Office.

Armenia's earlier domestic mechanism for implementation established in 2003 as part of the Ministry of Justice demonstrated less inclusiveness of other state and particularly non-state actors; however, also before 2018, Armenia had been gradually developing its institutional capacities and transparency over several years. In 2014, a decade after the establishment of the position of the Representative, a separate Division for Execution of the European Court of Human Rights Judgments was established, meaning additional human resources dedicated solely for implementation of ECtHR judgments. Although some further research is necessary to establish a causal connection, but following this enhancement in capacities, a number of communications from Armenia to the CM, its regular cooperation with the DEJ and a number of cases closed during 2015–2019, compared to 2007–2013, has grown significantly.[47] As the DEJ representative described it: 'our communication with Armenian counterparts is very regular and reciprocal, which, generally, ensures stability in cooperation on implementation'.[48] Armenia further enhanced transparency of the process by launching an official bilingual (Armenian and English) website of the Armenian Government Agent Office on 30 September 2015, the first one of such kind among all the CoE member states, and the only one among the three researched South Caucasus states to date.[49] As reiterated by the authorities, it was established in line with the Brussels' Declaration adopted in March 2015 by the CM aiming 'at enhancing the efficiency of the implementation', and contains information on all ECtHR judgments, including official submissions, statistics and other information relating to implementation.

---

46 CM/Rec(2008)2 on efficient domestic capacity for rapid execution of judgments of the European Court of Human Rights, adopted by the Committee of Ministers on 6 February 2008 at the 1017th meeting of the Ministers' Deputies.

47 HUDOC EXEC database filtered by 'Armenia, Action Plans/Reports', as of 1 December 2021; Armenia Country Factsheet (n 39); Government Official, ARM02, email communication, 12 May 2020; DEJ official, SXB04, Strasbourg, 30 November 2016.

48 DEJ official, SXB04, Strasbourg, 30 November 2016.

49 Government Official, ARM02, email communication, 12 May 2020; 9th Annual Report of the Committee of Ministers on Supervision of the Execution of Judgments and Decisions of the European Court of Human Rights, 2015 243.

Although Armenia's efforts to increase transparency and institutional capacities are significant, the existing domestic system offers no formal procedures or other ways for other actors, such as the national parliament, Human Rights Defender's Office or civil society organisations to get involved in the implementation process, an issue commonly observed in the whole region. The new Law establishes that the GA Office is obliged to submit to the Prime Minister its annual report, however, no further accountability mechanism focusing on ECtHR implementation is foreseen.[50] In the new setting, where the GA's Office forms a part of the Prime Minister's Office, which is accountable to the parliament and presents annual reports to its members, there is no clear normative framework for such accountability to be ensured as a formal procedure with regard to ECtHR judgments. It therefore leaves the issue of implementation of ECtHR judgments to the Prime Minister's discretion to decide if it should be included in its regular reporting to the parliament.

The new Law creates a general legal framework for the involvement of the civil society in the process in that it stipulates that the GA Office is authorised 'to cooperate with international and civil society organisations'.[51] The new Office is of a position that it 'appreciates' the role of civil society and 'emphasises the importance of cooperation', assuring that, as a way of example, their comments to NGO submissions to the CM 'are always provided to enhance that cooperation'.[52] The civil society representatives interviewed in 2020 however remained cautious referring to the need for the new Office to demonstrate its openness through actions: 'We can still see a rather hostile approach of the Office towards NGO submissions before the CM, for example, which indicates the opposite of the Office's stated enhanced openness and dialogue'.[53] The interviewee referred to two Rule 9.2 submissions from the civil society in two different cases in 2020, which the GA Office responded to by dismissing the NGO concerns as unsubstantiated or failing to be seen in a full picture of the Government's reforms.[54] It therefore remains to be seen how such enhanced

50 Law on the Representative of the Republic of Armenia before the European Court of Human Rights, adopted on 10 July 2020, unofficial translation, Article 12.

51 Ibid Article 10.

52 Government Official, ARM02, email communication, 12 May 2020.

53 CSO representative, ARM10, Yerevan, 27 April 2017.

54 Communication from NGOs Open Society Foundations-Armenia, Protection of Rights without Borders NGO, Helsinki Citizens Assembly of Vanadzor, Transparency International Anticorruption Center and Law Development and Protection Foundation (17/06/2020) and response from the Armenian authorities (25/06/2020) in the case of *Vardanyan and Nanushyan v. Armenia* (Appl. no. 8001/07); Communication from an NGO (Open Society Foundations – Armenia) (21/04/2020) in the case of *Mushegh Saghatelyan v. Armenia* (Appl. no. 23086/08) and response from the authorities (05/05/2020)

openness materialises in practice. All NGOs interviewed before the 2018 change of power unanimously asserted that they had no formal effective possibility to get involved in the implementation process, in absence of any formal procedures.[55] Among the challenges they mentioned their own insufficient level of knowledge of the implementation process, insufficient allocation of funds and human resources to implementation work, and, relatedly, lack of clarity of their roles in the domestic process and ways to engage when no established procedures or practices for such cooperation are in place. Two interviewed organisations expressed their dismay prior to 2018 in their attempts to engage in the Strasbourg supervision process for the lack of clear follow up to their submissions to the CM and the Government's dismissive responses to NGO recommendations, and insufficient clarity as to how NGOs can continue engaging.[56] While it remains to be seen how the new institutional setting, in the context of the optimistic post Velvet Revolution atmosphere, will enable the civil society to get involved in the implementation process in a more constructive and systemic way, in its turn, the civil society has taken some initiatives to increase its capacities by forming coalitions and building skills to integrate implementation work in their strategies.[57] As the research suggests, unified efforts of the civil society help ensure their stronger and more systemic contributions to the process (see 6.3.4).

4.2.2 *Armenia's Compliance with ECtHR Judgments: Good Practices and Challenges*

Armenia's overall performance in complying with the ECtHR judgments and engaging with the Strasbourg supervision process is regular, consistent and generally responsive to the supervision system. In statistical terms, since Armenia's accession, the successive governments have provided action plans/reports, or other updates to the CM. in all pending cases. In around 90% of all leading cases, action plans or reports were submitted either on time (within six months from the date a judgment became final) or within 1–1.5 years since the final date of the judgment.[58] The action plans generally comply with the

55 Lawyer, ARM06, Yerevan, 28 April 2017; Lawyer, ARM07, Yerevan, 28 April 2017; Lawyer, ARM08, online interview, 13 June 2017; CSO representative, ARM09, Yerevan, 28 April 2017; CSO representative, ARM10, Yerevan, 27 April 2017; CSO representative, ARM11, Yerevan, 27 April 2017.

56 Lawyer, ARM08, online interview, 13 June 2017; CSO representative, ARM11, Yerevan, 27 April 2017.

57 European Implementation Network, 'EIN trains Armenian civil society actors in tackling implementation challenges' (12 March 2020), accessed 20 July 2020.

58 HUDOC EXEC database, Armenia, as of 1 January 2022.

CM rules and procedures in that they entail information both on individual and general measures and set out the actions taken by the authorities. Such a pattern is observed in leading cases both under enhanced and standard supervision; however, similarly to the findings relating to Azerbaijan and Georgia, more frequent and substantive engagement is observed in the former type of cases, which is likely to be linked to a more frequent and formal engagement of the CM. Such a consistent pattern of engagement with the supervision procedures, the analysis of information obtained during the conducted interviews with the Armenian state officials and other actors, and that of other publicly available information entailing the authorities' official position indicate a consistent overall receptiveness by the Armenian authorities of their obligation to engage with the Strasbourg processes towards compliance with ECtHR judgments. The analysis of the conducted interviews with the relevant domestic and CoE actors suggest that compliance is generally perceived as a legally binding obligation by Armenian counterparts, which they have strong incentives to uphold, primarily driven by the need for such multilateral cooperation and support as a small country in its path to democratisation. As the interviewed Armenian representative to the CM described it:

> Differently from many other European countries, which also have EU, for Armenia as a new democracy the CoE is very important during this democratisation period. It provides us with the valuable support to organise our society, to set relevant legislation in line with the European standards, and to have more effectively operating state institutions, particularly the judiciary.[59]

The various domestic actors expressed particular respect and credibility towards the ECtHR for its standard setting, support in identifying and addressing systemic human rights issues, and its adjudication of individual justice to victims of human rights violations. As one of the interviewed human rights lawyers has put it:

> CoE membership has helped us start the process of changing the perceptions among the Armenian people of the relationship between the state and the people, human values and individual freedoms, and although there is still a long way to go, that important debate was started.[60]

59 Governmental Official, ARM01, Strasbourg, 23 May 2017.

60 CSO representative, ARM09, Yerevan, 28 April 2017.

All civil society members interviewed pre-2018 have unilaterally affirmed that litigation before the ECtHR and the implementation process has enabled them to enter into dialogue with the authorities on human rights matters, which was not otherwise possible in the absence of established procedures or practices for such debates.[61] Many of them confirmed however that their involvement in the implementation process is significantly lower than in the litigation, however, admitting that there was no strong reason for such a differentiation and that their focus on implementation should be enhanced.[62]

Although an overall pattern of consistent engagement of the authorities with the Strasbourg supervision process is a strong indicator of the state's willingness to abide with its obligations stemming from Article 46 of the Convention and cooperate with the CoE mechanisms, compliance with ECtHR judgments is best measured by the observance of substantive change on the domestic level stemming from the implementation process. Below I discuss some of such developments and the factors that predetermine, or preclude, such changes on the ground.

4.2.2.1 Factors Defining Compliance with ECtHR Judgments

In this Section, I analyse the substance of the Armenian authorities' submissions on its steps taken to comply with selected ECtHR judgments, and how it materialises in practice, on the basis of the implementation process of five selected judgments or groups of judgments representing a variety of human rights issues. These five groups of cases have been implemented and/or continue being implemented at different periods of time since Armenia's accession and were/are supervised by the CM under both, enhanced or standard, procedures to allow wider representation of various factors that affect the process. As noted in Section 1.3.1, the five selected cases include the Ashot *Harutyunyan* group, which concerns detention conditions and medical care in prisons in particular; the *Virabyan* group of cases relating to ill-treatment and/or torture in custody, actions of security forces and the issue of effectiveness of investigations; the *Chiragov and Others* case relating to protection of property

61 Lawyer, ARM06, Yerevan, 28 April 2017; Lawyer, ARM07, Yerevan, 28 April 2017; Lawyer, ARM08, online interview, 13 June 2017; CSO representative, ARM09, Yerevan, 28 April 2017; CSO representative, ARM10, Yerevan, 27 April 2017; CSO representative, ARM11, Yerevan, 27 April 2017.

62 Lawyer, ARM05, Yerevan, 28 April 2017; Lawyer, ARM07, Yerevan, 28 April 2017; Lawyer, ARM08, online interview, 13 June 2017; CSO representative, ARM09, Yerevan, 28 April 2017; CSO representative, ARM10, Yerevan, 27 April 2017; CSO representative, ARM12, email communication, 9 September 2020.

for displaced persons in the context of the Nagorno-Karabakh conflict; the *Mkrtchyan* case, in which the first judgment against Armenia was made by the ECtHR, relating to exercise of freedom of assembly; and the *Bayatyan* case relating to freedom of religion and alternative service for conscientious objectors.[63] The two latter cases were closed by the CM in 2008 and 2014 respectively, a year and three years after the final dates of their respective judgments. The rest of the cases have been pending implementation for more than five years, since 2010, 2013 and 2015 respectively, all under the enhanced supervision of the CM, indicating the existence of systemic structural problems.[64]

Against the background of Armenia's overall willingness to engage with the CM supervision process, which led to over 70% of leading cases against Armenia closed to date, the findings of the analysis suggest that two factors affect timely and effective implementation of ECtHR judgments in Armenia: active political resistance and high financial costs. These two factors were dominant in cases where the implementation progress faced significant delays, passivity or other obstacles obstructing smooth implementation process. A third factor that was also observed, but to a lesser extent, is the traditional societal values, which clash with the ideologies promoted through human rights standards protected by the Convention, such as equality and tolerance. I discuss each factor in the domestic context of Armenia below.

4.2.2.1.1 *Political Resistance*

Political will is widely recognised as playing a fundamental role in defining the success of the implementation process of ECtHR judgments, particularly in domestic contexts short of strong democratic practices and lacking well established implementation mechanisms and procedures (see 1.2 and 2.2). In the pre-2018 Armenian context, which I predominantly research in this book, the issue of political willingness would complicate the implementation process in cases where there is active political resistance from certain state structures to full compliance with an ECtHR judgment that requires measures entailing high political costs in the domestic system. In other words, overall political willingness to abide by ECtHR judgments, as part of the Convention obligations, is observed, unless the judgment exposes domestic political or structural issues that require measures rendering domestic costs as *too* high. It is too early to conduct a comprehensive assessment of what change the post

63 *Ashot Harutyunyan v Armenia*, Appl. no. 34334/04 (ECtHR15 June 2010); *Virabyan v Armenia*, Appl. no. 40094/05 (ECtHR 2 October 2012); *Chiragov and Others* (n 213); *Mkrtchyan* (n 327); *Bayatyan v Armenia*, Appl. No. 23459/03, 7 July 2011.

64 Armenia Country Factsheet (n 39).

Velvet Revolution context will bring in that regard in practice, where the new Government has signaled its willingness to enhance compliance with ECtHR judgments, as a result of which I mainly focus on the pre-2018 developments, with references to post-2018 events where possible in this analysis.[65] Such costs derive from political sensitivity around the issue or measures needed to address it, and / or disagreement with measures needed or the wider political contextual background of the issue involving interstate solution, such as the frozen Nagorno Karabakh conflict. Such political resistance may include inability of the authorities responsible for coordination of implementation of ECtHR judgments to ensure that the responsible authorities take on the necessary steps or reforms, political unwillingness of certain authorities to take certain measures as those going against their own personal political interests, or involves acting in 'bad faith', all of which I discuss through specific examples.

For example, in the *Virabyan* case, relating to ill-treatment of a political opposition member in police custody, effective and timely investigation, as a fundamental requirement of the international law in such cases, has become politically complicated in the domestic context. It implied a duty to effectively investigate serious allegations of torture inflicted by police officers who acted in 'bad faith', following the applicant's claims to have been interrogated about his participation in the opposition protest and not the charges in relation to which he was summoned, and was eventually ill-treated. Such an obligation also meant prosecuting police officers belonging to the same law enforcement structure under the Armenian criminal justice system, known for its wide institutional powers, and bringing them to justice for very serious charges when the initial investigation was only limited to charges against the applicant and did not involve any effective investigation into torture allegations. Against this context of repression of the opposition members exercising their freedom of assembly in 2004 in the aftermath of the Presidential elections, the issue of political willingness was further compromised by the fact that the authorities were found by the ECtHR to have failed to investigate any political motives underlying Mr Virabyan's ill-treatment, in a discriminatory manner, following his attendance of the opposition rally protesting the re-election of the then incumbent President of Armenia.[66] The very use of the law enforcement system to interrogate and pressure the applicant as the opposition member for his

65 Government Official, ARM02, email communication, 12 May 2020.

66 *Virabyan v Armenia* (n 63) [36, 218–225]; Human Rights Watch Briefing Paper, Cycle of Repression: Human Rights Violations in Armenia (4 May 2004), accessed 20 July 2020; Europe and Central Asia: Summary of Amnesty International's Concerns in the Region, January-June 2004, accessed on 20 July 2020.

involvement in peaceful assembly, leading to causing him severe physical harm to his health significantly reduced the likelihood of effective criminal investigation of those responsible by the same criminal justice system. The ECtHR did not only establish the fact of ill-treatment of the applicant, which it considered to amount to torture, but also set out multiple fundamental failings of the investigatory authorities in investigating the applicant's torture allegations such as reliance only on the testimonies of police officers who the applicant indicated as those who ill-treated him, disregarding the applicant's testimony without any justification.[67] Such failings represent the underlying structural issues in Armenian's legal and judiciary system identified by the CoE during its compatibility studies of Armenia upon its accession. In 2004, when the applicant's ill-treatment in custody took place, Armenia was in the process of transferring its penitentiary system from the control of the Ministry of Justice to the Ministry of Internal Affairs to reform the Soviet heritage notorious for its 'hierarchical administrative structure, and a mentality not conducive to the protection of human rights', and there were 'very credible allegations of beatings, torture, even killings' reported by NGOs at that time.[68] Another structural problem lies in the fact that the criminal investigations were conducted by the prosecution, which enjoyed extensive institutional powers since the Soviet era and did not conduct an independent effective oversight over actions of the penitentiary services. This led to very few if any cases being prosecuted through courts, encouraging, as concluded by the PACE report, a 'feeling of impunity amongst perpetrators of such crimes'.[69] At that time, the Armenian authorities admitted that there were problems with implementation of the legislation ensuring independence of the judiciary and proper functioning of courts, particularly in light of the criticism leveled at the influence exerted on the courts by public prosecutors and the executive.[70] It was in this politically hostile context that the ECtHR judgment in the *Virabyan* case brought this issue back to the domestic table as a legal obligation under the Convention almost a decade later, in 2013, years after the domestic case of the applicant

---

67 *Virabyan v Armenia* (n 63) [165–179].

68 PACE Legal Affairs and Human Rights Committee report, Doc. 8756, Armenia's application for membership of the Council of Europe (6 June 2000) [18]; Report of the PACE Committee on the Honouring of Obligations and Commitments by Member States of the Council of Europe, Doc. 10163, Explanatory memorandum, 27 April 2004.

69 Ibid PACE Legal Affairs and Human Rights Committee report [18]; Communication from NGOs in the cases of *Harutyunyan* and *Virabyan* against Armenia, Appl. no. 34334/04 and 40094/05, 25 September 2013; Concluding Observations of the UN Committee against Torture on Armenia at its 48th session, 6 July 2012 [12].

70 Report of PACE Political Affairs Committee on Armenia's application (n 9) [74–75].

was closed as groundless. The judgment served as the external factor offering a legal framework to the authorities to address this systemic problem, however, equally, exposing deep political sensitivities around such reforms, which triggered the Government's political resistance to comply with the ECtHR judgment in a timely, full and efficient manner.

Although the authorities have regularly reported to the CM on their actions both in terms of individual and general measures since 2013 in this case, the authorities' obligation to conduct an effective investigation under the judgment has not been fulfilled as of March 2020: two police officers who were eventually charged for ill-treatment of the applicant four years after the ECtHR judgment, in 2017, and were found guilty for exceeding official power accompanied by violence by court in February 2019 benefited from the statute of limitations in their case and remained unpunished.[71] In their action report of January 2020, the authorities reported to the CM that the police officers could not be found guilty of torture as the Armenian legislation did not provide a definition of torture at the time; however, in its earlier action report of October 2016 it reported that torture was criminalised in the domestic legislation and the relevant amendments entered into force on 18 July 2015.[72] The interviewed member of the legal team of Mr Virabyan explained it with the existence of the deeper structural problem relating to the judiciary's inability to conduct any investigation of its own.[73] The evidence such as one relating to severity of bodily injuries recorded in expert opinions, which predetermine the nature of the charges, and the decision regarding charges were finalised by the prosecution, known for its wide institutional and political powers in the state's organisation and the justice system in particular. He also indicated the highly sensitive political context of this case as a decisive factor in the investigation outcomes referring to the fact that one of the policemen whom Mr Virabyan named among those who ill-treated him, instead of being subjected to immediate investigation, was appointed to a high ranking position of a police chief of Yerevan city, post ECtHR judgment, 'as a signal of acknowledgment to those loyal to the Government' in pre-2018 Armenia.[74]

A number of the Armenian human rights lawyers interviewed in 2017 noted that the implementation process of this group has brought several positive

71 Updated action plan concerning *Virabyan* group of cases submitted by the Government of Armenia, 24 January 2020 3.

72 Action plan concerning the *Virabyan* group of cases, 14 October 2016 7; Updated action plan concerning *Virabyan* group of cases, 24 January 2020, 3 footnote 3.

73 Lawyer, ARM05, Yerevan, 28 April 2017.

74 Ibid.

developments as general measures (discussed below); however, the politically sensitive context of the individual case affects the application of such reforms in practice, indicating that clear political resistance to ensure effective investigation of such serious allegations superseded the legal obligations of the pre-2018 authorities.[75] The lengthy period of time that it took for the pre-2018 authorities to bring charges against two police officers and for the domestic courts to examine the case, and the new Government's request of January 2020 to close the case even before the domestic judicial proceedings are finalized, are further indicators of the Government's resistance even after the Velvet Revolution to take all necessary measures in full, timely and effective manner.[76]

As for the general measures taken so far at the time of the research, which have been welcomed by the CM, such as those leading to criminalisation of torture and imminent plans to install cameras in police stations, the interviewed domestic human rights groups raised concerns that they are not sufficient to address the deeper structural problem of absence of culture to effectively prosecute public officials for such crimes as torture or ill-treatment. They reported that in practice in the last few years, many of such cases led to charges of abuse of official powers rather than torture or ill-treatment as the investigation often concludes that the inflicted harm does not reach the threshold of torture and that ill-treatment is not defined as a separate crime in the Armenian legislation.[77] As for torture charges, the CM's reiterated calls to the Armenian authorities to exclude the crime of torture from the statute of limitations, as part of general measures, remained unaddressed as of its latest review of Armenia's actions in March 2020, with a new deadline indicated by the authorities for the end of 2020.[78] Such multiple unexplained delays in the above context are suggestive of insufficient willingness of the political decision makers, both pre and post 2018 political changes, to genuinely advance the reforms, which, although admittedly structural and complex, would be expected to have born fruit as a result of the process that was initiated in 2013.

---

75 Lawyer, ARM06, Yerevan, 28 April 2017; Lawyer, ARM07, Yerevan, 28 April 2017; Lawyer, ARM08, online interview, 13 June 2017; CSO representative, ARM09, Yerevan, 28 April 2017; CSO representative, ARM10, Yerevan, 27 April 2017.

76 Updated action plan concerning *Virabyan* group of cases, 24 January 2020.

77 Lawyer, ARM05, Yerevan, 28 April 2017; Lawyer, ARM06, Yerevan, 28 April 2017; Lawyer, ARM07, Yerevan, 28 April 2017.

78 CM decision in the *Virabyan* group of cases adopted at its 1369th meeting on 3–5 March 2020.

A contrasting example where implementation did not face such political resistance is the *Mkrtchyan* case relating to the arrest of another political opposition member during a demonstration in Yerevan in 2002, jointly organised by a number of opposition parties.[79] In this case, the Court found a violation of the applicant's right to freedom of assembly under Article 11 of the Convention in that there was no appropriate domestic law at the time setting out the rules for holding rallies, which the applicant was found to have violated. Following the dissolution of the USSR there was no legal act on assemblies applicable in Armenia, and the relevant law was adopted only on 28 April 2004, as part of the legislative plan set up with the support of the CoE, without any legal framework in the transition period. The Court noted in the judgment that a delay of almost thirteen years since the break out from the Soviet Union to adopt the law was not justifiable, highlighting the importance of freedom of assembly as a fundamental right indicating Armenia's failure to put the necessary legislative reforms in place in a timely manner.[80] This case, although, like *Virabyan*, it relates to rallies of the opposition parties, did not meet any political resistance; this may be due to the fact that the measure required as part of the implementation process concerned the adoption of a law that Armenia was already committed to adopt, and that did not generate any political sensitivities within the domestic system. Armenia had, in fact, adopted the law by the time the ECtHR judgment was published, as part of its CoE accession package, suggesting no high political costs of such measures for the domestic authorities. Additional research would be needed to examine if the implementation of these provisions bears any political sensitivities when applied in cases of political or otherwise 'sensitive' rallies.

Another case featuring political resistance of the domestic authorities to full and timely dedication to implementation of the ECtHR judgment is the case of *Chiragov and Others* of 2015, a twin judgment to *Sargsyan v Azerbaijan*, discussed in Section 3.2.3, concerning violations of property rights of displaced people as a result of the Nagorno Karabakh conflict.[81] In this judgment, pending implementation since 2015, the ECtHR indicated that Armenia (as well as Azerbaijan in its mirror case) should establish a property claims mechanism as a specific domestic remedy, highlighting at least a thousand similar cases pending before the Court.[82] It indicated that such a mechanism is particularly important 'pending a comprehensive peace agreement' and that it should

79 *Mkrtchyan v Armenia* (n 35).

80 Ibid [43].

81 *Chiragov and Others v. Armenia*, App. no. 13216/05 (ECtHR 15 June 2015).

82 Ibid [199].

be 'easily accessible and provide procedures operating with flexible evidentiary standards, allowing the applicants and others in their situation to have their property rights restored and to obtain compensation for the loss of their enjoyment'.[83] As of 1 January 2022, more than six years since the adoption of the judgment, the measures explicitly indicated by the Court remain unaddressed: no progress has been made in setting up the property claims mechanism by Armenia (or Azerbaijan) and the applicants have not been paid just satisfaction ordered by the Court in its separate judgment on just satisfaction in December 2017.[84] Although Armenia's involvement with the DEJ in the discussions on the implementation of this case appears to be significantly more extensive than the one of the Azerbaijani counterparts (at 3.2.3), the various arguments provided by the Armenian Government as to why this judgment cannot be implemented before a solution to the conflict is found do not release it from its human rights obligations under the Convention or justify its failure to comply with the judgment. Quite the opposite, it is suggestive of insufficient political willingness to take on measures clearly stipulated by the Court and therefore requiring no specific interpretation in such a complex conflict context, particularly in light of the emerging escalations of the conflict.[85] The Government provides no explanation of its failure to pay just satisfaction to the applicants for almost three years, particularly given its good record of timely payments of just satisfactions, which the Government highlights to the CM in its communication in December 2019 as an indicator of Armenia's commitment to its obligation to comply with ECtHR judgments.[86] With the letter from the applicants' representative providing information on the bank details to the Government in January 2018, a month after the Court's judgment on just satisfaction, it is unlikely the Government of Armenia would have had any technical hurdles that would have prevented making the payment to the applicants for almost three years.[87] As the CM reiterated in December 2019 when it examined the case, the obligation to pay the just satisfaction awarded by the Court to the applicants in December 2017 is unconditional, and urged

83 Ibid.

84 HUDOC EXEC database *Chiragov and Others v Armenia*, Appl. no. 13216/05, 'Status of execution' accessed 23 November 2020.

85 International Crisis Group, 'The Nagorno-Karabakh Conflict: A Visual Explainer', accessed 15 December 2021. Thomas de Waal, 'Why the Long Conflict over Nagorno-Karabakh Could Heat up Again' (World Politics Review 18 October 2019), accessed 23 November 2020.

86 Communication of the Government of Armenia on the actions taken and anticipated concerning the case of *Chiragov and Others v Armenia*, November 2019 11.

87 Rule 9.1 communication from the applicant in the case of *Chiragov and Others v Armenia*, 29 November 2019.

Armenia to pay it without further delay, however, bearing no response from the Armenian authorities as of December 2021.[88]

Further indications of Armenia's political resistance to take concrete tangible actions towards compliance with the judgment stems from its argumentation to the CM as to why establishment of a property claims mechanism is not possible, put in a highly politicised context of the conflict and explained primarily as deriving from the ongoing hostilities from the Azerbaijani side.[89] In its submission, Armenia referred to 'xenophobia against Armenians', 'destruction of historical [Armenian] monuments', 'impediments to economic and wealth-generating activities' of residents of Nagorno Karabakh who cannot travel to Azerbaijan, and 'permanent border line incidents' as factors that prevent timely and effective implementation of the ECtHR judgment, which however do not sufficiently explain why this puts Armenia is a position to not being able to adopt the necessary measures on its side.[90] As the interviewed representative of the Armenian Government to the CM described their challenge to engage in a constructive debate in 2017, 'Azerbaijan misuses this case for political purposes to raise the issue of the occupied territories', which further indicates that the Government sees the implementation as a two-party political process where unilateral legal or technical steps towards remedying victims are not possible.[91] Although political scientists focusing on this conflict saw the new post Revolution period as a new chance for the conflict, as violence reduced significantly in 2018, and the promise of both leaders to 'prepare populations for peace' came in 2019, these expectations have not been materialised with sufficient action.[92] The political and security context of this conflict of many years since ceasefire was achieved in 1994 is certainly significant to ensuring respect for individual rights of victims of the conflict, and the Court has recognised it in the judgment. It however also emphasised in both judgments that the mere fact that peace negotiations were on-going did not absolve the Government from taking other, human rights

88 CM notes on the *Chiragov and Others* case from its 1369th meeting held on 3–5 December 2019.

89 Communication of the Government of Armenia on the actions taken and anticipated concerning the case of *Chiragov and Others v Armenia*, November 2019 11.

90 Ibid 6–11.

91 Governmental Official, ARM01, Strasbourg, 23 May 2017.

92 Press Statement by the Co-Chairs of the OSCE Minsk Group (16 January 2019), accessed 20 July 2020; Thomas de Waal article (n 85); Tweets by Thomas de Waal, Carnegie Europe 15 July 2015 https://twitter.com/Tom_deWaal/status/1283310609094909952, accessed 20 July 2020; Tweets by Zaur Shiriyev, International Crisis Group, https://twitter.com/ZaurShiriyev/status/1283356572710850562 accessed 20 July 2020.

oriented measures, especially when negotiations had been pending for such a long time, without leading to tangible results.[93] Although ideally the property claims mechanism would lead to restoration of property rights through restitution, the Court has also recognised that return may not be possible, particularly given the failure of many years of the parties to the conflict to negotiate a peace settlement. The European Human Rights Advocacy Centre, which represented the applicant in the mirror case against Azerbaijan, submitted a Rule 9.2 report setting out the relevant international standards on property rights and analysed in detail the issues that the property claims mechanisms would need to address in order to provide effective remedies to displaced victims of the Nagorno-Karabakh conflict, one of them referring to the compensation element where return of property is not possible.[94] The Armenian Government did not address any of the points made in the respective submission offering very specific legal and technical guidance to establishing the required mechanism and specific steps that each Government can take regardless of the failure to engage in the political negotiations on the peace agreement, and nor does it seem to see this judgment as a new incentive to seek for ways to offer remedies to huge number of victims of the conflict. As these cases mark the first time, after more than twenty five years, that the violations of the victims' rights have been recognized with the compensation offered, and the obligation for the respective states to offer redress through a property claim mechanism to the applicants was established, the two Governments can no longer hide their political unwillingness to take tangible measures to compensate the victims behind the wider political context of the conflict. Due to the absolute nature of both states' legal obligations to comply with ECtHR judgments, the judgments may create a new platform for highly politicized negotiation processes if used willfully and determinedly. This case is also likely to be an example of a case in relation to which challenges of high financial costs are possible in ensuring effective functioning of the compensation mechanism once the hurdle of insufficient political will is overcome.[95]

4.2.2.1.2 *High Financial Costs*

A state's financial capacities to remedy for violations identified by the ECtHR is a significant factor that may emerge as an obstacle to timely, full and effective implementation if the financial burden is overly costly to the state's budget.

93 *Chiragov and Others*, (n 84) [198].

94 Rule 9.2 communication in the case of *Chiragov and Others v Armenia*, 1 November 2016 [44].

95 Lawyer, ARM05, Yerevan, 28 April 2017; CSO representative, ARM09, Yerevan, 28 April 2017.

Such state budget expenses may rise from large amounts of compensation ordered to be paid to applicants by the Court, or accumulate from multiple judgments adjudicated by the Court against the same country within a relatively short period of time. For example, in the case of Armenia, in 2019, the Court awarded EUR 2,130,858 in damages to be paid to applicants compared to almost EUR 200,000 in 2018, which constitutes a significant proportion of the state budget of around 3 billion EUR.[96] This issue is also particularly relevant where the implementation process includes general measures that require extensive structural reforms that are financially costly, such as building new detention facilities to improve detention conditions, create new institutions or set up any other institutional mechanisms that require vast financial resources. In Armenia, which, following the collapse of the Soviet Union, emerged as an economy relying extensively on foreign investment and contributions from Armenian diaspora abroad, and suffered immensely during the 2008 financial crisis, remains a volatile economy, in the context of which budgetary allocations stemming from ECtHR judgments are likely to be carefully scrutinised.[97] It is, however, difficult to trace the amounts allocated for implementation of general measures stemming from ECtHR judgments as the funds allocated for such measures do not fall under the same budget line as payments of just satisfaction and are covered by budgets for programmatic work of different involved institutions (which I discuss in this Section below).

One example of the impact of high financial costs as the factor influencing the implementation process is the *Ashot Harutyunyan* group of cases, where the need for substantial financial resources formed a huge part of the state's ability to comply with the judgments. This group of cases concerns the state's denial of adequate medical care to prisoners who suffered from various serious medical conditions from 2003 to 2006.[98] Mr. Harutyunyan, applicant in one of the three cases in this group, died from a heart attack in prison, having previously complained of serious health condition.[99] The general measures required in this group of cases included, as described by the CM, 'a large scale reform of the prison health care system to bring it into conformity with the relevant international standards'.[100] In addition to measures requiring creation of

---

96 CM Annual Report 2019 (n 3) 77; Radio Free Europe/Radio Liberty',Armenia's 2019 Budged Approved by Parliament' (22 November 2018), accessed 15 June 2020.

97 World Bank Economy Overview: Armenia, accessed 15 June 2020.

98 *Ashot Harutyunyan v Armenia* (n 63); *Piruzyan v Armenia*, Appl. no. 33376/07 (ECtHR 26 September 2012); *Davtyan v Armenia*, Appl. no. 29736/06 (ECtHR 30 June 2015).

99 *Ashot Harutyunyan v Armenia* (n 63) [70].

100 HUDOC EXEC database (n 157), 'Status of execution' of the *Ashot Harutyunyan* group of cases, accessed 1 November 2020.

necessary legislative frameworks and other legal and policy changes, the identified reforms included provision of adequate medication and medical equipment to prisons across the country, ensuring independence and qualification of medical staff through creation of a new independent institution, series of trainings to medical and prison staff, and establishing a compensation mechanism for victims alleging denial of adequate medical care in prison.[101] When asked about an example where the implementation process has been challenging, the interviewed Armenian representative to the CoE named this group of cases as 'requiring vast financial resources, and changing the existing practices, which is a long and challenging issue'.[102] The analysis of the information available on the implementation process of this group before the CM demonstrates that the implementation process was significantly advanced with the initiation of a joint CoE-Armenia project funded by the CoE and the EU, which provided vast financial and programmatic support for health care reforms in prisons in Armenia in 2015–2018.[103] With the budget of 1.2 million euros, the project helped Armenia establish a new Penitentiary Medicine Centre as an independent medical institution for prisons, purchase new medical equipment for the majority of prisons in the country, train 775 medical and non-medical staff of prisons on relevant European standards on health care in prisons and assistance in reviewing penitentiary healthcare legislation, all these reforms being in line with the general measures required under the *Ashot Harutyunyan* group of cases.[104] To compare the scope of measures initially taken by Armenia by June 2015, when it first submitted its action report five years after the first judgment in this group became final, it primarily reported to the CM on the awareness raising and educational activities among relevant domestic institutions, and steps taken towards improving the domestic legislation as a framework to ensure prisoners' rights to access adequate health care, the costs of which were significantly lower compared to the reforms identified later.[105]

As for the measures aimed to improve the material conditions and the provision of health care assistance in prison, the authorities primarily relied on

101 Communication from Armenia concerning the *Ashot Harutyunyan* group of cases (Appl. no. 34334/04), Action plan, 18 January 2019.

102 Governmental Official, ARM01, Strasbourg, 23 May 2017.

103 CoE/EU joint project 'Penitentiary reform – Strengthening Healthcare and Human Rights Protection in Prisons in Armenia', 2015–2018, accessed 1 September 2020.

104 'European Union and Council of Europe strengthening health care and human rights protection in prisons in Armenia 2015–2018', project infographics, accessed 1 September 2020.

105 Communications from Armenia concerning the cases of *Ashot Harutyunyan and Piruzyan against Armenia* (Appl. nos. 34334/04, 33376/07), Action plan of 16 April 2015 and Action report of 24 July 2020.

the support of the respective CoE-EU project providing significant support to the above-mentioned fundamental reforms, developed on the basis of the recommendations of the European Committee for Prevention of Torture (CPT), as reported by the authorities, following the CPT visit to Armenia in 2015.[106] Significant progress, involving the creation of a new Penitentiary Medicine Centre, a strong legislative basis for adequate medical care and services in prisons in compliance with CPT recommendations, establishment of domestic complaint procedures and ensuring prosecutorial monitoring of such procedures, is noticeable in the Government's subsequent action report in 2019 and 2020. This reported progress, the effectiveness of which in addressing the key systemic issues still remain to be seen in practice, followed the completion of the joint CoE-EU project in Armenia where a number of tangible deliverables have been reported to the CM as general measures in the *Ashot Harutyunyan* group of cases.[107] Although a number of significant steps remain to be taken by the Armenian authorities in this group of cases, the issue of the financial burden, which affected adequate and timely implementation process, was overcome with the support of the CoE-EU support, and serves as an example of an effective complementarity of the various CoE platforms and programmes to support its member states in advancing compliance with the Convention standards (which I discuss further in 4.3).

4.2.2.1.3 *Traditional Values or Other Deeply Entrenched Societal Views*

One other factor observed as an impediment to smooth and efficient implementation process of ECtHR judgments in Armenia is the deeply entrenched societal adherence to what are perceived as 'traditional values'. Although this concept is highly ambiguous, in that its perception often relies on prevailing cultural, religious and societal ideologies within the national borders of states, it has been increasingly relied on by more conservative states as a factor to be taken into consideration in the human rights discourse, with the Russian Federation being among the states actively promoting the need to address this contradiction in the international arena.[108] In Armenia, particularly observed

106 Ibid; Report to the Armenian Government on the visit to Armenia carried out by the European Committee for the Prevention of Torture and Inhuman or Degrading Treatment or Punishment (CPT) from 5 to 15 October 2015, CPT/Inf (2016) 31.

107 Communications from Armenia concerning the *Ashot Harutyunyan* group of cases v. Armenia (Appl. no. 34334/04), Action plan of 18 January 2019 and Action report of 24 July 2020.

108 Maggie Murphy, "Traditional values' v human rights at the UN' (Open Democracy 18 February 2013), accessed 1 September 2020; Human Rights First, Russia's 'Traditional Values' Leadership (1 June 2016), accessed 1 September 2020.

in its pre-2018 period, similarly to many other former Soviet Union states, this argument is often raised in justifying the dilatory progress in ensuring respect for human rights in practice, largely affecting such marginalised groups as women, children, LGBTI groups or communities of unconventional religions, and has been observed as a factor influencing the implementation process of a number of ECtHR judgments. For example, in the above-discussed *Ashot Harutyunyan* group of cases, firmly embedded societal attitudes marginalising prisoners as individuals who 'do not deserve adequate human treatment' as a result of their criminal behaviour were named among the factors affecting the dilatory implementation process.[109] The interviewed Armenian representative to the CoE described this phenomenon in 2017 as a 'big challenge in changing people's mentality that prisoners are not social outcasts without any rights', which in turn affects the authorities' efficiency and eagerness to pursue the necessary reforms to improve the prisoners' health care situation.[110] One of the interviewed human rights lawyers in 2016 working on rights of prisoners in Armenia referred to this issue as an example of how the public's perception of certain social groups influences the authorities' performance in light of its human rights obligations and at times even supersedes the clearly stipulated legal obligations.[111] These matters are not explicitly addressed in the Government's action plans, that would allow considerations of this factor as in the CM monitoring process, with the empirical data indicating the importance of such motivational attitudes to be raised by other actors, such as the civil society or the national human rights institution (NHRI) (whose contributions I discuss in 4.3).

Another example where the prevailing societal values served as a factor affecting the implementation process was a group of cases relating to conviction to prison of members of Jehovah's Witnesses as conscientious objectors, as part of the systemic repressive practice that the Court addressed with regard to a number of the FSU member states of the CoE.[112] Jehovah's Witnesses is a religious group whose beliefs include the conviction that service, even unarmed,

---

109 Governmental Official, ARM01, Strasbourg, 23 May 2017.

110 Governmental Official, ARM01, Strasbourg, 23 May 2017.

111 Lawyer, ARM05, Yerevan, 28 April 2017.

112 *Bayatyan* (n 355); see also *Jehovah's Witnesses of Moscow and Others v Russia*, Appl. no. 302/02 (ECtHR 10 June 2010); *97 members of the Gldani Congregation of Jehovah's Witnesses and 4 Others v. Georgia*, Appl. no. 71156/01 (ECtHR 3 May 2007); *Religious Community of Jehovah's Witnesses of Kryvyi Rih's Ternivsky District v. Ukraine*; Appl. no. 21477/10 (ECtHR 3 September 2019); *Religious community of Jehovah's Witnesses v Azerbaijan*, Appl. no. 52884/09 (ECtHR 20 February 2020); Human Rights Watch, Russia: Escalating Persecution of Jehovah's Witnesses (9 January 2020), accessed 1 September 2020.

within the military is to be opposed, which led to their criminal prosecution under charges of evasion of military service until Armenia ensured a properly operating alternative service mechanism.[113] Although eventually Armenia has put the necessary domestic law in place, which in practice ensured that conscientious objectors are no longer criminally prosecuted and have the opportunity to choose alternative service instead, it took three years until the case was closed as implemented and there was almost a 10-year delay until Armenia complied with its obligation to adopt a law on alternative service in line with the European standards, which it had pledged upon accession to the CoE.[114] At the accession time, it has also committed to 'pardon all conscientious objectors sentenced to prison terms ... allowing them instead ... to perform ... alternative service', whereas the ECtHR judgments in the *Bayatyan* group of cases relate to conviction of at least 37 conscientious objectors following Armenia's accession to the CoE.[115] Regardless of Armenia's explicit commitment to the CoE in that regard, the delay to comply with it on time presupposes other factors that affected the dilatory process. The research and the findings of the interviews suggest that among those factors is Armenian society's perception of their religion, the Armenian Orthodox Church, as a prevailing one, setting the societal conservative values as the basis for the society's organisation of life, with little tolerance for other religious communities or their particular needs as they occur. As the interviewed Armenian representative to the CoE explained it, 'given the popular view that our religion is very different and unique, there is resistance from the society to have alternative service created for conscientious objectors as members of another religion, which in turn influences the debates among the authorities on this issue'.[116] As the Armenian society is ranked as the second most religious one among the European states, meaning that the major part of popular support comes from religious part of the nation, this likely strengthens the stance of this factor in the authorities' eyes when considering the adoption of unpopular reforms.[117]

Although eventually in this case, the domestic political costs did not overrule Armenia's international human rights obligations (to adopt the law on alternative service), other human rights reforms unpopular among the Armenian society may face stronger clashes with the domestic 'traditional

113 *Bayatyan v Armenia* (n 63) [127].

114 PACE Opinion 221 (2000) on Armenia's application for CoE membership (n 3) [13.4(d)].

115 *Bayatyan v Armenia* (n 63) para 127.

116 Governmental Official, ARM01, Strasbourg, 23 May 2017.

117 Pew Research Centre, 'How do European countries differ in religious commitment? Use our interactive map to find out' (5 December 2018), accessed 5 August 2020.

values', depending on the level of prevalence of societal values 'challenged' by a particular ECtHR judgment, the timing and the political costs. One interviewed Armenian human rights lawyer litigating cases before the ECtHR suggested that issues such as violations of LGBTI rights or domestic violence in Armenia, which are widely entrenched in and justified with 'traditional values' in the Armenian society, once addressed by the ECtHR, will face much stronger resistance, which will also affect the political determination to pursue the necessary reforms.[118] Another interviewed NGO representative referred to the propitious timing when the reforms relating to the *Bayatyan* case were high on the political agenda in Armenia as they formed a part of Armenia's CoE accession package; since accession was considered as a primary geopolitical priority at that time, and was perceived favourably by the public, this in turn diminished the likelihood of the domestic sensitivity around the *Bayatyan* reforms.[119] This suggests a conclusion that the impact of the 'traditional values' argument in the context of implementation of ECtHR judgments in Armenia is defined by the level of popular support, or public's rejection, as a relevant factor for the ruling political decision makers to maintain their public support. This factor cannot be disregarded in assessing compliance with ECtHR judgments as it may contribute to generating – or preventing – the necessary political will for adequate compliance, as the above cases show.

4.3 Strasbourg's Contributions to Compliance with ECtHR Judgments in Armenia

The analysis of lifespans of the selected groups of cases against Armenia before the CM offers two key findings, which are discussed in this Chapter:

- The CM's enhanced supervision of the implementation process of cases leads to more frequent and substantive engagement by the authorities; and,
- The involvement of other CoE bodies and domestic actors significantly facilitates implementation.

4.3.1 *CM's Engagement with the Supervision of Armenian Cases*

Similarly to the findings in Azerbaijani and Georgian cases, the CM's enhanced follow up to the Armenian authorities' progress in complying with ECtHR

118 Lawyer, ARM08, online interview, 13 June 2017.

119 CSO representative, ARM09, Yerevan, 28 April 2017.

judgments resulted in more timely and frequent engagement by the Armenian counterparts. Although, as discussed in 4.2.2, Armenia is generally compliant with the CM supervision procedures and timeframes, the impact of the CM's enhanced involvement is significant both in terms of engagement and actual domestic steps. In Armenian cases, such engagement has not only increased in communication between the Armenian counterparts and the CM/DEJ but also led to more substantive progress regarding the necessary reforms. Although Armenian cases do not appear on the CM indicative list of cases as frequently as Azerbaijani or Georgian cases, meaning that individual CM delegations have fewer opportunities to pose questions to the Armenian authorities on the implementation progress, such closer supervision of the CM is nevertheless observed through official CM decisions where specific input and recommendations are provided to the Armenian authorities.

For example, from 2011, when the CM-DH agendas became publicly available, until 2014, no Armenian cases were put on the CM agenda in, except for one case in 2013. Since 2015, at least one case a year has been placed on the agenda, and this increased to three cases per year in 2019 and 2020, although the majority of them were not tabled for a debate before the CM.[120] As a result of this – still relatively infrequent – appearance of Armenian cases on the CM agenda, individual CM delegations engage with supervision of Armenian cases little if at all, since all the communication and CM decision drafting is done by the DEJ, and decisions are adopted in a written process. As one interviewed CM delegate from a Western European country actively involved in the CM supervision process noted, 'in my several years' experience at the CM, we have never discussed any Armenian cases, except for the Nagorno Karabakh case, which is highly political, and this allows me to assume that Armenia is performing well'.[121] Similar insights were shared by two other interviewed CM delegates actively involved in the CM supervision work who related the absence of Armenian cases on the agenda with its alleged satisfactory compliance performance.[122]

Although Armenian cases are rarely formally examined by the CM, Armenia's responsiveness to the CM formal decisions on the implementation progress in a number of cases has been positive and led to state reporting on tangible steps being taken by the authorities domestically. In the majority of

120 All CM-DH agendas and decisions adopted at each meeting available at https://www.coe.int/en/web/execution/committee-of-ministers-human-rights-meetings.

121 CM member state representative, SXB01, Strasbourg, 23 May 2017.

122 CM member state representative, SXB02, Strasbourg, 23 May 2017; CM member state representative, SXB03, Strasbourg, 23 May 2017.

such cases, the appearance of a case on the CM agenda was followed by a new or revised action plan or action report by the authorities providing updates on the progress. For example, in the case of *Ashot Harutyunyan* group of cases, out of all five action plans/reports provided by the authorities, three of them have been submitted just ahead of the CM meetings where this group of cases was put on the agenda in 2016, 2017 and 2019.[123] All three action reports addressed the specific questions raised by the CM in its decisions, which ensured the continuity of the communication on the implementation process. For example, in its December 2017 decision, the CM requested the Armenian Government to provide 'precise information on the remedy available to detainees to enable them to obtain direct redress in respect of complaints concerning access to appropriate health care in prison', which was not reported on by Armenia in its earlier action plans and which it responded to in its subsequent action plan in January 2019.[124] There have been, however, no further updates until July 2020, when Armenia has further reported on the respective developments and requested the CM to close the case, following which the CM has asked for further updated information from Armenia. This further reinforces the conclusion on the causal connection between CM formal reviews and Armenian Government's submissions.

Similar tendencies are observed in the *Virabyan* group of cases where over 60% of all the Government's submissions made during 2013–2020 have been submitted a couple of months before the CM-DH meetings where this group of cases was on the agenda.[125] Such continuous exchange of updates and feedback by the CM ensured, for example, that the issue of effective investigation in Mr. Virabyan's individual case, as one of the most sensitive issues in this group, remained on the agenda of this communication and led to Armenia's updates in this regard in every action plan.[126] Similarly to the other cases, no written communication was submitted by the authorities in this group of cases during the longer periods between the CM-DH meetings, e.g. during June 2018-March 2020 or December 2016-March 2018, which indicates the momentum that CM decisions create for state's enhanced involvement.

---

123 HUDOC EXEC database, information on the *Ashot Harutyunyan* group of cases, last accessed on 15 December 2021.

124 CM decision in *Harutyunyan Ashot* group v. Armenia (Appl. no. 34334/04), adopted at its 1302nd meeting, 5–7 December 2017; Communication from Armenia concerning the *Ashot Harutyunyan* group of cases v. Armenia (Appl. no. 34334/04), 18 January 2019

125 HUDOC EXEC database, information on the *Virabyan* group of cases, accessed on 15 December 2021.

126 Government action plans in the *Virabyan* group of cases submitted to the CM on 16 February 2015, 14 October 2016, 22 February 2018, 30 March 2018, and 24 January 2020.

Such findings relating to enhanced communication between the CM and the authorities demonstrate that the formal inclusion of cases on the CM agenda is beneficial not only in cases where additional political pressure or encouragement is needed, as often perceived by the DEJ or CM members.[127] These examples in the Armenian cases suggest that such inclusion of cases is likely to be valuable in ensuring more regular and consistent communication and substantive reporting on the progress as some sort of guidance or a reminder to respondent states in more 'standard' circumstances, and not only in cases where there is obvious political resistance from states to adopt the necessary measures. On that basis, I suggest that standard regular formal attention on cases from the CM is likely to ensure more regular continuous reporting by states, and, in that way, their better socialisation with the Strasbourg norms and procedures. This undoubtedly raises questions about the capacity of the CM, and the DEJ as a secretariat body, to include more cases on the formal CM agenda of each DH meeting; since the DEJ already maintains bilateral communications with respondent domestic institutions on the progress of all country cases on a regular basis, such consideration would not appear unfeasible.

The *Chiragov and Others* case, on the other hand, is a good example indicating how the absence of sufficient CM involvement in the supervision process likely affects the progress in effective communication, particularly where the conflict context is politically sensitive on both sides. Although Armenia asserts its determination to hold consultations with the DEJ on the execution of the case through bilateral meetings, the outcomes of which remain behind closed doors and therefore unknown to public, formal written submissions from Armenia have been limited to one communication in December 2019, more than four years after the judgment has become final. Although the ongoing dialogue with the DEJ is a positive development, its informal unwritten nature hinders the applicant and other relevant state bodies and actors, such as national parliament members, civil society, Human Rights Defenders' Office from scrutinising the process. Rather than focusing on complying with the Court's indicated measure to establish a property restitution mechanism, as discussed above, the submission sets out the obstacles, which 'objectively hinder the execution of the judgment', referring to the parties' failure to reach a peace agreement.[128] The Armenian Government has to date failed to submit any information on its efforts to examine how such a property compensation mechanism should look like in the domestic system legally and technically,

127 DEJ official, SXB04, Strasbourg, 30 November 2016.

128 Communication from the authorities (02/12/2019) in the case of *Chiragov and Others v. Armenia* (Appl. no. 13216/05).

and how its operation would be ensured, nor did it provide any update on the individual measures, including the payment of compensation to the applicants. In light of Armenia's overall responsiveness to the CM enhanced supervision, I argue that such a standstill in communication in this case is likely to be overcome by more frequent formal reviews of this case by the CM, which has so far largely remained outside any formal examination of this case. The CM has formally examined this case, together with its mirror case against Azerbaijan, only once during the five years of implementation pending before the CM, at its March 2017 meeting, and limited its decision to an invitation to the Armenian authorities to provide an action plan.[129] Enhanced CM attention to the case would create a formal platform for engagement encouraging Armenia to provide formal updates on its progress, which, as the analysis of the Armenian practice suggests, it is conducive to.

4.3.2 *Contributions of other CoE Bodies and Domestic Actors to Compliance*

The research findings indicate supplementary contributions of other CoE bodies and the NHRI to the progress in the implementation of ECtHR judgments by Armenia. It is not only the involvement in the implementation process that is observed but also their ability to effectively contribute to the process, positively received by the Armenian authorities in a number of cases. In the analysed cases, the roles of the CPT and the Venice Commission are particularly observed, and, at the domestic level, the involvement of the Armenian Human Rights Defender's Office (the Armenian NHRI) as those that had valuable contributions to the process. A case in point is the *Bayatyan* group of cases relating to conscientious objectors, where the main necessary reform concerned the adoption of a law on alternative service providing conscientious objectors with an opportunity to refuse from military service and to not be criminally prosecuted. Although Armenia adopted the law on alternative service in 2004, it did not meet the CoE requirements on a number of counts, primarily on the fact that the civil service remained under military control. Following the ECtHR judgment in *Bayatyan* case in July 2011, the Armenian parliament sought an opinion from the Venice Commission on the draft amendments to the Law on Alternative Service, which assisted Armenia in developing the scope of alternative service, its term, procedure and conditions.[130] Effective incorporation

129 CM decision in the case of *Chiragov and Others v Armenia* (Appl. no. 13216/05), adopted at its 1280th meeting on 7–10 March 2017.

130 Opinion on the Draft Law on Amendments and Additions to the Law on Alternative Service of Armenia, adopted by the Venice Commission at its 89th Plenary Session (Venice, 16–17 December 2011), Opinion no. 644/2011.

of the Commission's recommendations into the amended law also ensured that military control was fully eliminated from this mechanism as one of the key reforms that Armenia had to ensure as part of the compliance with the ECtHR judgment.[131]

Another successful example of such complementarity of efforts of CoE bodies is observed in the *Ashot Harutyunyan* group of cases, requiring substantial domestic reforms concerning health care in prisons. The health care system reform that is being implemented under this group of cases has been prepared on the basis of the 2015 CPT recommendations to Armenia, which the authorities were encouraged to rely on by the CM, together with the indications from the Human Rights Defender of Armenia as a domestic monitoring body, which Armenia has taken into account.[132] Further substantial reforms were initiated with the support of the joint EU-CoE project "Strengthening Health Care and Human Rights Protection in Prisons in Armenia", which the CM has urged Armenia 'to take full benefit from' in implementing this group of judgments, the contributions of which I addressed above (see 4.2.2.1.2).[133] Such receptive reliance on the support of other bodies and actors did not only enable Armenia to introduce some of the highly financially costly reforms but also offered expert support in developing the substantive plan for such substantial structural reforms, all resulting in efficient complementarity of efforts and socialisation of the respective institutions for the same cause.

A less responsive approach by the Armenian authorities is noticeable with regard to contributions from the domestic and international civil society organisations, which primarily aim to provide their input and recommendations to facilitate the state's efforts towards general measures. For example, the NGO submission in the *Chiragov and Others* case by the European Human Rights Advocacy Centre, setting out the international standards relating to property claims mechanisms, could serve a similar purpose as the other above mentioned actors if taken into consideration by the Armenian authorities, however, remains to be responded on by Armenia (as well as Azerbaijan in its

131 Communication from Armenia concerning the *Bayatyan* group of cases against Armenia (Appl. no. 23459/03), 25 February 2013, Part II.

132 CM decision in the *Ashot Harutyunyan* group v. Armenia (Appl. no. 34334/04), adopted at the 1302nd meeting, 5–7 December 2017 [2].

133 CM decision in the *Ashot Harutyunyan* group v. Armenia (Appl. no. 34334/04), adopted at the 1250th meeting, 8–10 March 2016, para 6; Communication from the Human Rights Defender of Armenia (21/01/2019) and reply from the authorities (01/02/2019) in the case of *Ashot Harutyunyan v. Armenia* (Ashot Harutyunyan group) (Appl. no. 34334/04).

mirror case).[134] Furthermore, although the CM took note of this submission and its content in its official notes on the status of execution of this case, it did not formally rely on the referred international standards as guidelines for developing the mechanism in formulating its recommendations in its subsequent communication on this case, as it did in other above mentioned cases. If it did so, it may have served as an additional encouragement on the Armenian authorities to take into consideration and build on the support offered by the civil society.[135]

A similarly unresponsive approach is observed in other cases where NGO submissions have been made. As to the NGO submissions on general measures by two different domestic organisations in the *Virabyan* group of cases in 2013, 2014 and 2016, the Armenian Government has largely dismissed their allegations and recommendations as either ungrounded or irrelevant to this group of cases, or has not responded to them at all, with little or no indication of engagement with the substance of the submissions.[136] For example, in the first NGO submission in this group made by the Rule of Law NGO in September 2013, where it set out recommendations for the necessary criminal procedure reforms in the domestic system to prevent similar violations in the future, the authorities baldly responded in their written reply that such recommendations had no concern with this judgment and that 'the process of execution of judgments should not be used as a platform for irrelevant discussions'.[137] It did not deem it necessary or useful to engage in a more detailed discussion as to why such recommendations were not relevant in their eyes leaving no further window for further contributions for the civil society (which led to no further submissions from this NGO in this group during the research period). No formal mention of any of these submissions is observed by the CM in its

134 Communication from a NGO (EHRAC) (02/11/2016) in the cases of *Chiragov against Armenia* (Appl. no. 13216/05) and *Sargsyan against Azerbaijan* (Appl. no. 40167/06).

135 CM notes on the Agenda in the case of *Chiragov and Others v. Armenia*, CM/Notes/1362/H46-1, 1362nd meeting, 3–5 December 2019.

136 Communication from a NGO (Helsinki Citizens' Assembly-Vanadzor) (07/11/2016) and reply from the authorities (17/11/2016) in the case of *Nalbandyan* (*Virabyan group*) *against Armenia* (Appl. no. 9935/06); Communication from a NGO (Helsinki Citizens' Assembly-Vanadzor) (26/09/2014) in the case of *Virabyan against Armenia* (Appl. no. 40094/05); Communication from NGOs (Helsinki Citizens Assembly – Vanadzor and Spitak Helsinki Group) (25/09/13) in the cases of *Harutyunyan and Virabyan against Armenia* (Appl. no. 34334/04 and 40094/05) and reply of the authorities (08/10/2013); Communication from a NGO (Rule of Law) (25/09/2013) in the case of *Virabyan against Armenia* (Appl. no. 40094/05) and reply of the authorities (08/10/2013).

137 Communication from an NGO (Rule of Law) (25/09/2013) in the case of *Virabyan against Armenia* (Appl. no. 40094/05) and reply of the authorities (08/10/2013).

written communications either, which, as suggested above, may have otherwise encouraged the authorities to engage with the NGO suggestions. The two interviewed NGO groups expressed their uncertainty as to what impact they had to the process, if any, and if they should continue focusing their limited financial and human resources in preparing similar submissions to the CM.[138] This suggests that the civil society will not be incentivized enough to engage in the process if the CM itself and the domestic authorities do not accord visible weight to civil society submissions.[139] This risks diminishing the CM's access to crucial alternative sources in assessing the effectiveness and sufficiency of the steps taken by the domestic authorities, and therefore potentially undue reliance on the state's position may be made.

Such contrasting approach by the authorities towards NGO submissions, as opposed to other actors, may be partly explained by the broader perception of the limited role of the civil society in the country in such matters and their involvement in the implementation process, or any other decision making on issues of state governance, rule of law or human rights. As discussed in Section 4.2.1 on domestic implementation system above, there is no established practice of any formal consistent NGO involvement in matters of public interest, nor any procedures or other frameworks to encourage such involvement. The NGOs interviewed in the pre-2018 period unanimously confirmed that it is very difficult for them to get involved in such processes and their contribution is rather sporadic, often based on individual contacts in certain state institutions and bodies.[140] Admittedly, many of them confessed that there is space for their enhanced focus on the implementation and not litigation only, and that they should prioritise it better in their strategic plans, as part of their programmatic work. As one of the interviewed NGOs described, 'there is no wider dialogue between the authorities and the civil society on ECtHR judgments, but since this is perceived as a very specific narrow area, the civil society needs to increase its interest and prioritise this issue better too'.[141] As, similarly to the case of Georgia, the post Velvet Revolution has allowed for a

138 Lawyer, ARM08, online interview, 13 June 2017; CSO representative, ARM12, email communication, 9 September 2020.

139 Alice Donald, Debra Long, and Anne-Katrin Speck, 'Identifying and Assessing the Implementation of Human Rights Decisions' (2020), Volume 12 Issue 1, Journal of Human Rights Practice, 1–24 [2.2.2].

140 Lawyer, ARM05, Yerevan, 28 April 2017; Lawyer, ARM06, Yerevan, 28 April 2017; Lawyer, ARM07, Yerevan, 28 April 2017; Lawyer, ARM08, online interview, 13 June 2017; CSO representative, ARM09, Yerevan, 28 April 2017; CSO representative, ARM10, Yerevan, 27 April 2017; CSO representative, ARM11, Yerevan, 27 April 2017.

141 CSO representative, ARM10, Yerevan, 27 April 2017.

number of civil society members to take up governmental positions, and the newly established implementation structure appears to be more receptive of the civil society involvement, Armenia will be an interesting test case in this regard.

4.4 Conclusion

Two decades into the CoE membership, Armenia's compliance performance is most progressive in statistical terms among the South Caucasus states. It has got the highest number of cases closed as implemented by the CM in total numbers and its number of leading cases pending implementation under enhanced supervision procedure is the lowest among the three states. Largely motivated by the support of and a sense of belonging to the 'European family', Armenia generally engages with the Strasbourg supervision procedures and is conducive to socialisation by the existing Convention system. Its domestic implementation system is marked by gradual increase of institutional capacities and transparency, and the 2019 reforms offer some further positive insights if implemented to the letter.

In order to effectively assess the state's implementation efforts and the eventual impact of ECtHR judgments, however, it is equally important to identify what qualitative change such efforts have on the domestic level and how effective they are in putting an end to similar violations. The research analysis suggests that although generally Armenia is willing to comply with ECtHR judgments, certain underlying structural domestic factors predetermine the prevalence of domestic interests over its Convention obligations to comply with ECtHR judgments in a timely, full and effective manner. They include clear political unwillingness to comply with a judgment, exposing hidden individual political interests of certain authorities or their acting in bad faith, and the entrenched institutional power balance, inherited from the Soviet Union. It also includes high financial costs of full compliance with ECtHR judgments, and deeply rooted traditional values and other widely popular societal views, which some ECtHR judgments challenge, and put the public support of political powers at risk. Such underlying factors are common in countries where the culture of genuine respect for individual human rights, rule of law and democratic values is not yet well embedded in the organisation of the state and the society, and is known as 'the problem of democratising states' of the CoE. States like Armenia serve as a litmus test for the CoE, whose successful integration, started with the open door policy, requires consistent targeted support to ensure real adequate socialisation with the norms the state adhered to. The case of Georgia, as the third state in the South Caucasus region, which I discuss in the next Chapter, presents yet further particularities of domestic compliance with ECtHR judgments, allowing drawing some further findings from the region.

CHAPTER 5

Georgia as Council of Europe's Success Story in the South Caucasus?

This Chapter discusses Georgia's compliance with judgments of the European Court of Human Rights (ECtHR) and analyses its compliance behavior in the domestic context. Similarly to the previous country chapters, this analysis is made against the backdrop of Georgia's historical and geopolitical background both upon its accession to the Council of Europe (CoE) and throughout its membership that set the ground for Georgia's compliance behaviour (see 5.1). I analyse compliance both by assessing the existing domestic system for implementation as the institutional framework for implementation, and the role that various domestic actors play in that regard (see 5.2). I further analyse the implementation of five selected Georgian cases, or groups of cases pending implementation before the Committee of Ministers (CM), which allows to derive more generalized findings on factors that affect Georgia's performance (see 5.3). I focus both on the domestic factors and the effectiveness of the Strasbourg compliance supervision processes to Georgia's respective behavior, and critically assess their role in Georgia's compliance with ECtHR judgments. The analysed cases/groups of cases, *Ghavtadze* group of cases, *Gharibashvili* group of cases, *Klaus and Yuri Kiladze* case, *Gorelishvili* case, and *Identoba and Others* case, address a variety of systemic human rights issues exposing various structural systemic problems in the domestic system that require adoption of various individual and general measures, allowing for consideration of a wide range of factors and situations in Georgia's compliance studies.[1]

1 *Ghavtadze* group of cases: *Ghavtadze v. Georgia*, Appl. no. 23204/07 (ECtHR 30 March 2009); *Poghosyan v. Georgia*, Appl. no. 9870/07 (ECtHR 24 February 2009); *Makharadze and Sikharulidze v. Georgia*, Appl. no. 35254/07 (ECtHR 22 November 2011); *Irakli Mindadze v. Georgia*, Appl. no. 17012/09, (ECtHR 11 December 2012); *Jeladze v. Georgia*, Appl. no. 1871/08 (ECtHR18 December 2012); *Ildani v. Georgia*, Appl. no. 65391/09 (ECtHR 23 April 2013): Gharibashvili group of cases as of December 2016: *Gharibashvili v Georgia*, Appl. no. 11830/03 (ECtHR 29 October 2008), *Khaindrava and Dzamashvili v Georgia*, Appl. no. 18183/05 (ECtHR 08 September 2010); *Mikiashvili v Georgia*, Appl. no. 18996/06 (ECtHR 09 January 2013); *Dvalishvili v Georgia*, Appl. no. 19634/07 (ECtHR 18 March 2013); *Tsintsabadze v Georgia*, Appl. no. 35403/06 (ECtHR 18 March 2011); *Enukidze and Girgvliani v Georgia*, Appl. no. 25091/07 (ECtHR 27 July 2011); *Ramin Kirizia v Georgia*, Appl. No. 4728/08 (ECtHR 11 March 2014); *Baghashvili v Georgia*, Appl. no. 5168/06 (ECtHR 18 March 2014); *Otar; Sulkhan Molashvili v Georgia*, Appl. no. 39726/04 (ECtHR 30 September 2014); *Malkhaz Mzekalishvili v Georgia*,

 | DOI:10.1163/9789004538214_006

5.1 Georgia's Accession and Its Membership in the CoE

Today, more than two decades into the CoE membership, Georgia is seen as the most advanced country among the South Caucasus states in its democratisation path both by the CoE representatives and domestic actors.[2] It was the first to be accepted to the CoE among the three states, on 27 April 1999, perceived as having demonstrated its readiness and willingness to join the European system and uphold its values.[3] In the early 1990s, however, Georgia was one of the emergent independent countries after the collapse of the Soviet Union, with Soviet-inherited weak separation of powers and judicial system, and having experienced two armed conflicts with the de facto independent, partly recognised republics of Abkhazia in 1992–94, and South Ossetia in 1990–93, that embarked on the road to independence and democratic transition.[4] Following the proclamation of independence through a referendum of 31 March 1991 and the election of a former dissident, Zviad Gamsakhourdia in the presidential elections, Georgia soon found itself drifting into nationalism and authoritarianism.[5] The coup d'etat in January 1992, which led to the establishment of the military council as the highest governing body, led the country into chaos, further deepened by the escalating conflicts with Abkhaz and South Ossetian separatists.[6] Unable to control the situation, the military council approached

Appl. no. 8177/12 (ECtHR 10 February 2015); *Emzar Kopadze v Georgia*, Appl. no. 58228/09 (ECtHR 10 March 2015); *Lasha Lanchava v Georgia*, Appl. no. 28103/11; *Studio Maestro Ltd and Others v Georgia*, Appl. no. 22318/10 (ECtHR 30 June 2015); *Davit Chantladze v Georgia*, Appl. no. 60864/10 (ECtHR 30 June 2015); *Giorgi Bekauri and Others v Georgia*, Appl. no. 312/10 (ECtHR 15 September 2015); *Vazha Gegenava and Others v Georgia*, Appl. no. 65128/10 (ECtHR 20 October 2015); *Klaus and Yuri Kiladze v Georgia*, Appl.no. 7975/06 (ECtHR 2 February 2010); *Gorelishvili v Georgia*, Appl.no. 12979/04 (ECtHR 5 June 2007); *Identoba and Others* group v Georgia, Appl. no. 73235/12 (ECtHR 12 May 2015).

2 CM member state representative, SXB01, Strasbourg, 23 May 2017; CM member state representative, SXB02, Strasbourg, 23 May 2017; CM member state representative, SXB03, Strasbourg, 23 May 2017; DEJ official, SXB04, Strasbourg, 30 November 2016; Governmental Official, GEO01, Strasbourg, 30 March 2018; Georgian MP, GEO05, Tbilisi, 16 September 2015; Governmental Official and former human rights lawyer, GEO04, Tbilisi, 17 September 2015.

3 PACE Opinion 209 (1999), Georgia's application for membership of the Council of Europe, 27 January 1999.

4 PACE Recommendation 1247 (1994) on Enlargement of the Council of Europe (n 304); PACE report on 'Georgia's application for membership of the Council of Europe', Doc. 8275, prepared by the Political Affairs Committee and its rapporteur Mr Terry Davis (UK, Socialist Group), 2 December 1998.

5 Explanatory memorandum to the report of PACE Political Affairs Committee on 'Georgia's application for membership of the Council of Europe', Doc. 8275, prepared by its rapporteur Mr Terry Davis (UK, Socialist Group), 2 December 1998 [8].

6 Ibid [8–11].

Eduard Shevardnadze, the Minister of Foreign Affairs of the Soviet Union of 1985–1991, who returned to Georgia after its independence, and future President of Georgia, to form a new state council in March 1992, which led to the parliamentary elections resulting in Shevardnadze's election as the Chairman of the Parliament with extensive semi-presidential powers. It was the adoption of the Georgian Constitution in August 1995 and the parliamentary elections in November 1995 that marked, according to the Parliamentary Assembly of the Council of Europe (PACE), the beginning of establishing 'solid foundations for properly functioning democracy in Georgia', which paved the way for Georgia's accession to the CoE on 27 April 1999.[7]

Although the political upheaval was brought to an end and, as concluded by the ad hoc PACE committee in 1998, 'the "official" political landscape appeared to operate in a normal democratic way', Georgia's political system remained deeply fragile, featuring challenges to the legitimacy of the ruling regime and the prosecution of political opponents.[8] Furthermore, relations with Abkhaz separatists remained volatile despite the ceasefire agreement in May 1994, with 250,000 people in need of protection as refugees and internally displaced people, many reliant on humanitarian aid. Further hostilities erupted in August 2008 leading to a so called five-day war that broke out following the worsening relations between Russia and Georgia and the tensions in South Ossetia that soon involved Russia, South Ossetian and Abkhaz military units.[9]

It was against this context that Georgia started its negotiations with the CoE for its membership that was largely based on the CoE's open door policy towards newly emerging independent aspiring democracies in the East. The CoE, then largely consisting of Western democracies, was willing to open its doors to Georgia on the basis of the country's expressed willingness to abide by the key principles and norms of the CoE. As Andrew Drzemczewski, former Head of the Secretariat of PACE Committee on Legal Affairs and Human Rights, noted, the doors could not have been slammed to those wishing to join the democratic club and the enlargement to the East, although it may have been precipitate, at the time appeared to be politically inevitable.[10] In its report on the conformity of Georgia's legal order with the CoE principles in 1998, following its two visits to Georgia, the PACE Political Affairs Committee

7 Ibid [11].

8 Ibid [15–16].

9 Report 'Independent International Fact-Finding Mission on the Conflict in Georgia', established by the Council of the European Union, September 2009 10, 15.

10 Inaugural lecture of Andrew Drzemczewski, a Visiting Professor of the Middlesex University, School of Law 'Human Rights in Europe: an Insider's View', 18 January 2017.

and its legal experts were of the opinion that Georgia's willingness and assurances to engage in further reforms demonstrated its readiness to join the CoE.[11] In their view, such factors as the parliamentary elections of November 1995, which passed 'reasonably normally and lawfully', and Georgia's readiness to peacefully settle the two conflicts, were strong indicators of Georgia's promising efforts to become a 'pluralist democracy'.[12] Although the PACE recognised the existence of various legislative and policy gaps and deep-rooted problems, including corruption and alleged persecution of political opponents, the CoE welcomed Georgia on the basis of their promise and willingness to progress, as 'it would not have been realistic to expect a better result so soon after the end of the totalitarian Soviet regime'.[13] Rather than waiting for Georgia to reach compliance with the European standards in its domestic system, the CoE embarked on its role to serve as a platform to assist Georgia to achieve this objective on the basis of its expressed willingness and readiness 'to continue the democratic reforms in progress in order to bring all the country's legislation and practice into line with the principles and standards of the Council of Europe'.[14]

Georgia's political leadership embraced the aspired European opportunity for its 'aspiration to become a part of the European family' and create 'an independent and prosperous country given its geopolitical situation'.[15] As its late Prime Minister, Zurab Zhvania, noted in the CoE in 1999: "I am Georgian and therefore I am European".[16] A number of interviewed domestic actors both from the state authorities and the civil society suggested that Georgia's geopolitical situation and its Soviet legacy at the time predetermined its Europe-oriented vision. A lawyer at the ECtHR described it as the most sought aspiration for the Georgian society at the time, and it remains strong today: 'to become a part of the European family'.[17] As one human rights lawyer from Georgia put it, 'Georgia did not and does not have any other way but to abide by the European

11 PACE Political Affairs Committee report on Georgia, Explanatory memorandum (n 5) [90].

12 Ibid [45, 86, 89].

13 Ibid Annex II, [7].

14 PACE report on Georgia's application for CoE membership (n 4) [90].

15 Governmental Official, GEO04, Tbilisi, 15 September 2015; Governmental Official and former human rights lawyer, GEO04, Tbilisi, 17 September 2015; Georgian MP, GEO05, Tbilisi, 16 September 2015; Judge of Georgian Constitutional Court, GEO06, Tbilisi, 9 December 2016.

16 The Caucasus Research Resources Center Georgia, survey report 'Knowledge and Attitudes towards the EU in Georgia: Changes and Trends 2009–2013' 14.

17 CSO representative, SXB10, London, 23 November 2016.

human rights standards and cooperate with the European institutions because the only other direction would be Russia'.[18] Such a view refers to Russia as the powerful neighbor in the north of Georgia dissatisfied with the geopolitical changes after the collapse of the Soviet Union, including the 'spread' of the European values. Russia consequently became more adamant in imposing its influence upon its 'near abroad'.[19]

In 1994, following the CoE's debate on enlargement and its decision to open up to newly emerging democracies, Georgia, together with Armenia and Azerbaijan, was invited to apply for membership of the CoE, 'provided they clearly indicate their will to be considered as part of Europe'.[20] Ahead of its accession, Georgia was required to undergo certain reforms such as the creation of the new necessary legal framework and ensuring effective domestic systems, such as improving the judicial system, the prison system and law enforcement bodies, and fighting corruption in the judiciary and law enforcement agencies. The adopted laws included the adoption of the Constitution, and laws on the courts, the Ombudsman, referenda, local self-government and local administration, the Prosecutor's Office, as well as the codes of criminal and civil procedure and the civil code, with the expert support of the CoE, its democratic member states and other international organisations.[21] The list of obligations also included the ratification of a number of CoE treaties, including the European Convention on Human Rights (ECHR) and its protocols, and the European Convention for the Prevention of Torture and Inhuman or Degrading Treatment or Punishment and its protocols; and initiating legislative reforms to secure compliance with the treaties' norms.[22] Some major commitments such as eradicating corruption in the judiciary and police, stemming from the deep-rooted Soviet legacy, required changes in institutional and societal attitudes, and hierarchical subordination, necessitating stable and long lasting political will, time and effective monitoring and accountability mechanisms, which require a lot of time and were not as easy to measure at the time.

Although many laws were adopted, the application of the new legislation and policies, however, remained of great concern, largely due to deep-rooted problems arising from the totalitarian Soviet past and the economic situation.[23]

---

18 CSO representative, GEO08, Tbilisi, online interview, 12 December 2016.

19 Inaugural lecture of Andrew Drzemczewski (n 10).

20 PACE Recommendation 1247 (1994) on Enlargement of the Council of Europe (n 304); PACE Political Affairs Committee report on Georgia, Explanatory memorandum (n 4) [8].

21 PACE Political Affairs Committee report on Georgia, Explanatory memorandum (n 4) [49].

22 Ibid [10].

23 Ibid [88].

As one interviewed lawyer described it: 'laws have been changed with the support of the CoE, and it was a huge progress, but changing deeply rooted practices and societal attitudes takes time and strong political willingness, which is a longer process'.[24] Corruption remained prevalent in law enforcement agencies and the judiciary, as the legacy of the Soviet legal system, and as an underlying problem to establishing rule of law, which state institutions were not strong enough to effectively tackle.[25] Reports of human rights groups about politically motivated arrests and imprisonment, widespread abuses by police, and restrictions on the exercise of the right to freedom of assembly for political opponents raised serious doubts about the proper functioning of the justice system and the independence of the judiciary.[26] Poor detention conditions and the observance of prisoners' human rights were among reported issues of concern, which, in the view of PACE, had to be closely monitored after Georgia's accession.[27] Effective implementation of commitments related to the peaceful settlement of the two conflicts, such as determining the status of autonomous territories, and prosecuting perpetrators of war crimes committed during the conflicts in Abkhazia and South Ossetia, entailed complex political decision-making processes and negotiations, as well as an effective application of the criminal justice system. The geopolitical context of the two conflicts, with Russia's interest in and support to the autonomous territories, and its overall intention to remain influential in the region, meant that the settlement process remained fragile.[28]

At that time, the 'European future' for Georgia, which included aspirations for membership of several regional organisations, including the European Union (EU) and the North Atlantic Treaty Organisation (NATO), has increasingly became the subject of the public debates and has often been dominant in the popular speeches of various Georgian political groups.[29] The Georgian population has generally been enthusiastic about the European idea since the independence from the Soviet Union[30] and particularly the Rose Revolution

24 Human rights lawyer, GEO010, Tbilisi, online interview, 19 February 2017.

25 PACE Political Affairs Committee report on Georgia, Explanatory memorandum, Annex II, [5].

26 Ibid [55, 62, 63]; Freedom House report 'Nations in Transit: Georgia', 2003, sections on Judicial Framework and Independence, and Corruption, accessed 3 August 2020.

27 PACE Political Affairs Committee report on Georgia, Explanatory memorandum (n 4) [69].

28 Report 'Independent International Fact-Finding Mission on the Conflict in Georgia' (n 9) 14.

29 The Caucasus Research Resource Center Georgia, 'Knowledge and attitudes toward the EU in Georgia' 2015 accessed 22 January 2017 14.

30 Ibid 14.

that led to a pro-Western peaceful change of power in November 2003 and the emergence of the United National Movement (UNM) as the dominant ruling party and Mikheil Saakashvili, UNM leader and Georgia's President in 2004–2012.[31] That period marks Georgia's pro-Western foreign policy era in building relations with the EU, NATO, the United States and other Western democracies and positioning integration with Europe as its key priority.[32] This period contributed to laying the foundations for Georgia's democratisation, with an influx of foreign aid, wide economic and government reforms, successful measures to tackle corruption[33] and high crime rates, the emergence of an enabling environment for vibrant, strong and independent non-governmental organisations and media. The administration's harsh policies on fighting corruption and high crime rates, however, led to an excessively abusive and punitive justice system, which drastically increased the prison population and conviction rates, resulting in routine prison overcrowding and abusive treatment of prisoners by law enforcement officers acting with apparent impunity.[34]

Saakashvili's 8-year pro-European era and willingness to engage with international and European institutions created favourable conditions for Georgia's overall socialisation with various human rights bodies, including the CoE. Strong pro-European rhetoric, however, shifted with the arrival of the Georgian Dream party and its leader, the billionaire businessman Bidzina Ivanishvili, who was elected in November 2012 following the growing popular dissatisfaction about the increasing concentration of power by Saakashvili and reports of political corruption.[35] The Georgian Dream coalition that demonstrates a stronger nationalistic and conservative position, and divergent foreign policy priorities, including favourable relations with Russia, secured a second term, with an overwhelming increase in votes, in 2016, indicating its growing popular support. It secured the public vote despite increasing allegations of corruption and lack of transparency in the government, and economic stagnation.[36] The UNM defeat may have been affected by the ongoing prosecution of its leadership under multiple criminal charges, which it claimed to be politicised.[37]

---

31 Freedom House, Nations in Transit 2016: Georgia, accessed 9 January 2017.

32 Ibid.

33 Georgia's ranking in the Corruption Perceptions Index by Transparency International improved dramatically from rank 133 in 2004 to 67 in 2008 and to 51 in 2012.

34 Freedom House, Nations in Transit 2016: Georgia (n 31).

35 Ibid.

36 Ibid.

37 In the case of Merabishvili v Georgia (Appl. no. 72508/13, ECtHR 28 November 2017), former Prime Minister of Georgia under the UNM leadership in 2012, the ECtHR found that his pre-trial detention was used to exert pressure on him and lacked reasonableness.

Strong public unease over allegations of ill-treatment of prisoners in custody and the continuous failure to effectively investigate it under the UNM government, with a video documenting sexual abuse committed by law enforcement agents leaked just before the 2012 elections, is believed to have served as another factor that had shaped the public opinion.[38] Such political power shifts have deepened the division of the population, with the various groups attempting to find ways to voice their political positions in the streets, leading to violent clashes with the law enforcement agents in 2019–2020.[39]

It is against this volatile political and legal context that I examine Georgia's compliance with ECtHR judgments, which undoubtedly influence the process as the domestic platform within which compliance takes place. The ECtHR addressed many of the above-mentioned remaining challenges in its judgments, the implementation of some of which I analyse below.

5.1.1 *Georgia and the ECtHR*

During Georgia's two decades of CoE membership, the ECtHR has grown in its popularity among the Georgian population as an effective judicial mechanism for remedies for human rights violations and delivered judgments that led to significant changes on the ground. As one litigating human rights lawyer described it, 'the Court is very well known among ordinary people, as a court of last resort when the domestic courts do not ensure expected remedy, and not only – we also hear politicians referring to the option of going to the Court when they claim their rights being violated'.[40] In 2018, Georgia was among ten member states, out of 47, that accounted for 85% of the total caseload of pending cases before the Court, constituting 3.3% (1,850 cases) of such applications.[41] The Court's popularity steadily grew throughout years, with 42

See the press release of the European Human Rights Advocacy Centre 'European Court: Former Georgian Prime Minister's pre-trial detention used to exert pressure on him', 14 June 2016; Freedom House, Nations in Transit 2016: Georgia (n 31).

38 Freedom House, Nations in Transit 2016: Georgia (n 31); The *Gharibashvili* group of cases under the supervision of the Committee of Ministers includes cases documenting events dated 2005.

39 BBC News, 'Georgia protests: Thousands storm parliament over Russian MP's speech' (BBC 21 June 2019), accessed 29 November 2019; Reuters, 'Thousands gather in Tbilisi for protest against Georgian government' (20 September 2019), accessed 29 November 2019; Human Rights Watch, 'Protests erupt in Georgia over failed electoral reforms' (15 November 2019), accessed 29 November 2019; Agenda.ge, 'PM Gakharia on anniversary of June protests: 'no matter how many years pass, we prevented destabilisation'', (18 June 2020), accessed 29 November 2019.

40 CSO representative, GEO08, Tbilisi, online interview, 12 December 2016.

41 ECHR Analysis of Statistics 2018, published in January 2019, accessed 20 July 2020 169.

applications lodged in 2002, followed by a sharp increase to 1,771 applications in 2008 and 2,122 applications in 2009, likely related to the mass applications brought to the Court against Russia following the August 2008 Georgia-Russia war, which have likely further enhanced the Court's credibility for Georgians as a forum to raise complaints against Russia.[42] It later continued with the gradual increase to 99 in 2018, 131 in 2019 and 130 in 2020.[43] As of January 2022, 163 ECtHR judgments against Georgia have been transferred for the supervision of the CM, addressing violations of the Convention varying from Article 3 (prohibition of torture), Article 6 (right to a fair trial), Article 5 (right to liberty and security), Article 2 (right to life), Article 8 (right to respect for private and family life) to Article 13 (right to an effective remedy) and Article 14 (prohibition of discrimination), and others (Figure 10).[44]

As of the same date, 58 judgments against Georgia, constituting 38% of all adjudicated Georgian cases, were pending implementation before the CM, out of which 25 were 'leading cases' identifying structural systemic human rights issues, with 5 of them supervised by the CM under the 'enhanced supervision' procedure (Figures 11 and 12). 63% of all the leading cases have been closed as implemented by the CM as of 1 January 2022 (Figure 12). The length of time that cases have been pending implementation under enhanced supervision varies from 3 to 13 years, whereas the cases under standard supervision are relatively new, with the majority having been adopted in 2014–2015, and one case in 2005 and in 2012.[45] The five pending cases, or groups of cases, under enhanced supervision procedure, constituting 20% of all Georgian leading cases pending implementation, concern systemic complex human rights problems. It includes issues of lack of effective investigations into allegations of violations of the right to life or ill-treatment by law enforcement agents and a systemic failure to ensure that LGBTI groups are able to effectively exercise their right to freedom of assembly, and are adequately protected, that the CM has been closely scrutinising, and which I analyse in 5. 3.

---

42 European Court of Human Rights Annual report 2004 118; European Court of Human Rights Annual report 2008 130; European Court of Human Rights Annual report 2009 142, accessed 12 July 2019; Steering Committee for Human Rights (CDDH), Draft CDDH report on the effective processing and resolution of cases relating to inter-State disputes, DH-SYSC-IV(2020)04 08/07/2020, accessed 12 August 2020.

43 Ibid European Court of Human Rights Annual report 2019 132, European Court of Human Rights Annual report 2021 184.

44 HUDOC database accessed on 20 December 2021; Country Factsheet for Georgia developed by the Department for the Execution of Judgments of the European Court of Human Rights, updated on 15 March 2021, accessed 20 September 2021.

45 HUDOC EXEC database, accessed on 1 December 2021.

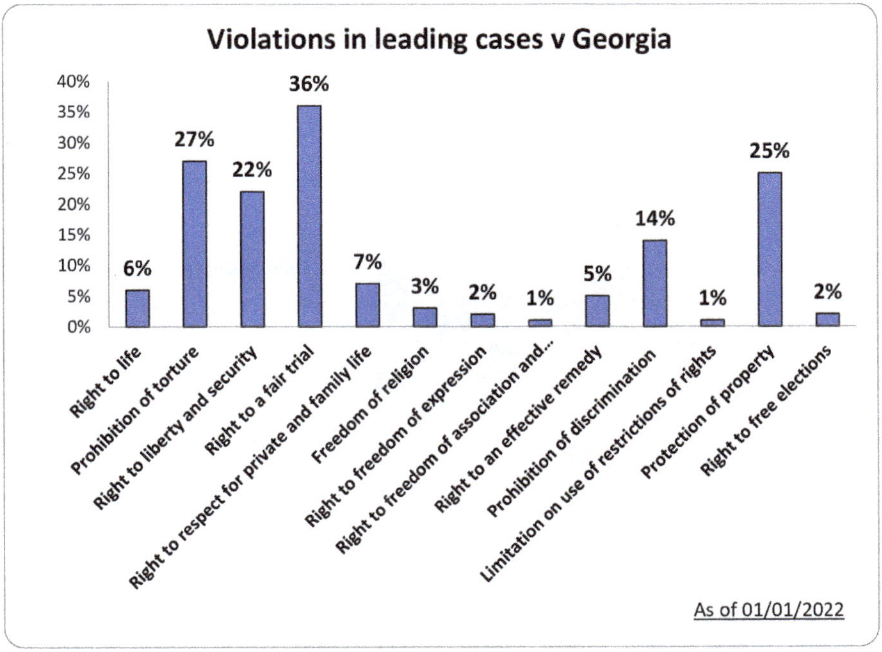

FIGURE 10 Violations in ECtHR cases against Georgia
SOURCE: HUDOC DATABASE, AS OF 1 JANUARY 2022

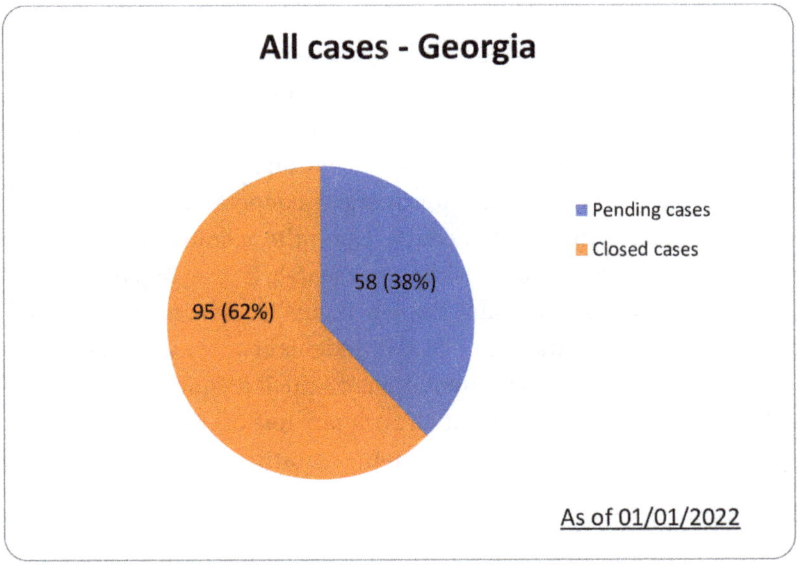

FIGURE 11 All ECtHR cases against Georgia
SOURCE: HUDOC EXEC DATABASE, AS OF 1 JANUARY 2022

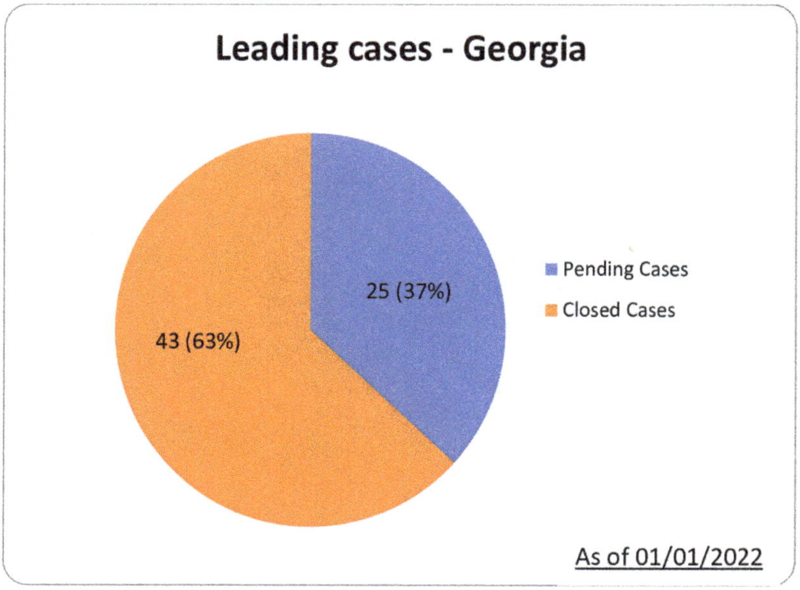

FIGURE 12 All leading cases against Georgia
SOURCE: HUDOC EXEC DATABASE, AS OF 1 JANUARY 2022

5.2 National System for the Implementation of ECtHR Judgments in Georgia

The following section analyses the existing domestic framework for implementation in Georgia and discusses factors that influence its effectiveness. The domestic implementation of ECtHR judgments in Georgia falls under the responsibility of the executive power, and is coordinated by the Ministry of Justice (MoJ) as a part of its mandate for Georgia's cooperation with the international and regional human rights courts. Upon the initiative of the (then) Government Agent, a separate division was created in the Department for Representation before International Human Rights Courts in 2008, entirely dedicated to the implementation of ECtHR judgments, to ensure 'sufficient efforts and resources' for the implementation of ECtHR judgments.[46] As stipulated in the charter of the Department, the primary role of the division, run by the Government Agent, Georgia's official representative before the ECtHR, is

46 Governmental Official, GEO04, Tbilisi, 15 September 2015; Former Governmental Official and former human rights lawyer, GEO03, online interview, 15 October 2016.

to 'lead and coordinate' the implementation work of ECtHR judgments.[47] The responsible division's coordination work is well established and largely materialises in the form of delegated tasks or inquiries with domestic institutions identified as relevant for implementation of specific judgments by the MoJ. Once an ECtHR judgment becomes final, the division examines a judgment and prepares an action plan, in line with the working procedures of the CM, as to what it considers necessary for the implementation of the judgment. The initial internal action plan identifies relevant state institutions to be responsible for, or otherwise involved, in the implementation process and measures to be taken before it is sent to the CM. This practice has been introduced in line with the new rules and methods established by the CM in 2010 requiring member states to provide action plans, indicating Georgia's willingness to comply and 'socialise' with the CM procedural rules.[48] In the absence of any established formalized procedures for the involvement of other domestic actors, in practice, however, the MoJ is often provided with a wide discretion to decide which domestic institutions will be involved in the implementation process and what measures shall be proposed, which, as I discuss further below, has its drawbacks affecting the implementation processes.

The analysis of the domestic system indicates that it draws a distinction between individual and general measures to be taken for the implementation of ECtHR judgments, with a rather formalised procedure in place for the former, which has tended to ensue full and timely compliance. The existing procedure for payments of compensation as individual measures normally indicated in ECtHR judgments, for example, is a straightforward one and is set out in the regulations on payment of compensation, which Georgia, as a rule, complies with.[49] Another normative procedure relating to individual measures is the re-opening of civil and criminal proceedings by domestic courts established in the domestic legislation. Both the civil and the criminal procedural codes recognise ECtHR judgments as 'newly discovered circumstances', which serve

47 Charter of the Department for Representation before International Human Rights Courts, unofficial translation, provided by an interviewed Government Official, date not indicated.

48 Governmental Official, GEO01, Strasbourg, 30 March 2018; Committee of Ministers 13th Annual report on Supervision of the Execution of Judgments and Decisions of the European Court of Human Rights (2019) 80; Committee of Ministers 11th Annual report on Supervision of the Execution of Judgments and Decisions of the European Court of Human Rights (2017) 83.

49 Ministry of Justice of the Republic of Georgia, Regulations on payment of compensation (2013) No 132.

as a basis for the reopening of domestic cases.[50] Such provisions do not only indicate Georgia's recognition of the legally binding nature of ECtHR judgments and the domestication of its international obligation to abide by such judgments but also offer normative institutionalised guarantees for applicants to seek for individual remedies in their cases post ECtHR judgments. The latter remedy also ensures that a decision on the re-opening of domestic proceedings is not left at the discretion of the prosecution, as a significant guarantee in the implementation process. As one litigating lawyer suggested, 'it is the only legally embedded tool for applicants and their representatives to seek for the implementation of ECtHR judgments in Georgia'.[51] The effectiveness of such proceedings, however, remains to be assessed in each individual case as the re-opening does not necessarily guarantee the effective re-examination of a case (see, for example, 5.3.2.1).

As for the general measures, which may involve legislative or policy reforms, and are not normally indicated by the ECtHR, the existing Georgian system leaves it at the wide discretion of the MoJ. The MoJ division coordinating the implementation of ECtHR decides on the necessary measures and enquires about the issues addressed in the judgments from other relevant domestic institutions, when 'it is not clear from a judgment if the violation concerns a systemic or structural problem in Georgia and whether further reforms are needed' indicating that such prescription would be appreciated.[52] As there is often no guidance or indications as to what measures are needed from the ECtHR, a clearly established procedure for involvement of other domestic actors that would allow for synergies to decide on such measures is of significant value. The absence of procedures allowing for exchanges of views on necessary measures with other relevant actors, such as other executive bodies, the national parliament and its committees, the Ombudsman's office or the civil society, prevents these actors from contributing to the implementation process in a systemic manner and leaves it to the discretion of the MoJ to cooperate with such actors. Reforms necessitating from ECtHR judgment are often of huge public interest or which may affect large sections of the population, which makes the involvement of respective actors all the more relevant. It further prevents them from pursuing 'checks and balances' over the executive's efforts to implement ECtHR judgments, which is of particular relevance

---

50 Criminal Procedure Code of the Republic of Georgia (2009) No 1772 II, Article 310; Civil Procedure Code of the Republic of Georgia (1997) No 1106 IS, Article 423.

51 CSO representative, GEO08, Tbilisi, online interview, 12 December 2016.

52 Former Governmental Official and former human rights lawyer, GEO02, Tbilisi, 15 September 2015.

in cases where there is insufficient political will to engage in the necessary reforms. Such a mechanism would also help address the resistance of certain institutions that may occur in the implementation process, as suggested by one of the former Government Agents: 'It is sometimes difficult to involve those that are technically responsible for implementation of a specific judgment, especially when judgments are not very clear as to what measures need to be taken'.[53]

Although all the interviewed former and present MoJ representatives assured favoring cooperation with other domestic actors, in the absence of the domestic mechanism or procedures institutionalising such interaction, in practice their involvement is rather ad hoc and often done under their own initiative and on a case-by-case basis. This is particularly the case for those that do not form a part of the executive power, such as the Ombudsman Office or the civil society.[54] Some interviewed Georgian lawyers suggested that in certain cases they found it more effective to communicate directly with the institution responsible for certain issues addressed by ECtHR judgments rather than the MoJ as a coordinating institution due to the absence of existing procedures for such communication.[55] Such ad hoc involvement, however, does not guarantee their regular systemic contributions and is dependent on their individual contacts with those institutions, preventing their consistent systemic involvement. Below, my analysis offers a number of findings into factors that prevent such effective involvement in absence of clear domestic procedures (in cases of the Ombudsman's Office and the civil society), or ineffective use of existing procedures (in the case of the national parliament).

5.2.1 *Absence of Strong Culture of Accountability, and Politicization of the Process*

Research findings suggest that the effectiveness of the domestic implementation system in Georgia could be enhanced with increased accountability and safeguards to address politicization. Up until 2016 there has been no formal parliamentary oversight mechanism over the Government's actions relating to implementation of ECtHR judgments. The Parliament's role in the implementation process was limited to considering legislative proposals submitted

53 Former Governmental Official and former human rights lawyer, GEO02, Tbilisi, 15 September 2015.

54 Former Governmental Official and former human rights lawyer, GEO02, Tbilisi, 15 September 2015; Governmental Official, GEO04, Tbilisi, 15 September 2015.

55 Ibid. 7; CSO representative, GEO08, Tbilisi, online interview, 12 December 2016; CSO representative, GEO09, Tbilisi, online interview, 15 November 2016.

by the executive, as a part of the implementation process, which would only reach the parliament once it is developed by the executive power as a proposed necessary measure.

In 2016, following the amendments to the Rules of the Georgian Parliament, a procedure for oversight of implementation of judgments of international mechanisms was established entitling the parliament with a mandate to scrutinize the Government's actions.[56] It obliges the Government of Georgia to provide annual reports on compliance with judgments and decisions of ECtHR and the United Nations Treaty Bodies, before 1 April each year, to the Parliament of Georgia. The institutionalization of such supervisory role of the parliament over the implementation process is a significant development towards improving the domestic implementation system, the effectiveness of which, however, lies in the effective use of this mechanism by the parliament and the favourable political context. The Georgian civil society has raised concerns that the new parliamentary procedure has not yet been actively used by the members of the parliament, suggesting this is due to absence of a clear designation as to which parliamentary committee is to take on this role.[57] For the first three years of the new procedure in 2017–2019, two committees, the Legal Committee and the Committee of Human Rights and Civic Integration, were assigned to co-share the roles, without a clear lead committee that would ensure the continuation and ownership of the process. Furthermore, the deliberations did not include other responsible executive institutions beyond the representatives of the Ministry of Justice, whose presence would enable a more substantive discussion of measures being taken, such as the Office of Prosecutor General or the Ministry of Internal Affairs in cases concerning effective investigations, for example.

Existence of favourable political climate to effectively employ such a mechanism is significant to the effective scrutiny. Although generally, there appears to be a uniform recognition of the importance of coordinated actions of the executive and the legislative power to enhance effective implementation of ECtHR judgments in Georgia, the research suggests that absence of an overall tradition of the executive's accountability to the parliament hinders it from materializing into a fully effective practice of cooperation. One interviewed parliament member representing political opposition in 2016 described it as part of 'the problem of the Georgian democracy', referring to absence of tradition of the parliament's effective oversight over Government's actions:

56 NGO Article 42 of the Constitution, 'Report on Execution of Rulings of the European Court of Human Rights and the United Nations Treaty Bodies in Georgia' (January 2020) 27.

57 Ibid 27.

> In Georgia, the Government is not used to being overseen by and accountable to the parliament and that applies to its actions to comply with ECtHR judgments too. This in turn leads to Parliament's passivity in that regard, largely affected by the fact that the agenda is being set by the political majority. We certainly need a mechanism that would allow avoiding any political fragility in cases of change of power and effectively supervise the Government's actions.[58]

Against such context, some of the interviewees suggested that the success of the parliamentary mandate to follow up on ECtHR judgments largely depends on the salience of the particular case.[59] If a certain ECtHR judgment challenges the ruling power's accountability for certain systemic human rights violations, or exposes its deep failures to prevent them, such as, for example, issues related to ineffective investigations into ill-treatment allegations of prisoners against law enforcement agents, it is less likely that the political majority in the parliament will take an initiative to raise this issue with the executive represented by the same political power. Likewise, as suggested by an opposition MP, the executive, in the absence of the culture of accountability, will feel less inclined to respond to inquiries by the opposition members to defend the position of the ruling power to account for issues addressed by the ECtHR.[60] For example, one interviewed opposition MP appealed to the MoJ requesting for information on the implementation of the case of *Merabishvili v Georgia*, relating to the pre-trial detention of the former Prime Minister from her political party, which the ECtHR found to involve an ulterior purpose, but her request remained unaddressed.[61] Similarly, as noted by the interviewed MoJ representative, such individualized parliamentary initiatives do not emerge in relation to less politically salient cases where there is no direct political interest by one or another political power in the parliament: 'in my experience, parliament members show interest in those cases only where there is a political aspect, sometimes used for political manipulations, otherwise, there is no interest in the overall implementation process'.[62] The monitoring of the parliamentary

58 Georgian MP, GEO05, Tbilisi, 16 September 2015.

59 CSO representative, GEO08, Tbilisi, online interview, 12 December 2016; Former Governmental Official and former human rights lawyer, GEO02, Tbilisi, 15 September 2015; Former Governmental Official and former human rights lawyer, GEO03, online interview, 15 October 2016.

60 Georgian MP, GEO05, Tbilisi, 16 September 2015.

61 Ibid.

62 Governmental Official, GEO04, Tbilisi, 15 September 2015.

deliberations in 2019 conducted by the Georgian civil society suggested similar findings indicating that observations made by MPs were limited to the positive outcomes achieved by the Ministry with no critical comments or substantive in-depth questions made in relation to any of the cases raising systemic structural human rights problems.[63] Such politicized context is among the major obstacles in establishing healthy parliamentary oversight practices over the actions of the executive, and the adoption of formalized procedures should potentially neutralize or at least reduce the political sensitivities in such domestic processes in Georgia if effectively employed.

Similar hindrances are observed in the Georgian civil society's attempts to get involved in the implementation process, as, although being very vibrant, active and well engaged in public debates and initiatives, the civil society is yet to be granted a role of an equal or a significant actor whose considerations concerning implementation of ECtHR judgments as human rights judgments would be taken into account.[64] In the absence of any formal procedure for civil society to get engaged in the execution process, many interviewed NGOs reported getting involved on an ad hoc basis, often due to their established connections with the Government Agent's Office as active litigators of human rights cases, or directly with other institutions involved with the human rights issues addressed by the ECtHR, but not as part of the formal domestic implementation process. One interviewed lawyer noted that although their NGO actively litigates cases, they do not always pursue their advocacy strategies within the framework of the implementation of ECtHR judgments addressing the exact issues that they advocate, largely due to absence of the framework for such engagement and very limited access to information on the domestic level.[65] In some cases, NGOs would instead initiate contacts directly with the institutions responsible for issues addressed by ECtHR or limit their work to focusing on individual measures. For example, in the case of the issue of effective investigations addressed by the *Gharibashvili* group, domestic NGOs have been holding discussions to present their positions with the Prosecution Office directly without the involvement of the MoJ. Some lawyers, however, recognised the importance of the accessibility of the Government Agent that allow discussion of the issues addressed in ECtHR judgments and the measures

---

63 NGO Article 42 of the Constitution report (n 56) 30.

64 Freedom House report 'Nations in Transit: Georgia', 2003, section on civil society, accessed 25 January 2017; Freedom House, Nations in Transit 2016: Georgia, accessed 9 January 2017.

65 CSO representative, GEO09, Tbilisi, online interview, 15 November 2016.

to be taken in order to ensure effective compliance beyond formal written submissions:[66]

> This may sound like a basic thing but the accessibility of the Government Agent and effective communication on the implementation of ECtHR judgments, including the informal discussions, beyond written submissions, is crucial. The response may not be exactly the one we may want but it would be possible to have a sensible discussion about substantive issues of cases.

As another lawyer suggested, this could be explained by Georgia's genuine respect for the Convention system and the ECtHR and the 'absence of the general hostility towards the system, as is the case in some CoE member states these days'.[67] As the two latest elections in Georgia showed, people committed to advancing the human rights situation in Georgia have had a chance to take positions in various state and non-governmental structures and to push their agendas.[68] This includes the position of the Government Agent that has been taken up by individuals with a legal, human rights and/or civil society background in the last fifteen years.[69] The aspiration of Georgia and especially its younger generation who has been brought up and educated on the Convention system for Europe allowing Georgia to position itself outside Russia's orbit has certainly played a role in shaping Georgia – both its institutions and its public – as a country willing to be perceived as a human rights respecting state.[70]

Such communication is, however, dependent on the individual who takes up the position of the Government Agent and his/her willingness and initiative to engage with NGOs. Institutionalising such interaction by creating procedures for the civil society as an 'alternative' voice and often representing certain groups of the society to get involved in the implementation process with the executive power would ensure that it continues after the departure of certain individuals. An example of such interaction could be the invitation to NGOs litigating discussed cases before the ECtHR to provide their input in the form of a written submission or participation in a discussion, similarly to the one established as part of the parliamentary supervision procedure in 2016.

66 CSO representative, GEO08, Tbilisi, online interview, 12 December 2016.
67 CSO representative, SXB10, London, 23 November 2016.
68 Ibid.
69 Governmental Official, GEO01, Strasbourg, 30 March 2018.
70 Former Governmental Official and former human rights lawyer, GEO02, Tbilisi, 15 September 2015.

The latter procedure, allowing NGOs to provide alternative reports to the parliament, along the Government's reports on the implementation, however, still needs to find its place in the process of the parliamentary scrutiny. The deliberations of the first NGO report of this kind submitted to the parliament in 2019 was only attended by very few MPs and no questions were asked by MPs to make effective use of alternative views provided by the civil society that would in turn better enable MPs in their new role.[71]

5.2.2 *Insufficient Access to Information on the Implementation Process*

Adequate access to information is a significant and perhaps primary factor defining the ability of domestic actors, who are not a part of the institutionalized domestic implementation system, to get involved in the process. While the Georgian parliament is now provided with annual reports from the Government since 2017, which are publicly available, the absence of adequate full access to information throughout the year significantly hinders the involvement of such Georgian domestic actors as the Public Defender Office (PDO) or the civil society in individual cases at a stage when specific measures are being considered, or could be suggested. A significant number of the interviewed domestic actors noted that their ability to engage and to access information is primarily dependent on the information available on the HUDOC EXEC database containing information on the progress of the government's actions in implementing ECtHR judgments.[72] Another way to attempt to obtain information is individual information requests to relevant domestic institutions, this, however, being limited in their effectiveness depending on the timeliness and substance of the response.[73] One interviewed MP particularly highlighted the importance of the information available on the CM website as not only enabling them to access information as measures are being taken but also bringing more transparency to the process: 'The CM supervision process provides for more transparency to the implementation process ..., as the Ministry does not publish any information on the pending cases before they are closed'.[74] The interviewed lawyers and civil society organisations limited in their ability to access information and engage in the implementation process expressed their strong support for the parliament's involvement in the implementation

71 NGO Article 42 of the Constitution Report (n 56) 30.

72 CSO representative, GEO08, Tbilisi, online interview, 12 December 2016; CSO representative, GEO09, Tbilisi, online interview, 15 November 2016; Human rights lawyer, GEO010, Tbilisi, online interview, 19 February 2017.

73 CSO representative, GEO08, Tbilisi, online interview, 12 December 2016.

74 Georgian MP, GEO05, Tbilisi, 16 September 2015.

process not only for the sake of parliamentary oversight but also for its broader role in the society:

> It is fundamental that the parliament gets involved in the implementation process. ECtHR judgments often raise problematic issues of concern for wider groups of the society and it is pretty obvious that such matters should be of relevance for lawmakers.[75]

One Georgian MP interviewed before the domestic supervisory procedure was introduced in 2016 indicated their reliance on Strasbourg processes, that, apart from the CM, include the efforts taken by PACE to engage national MPs in the process. Such initiatives include regular PACE reports on implementation of ECtHR judgments or regional seminars and other awareness raising and capacity building activities organized for MP members and their assistants.[76] For example, the PACE regional seminar organized in Tbilisi in September 2015 has brought together MPs from relevant parliamentary committees responsible for human rights issues from the Eastern Partnership countries has created a unique platform for MPs to exchange views and raise awareness of MPs in the implementation process, particularly where no formal procedures for such scrutiny is in place.

The reforms introduced with the adoption of Protocol 14 to the ECHR in 2010 that brought more transparency to the supervision process over the implementation of ECtHR judgments by the CM and a more formalised role for NGOs and national human rights institutions (NHRIs) in contributing to the implementation process has created more space for their involvement in Georgia.[77] All interviewed lawyers and NGO representatives recognised the importance of the CM supervision process in bringing more transparency to

75 CSO representative, SXB10, London, 23 November 2016.

76 Georgian MP, GEO05, Tbilisi, 16 September 2015; PACE Committee on Legal Affairs and Human Rights, Implementation of Judgments of the European Court of Human Rights – Extracts from the Minutes of hearings, organised by the Committee in April 2012, in June 2012, in October 2012 and in January 2013, AS/Jur (2013) 13, 28 March 2013; PACE regional seminar on the role of national parliaments in implementing the standards of the European Convention of Human Rights, Tbilisi, 21–22 September 2015 (in attendance).

77 Rules of the Committee of Ministers for the supervision of the execution of judgments and of the terms of friendly settlements, adopted on 10 May 2006 at the 964th meeting of the Ministers' Deputies and amended on 18 January 2017 at the 1275th meeting of the Ministers' Deputies): according to Rule 9 of the Rules of the Committee of Ministers, NGOs, National Human Rights Institutions (NHRIs) and applicants have a possibility to communicate with the Committee of Ministers and provide with information on the implementation of the judgment at the national level.

the process and enabling them to engage and conduct public oversight over the Government's actions domestically as they were provided with more information as to what steps have been taken or were planned being taken by the Georgian authorities. As one of them noted, 'If there is no action plan on the CM website, we often do not have any other way to get information on what is being done by the authorities in terms of implementation'.[78] Although this provides them with knowledge on the status of the cases, and the measures being taken, however, it does not sufficiently enable them to engage directly with the domestic authorities: 'We receive valuable information from the action plans and reports provided by the Government to the CM, however, they often relate to measures already taken by the authorities when it is too late for us to provide any input in developing them domestically, particularly when it comes to deep systemic reforms'.[79] As a result, only in the recent years the number of submissions from NGOs and the Public Defender's Office has been steadily growing, with the increased access to information and awareness of this role. During the interview with a representative of the Georgian Public Defender's Office in 2015, for example, when asked about their involvement in the domestic implementation process and the engagement with the CM, she confirmed that the Office was not involved in any of these activities at all and had little information.[80] Since 2017, however, the PDO has increasingly made submissions to the CM in groups of cases under enhanced supervision.[81]

All the above factors speak to the need to better enable the civil society and other non-state actors with knowledge and tools to build their capacities to effectively use ECtHR judgments as advocacy tools and systematically engage in the process, particularly given Georgia's rather receptive political climate. The existence of clear formal procedures in the domestic system allowing for their involvement, through written submissions or participation in working groups, as some of the examples, would not only enable their timely engagement but would also ensure that it is done in an institutionalized consistent way, reducing any political sensitivities or other possible triggers to exclude the public voice in these debates.

---

78 CSO representative, GEO08, Tbilisi, online interview, 12 December 2016.

79 Human rights lawyer, GEO010, Tbilisi, online interview, 19 February 2017.

80 NHRI representative, GEO07, Tbilisi, 16 September 2015.

81 See, for example, communication from a Public Defender of Georgia in the selected cases of *Identoba and Others v Georgia*, Appl. no. 73235/12, 18 August 2017; communication from a Public Defender of Georgia in the cases of *Makharadze and Sikharulidze, Tsintsabadze, Identoba and Others v Georgia*, (Appl. no. 35254/07, 35403/06, 73235/12), 7 December 2017. Submissions by the PDO have also been made in the case of *Merabishvili v Georgia* (Appl. No. 72508/13) on 29 January 2020, 24 January 2020 and 13 October 2020.

5.3 Georgia's Compliance with ECtHR Judgments

In this Section I discuss Georgia's engagement with the Strasbourg supervision process and the factors that influence the extent and the substance of such engagement. I do so on the basis of the analysis of all the available official information on the HUDOC EXEC database relating to all the leading Georgian cases pending implementation as of 1 January 2022, as well as the empirical data, with a particular focus on the five selected groups of cases. I further discuss the change that the five selected groups of cases have led to on the domestic level, as a result of the implementation efforts, and the role that the various factors play in this context. The selected cases present a wide spectrum of human rights issues, varying from inadequate medical treatment in prison (*Ghavtadze* group of cases) and investigations into ill-treatment by state agents (*Tsintsabadze* group of cases) to absence of compensation for Georgian victims of Soviet repression (*Klaus and Yuri Kiladze* case) to malicious laws on defamation (*Gorelishvili* case), and a failure to protect demonstrators against homophobic violence by religious groups (*Identoba and Others* case).

5.3.1 *Georgia's Engagement with the CM Supervision Process*

The research analysis suggests that Georgia's, like Armenia's, engagement with this process is highly dependent on the type and intensity of supervision by the CM procedures. Although Georgia is bound to comply with the existing CM supervision rules, including the requirement to submit action plans and reports, the socialization effect of this process is much more prevalent in cases monitored under enhanced supervision where the CM and DEJ follow up is more consistent and regular compared to cases under standard supervision. The analysis of the information available on the HUDOC EXEC database demonstrates that Georgia's engagement with the CM amounts to 100% in leading cases under enhanced supervision whereas in the other cases, pending under the standard supervision, the authorities complied with the basic CM rules to provide an action plan in only 46% of cases, and in none of these cases it provided an action plan on time, with the delay varying from 6 months to 12 years.[82] In other words, in more than 50% of cases under standard supervision the Georgian authorities failed to provide any action plans or updates on the implementation process. In none of the leading cases under standard supervision has the CM adopted any written formal decisions to follow up on any of the action plans or other reported progress, and only one submission

82 HUDOC EXEC database, leading cases against Georgia, accessed 30 December 2021.

was made by an applicant and one submission by the PDO.[83] The only formal reference to the Strasbourg position on these cases included a note in the summary of the status of execution of these cases on HUDOC EXEC that 'updated information' was requested by the DEJ from the authorities or that 'feedback regarding action plan' has been sent, noted in the files of about a half of these cases; however, there is no further information as to what the status of implementation of these cases is, preventing any further follow up by applicants or other interested domestic actors.[84] In contrast, in all leading cases under enhanced supervision, the Government submitted from three to five action plans, reports or other communications on average, with applicants' submissions varying from one to nine. Submissions by the PDO were made in 80% of the cases, and at least two CM decisions with specific follow up recommendations per case were adopted.[85] The duration of time that the leading cases have been pending implementation is similar under both types of supervision procedures and varies significantly: from four to 13 years among cases under enhanced supervision and between one to 15 years among the rest. This huge disparity in engagement with the CM processes by the Georgian authorities suggests a causal link between the scope and intensity of socialization by the CM and other implementation actors and the authorities' involvement in the process. Although Georgia has a clear obligation to abide by the CM rules and procedures, in practice, its compliance rate with these rules is much higher when the CM and DEJ support is enhanced beyond these general written CM rules.

It is further suggested that the inclusion of Georgian cases on the agenda of the CM human rights quarterly meetings, and their formal review by the CM delegations, further enhanced the Georgian Government's engagement on these cases as more salient cases in the Strasbourg context. As noted by the interviewed former Government Agent:

> In light of our overall strong commitment to comply with ECtHR judgments, the formal examination of a case always encourages us to deliver

---

83 HUDOC EXEC database, leading cases under 'standard supervision' against Georgia, accessed 30 December 2021.

84 See, for example, the 'status of execution' of cases *Sarishvili-Bolkvadze v Georgia*, Appl. no. 58240/08, 19 October 2018; *Kartvelishvili v Georgia*, Appl. no. 177116/08, 7 September 2018; and *Jugheli and Others v Georgia*, Appl. no. 38342/05, 13 October 2017 on HUDOC EXEC as of 1 November 2021.

85 HUDOC EXEC database, leading cases under 'enhanced supervision' against Georgia, accessed 30 December 2021.

> in the eyes of our European colleagues, and the CM's feedback to the progress brings clarity to the process and the expectations from the CM towards us.[86]

During the period of 2010–2020, Georgian cases appeared on the agenda of the CM's quarterly human rights meetings 20 times in total, at least once year, with an increase to three times a year in 2016–2020 (except for 2017 when Georgian cases were reviewed twice).[87] Among all the reviewed cases, the vast majority were the groups of leading cases under enhanced supervision: the *Tsintsabadze* group (formerly reviewed as the *Gharibashvili* group until 2017), the *Identoba and Others* group, and the *Merabishvili* case, and two repetitive cases that are grouped with the above mentioned groups of cases. All these cases were pending implementation at the time of this research, except for 2011 when two other groups of cases, since closed, were reviewed by the CM.[88] Particularly in 2016–2020, the three mentioned groups of cases have been reviewed by turns by the CM, one case at a time at one of the CM meetings each year, with no other Georgian cases put on the CM agenda either for a debate or a written formal review. The research finds that the engagement of the Georgian authorities with the CM on those cases was most frequent and regular among all pending leading cases. The inclusion of a Georgian case on the CM human rights meeting agenda, which is made public in advance, has led to an advance submission of an updated plan or report by the authorities in *all* these cases ahead of each CM meeting when the respective cases were examined. For example, the selected *Identoba and Others* case of 12 August 2015 was put on the CM agenda in December 2016, June 2018, September 2019 and September 2020. The authorities submitted action plans ahead of each of these meetings providing updates on the implementation progress that was taken into consideration during each CM meeting.[89] In contrast, in 2017 when this case was not on the CM agenda, no updates have been provided by the authorities throughout the year and until the meeting of June 2018 when it

86 Governmental Official, GEO01, Strasbourg, 30 March 2018.

87 List of CM Human Rights meetings available at https://www.coe.int/en/web/execution/committee-of-ministers-human-rights-meetings accessed 1 June 2020.

88 The two other groups of cases reviewed in 2011 were the *Klaus and Yuri Kiladze* case, Appl. no. 7975/06, one of the selected cases for this research, closed on 11 March 2015, and *Pandjikidze and Others v Georgia*, Appl. no. 30323/02, closed by the CM on 24 September 2012.

89 HUDOC EXEC database, *Identoba and Others v Georgia*, action plans and action reports under 'Case documents': communications from the Georgian authorities on 25 June 2020, 10 July 2019, 16 April 2018, 15 November 2016, 26 April 2016.

was next reviewed. The same patterns are observed in the *Merabishvili* case first examined by the CM in December 2018 and in the selected *Tsintsabadze* group of cases, first put on the CM agenda for its meeting in September 2014.[90] In the leading case of *Enukidze and Girgvliani v Georgia*, for example, which was twice examined by the CM at its December 2012 and March 2013 meetings, an action plan was submitted before the 2012 meeting, later withdrawn by the newly elected Government, and a new updated report was submitted on 20 January 2015, with no other updates provided to date, and it has not been on the CM agenda since then.[91]

Such quantitative analysis of all the submissions to the CM by the Georgian authorities and CM's various formal engagements with the Georgian cases suggests a finding, similar to the one I arrived to in the case of Armenia, that the level of Georgia's engagement with the process is directly linked to the CM's formal involvement with the cases: the more regular and frequent the CM follow up is, the more engaging and delivering the Georgian authorities are on the implementation process. Although Georgia is not consistently compliant with the normative CM rules and regulations concerning implementation, the above findings are indicative of a strong socialisation effect of the enhanced CM engagement with Georgia through its existing procedures, endorsing the constructivism theory, which explains states' compliance with the international law and institutions.

5.3.2 *Domestic Factors Shaping Georgia's Engagement with Strasbourg Processes*

In the proceeding sections, I further suggest that such evident socialisation is not absolute and at times is confronted by other factors that affect the implementation progress, which requires further qualitative analysis. By doing so, I affirm my hypothesis that Georgia's compliance with ECtHR judgments as a

---

90 HUDOC EXEC database, *Merabishvili v Georgia*, action plans and action reports under 'Case documents': communications from the Georgian authorities on 29 June 2020, 30 September 2019, 29 March 2019, 26 October 2018, 4 June 2018; *Tsintsabadze group v Georgia*, action plans and action reports under 'Case documents': communications from the Georgian authorities on 25 October 2019, 13 July 2018, 5 December 2016, 20 January 2015; and *Gharibashvili* group v Georgia, action plans and action reports under 'Case documents': communications from the Georgian authorities on 16 August 2017, 7 September 2017, 15 November 2016, 28 October 2016, 1 June 2016, 1 March 2016, 3 June 2015, 17 July 2014.

91 HUDOC EXEC database, *Enukidze and Girgvliani v Georgia*, action plans and action reports under 'Case documents': communication from the Georgian authorities on 20 January 2015; the action report of 2012 has been removed from the database following the withdrawal.

country in the democratisation process is best explained by a synergy of constructivism and rational choice theories, the latter referring to certain material and other incentives that influence the authorities' behaviour. I demonstrate it through the qualitative analysis of the implementation progress made in five selected groups of cases and suggest a number of factors that define the authorities' performance. The selected cases include two cases pending implementation under enhanced supervision before the CM at the time of the writing of this book (*Tsintsabadze* group and *Identoba and Others*) and three cases that the CM has considered to be implemented and terminated the supervision of in recent years.[92] Compliance with specific judgments is often motivated by a number of factors, and as Çalı and Alice Wyss suggest, a balance of reasons need to be studied to explain the state's conduct in complying with specific human rights judgments.[93] Below I identify several factors that appear to be shaping Georgia's behaviour in complying with ECtHR judgments.

The below qualitative discussion on Georgia's compliance with ECtHR judgments is set against the background of strongly expressed overall willingness of the domestic structures to abide by this human rights obligation, documented both in official submissions and interviews. A strong support to international human rights norms, including human rights judgments, and the principle of rule of law was expressed by the interviewed domestic actors in shaping Georgia's identity as a 'learning democracy', which was significantly more remarkable among the Georgian interviewees, compared to other two countries.[94] I, however, recognise that the interviewees selected for this research may have a higher understanding and respect for the Convention system, and that they were more accessible than in Armenia or Azerbaijan. Such a unified vision was described to set the basis for the new normative framework for independent Georgia but also for shaping the attitudes of the Georgian society

---

92 *Ghavtadze* group was closed by the CM by its final resolution of 5 November 2014; Klaus and Yuri *Kiladze* case was closed on 11 March 2015 and the *Gorelishvili* case was closed on 30 November 2011.

93 Başak Çalı and Alice Wyss, 'Why Do Democracies Comply with Human Rights Judgments? A Comparative Analysis of the UK, Ireland and Germany' (2009), SSRN e-Library.

94 Governmental Official, GEO01, Strasbourg, 30 March 2018; Former Governmental Official and former human rights lawyer, GEO02, Tbilisi, 15 September 2015; Former Governmental Official and former human rights lawyer, GEO03, online interview, 15 October 2016; Governmental Official and former human rights lawyer, GEO04, Tbilisi, 17 September 2015; Georgian MP, GEO05, Tbilisi, 16 September 2015; Judge of Georgian Constitutional Court, GEO06, Tbilisi, 9 December 2016; NHRI representative, GEO07, Tbilisi, 16 September 2015; CSO representative, GEO09, Tbilisi, online interview, 15 November 2016; Human rights lawyer, GEO010, Tbilisi, online interview, 19 February 2017.

that emerged after the decades of the Soviet mentality towards human rights values, and individual justice. As one Georgian lawyer described it:

> Georgia is still learning from the Council of Europe. We are a young democracy and we are still in the process of harmonizing our laws with the European standards, changing attitudes and getting used to the rules of behaviour in a democratic framework, which are very important for the democratization process.[95]

Although such overall adherence to the Convention system is fundamental in creating the overall human rights conducive culture in a newly emerged aspiring democracy, a strong self-perception of it being an ongoing learning process indicates the existence of factors as possible challenges to compliance with such international obligations.

5.3.2.1 Political Willingness as an Underlying Factor for Compliance

The existence of political incentives to abide by ECtHR judgments is an underlying precondition to effective compliance and particularly so in countries as Georgia that are undergoing a democratization process, where a creation of the human rights and rule of law culture is a part of that process. The absence of strong accountability and judicial oversight mechanisms, and the fact that there is not sufficient institutionalization of compliance with ECtHR judgments, further enhances the significance of political will to successful compliance as it becomes more difficult to tackle lack of such will without strong domestic tools. As the analysis demonstrates, certain ECtHR judgments can serve as important catalysts to generate progress on certain human rights issues, whereas others may lead to stalled advancement depending on the existence of political willingness, or rather insufficient political willingness or even political resistance from the authorities. As prof. Korkelia, the former Permanent Representative of Georgia to the CoE has noted, the Convention's impact is highly dependent on the state's efforts: 'The Convention may have influence on legislation and practice of the state and strengthen the system of human rights protection in Georgia; to have such influence, measures aimed at establishing practice of applying the European Convention are to be taken by the state'.[96] The reasons for insufficient political will or political resistance vary

95 ECtHR representative, SXB06, Strasbourg, 4 September 2017.

96 Prof. Konstantine Korkelia, *Application of the European Convention on Human Rights in Georgia*, Summary in English (2003) 345.

from high political costs, to prioritization of domestic interests challenged by ECtHR judgments, to securing political votes by avoiding unpopular reforms.

The landmark case of *Klaus and Yuri Kiladze v Georgia* of 2010, which I selected for this research, is one such example of the authorities' political willingness leading to significant domestic reforms on the basis of the ECtHR judgment, with the support of the CM and strategic consistent follow up by NGOs that litigated the case. The case related to two applicants whose father was shot, after having been tried for sabotage and terror in 1938, and whose mother was imprisoned for propaganda and for agitating to overthrow the Soviet regime and sent to a GULAG camp, and had their flat in Tbilisi confiscated. The two applicants, then 12 and 10, were held in detention, malnourished and kept in unhygienic conditions, then transferred to orphanage in Russia and continuously abused as children of 'traitors of the Motherland'. Although the domestic legislation providing for recognition of a status of a victim of political repression and a right to seek compensation has been adopted in 1997, the absence of domestic mechanism to determine the sum of such damages effectively prevented the applicants from benefiting from such legal guarantees. The ECtHR, referring to the problem of the legislative void that had to be addressed fearing there may be up to 16,000 other victims, which may cause a large number of applications to ECtHR, ruled that necessary legislative, administrative and budgetary measures had to be rapidly taken as general measures to comply with the ECtHR judgment. As a result, the reforms paved the way for thousands of Georgian victims of the Soviet political repression to receive compensation from the state. Following the ECtHR judgment, on 18 May 2011, the respective law and the Code on Administrative Procedure were amended to enable victims and their first generation heirs to apply for compensation to Tbilisi City Court.[97] It was however left for the Tbilisi City Court to decide on the amount of the compensation in each case, having regard its particular circumstances, ranging between 92 EUR and 230 EUR in 6,914 applications that were granted by the end of 2014.[98] Unsatisfied with the implementation of the newly adopted amendments, leading to derisory compensations,

97 Action report of the Georgian Government on the execution of the judgment in the case of *Klaus and Yuri Kiladze* (Appl. no. 7975/06), submitted to the Committee of Ministers, 5 December 2014 [13–14].

98 Action report of the Georgian Government on the execution of the judgment in the case of *Klaus and Yuri Kiladze* (Appl. no. 7975/06), submitted to the Committee of Ministers, 5 December 2014 [16]. In their submission to the CM, received on 24 January 2012, the two NGOs representing clients submitted that the compensation ranged between 46 EUR and 230 EUR.

delays caused at the admissibility stage and the fact that such compensation could only be sought from the Tbilisi City Court, the two NGOs representing the applicants contested the new mechanism and called for further reforms as a part of full and effective implementation of the ECtHR judgment in their submission to the CM, and closely followed the domestic progress.[99] [100] As a result, the relevant laws were once again amended on 31 October 2014 to enable victims to receive higher awards, ensuring that applications can be lodged by the victim, his/her first generation heir or an appointed representative, and they can be submitted to a number of district courts across the country, and taking necessary budgetary measures to secure timely implementation of such reforms.[101]

This implementation process in the *Kiladze* case, closed by the CM as fully implemented in 2015, well illustrates the effect of the concerted efforts of the various implementation actors seeking effective implementation of the judgment, with the sufficient political receptiveness of the Georgian authorities to engage in such reforms. The political willingness set the ground for the necessary reforms to materialise, in response to the ECtHR judgment, which did not only establish the violations of the applicants' rights but also indicated to the state the core problems in the domestic system, addressed through the necessary reforms with the close oversight of the litigants, within the CM supervision framework. Unanimously named as one of the key examples of successfully implemented ECtHR judgments by the interviewed Georgian actors, the success of this case in terms of the existence of the political will is explained by absence of any political or social controversy around the issue addressed in the judgment, which would compromise the state's overall willingness to act as a human rights compliant state.[102]

The *Ghavtadze* group of cases, another case selected for this research, consisting of six judgments from 2009–2013 and addressing structural inadequacy of medical care for detainees suffering from contagious diseases, and

99 Submission by the Georgian Young Lawyers Association (GYLA) and the European Human Rights Advocacy Centre (EHRAC) to the CM on the implementation in the case of *Klaus and Yuri Kiladze* (Appl. no. 7975/06), received on 24 January 2012.

100 European Humn Rights Advocacy Centre news 'Georgia amends legislation following European Court case' (13 November 2014), accessed 23 June 2020.

101 Action report of the Georgian Government on the execution of the judgment in the case of *Klaus and Yuri Kiladze* (Appl. no. 7975/06), submitted to the Committee of Ministers, 5 December 2014.

102 CSO representative, GEO08, Tbilisi, online interview, 12 December 2016; CSO representative, GEO09, Tbilisi, online interview, 15 November 2016; Human rights lawyer, GEO010, Tbilisi, online interview, 19 February 2017.

the ineffectiveness of the complaint procedure feature similar political receptiveness of the Georgian authorities to undertake the necessary structural reforms and comply with these judgments. Similarly to the above example, the ECtHR found the identified violations to be of systemic nature in Georgia and indicated the Government to take urgent legislative and administrative measures to address the problem, under the supervision of the CM.[103] Following the first judgments in this group, the Georgian Government reported on the first reforms in the administration of medical and other conditions as early as in 2011, with the adoption of a new Prison Code, which the ECtHR acknowledged as a positive development in a similar case of *Goginashvili v Georgia* adjudicated in October 2011.[104] The Prison Code, which entered into force on 1 October 2010, established a detainee's right to health care in prison as an independent right and described the procedure for submitting complaints if a detainee considered that his rights, including that to health care, was not being duly respected by the prison authority.[105]

Other extensive reforms in the penitentiary health system, in line with the standards set down in the 'European Prison Rules' and the recommendations of the European Committee for the Prevention of Torture (CPT) introducing prevention, diagnostics and treatment programmes for tuberculosis and hepatitis C, the improved medical infrastructure and the adoption of the Strategy of Development of the Penitentiary Health Care System 2014–2017 indicated the Government's political willingness to abide by the judgment and undertake substantive reforms. Although resource intensive, the necessary measures did not cause any political or social resistance from any political groups and the Government has regularly communicated its progress to the CM.[106] The ECtHR judgments helped bring the systemic issue of the lack of medical care in prisons on the political agenda and aided the Government in pursuing the necessary reforms. As noted by a former Georgian Government Agent, it created a framework to develop and implement an action plan in order to undertake the necessary reforms, identified by the ECtHR, which otherwise may not have

103 *Ghavtadze*, paras 105–106.

104 Consolidated action plan of the Government of Georgia concerning the execution of cases of *Ghavtadze v. Georgia*, Appl. no. 23204/07, 3 March 2009, *Poghosyan v. Georgia*, Appl. no. 9870/07, 24 February 2009, *Makharadze and Sikharulidze v. Georgia*, Appl. no. 35254/07, 22 November 2011, *Irakli Mindadze v. Georgia*, Appl. no. 17012/09, 11 December 2012, *Jeladze v. Georgia*, Appl. no. 1871/08, 18 December 2012, *Ildani v. Georgia*, Appl. no. 65391/09, 23 April 2013, 8 January 2014 3.

105 *Goginashvili v Georgia*, Appl. no. 47729/08 (ECtHR 4 October 2011) [55].

106 Government reports to the CM on 27 January 2014, 4 August 2014, 30 September 2014, accessed on HUDOC EXEC database on 7 February 2017.

been possible or as efficient.[107] As the interviewed Government Agent who held the position at the time noted: 'When I was appointed to this position in 2008, I realised that 80% of all the pending cases concerned medical treatment of prisoners and prison conditions in the penitentiary, but following this group of judgments, the situation was significantly improved'.[108] The effectiveness of the measures taken as part of this group of cases, closed by the CM in 2014, is further indicated by the fact that no further applications on similar issues as repetitive cases have been filed to the ECtHR, suggesting the effective dealing of such cases by the domestic mechanism. In his report of 1 December 2015 following a visit to Georgia, the UN Special Rapporteur on torture and other cruel, inhuman or degrading treatment or punishment found the medical care in Georgian prisons 'satisfactory' without any references to issues addressed in the *Ghavtadze* group of cases, further reaffirming the progress made.[109]

These two groups of cases well illustrate how absence of any factors, such as domestic interests or sensitivities around cases, that would overrule the Government's political willingness to position itself as compliant with the European human rights standards can lead to Georgia's genuine willingness to engage with the ECtHR judgments and undertake the necessary reforms. Unless such factors put certain domestic interests at stake, the research findings suggest that Georgia shall normally comply with ECtHR judgments to position itself as a democratic and human rights respecting state, as part of its broader aspiration for the European integration and Europe's perception of Georgia as a European state. As one Georgian lawyer has put it, 'It is all about the European inspiration – the state needs to prove to Europe that it can become its member and reputation matters very much'.[110] The research results find strong evidence in Georgia's efforts to avoid 'international embarrassment', a factor suggested by Çalı and Wyss, by failing to comply with ECtHR judgments.[111] As one of the interviewed representatives of a Western member state to the CM described Georgia's efforts in that regard: 'The representatives of the Georgian authorities always put efforts to demonstrate that compliance is their priority so even if there were some other hidden priorities, there is

107 Former Governmental Official and former human rights lawyer, GEO03, online interview, 15 October 2016.

108 Ibid.

109 Report of the UN Special Rapporteur on torture and other cruel, inhuman or degrading treatment or punishment on his mission to Georgia, 1 December 2015, UN Human Rights Council, A/HRC/31/57/Add.3 [105].

110 CSO representative, GEO09, Tbilisi, online interview, 15 November 2016.

111 Çalı and Wyss (n 93).

nothing indicating that they are not willing to cooperate and engage'.[112] This strong aspiration however is not always absolute and is faced with a variety of other factors in practice, as other case examples demonstrate.

One such example of a group of cases questioning the existence of sufficient political willingness of the authorities to comply with the ECtHR judgments is the *Tsintsabadze* group of cases (also known as the *Gharibashvili* group until September 2017 when the *Gharibashvili* case was closed with regard to its individual measures).[113] This group of cases, consisting of over 30 cases, including 11 friendly settlements, a procedure allowing the parties to agree on the terms of the settlement of the dispute under Article 35 of the ECHR, concerns ineffective investigations into allegations of breaches of the right to life, torture and other forms of ill-treatment imputable to state agents from multiple state institutions, among those the Ministry of Internal Affairs, the Ministry of Corrections, the Ministry of Justice and the Public Prosecutor's Office, some of them dating back as early as 2002.[114] This group of cases is the biggest one among all pending groups of cases against Georgia and represents a complex structural deeply rooted domestic issue: ill-treatment and torture in detention and prisons, and the inability of the domestic system to effectively address it. Although some of these cases date back to events in the early 2000s, the issue of lack of effective investigations has reached the peak of public unease when the video showing sexual abuse committed by law enforcement agents under the UNM government was leaked in 2012, which significantly enhanced the focus on this issue in the Government's political agenda and has been closely scrutinised by civil society and the media in Georgia.[115] In the past five years, the implementation of this group has been on the CM's agenda on a regular basis, and further scrutiny is ensured by consistent follow up and submissions from applicants, the civil society and the PDO.[116] Although the Government's engagement with the CM process has been generally regular and responsive in this group, the supervision process has so far lasted for over ten years, with

112 CM member state representative, SXB01, Strasbourg, 23 May 2017.

113 Resolution CM/ResDH(2017)287 in the case of *Gharibashvili v Georgia*, Appl. no. 11830/03, adopted by the Committee of Ministers on 21 September 2017 at the 1294th meeting of the Ministers' Deputies.

114 HUDOC EXEC database, Tsintsabadze group of cases, 'Leading case', accessed 8 August 2020.

115 Freedom House, Nations in Transit 2016: Georgia (n 56).

116 Communication of the Public Defender of Georgia to the Committee of Ministers in the *Gharibashvili* group of cases, 28 November 2016; Communication of the Public Defender of Georgia to the Committee of Ministers in the *Tsintsabadze* group of cases, 7 December 2017, accessed on HUDOC EXEC database on 28 September 2019.

no sufficient tangible progress in ensuring individual justice to applicants or addressing the systemic nature of this problem to date, which I discuss further below.[117]

In cases of ineffective investigations of ill-treatment allegations, which this group of cases concerns, individual measures, along the payment of compensation ordered by the ECtHR, shall be ensured through re-opening of domestic investigations and effective re-investigation. In this group of cases, the authorities re-opened the investigations, with the majority of them however leading to termination of investigations due to lack of evidence or lapse of time to obtain new evidence, and only four investigations have led to identification of perpetrators.[118] The authorities' actions in the four latter cases are further questioned by the CM and the PDO for the classification of ill-treatment related crimes as often law enforcement agents are charged with abuse of official powers rather than the more serious charge of torture or other forms of ill-treatment.[119] In other cases, the investigations have been pending for more than five years since the re-opening without any tangible results. For example, in the cases of *Bekauri and Others v Georgia*, and *Studio Maestro LTD v Georgia*, there have been a series of actions taken by the investigative authorities since the renewal of investigations in April 2015 into the events that took place in June 2009; however, no tangible outcomes have so far been observed, which questions the effectiveness and relevance of such actions, given the urgency of obtaining evidence after such a long lapse of time.[120] Although the investigations appear to be continuing, including the questioning of over 100 witnesses,

117 Action plans by the Government of Georgia to the Committee of Ministers in the *Tsintsabadze* group of cases on 25 October 2019, 13 July 2018, 5 December 2016, 20 January 2015; Actions plans by the Government of Georgia to the Committee of Ministers in the *Gharibashvili* group of cases on 16 August 2017, 7 September 2017, 15 November 2016, 28 October 2016, 1 June 2016, 3 June 2015, 17 July 2014, accessed on HUDOC EXEC database on 28 September 2019.

118 Updated action plan concerning individual and general measures in respect of the execution of cases of *Tsintsabadze* group, 25 October 2019, accessed on HUDOC EXEC database on 28 September 2019.

119 2018 Annual report of the Public Defender of Georgia 71, accessed 29 September 2019; CM Notes on the *Tsintsabadze* group of cases from its 1362nd meeting held on 3–5 December 2019, accessed on HUDOC EXEC database on 28 September 2019.

120 Consolidated action plan of the Government of Georgia to the CM concerning individual and general measures in respect of the execution of the following cases: *Bekauri and Others*, Appl. no. 312/10 final on 08.10.2015, *Studio Maestro LTD and Others*, 22318/10 final on 23 July 2015, *Chantladze*, 60864/10 final on 23 July 2015, 28 October 2016.

there is very little information available to the applicants and their lawyers on what led the investigation to such delays or who those witnesses are.[121]

Another strategy that the Georgian Government employed in these types of cases was undertakings under 'unilateral declarations', a procedure allowing the authorities to make a declaration acknowledging violations and to give an undertaking to provide adequate redress, which the ECtHR favored in a number of such cases, such as the *Tsintsabadze* group (effective use of force by police/in custody and lack of effective investigations). This initially offered an indication of the Government's determination to willingly address the issue of ineffective investigations acknowledging that there has been a violation and undertaking to carry out an effective investigation.[122] Five years later, however, the investigations, closely monitored by a number of litigating organisations in the country, appear to involve no investigative actions that could be described as effective investigations.[123] Such unexplained delays of compliance, when the Government has willingly undertaken to conduct effective investigations, raises concerns of the genuineness of the Government's actions and is suggestive of absence of sufficient political will to abide by its own undertakings, particularly given that the implementation of the unilateral declarations are not monitored by the CM, with the burden of scrutiny falling on the applicants.[124] Although the ECtHR seems to have been favoring such settlement of cases with Georgia, such delays cast a shadow over the Government's intentions failing to use this as an opportunity to offer timely and effective remedies to the victims. As one litigating lawyer suggested:

> When the Government makes a commitment to conduct effective investigation on the basis of its own initiated unilateral declaration and fails to do so, I do not see any other reason for it to do so but to avoid taking any effective measures, given the complexity of the issue. As not all victims may follow up on the promised investigations, offering monetary

121 CSO representative, GEO08, Tbilisi, online interview, 12 December 2016; CSO representative, SXB10, London, 23 November 2016.

122 See, for example, *Bekauri and Others v Georgia*, Appl. no. 312/10, 08 October 2015, *Menabde v Georgia*, Appl. no. 4731/10, 13 October 2015; *Egiazaryan v Georgia* Appl. no. 40085/09, 24 November 2015; *Tedliashvili and others v Georgia* Appl. no. 64987/14, 24 November 2015.

123 Nino Jomarjidze and Philip Leach, 'What future for settlements and undertakings in international human rights resolution?' (Strasbourg Observers 15 April 2019), accessed 23 September 2019.

124 CSO representative, GEO08, Tbilisi, online interview, 12 December 2016; CSO representative, SXB10, London, 23 November 2016.

> compensation to them with a promise to re-investigate may allow the state to position itself as a winner without engaging in any structural reforms.[125]

As such undertakings are not being supervised by the CM, the authorities' actions are not subjected to any formal systemic scrutiny, unless the applicants themselves challenge the Government's failings before the ECtHR with a new application.[126] This, however, being a lengthy and demanding process for the applicants, risks leaving the authorities without adequate oversight.

Similar issues with political will are also observed with regard to adoption of general measures in this group of cases. Such measures primarily concern ensuring independence of investigatory bodies dealing with such cases, reforms to depoliticize the prosecutor office and the capacity building activities to law enforcement agents.[127] As an example of political reluctance of the domestic authorities to take timely adequate actions in this group of cases, securing the independence of investigatory bodies well illustrates what a significant role other actors can play in scrutinizing the authorities' performance (also discussed in 5.3.2.3) and addressing the issue of lack of adequate political willingness. In the context of the issues of use of force by law enforcement in police and prisons, the Georgian civil society and the PDO have actively advocated for the creation of an independent investigatory mechanism to examine such allegations, as part of the need to ensure its independence.[128] Such an independent and impartial mechanism, that would enjoy high public trust, would aim to ensure that investigations are carried out fully and effectively. As noted by the PDO in its submission to the CM, the creation of a new independent mechanism would ensure that such investigations of actions of employees of the Public Prosecutor's Office are not conducted by the same institution, significantly reducing the likelihood of its independence.[129] Such

125 CSO representative, GEO08, Tbilisi, online interview, 12 December 2016.

126 Jomarjidze and Leach (n 123).

127 Action plan of the Government of Georgia in the *Gharibashvili* group of cases to the CM, 14 November 2016; Consolidated action plan of the Government of Georgia to the CM concerning individual and general measures in respect of the execution of the following cases: *Giorgi Bekauri and Others*, Appl. no. 312/10, *Studio Maestro LTD and Others*, 22318/10, *Chantladze*, 60864/10 28 October 2016.

128 Communication of the Public Defender of Georgia to the Committee of Ministers in the *Gharibashvili* group of cases, 28 November 2016; CSO representative, GEO09, Tbilisi, online interview, 15 November 2016.

129 Communication of the Public Defender of Georgia to the Committee of Ministers in the *Gharibashvili* group of cases, 28 November 2016.

an initiative, proposed to the Government in the form of a draft law prepared by a coalition of NGOs for Independent and Transparent Judiciary has been met with reluctance, with the Government arguing that such a mechanism may lead to a potential overlapping of the mandate of the Prosecution and shortage of sufficient budgetary means.[130] In its 2016–2017 Human Rights Action Plan, however, the Government committed to exploring the possibility of establishing an independent mechanism, as the Georgian civil society continued advocating for this measure.[131] In its action plan of 25 October 2019, the Government of Georgia reported on the establishment and operation of the State Inspector's Service as a new independent investigative mechanism, whose investigative function became operational on 1 November 2019, as a positive step welcomed by the CM, the PDO and the CPT.[132] Nevertheless, relying on the CPT 2019 report on Georgia, the CM expressed its concern that the scope of the new legislation establishing the new mechanism is relatively narrow as it excludes senior officials, and the Prosecutor's Office retains full control over the investigation process, including which agency should carry out an investigation (the State Inspector's Service, the Prosecutor's Office, the Ministry of Internal Affairs or the Ministry of Justice).[133] The same concern was further expressed by the PDO in its submission in another case in January 2020.[134] The CM consequently urged the authorities to take legislative and/or other measures to further enhance the independence and effectiveness of the State Inspector's Service indicating that the general measures so far taken by the Georgian authorities have not yet met the expectations set by the CM.[135]

Despite the declared political determination to address the serious ill-treatment cases, the Government of Georgia has so far been unable to abide by its obligation to effectively investigate the majority of these cases and

---

130 CSO representative, GEO09, Tbilisi, online interview, 15 November 2016.

131 Communication of the Public Defender of Georgia to the Committee of Ministers in the *Gharibashvili* group of cases, 28 November 2016; CSO representative, GEO08, Tbilisi, online interview, 12 December 2016.

132 Updated action plan concerning individual and general measures in respect of the execution of cases of *Tsintsabadze* group, 25 October 2019, paras 246–264; CM Notes on the *Tsintsabadze* group of cases from its 1362nd meeting held on 3–5 December 2019.

133 Report to the Georgian Government on the visit to Georgia carried out by the European Committee for the Prevention of Torture and Inhuman or Degrading Treatment or Punishment (CPT) from 10 to 21 September 2018, CPT/Inf (2019) 16 [14]; CM Notes on the *Tsintsabadze* group of cases from its 1362nd meeting held on 3–5 December 2019.

134 Communication from an NHRI (24/01/2020) in the case of *Merabishvili v. Georgia* (Appl. no. 72508/13).

135 CM decisions in the *Tsintsabadze* group of cases, adopted at its 1362nd meeting on 3–5 December 2019 and at its 1390th meeting on 1–3 December 2020.

undertake adequate general measures, which questions its political determination. Although this group of cases represents a complex and systemic domestic issue exposing very serious human rights violations, which can be difficult to remedy for certain objective reasons, it is in these types of situations involving multiple domestic institutions and requiring change of deeply rooted culture where a strong political will of the Government is necessary to demonstrate its real willingness and ability to address such issues under ECtHR judgments. The research suggests that in these cases, absence of sufficient political stance of the executive may be explained by either insufficient political power to contest the entrenched powers of the Prosecution Office or the absence of such willingness to take adequate steps. The latter can be explained by long existing hierarchical subordination and institutional self-protection relations between the prosecution and the penitentiary as state institutions, historically formed throughout the years, particularly the soviet period of Georgia. Such a context may indicate the inability of the responsible authorities to deal with such highly political cases, which challenge the well-embedded institutional modalities in Georgia. As one Georgian lawyer suggested, the Government's inability to conduct effective investigations in what initially was several ill-treatment cases becoming 'systemic' in nature due to its political inability to address them:[136]

> In some specific cases, it may be impossible to effectively investigate due to the fact that it is not possible to obtain sufficient evidence anymore due to lapse of time that had already passed. In many other cases, however, we cannot ignore the possible lack of professionalism in investigating highly politically sensitive cases. It is simply wrong that the same prosecutors who were in their positions at the time when crimes were committed are now investigating cases of their colleagues.

Almost ten years since the first judgment in this group, the growing number of the investigations are about to be closed or remain pending without any progress, indicating the insufficient political willingness to put all efforts to address such serious allegations, which, with time, become objectively difficult to investigate.[137]

The discussed cases indicate how dependent the existence of political willingness is on the salience of certain ECtHR judgments and the nature of human

---

136 CSO representative, GEO08, Tbilisi, online interview, 12 December 2016.

137 CM decision in the *Tsintsabadze* group of cases, adopted at its 1362nd meeting on 3–5 December 2019 [3–4].

rights issues addressed. Political will is not an absolute factor in Georgia's compliance with ECtHR judgments and is conditional on the various levels of domestic political and institutional sensitivities and prevalence of domestic interests challenged by ECtHR judgments. The research further suggests that it is also determined by the existence, or absence, of public support to necessary measures, which I discuss in the next section.

5.3.2.2 Intrusion of 'Traditional' Values and Pervasive Discrimination as a Complex Political and Societal Issue

A significant number of ECtHR judgments against Georgia addresses systemic structural problems that require complex legal and policy reforms, and attitudinal changes, necessitating significant efforts from the authorities. Such judgments often require not only individual measures or adoption of a law but also the change of policies and practices, or attitudes of certain structure powers and the public as certain ECtHR judgments are seen as intruding existing 'traditional values' or expose pervasive phenomena of discrimination (which I also identified in the Armenian cases in 4.2.2.1). In such instances, ECtHR judgments identifying such issues are seen as raising high-perceived political costs where the public perception of the necessary reforms plays a significant role in the authorities' determination to that end. The executive as a political power being in charge of the implementation of ECtHR judgments is motivated to maintain the public support as part of its domestic political interest to remain in power, which may be challenged by the necessity to engage in unpopular human rights reforms, particularly at times of national elections. This issue is observed in the case of *Identoba and Others* concerning homophobic attacks on LGBT marchers by members and supporters of the Orthodox Church, whom the police failed to protect during a demonstration in the capital Tbilisi in 2012, in violation of Articles 3 and 14 of the ECHR. Although the Georgian Government has paid compensations to the victims ordered by the ECtHR, which indicates its acknowledging of the violations, domestic investigations into the attacks and prosecution of those responsible, however, have not yet been concluded over five years after the ECtHR judgment.[138] Similarly

---

138 Rule 9 submission to the Committee of Ministers by a Group of NGOs (Identoba, Women's Initiatives Support Group (WISG), Amnesty International and ILGA-Europe) in the case of *Identoba and Others v Georgia* (Appl. No. 73235/12), 16 November 2016; Communication from NGOs (Joint submission from The Human Rights Education and Monitoring Center, the Women's initiatives Support Group and ILGA-Europe) (02/08/2019) in the *Identoba and Others group of cases v. Georgia* (Application No. 73235/12), 2 August 2019; Communication from a NIHR (Public Defender of Georgia) (19/08/2019) in the cases of *Tsartsidze and Others, Begheluri and Others, Members of the Gldani*

to the situation in the *Tsintsabadze* group addressed above, the investigations have been opened under charges other than those relating to ill-treatment, regarding the encroachment on the right to assembly, which are subjected to a two-year prescription period that has elapsed 'even before the Court's judgment became final', as noted by in the Government's action report, and the investigations are therefore subject to termination.[139] This indicates that the ECtHR judgment did not only not lead to the re-opening of the domestic investigations but also did not lead to the reclassification of the charges against those responsible in light of the Court's findings of a violation of prohibition of ill-treatment and torture under Article 3 of the ECHR, suggesting the prioritization of other interests than compliance with this ECtHR judgment. As one interviewed Georgian lawyer described it, 'this case raises very sensitive societal issues, which require strong political leadership stance that is missing in Georgia due to the fear to lose electorate as these would be unpopular steps in light of prevailing homophobic views among the society'.[140] Another lawyer suggested that although some of these reforms can be explained to the public through the prism of public safety and prohibition of torture, the political will to do it is not sufficient among the political leadership: 'the authorities need to do diplomacy with the church, which is very influential in Georgia and plays a big role in forming the electorate's opinions, but there does not seem to be sufficient willingness to do it despite their authority to do it'.

In a highly hierarchical society with deeply ingrained traditional gender and family values, backed by the prevailing religions and its institutions, often generally attractive European values struggle to pave their way to their domestication. In light of this context, the implementation of general measures of in the case of *Identoba v Georgia* has been met with passivity and at times resistance among certain political groups and the public in Georgia due to the controversial nature of the issue in the Georgian society.[141] According to the European Commission against Racism and Intolerance (ECRI) report on Georgia published in 2015, in a survey on violence against LGBTI community following the events addressed in the *Identoba* case, 50% of survey respondents said that

Congregation of Jehovah's Witnesses and Others and *Identoba and Others group of cases v. v. Georgia* (Applications No. 18766/04, 28490/02, 71156/01, 73235/12), 19 August 2019.

139 Action report from Georgia concerning the case of *Identoba and Others v Georgia* (Appl. no. 73235/12), 10 July 2019 [11].

140 Human rights lawyer, GEO010, Tbilisi, online interview, 19 February 2017.

141 Alice Donald and Anne-Katrin Speck, 'The Dynamics of Domestic Human Rights Implementation: Lessons from Qualitative Research in Europe' (2020), Volume 12 Issue 1, Journal of Human Rights Practice 1–23; [4.1].

violence was acceptable towards people who "endanger national values, such as LGBTI persons".[142] The survey also established that nearly 60% of respondents thought that members of Orthodox clergy who participated in acts of violence against LGBTI people should not face trial and that about 50% said that the rights of sexual minorities should never be respected." The same report also refers to the hostile statements of the then Chairman of the Georgian Dream Parliamentary majority who 'blamed the LGBTI organisations themselves for the violence, portraying them as provocateurs'.

In May 2016, the Georgian parliament held debates on amending the Constitution to define marriage as a union between a man and a woman where many representatives of the ruling party expressed their support for such an initiative.[143] Given the sensitivity of the issue in Georgian society, including among the politicians, the Georgian Government has to balance securing high-level political attention to the issue within the framework of implementation of ECtHR judgment and at the same time ensuring the public support. Such hostile approach to human rights issues that remain sensitive to the traditional wider Georgian public, with the intolerance often conveyed by public figures to the general public, may well explain the dilatory progress with the necessary measures in the *Identoba and Others* case.[144] Although some progress has been made by the authorities, particularly in relation to legislative amendments aimed at creating adequate legislative framework to address discrimination more generally, the complex societal and political nature of the issue of fighting homophobia has led to little change in practice: both the civil society and the PDO reported offensive attitudes of police officers towards LGBTI victims, low numbers of investigations of hate crimes against LGBTI persons and inability to hold LGBTI marches in safety on IDAHOT Day to date.[145]

142 The European Commission against Racism and Intolerance report on Georgia (8 December 2015) [104], accessed 23 September 2019.

143 Civil.ge, 'MPs Debate Constitutional Ban of Same-Sex Marriage' (27 May 2016), accessed 23 September 2019.

144 Communication from a NHRI (Public Defender of Georgia) (19/08/2019) in the cases of *Tsartsidze and Others, Begheluri and Others, Members of the Gldani Congregation of Jehovah's Witnesses and Others* and *Identoba and Others group of cases v.* v. *Georgia* (Appl. no. 18766/04, 28490/02, 71156/01, 73235/12), 19 August 2019.

145 Communication from NGOs (Joint submission from The Human Rights Education and Monitoring Center, the Women's initiatives Support Group and ILGA-Europe) (02/08/2019) in the *Identoba and Others group of cases v. Georgia* (Appl. no. 73235/12), 2 August 2019; Communication from a NIHR (Public Defender of Georgia) (19/08/2019) in the cases of *Tsartsidze and Others, Begheluri and Others, Members of the Gldani Congregation of Jehovah's Witnesses and Others* and *Identoba and Others group of cases v.* v. *Georgia* (Appl. no. 18766/04, 28490/02, 71156/01, 73235/12), 19 August 2019.

In Georgia's domestic context, which featured multiple institutional, legal and political vulnerabilities in the state's organization upon its accession to the CoE, the respective ECtHR judgments do not only assist in identifying the necessary reforms but also reflect on the existing domestic challenges, that is very likely to require systemic assistance to the state authorities to address. Such assistance will vary from political and public pressures to political and financial incentives or programmatic and expert support, some of which I discuss below.

5.3.2.3 'External' Support to Compliance with ECtHR Judgments

The research findings suggest that a number of 'external' factors that come into play as a form of support to the authorities' compliance efforts can enhance the domestic implementation progress, particularly in cases, in which such progress would otherwise be likely slower, lesser or non-existent. Such factors vary from the CM supervision and follow up to engagement of the civil society and the PDO to programmatic and expert support from other CoE bodies to the ECtHR's prescriptive measures in the judgments against Georgia to incentives stemming from other international collaborations such as the EU-Georgia Association Agreement.

The significant impact of the CM's regular enhanced engagements with Georgian cases on Georgia's overall compliance with the CM rules and procedures has been addressed in 5.3.1. Here I discuss some examples in specific cases demonstrating the CM's impact on the taken domestic measures or the continuation of the implementation process, often further enhanced with the submissions from the civil society or the PDO, allowing the CM to assess the effectiveness or relevance of the authorities' actions. For example, in the *Tsintsabadze* group of cases, in the initial action plans submitted in 2015, the Georgian authorities referred to payments of compensation, re-investigations of individual cases, the legislative amendments ensuring the participation of the victim in the criminal proceedings as the necessary measures taken in these cases, capacity building of law enforcement agents and the judiciary, and the development of the action plan to combat torture and ill-treatment, however, making no reference to the necessity of any reforms to ensure the independence of the whole investigatory mechanism.[146] It was when the PDO and a group of NGOs as a Coalition for an Independent and Transparent Judiciary

146 Communication from Georgia concerning the case of *Enukidze and Girgvliani* (*Gharibashvili* group) *against Georgia* (Appl. no. 25091/07), 20 January 2015; Communication from Georgia concerning the *Gharibashvili group* of cases against Georgia (Appl. no. 11830/03), 3 June 2015.

introduced an idea to establish an independent investigatory body entitled to conduct investigations and bring charges in cases involving the violations of Articles 2 and 3 of the ECHR in November 2016 and in March 2017 respectively that this issue was taken into consideration by the CM and raised with the Georgian authorities in the CM decision of 6–8 December 2016.[147] The PDO's proposal was translated into a CM recommendation to the Georgian authorities 'to provide further information on how the institutional independence of investigating bodies, in particular the Prosecutor's Office, is henceforth guaranteed in law and in practice', which eventually led to the establishment of the State Investigator's Service as an independent investigative mechanism on 20 July 2018.[148] As this new mechanism is being set into operation in practice, the CM continues reviewing its effectiveness in light of the concerns expressed by NGOs and the PDO.[149] It is their submissions to the CM, as a form of their contribution to the domestic implementation process, that assist the CM in effectively scrutinizing the effectiveness of the authorities' actions, particularly the very implementation of adopted measures.

Similar efforts have ensured that questions relating to investigations of individual cases in this group, including the question of classification of acts, remains high on the CM agenda with the aim to ensure that the authorities comply with their Convention obligation to conduct effective investigations into such serious allegations under Articles 2 and 3 of the Convention.[150] In the *Identoba and Others* case, for example, such coordinated enhanced engagement of the CM, the PDO and the civil society ensured that the implementation debates between the authorities and the CM/DEJ included not only the obligation to investigate the homophobic attacks as such but also questioned the relevance and adequacy of the classification of acts, i.e. the encroachment on the right to assembly, on the basis of which the Georgian authorities appear to aim

147 Communication from the Public Defender of Georgia in the *Gharibashvili* group of cases against Georgia (Appl. no.11830/03), 28 November 2016; Communication from a NGO (Coalition for an Independent and Transparent Judiciary) (07/03/2017) and reply from Georgia (22/03/2017) in the *Gharibashvili* group of cases against Georgia (Appl. no. 11830/03), 7 March 2016; CM decision in the *Gharibashvili* group v. Georgia (Appl. no. 11830/03), adopted at its 1273th meeting on 6–8 December 2016.

148 CM decision in the *Gharibashvili* group v. Georgia (Appl. no. 11830/03), adopted at its 1273th meeting on 6–8 December 2016; Communication from Georgia concerning the case of *Tsintsabadze v. Georgia* (Appl. no. 35403/06), 13 July 2018.

149 Communication from an NGO (03/09/2018) and reply from the authorities (13/09/2018) in the cases of *Bekauri and Others, Studio Maestro Ltd and Others and Tsintsanadze v. Georgia* (Appl. no. 312/10, 22318/10, 35403/06).

150 CM decision in the *Tsintsabadze* group v Georgia, adopted at its 1362nd meeting held on 3–5 December 2019 [10].

to terminate the investigations.[151] The contributions of 'Rule 9' submissions are also noticeable in that it ensured that the case was not closed by the CM prematurely, allowing the CM to establish certain benchmarks for satisfactory implementation.[152] In September 2019, the Georgian authorities attempted to convince the CM that it has taken all the necessary measures implying the possibility to have the supervision of this case closed, which was followed by a joint NGO submission raising concerns that such a decision would be premature. The latter indicated series of steps that the authorities should take to ensure that the deeply structural problem of discrimination would be effectively addressed, which the CM has concurred with.[153]

These examples well demonstrate the significance of the concerted efforts by other implementation actors, enabling their contributions to the process, and which allow creating the necessary support, scrutiny or pressure on the domestic authorities in their compliance with ECtHR judgments.

Another type of tools to support the authorities in their implementation work is observed through the programmatic work of other CoE bodies, such as CPT or the Venice Commission, or CoE Action Plans developed for individual member states, which is often extended to countries undergoing multiple reforms as part of their democratisation process and in need of such support. The research finds that such support is particularly effective in supporting compliance with ECtHR judgments where it closely corresponds with the issues identified as necessary general measures, as it ensures not only the expert support but also provides the financial assistance, which relieves some of the financial burden on the state. For example, in the *Ghavtadze* group of cases, where the authorities have taken numerous reforms to improve health care in prisons, significant support was provided to the authorities by the CoE bodies to implement the measures. The national action plans and strategies

---

151 Action report from Georgia concerning the case of *Identoba and Others v Georgia* (Appl. no. 73235/12), 10 July 2019 [11]; Communication from a NIHR (Public Defender of Georgia) in the cases of *Tsartsidze and Others, Begheluri and Others, Members of the Gldani Congregation of Jehovah's Witnesses and Others and Identoba and Others* (*Identoba and Others* group) *v. Georgia* (Appl. no. 18766/04, 28490/02, 71156/01, 73235/12), 19 August 2019 8.

152 Alice Donald, Debra Long, and Anne-Katrin Speck, 'Identifying and Assessing the Implementation of Human Rights Decisions' (2020), Volume 12 Issue 1, Journal of Human Rights Practice, 1–24 [3.1.5].

153 Communication from Georgia concerning the case of *Identoba and Others v. Georgia* (Appl. no. 73235/12); Communication from NGOs (Joint submission from The Human Rights Education and Monitoring Center, the Women's initiatives Support Group and ILGA-Europe) (02/08/2019) in the *Identoba and Others* group of cases v. Georgia (Appl. no. 73235/12).

for the reforms were prepared on the basis of the European Prison Rules and the findings of the CPT reports on Georgia, and significant financial support through the Joint CoE/EU Programme 2013–2015 enabled the improvement of the material conditions and reduce mortality and tuberculosis rate in Georgian prisons.[154] Similar support was provided in Georgia's continuing efforts to combat discrimination and ensure protection of vulnerable groups, in line with the general measures identified in the *Identoba and Others* case. The CoE Action Plan for Georgia 2016–2019 has assisted the PDO, Ministry of Justice, judiciary, prosecution and law enforcement in bringing legislation and practice on anti-discrimination, hate crime and hate speech further in line with the European standards, as also recognised by the ECtHR judgment, which, given Georgia's dilatory progress in these cases, have also served as an encouragement for progress.[155] The Georgian authorities recognised the importance of such support to its actions to improve investigation of hate crimes in its action plans to the CM in 2019 and 2020, indicating the receptiveness of such assistance in the complex domestic context of this case.[156] As one of the interviewed former Government Agents noted, 'the CoE/EU cooperation projects and the wider EU-Association Agreement context, where anti-discrimination efforts are prioritised as a condition, certainly play a role in Georgia's performance in that regard – it serves as a strong incentive to deliver as the gain is high'.[157] The continuity of such concerted support from various actors and programmes creates a consistent oversight of Georgia's efforts to adopt the necessary general measures as identified within the framework of these ECtHR judgments and ensures additional incentives or pressures when such a need emerges in light of the complex domestic political context within which such reforms take place.

154 Communication from Georgia concerning the *Ghvatadze* group of cases against Georgia (Appl. no. 23204/07), 27 January 2014; Communication from Georgia concerning the *Ghvatadze* group of cases against Georgia (Appl. no. 23204/07), 30 September 2014; Council of Europe Action Plan for Georgia 2013 – 2015 Final Report, GR-DEM(2016)16, 6 June 2016, 16.

155 Council of Europe Action Plan for Georgia 2016-2019, accessed 19 January 2020 Final Report (1 January 2016 – 31 October 2019), GR-DEM(2020)2, 19 December 2019 accessed 19 January 2020.

156 Communication from Georgia concerning the case of *Identoba and Others v. Georgia* (Appl. no. 73235/12), 10 July 2019; Communication from Georgia concerning the case of *Identoba and Others v. Georgia* (Appl. no. 73235/12), 25 June 2020.

157 Former Governmental Official and former human rights lawyer, GEO03, online interview, 15 October 2016.

Finally, one more factor identified in the Georgian context as potentially contributing to enhancing compliance with ECtHR judgments is the prescriptiveness of measures in the ECtHR judgments. The ECtHR remains very clear on this primary obligation of the member state to abide by its judgments, but in recent years it has taken an increasingly more active role in interpreting Article 46 of the Convention by indicating more specific individual and general measures to be taken by respondent states, at the expense of their margin of appreciation (see 2.3). Although this has created some dissatisfaction about the perceived ECtHR 'interference' into domestic issues and the political resistance to the Convention system by some established democracies, in the Georgia context, the prescription of measures by ECtHR is perceived as a factor facilitating the implementation process. The idea of the ECtHR being more prescriptive in its judgments did not raise any concerns among any of the interviewed Georgian actors regarding the possible breach of the principle of the margin of appreciation by the ECtHR, which could potentially lead to growing resistance to implementing its judgments.[158] It was suggested that the lack of prescription or clarity on measures in judgments may delay the implementation process as the more debate over what measures are necessary among various domestic institutions, the longer the implementation may take, especially where there is no political will to implement certain judgments. The only skepticism over the ECtHR's prescription referred to the possible failure of the ECtHR to consider all relevant developments that may occur during the examination period of a case by the ECtHR, often lasting several years, which may affect the relevance of suggested measures.[159] One of the former Government Agents suggested that this was why Georgia, perhaps just like many other member states, is normally compliant with individual measures in a timely manner as the ECtHR normally indicates what compensation is to be paid to applicants and what other individual measures should be taken (e.g. reopening of a case).[160] Another former representative of the MoJ suggested

158 Governmental Official, GEO01, Strasbourg, 30 March 2018; Former Governmental Official and former human rights lawyer, GEO02, Tbilisi, 15 September 2015; Former Governmental Official and former human rights lawyer, GEO03, online interview, 15 October 2016; Governmental Official, GEO04, Tbilisi, 15 September 2015; Judge of Georgian Constitutional Court, GEO06, Tbilisi, 9 December 2016; NHRI representative, GEO07, Tbilisi, 16 September 2015; CSO representative, GEO08, Tbilisi, online interview, 12 December 2016; CSO representative, GEO09, Tbilisi, online interview, 15 November 2016; Human rights lawyer, GEO010, Tbilisi, online interview, 19 February 2017.

159 Former Governmental Official and former human rights lawyer, GEO03, online interview, 15 October 2016; Human rights lawyer, GEO010, Tbilisi, online interview, 19 February 2017.

160 Former Governmental Official and former human rights lawyer, GEO03, online interview, 15 October 2016.

that it would certainly help promote the human rights narrative and speed up the implementation process:

> From the perspective of the human rights protection it is always a [welcome] thing if the ECtHR is prescriptive enough, especially where political will or its absence comes into play. If the Government refrains from taking certain steps towards implementation, a clear message from the ECtHR would make them understand that there is no space for interpretation and that certain reforms need to be made.[161]

Lawyers representing victims of human rights violations in Georgia suggested that more prescriptive judgments would be particularly helpful in cases where endemic problems occur and where the Government can be unwilling or unable to take all necessary measures to address the issue.[162] For example, in cases where the ECtHR case law and the human rights standards are well developed on a particular issue, the ECtHR should support the Government to make necessary reforms by referring to those standards and indicating specific measures to be taken:

> We saw a similar approach of the Court when a pilot judgment procedure was introduced, which in part was an anticipated response of the Court to the governments' failing to implement similar judgments. The Court needs to be creative in using various ways to help member states better comply with judgments in certain areas, such as those exposing systemic violations. This may also help Government Agents, as in the case of Georgia, to persuade other institutions on what measures need to be taken, which, we hear, sometimes is a real problem. [163]

Among the five analysed Georgian cases, the two cases in which the implementation efforts can be considered as most complete, and the cases have been closed as implemented, were the ones in which the ECtHR indicated specific measures. Both in the case of *Klaus and Yuri Kiladze*, and the *Ghavtadze* group of cases, the ECtHR indicated that the Georgian Government should take necessary legislative and administrative measures to address the specific human rights issues identified by the ECtHR, which, combined with concerted follow up of the CM and NGOs, led to successful reforms (see 5.3.2.1). In the absence

161 Ibid.

162 CSO representative, GEO08, Tbilisi, online interview, 12 December 2016.

163 Human rights lawyer, GEO010, Tbilisi, online interview, 19 February 2017.

of any factors indicating strong political resistance to implement an ECtHR judgment, it is suggested that there is a causal link between the prescriptiveness of the ECtHR and the enhanced implementation efforts of the Georgian Government, further supported by the CM and the civil society.

5.4 Conclusion

Georgia is widely perceived as the success case in the South Caucasus region. This excitement stems from a combination of domestic developments such as the early Rose Revolution in 2003 that led to the first peaceful change of power in the region, a wide public support for European integration and a significant number of legal and policy reforms undertaken by the Georgian leadership with the support of its European partners. Georgia's general optimism is equally observed towards the role that the ECtHR plays in its Europeanization path. The research into the selected Georgian cases offers significant findings of their resulting in a number of effective domestic reforms, such as the two cases of *Kiladze* and *Ghavtadze* demonstrate, or in creating unique platforms for debates on often salient and complex human rights issues, such as pervasive homophobic discrimination identified in the *Identoba and Others* case, or ineffective investigations into ill-treatment or torture allegations in custody in the *Tsintsabadze* group of cases. It made significant contributions in ensuring that these structural systemic issues remain on the public and political agenda in Georgia and the CM supervision process has ensured a systematic attention to these issues. The CM process has also empowered the Georgian and international civil society with a useful tool to engage with these issues, through submissions to the CM, which in turn allows the CM to conduct a more comprehensive review and avoid premature decisions. The research findings suggested a strong causal link between a regular consistent CM engagement with Georgian cases and the level of response from the Georgian authorities, similarly to the case of Armenia.

An in-depth case-level research has also provided a unique possibility to look into the modalities of domestic implementation processes and identify a number of factors affecting smooth, timely and full compliance with ECtHR judgments. It suggests that although there are strong indications of overall willingness of the Georgian authorities to comply with the judgments, certain human rights issues exposed by the ECtHR judgments result in high perceived domestic political costs. Such challenges stem either from strong political interests of certain domestic political groups or state institutions, or the ruling power's concerns over public support on issues that are perceived by a large proportion of the population as clashing with 'traditional values'. In such cases, generating sufficient political will to indulge in the necessary reforms as part of compliance with ECtHR judgments becomes a matter of balancing between the international human rights obligations and other domestic interests. More than two decades into the CoE membership, the socializing role of the ECtHR judgments and the CM supervision system in Georgia proves to be a combination of encouragement, support and pressure that work in tandem to assist the Georgian authorities in addressing some deeply systemic human rights issues.

CHAPTER 6

Challenging the Unconditional Obligation

Partial Compliance with ECtHR Judgments in the South Caucasus States

In this Chapter, I argue that *partial compliance* is a very likely form of compliance in the South Caucasus states as new democracies continue to display various structural systemic vulnerabilities in the areas of human rights, rule of law and democracy today. I do so on the basis of the research findings into compliance with judgments of the European Court of Human Rights (ECtHR) in each domestic system, discussed in Chapters III–V introducing factors that explain the status quo against the background of the unconditional obligation to comply. I introduce the concept of partial compliance in the South Caucasus states as new democracies and propose types of partial compliance in the researched states that I identify on the basis of their compliance behaviour, and the motives that accompany it. I discuss the methodology of measuring compliance in the context and identify the various factors to be taken into consideration that indicate the likelihood of partial compliance. I conclude with a discussion on the key factors common across all three states as underlying points that predetermine the likelihood of partial compliance in the respective domestic contexts.

The analysis of the implementation of ECtHR judgments in the South Caucasus states in preceding Chapters Three-Five documents numerous instances of minimalistic, dilatory, protracted and contested compliance, pointing to the relevance of studying compliance as a spectrum rather than as a binary phenomenon. I suggest that the likelihood of such partial compliance in the respective states is presupposed by the following three factors: firstly, the complexity of human rights issues addressed by ECtHR judgments, often requiring complex systemic and often politically difficult changes; secondly, political, social or cultural sensitivity to the ECtHR findings in the domestic contexts, by the authorities and/or the broader public (that influences the political power's position). Thirdly, the absence of well institutionalised inclusive implementation mechanisms or procedures that would ensure synergies of various relevant domestic actors to address often complex and structural human rights issues hinders the institutionalisation and de-politicisation of domestic compliance with ECtHR judgments. I discuss it against the background of the incrementalist optimism of the Council of Europe (CoE) towards the South Caucasus states over the last two decades with which they

DOI:10.1163/9789004538214_007

have been invited to the CoE, and which has been challenged with a significant implementation backlog. Addressing serious systemic and structural problems, including 'bad faith' cases, the backlog questions the very essence of the states' democratisation, which makes the debate on partial compliance and its impact inevitable. Furthermore, recent years have witnessed instances of deepening contestation by certain states, such as Azerbaijan, which the Committee of Minister (CM) describes as 'situations of resistance'.[1] Azerbaijan has shown worrisome regression by explicitly refusing to adopt measures indicated by the CM when compliance becomes politically too 'costly', such as in the Ilgar Mammadov group, thus undermining its unconditional adherence with its selective approach.[2] This situation suggests that it is no longer sufficient to see compliance as a dichotomous concept defined by the two pillars of full compliance or no compliance with the pending implementation as merely an 'ongoing' process towards full compliance.[3]

6.1 What Is Partial Compliance?

Partial compliance is not a new concept in the legal scholarship and was first introduced by Hawkins and Jacoby in 2008 and updated in 2010 in relation to compliance with judgments of the ECtHR and the Inter-American Court of Human Rights (see 1.2).[4] They suggested four forms of partial compliance in 2010: 1) split decisions (states comply with part of the judgment but not with all parts) 2) state substitution (state offers a different response than the one the court ordered), 3) slow motion compliance (slow, delayed steps towards compliance), 4) ambiguous compliance amid complexity.[5] They argued that partial compliance is very common as states have strong incentives for both

1 Supervision of the Execution of Judgments and Decisions of the European Court of Human Rights, 11th Annual Report of the Committee of Ministers (2017) [13].

2 Interim Resolution of the Committee of Ministers on the execution of the judgment of the European Court of Human Rights in the case of *Ilgar Mammadov v Azerbaijan*, CM/ResDH(2017)429, 5 December 2017. The CM initiated the infringement proceedings and to refer the case to the ECtHR under Article 46(4) of the Convention as a result Azerbaijan's failure to comply with the CM repeated calls to release Ilgar Mammadov.

3 Anne-Katrin Speck, 'The European System of Human Rights Protection: No Rolls-Royce, but a Solid Engine Fit for the Future? In Conversation with Council of Europe Insiders' (2020) Vol. 12, Issue 1, Journal of Human Rights Practice 149–156.

4 Darren Hawkins and Wade Jacoby, 'Partial compliance. A Comparison of the European and Inter-American Courts of Human Rights' (2010) Volume 6, Journal of International Law and International Relations 35.

5 Ibid 77.

compliance and non-compliance, which suggest that partial compliance is a relatively stable end point. In relation to the ECtHR, they found that a substantial number of its cases are pending compliance for quite extended periods, which clearly show partial compliance, and in some instances partial compliance may be the long-term outcome. The latter point covers instances where CM adopts decisions to close cases on the basis of information provided by the respondent Governments where full compliance, i.e. the necessary changes have not yet been achieved on the ground. Hawkins and Jacoby conducted their analysis on the basis of the information available in the CM annual reports, decisions and interim resolutions on specific cases, and other publications, before the 2011 reforms entered into force.[6] It therefore does not reflect on changes brought by the reforms, aimed to enhance efficiency and transparency of the CM supervision process, which led to increased access to documentation provided by the member states and to 'alternative sources' provided by national human rights institutions and the civil society allowing for better *domestic context* analysis.

The concept of partial compliance initially introduced by Hawkins and Jacoby did not receive wider recognition in the legal scholarship, which largely relies on the premise that domestic systems generally accept and are socialised by the international laws.[7] The existing literature primarily focuses on well-established Western democracies and their motivations for compliance with ECtHR judgments and does so to a significantly lesser extent in relation to younger democracies of the CoE. I aim to revive and advance the so far limited scholarly debate on the concept of partial compliance in the context of international human rights law, and ECtHR human rights judgments, in particular on the basis of my findings in the South Caucasus states as states on a spectrum of democratization (from democratising states to those displaying authoritarian tendencies), which suggest the increasing relevance of this concept. I therefore aim to further induce the debate on partial compliance in light of the growing presence of various forms of compliance as a middle ground between the starting point and full compliance in democratising states such as the South Caucasus states. In this regard, the environment in which such states operate is rather unique as the level of democracy and its properties, such as

6 Ibid 66–70.

7 Janneke Gerards and Joseph Fleuren (eds), *Implementation of the European Convention on Human Rights and of the Judgements of the ECtHR in National Case-Law: A Comparative Analysis* (Cambridge University Press 2014) 3–5; Başak Çalı, Anne Koch and Nicola Bruch, 'The Legitimacy of the European Court of Human Rights: The View from the Ground' (2011), University College London 35–37.

separation of powers, respect for rule of law, including independence of judiciary, regular fair and free elections and other forms of citizen participation, are rather turbulent, affecting the states' domestic human rights compliance policies. The starting point of their socialisation process therefore differs from old democracies, which needs to be taken into consideration when assessing their compliance efforts.

Differently from Hawkins and Jacoby, I identify full compliance by a number of factors, including the formal closure of the cases by the CM as the CoE supervising body, which establishes that a state has taken all necessary measures by adopting a final resolution, but not as the sole decisive factor. I also consider the fact of repetitive cases pending before the ECtHR and reports on respective human rights issues by domestic human rights groups, such as non-governmental organisations (NGO), national human rights institutions (NHRI) and media, and regional and international bodies reflecting on the real time human rights situation in the country. This broader spectrum of criteria for assessment of compliance allows placing a particular ECtHR judgment, and its potential impact in the wider domestic human rights context, against the background of the human rights situation on the ground at the time of implementation. This domestic context oriented analysis also suggests a new form of partial compliance, *contested compliance*, in the South Caucasus states. I discuss all identified forms of partial compliance in the next section.

6.2 Forms of Partial Compliance

I employ the term of *partial compliance* as an overarching definition of the proposed forms of compliance behaviour of the respective states and break it down to three forms on the basis of the researched cases: minimalistic, dilatory and contested compliance. On this basis, I propose these forms of partial compliance in the South Caucasus states, which, although partly similar to those proposed by Hawkins and Jacoby,[8] also brings in the issue of motivation of the states, analysed on the basis of original empirical data, and are domestic context oriented. Furthermore, it specifically reflects on the particular tendencies in the domestic contexts within which implementation takes place in the South Caucasus states as states in the democratisation process, and yet featuring authoritarian tendencies. These three forms of compliance observed in the South Caucasus States demonstrate that partial compliance varies in forms

8 Darren Hawkins and Wade Jacoby (n 4).

and can overlap and apply to the same case. It is not suggested that they are exhaustive as they stem from the patterns observed in the compliance behaviour of the three analysed states but are aimed to reiterate that compliance can no longer be seen as a dichotomous concept and that it necessitates adequate attention to prevalence of partial compliance.

6.2.1 *Minimalistic Compliance*

In cases of minimalistic compliance, states take very minimal measures to remedy the situation for the applicant, which often do not extend beyond the payment of monetary compensation, commonly indicated by the Court in its judgments. This is a commonly observed form of partial compliance in the South Caucasus states, particularly with regard to cases under standard supervision, where the CM's engagement with the authorities is minimal (see 3.2.3.1, 4.3.1 and 5.3.1). For example, as already noted in respect of Azerbaijan, although the Government normally complies with its obligation to pay compensation, in only around 40% of its cases under standard supervision did it provide brief updates on individual measures, with 60% of cases still awaiting any information on the implementation status (see 3.2.3.1). Similarly, in the case of Georgia, which also has a record of timely compliance with the obligation to pay compensation on time, in more than 50% of the cases under standard supervision no further information on any other measures taken is available (see 5.3.1). As many interviewees across all three countries noted, payment of compensation is a clear and straightforward individual measure that does not put the Government in a spotlight even in politically sensitive or otherwise 'costly' cases as it does not involve any reforms or other complex or financially burdensome measures. It also provides applicants as victims of human rights violations with partial remedy, removing the immediate pressure from the authorities to redress the victims. It is suggested that in such cases, minimalistic compliance by the Governments with no enhanced engagement from the CM that would ensure close scrutiny of all the necessary measures is a common form of partial compliance, allowing them to initiate the implementation process and maintain it as an *ongoing* one before the CM.

The qualitative analysis of the selected cases, both under enhanced and standard supervision, offers further evidence of instances of minimalistic compliance, where further measures beyond payment of compensation have been taken by the authorities and scrutinised by the CM. In many such instances, the original action plans by the authorities from all three countries aimed to set the framework for implementation work, including reports on measures whose impact it is difficult to grasp without further data. They often involve measures such as the translation of judgments into national languages, dissemination of judgments among state institutions or trainings for relevant state officials; however, these documents rarely include specific plans and timeframes for other individual measures, such as re-opening of investigation, or general measures requiring more complex reforms, such as the adoption or amendments of the domestic legislation or change of existing policies. For example, in the *Identoba* case relating to violent attacks of participants of the march to mark the International Day Against Homophobia, Transphobia and Biphobia (IDAHOT) by homophobic groups, in its first action plan submitted in April 2016, the Georgian Government reported on the payment of compensation as an individual measure but made no reference to its obligation to ensure effective investigations into the attacks, an unconditional obligation stemming from the finding of a violation of Article 3 of the Convention.[9] Following the CM's December 2016 decision inviting the authorities to ensure that investigations are 'conducted in a prompt and effective manner and to keep the Committee informed of the progress accomplished in this respect', the authorities continued providing updates on the renewed investigations to the CM, as part of the supervision process.[10]

In the *Muradova, Mammadov (Jalaloglu) and Mikayil Mammadov* group of cases concerning unlawful physical use of force by security forces, with the first judgment dating back to 2009, the Government of Azerbaijan, in its first action report submitted in 2018, included no information on the investigations into actions of security forces in any of the 21 cases in this group. In its one-page action plan, the Government chose to inform the CM of the adoption of two executive orders by the President, and the Prosecutor General and the Minister of Internal Affairs on improvement of application of non-custodial measures of restraints and on the rights of arrested and detained individuals respectively, providing no further information on its practical impact in addressing the systemic problem of ill-treatment in custody.[11] In this group of cases, no further information on investigations has been provided by the authorities despite the CM's concerns 'regarding the lack of information on the investigations into

9 Communication from Georgia concerning the case of *Identoba and Others v Georgia* (Appl. no. 73235/12), 26 April 2016.

10 CM decision in the case of *Identoba and Others v Georgia* (Appl. no. 73235/12), adopted at its 1273rd meeting held on 6–8 December 2016.

11 Communication from the authorities (updated information) concerning the cases of *Muradova, Mamamdov (Jalaloglu) and Mikayil Mammadov v. Azerbaijan* (Appl. no. 22684/05, 34445/04, 4762/05), 20 February 2018.

deaths of the applicants' next of kin or ill-treatment allegedly imputable to law enforcement officers' in its subsequent decision of March 2018.[12]

Similarly, in the *Virabyan* case concerning torture in custody, in their first action plan submitted a year after the adoption of the judgment, the Armenian authorities limited their actions on the individual measures to the payment of compensation, with no reference to its obligation to investigate such egregious allegations (an investigation was later opened on the basis of the complaint from the applicant).[13] In the *Ashot Harutyunyan* case relating to the failure to provide adequate medical care in prison, which led to the applicant's death, the Armenian Government initially suggested that no other individual measures than the payment of compensation 'seem necessary', particularly given the fact that 'the applicants did not avail themselves of the right to apply for reopening of the cases at the national level'.[14]

In addition to the earlier mentioned examples of measures being limited to payments of compensation, these instances further indicate the preference of the Governments in the South Caucasus states to take minimalistic steps when implementing ECtHR judgments on their own initiative, particularly before they are scrutinised by the CM. These measures often concern steps that can be accomplished in a relatively simple and swift way and do not require significant efforts from the authorities. It is often when their actions are closely scrutinised by the CM and the Department for Execution of Judgments EJ, particularly with the involvement of the civil society and the national human rights institutions, that all the necessary measures aimed to fully remedy the victims and to prevent similar violations in the future become a part of the implementation process before the CM. The findings of the analysis also suggest that this concerns both individual and general measures and depends largely on the sensitivity and complexity of the measures to be taken. It is further suggested that the initiation of such measures does not necessarily guarantee their full and timely completion, which I discuss in the next section below.

12 CM decision in the cases of *Muradova, Mamamdov (Jalaloglu) and Mikayil Mammadov v. Azerbaijan* (Appl. no. 22684/05, 34445/04, 4762/05), adopted at its 1310th meeting held on 13–15 March 2018 (DH), CM/Del/Dec(2018)1310/H46-2.

13 Communication from Armenia concerning the case of *Virabyan v Armenia* (Appl. no. 40094/05), 29 November 2013; Communication from Armenia concerning the case of *Virabyan v Armenia* (Appl. no. 40094/05), 25 February 2014.

14 Communication from Armenia concerning the cases of *Ashot Harutyunyan and Piruzyan vArmenia* (Appl. no. 34334/04, 33376/07), 16 April 2015.

6.2.2 *Dilatory Compliance*

I categorise compliance as 'dilatory' in cases where the Governments engaged in the implementation process and have taken actions with respect to specific measures, either individual or general, but where the process of amending existing legislation or policy has been particularly protracted or where the measures did not, in practice, bring any tangible results to remedy the applicants' situation. This form of partial compliance is very common in the majority of the analysed cases, further supported by the wider statistical data indicating the high percentage of cases pending implementation for more than five years in the South Caucasus states. According to the official data of the CM, in 2021, 65% of all Azerbaijani pending leading cases, 35% of all Armenian pending leading cases and 33% of all Georgian pending leading cases have been pending implementation for more than five years.[15] Cases mentioned in 6.2.1 involving an obligation to ensure effective investigations following findings of violations of Article 3 of the Convention well illustrate such form of compliance in all three South Caucasus states as the vast majority of the re-opened investigations in the analysed cases have either been effectively stalled or have brought no tangible results to date. In some instances, the investigations led to their closure due to expiration of statutory limitations or are being conducted under inadequate charges (other than ill-treatment or torture).

For example, in the *Tsintsabadze* group of cases consisting of 21 cases of ill-treatment and torture allegations in custody in Georgia, the authorities re-opened the investigations on the basis of the ECtHR judgments; however, the majority were terminated due to lack of evidence or the lapse of time, which made it difficult to obtain new evidence, and only four investigations led to the identification of perpetrators. They were charged with abuse of official powers but not the more serious charges of torture or other forms of ill-treatment.[16] In other cases in this group, the investigations have been pending for more than five years since the re-opening without any tangible results or information about the investigation being given to the applicants.[17] Similarly, in the *Identoba* case, the investigations into attacks of the applicants at the LGBTI march that have been reported by the authorities to the CM as pending

15 Committee of Ministers 15th Annual report on Supervision of the Execution of Judgments and Decisions of the European Court of Human Rights (2021) 64.

16 Government updated action plan concerning individual and general measures in respect of the execution of cases of *Tsintsabadze* group, 25 October 2019; 2018 Annual report of the Public Defender of Georgia, accessed 29 September 2019 71; CM Notes on the *Tsintsabadze* group of cases from its 1362nd meeting held on 3–5 December 2019.

17 Human rights lawyer, GEO11, Tbilisi, online interview, 12 December 2018.

since 2016 have been opened under charges other than those relating to ill-treatment, regarding the encroachment on the right to assembly. The latter charges are subjected to a two-year prescription period that had elapsed 'even before the Court's judgment became final', as noted in the Government's action report two years later, in 2018.[18]

In the *Virabyan* case of 2012, in which, following the ECtHR judgment, the issue of investigation was brought back to the table in 2013, having previously been closed as groundless in 2004. As a result, only after four years the Armenian authorities reported having charged two police officers who were found guilty by the domestic court two more years later, in 2019. They were, however, convicted for exceeding official powers accompanied by violence, and not ill-treatment or torture (as found by the ECtHR) and eventually benefited from the statute of limitations in their case and remained unpunished.[19] In their action report of January 2020 the authorities reported to the CM that the police officers could not be found guilty of torture as the Armenian legislation did not provide a definition of torture at the time; however, in its earlier action report of October 2016, it had reported that torture *was* criminalised in the domestic legislation and the relevant amendments entered into force on 18 July 2015.

Similarly, dilatory implementation is observed in other types of analysed cases, requiring structural systemic reforms in the domestic systems, where the authorities report having initiated the process for necessary reforms, but where they are yet to deliver tangible results several years later, or where their effectiveness is difficult to measure. In the group of cases of *Mahmudov and Agazade* of 2009, relating to imprisonment of journalists under criminal defamation charges, as part of general measures, in 2012–2013, the Azerbaijani authorities initiated the process to bring its legislation on defamation in line with the European standards, including by seeking for the assistance of the Venice Commission, with the aim to decriminalise defamation.[20] Defamation has not, however, been decriminalised to date, and, on the contrary, its application has been extended to content published online.[21] The implementation

18 Communication from Georgia concerning the case *Identoba and Others v Georgia*, 16 April 2018.

19 Updated action plan concerning *Virabyan* group of cases, 24 January 2020 3.

20 *Mahmudov and Agazade* group of cases, Government communications examined during CM meetings on 4–6 December 2012, 4–6 June 2013 and 3-5 December 2013.

21 Communication from NGOs (Institute for Reporters' Freedom and Safety, International Media Support, Media Rights Institute and Legal Education Society) (26/02/2014) in the case of *Mahmudov and Agazade against Azerbaijan* (Appl. no. 35877/04), 25 February 2014.

process before the CM has been at a standstill since around 2015, despite the CM's repeated calls 'stressing anew the importance of finding solutions to the problems'.[22]

In the case of the twin judgments of *Chiragov and Others v Armenia*, and *Sargsyan v Azerbaijan*, which bring an additional complication of an unsolved conflict between the two countries to the implementation context, the dilatory and limited nature of the actions taken by both sides is clearly observed, despite the specific remedial measure indicated by the ECtHR in both judgments – the establishment of a property claims mechanism. In response, the two Governments employed different implementation strategies with the CM, none of which displayed any tangible progress towards effective compliance five years after the adoption of the judgments in 2015 (see 3.2.3 and 4.2.2.1.1). Azerbaijan reported to the CM in its only action plan in 2017 that such a mechanism already existed in the domestic system and that no other measures were necessary; however, when requested by the CM for further information as to how accessible it would be for persons in the applicant's situation, no further information was provided by the Government to the CM.[23] The Armenian Government reported prioritising bilateral meetings with the DEJ behind closed doors to look for possible solutions for implementation; however, its submissions focused on the alleged obstacles, which 'objectively hinder the execution of the judgment', referring to the parties' failure to reach a peace agreement in its so far only official submission to the CM made in 2019.[24] Four years after the adoption of the judgment by the ECtHR and the reported consultations with the DEJ, the Armenian government does not appear to have taken any practical, specific steps, such as considerations of the legal and technical nature of such a compensation mechanism in the domestic system.

The dilatory nature of the measures taken by the Governments in the analysed cases suggest two conclusions: that the authorities are not willing or able to take all the necessary measures in an efficient and timely manner (the reasons for which I discuss in Section 6.3 below), and, secondly and relatedly, that this requires the CM to conduct diligent and persistent scrutiny of these processes so as to be able to distinguish cases of dilatory compliance from genuinely time consuming measures, and respond to it adequately. In certain

22 *Mahmudov and Agazade v Azerbaijan*, CM decisions, accessed on 27 July 2019.

23 Government action plan in the case of *Sargsyan v Azerbaijan* (Appl. no. 40167/06), 6 March 2017; CM decision in the case of *Sargsyan v Azerbaijan* (Appl. no. 40167/06), adopted during its 1280th meeting on 7–10 March 2017.

24 Communication from the authorities (02/12/2019) in the case of *Chiragov and Others v. Armenia* (Appl. no. 13216/05).

cases, such dilatory compliance may also be an early indication of instances of contested compliance, discussed below.

6.2.3 *Contested Compliance*

Contested compliance is a relatively new phenomenon discussed in the context of the implementation of ECtHR judgments by CoE member states, and primarily emerged in relation to the implementation of 'Article 18' judgments, establishing 'bad faith' in the Governments' actions and in other highly politically sensitive contexts. It was in the CM Annual Report 2017 that Christos Giakoumopoulos, the Director General of the Directorate General of Human Rights and Rule of Law, first identified such instances as 'situations of resistance'; he was referring to the types of situations first identified in the 2016 report: cases disclosing complex structural problems; an absence of common understanding as to the scope of the execution measures required; slow or blocked execution; or a refusal to adopt the individual measures required or to pay just satisfaction.[25] While the 2016 report did not refer to any specific cases as examples, Giakoumopoulos, in the 2017 report, referred to the Azerbaijani Government's refusal to release Ilgar Mammadov as a situation of resistance that 'has not resolved', leading to the CM bringing infringement proceedings against Azerbaijan (discussed in 1.1). In 2019, the CM described resistance to implementation as a continuing issue of concern, adding that in 'an increasing number of instances' the CM 'has felt compelled to remind the respondent States of the unconditional obligation to abide by the Court's judgments'.[26] It again referred to the case of Ilgar Mammadov as the one specific example of such resistance, describing it as a 'situation of unprecedented gravity', adding that the applicant continued 'to be affected by the consequences of the violations of his Convention rights' despite the Court's judgment following the infringement proceedings (he was finally cleared of all negative consequences of the conviction in April 2020).[27] Although it took the CM four years to qualify Azerbaijan's failure to release Mr Mammadov as a 'refusal' to comply with the ECtHR judgment in light of Article 46(4) of the Convention, the CM 'finally

25 Supervision of the Execution of Judgments and Decisions of the European Court of Human Rights, 11th Annual Report of the Committee of Ministers (2017) 13; Supervision of the Execution of Judgments and Decisions of the European Court of Human Rights, 10th Annual Report of the Committee of Ministers (2016) 13.

26 Supervision of the Execution of Judgments and Decisions of the European Court of Human Rights, 13th Annual Report of the Committee of Ministers (2019) 19.

27 CM Annual Report 2019 (n 26) 20; Communication from Azerbaijan concerning the cases of *Ilgar Mammadov v. Azerbaijan* (Appl. no. 15172/13) and *Rasul Jafarov v. Azerbaijan* (Appl. no. 69981/14), 23 April 2020.

deemed it necessary to initiate the infringement procedure'. Its recognition of Azerbaijan's response as a 'situation of resistance' is significant in that it follows the Court's growing findings of ulterior purpose and bad faith in Azerbaijan's actions and potentially lays the ground for more persistent examination of compliance with other eight 'Article 18' judgments against Azerbaijan as of July 2020.[28] The growing number of 'Article 18' cases from the region, including Azerbaijan, Georgia and Turkey, totaling 13 by the end of 2021, as a testimony to the authorities' acting in bad faith in limiting rights of individuals 'unfavoured' by the authorities (political opposition, journalists, activists, human rights defenders), suggest that instances of contested compliance may grow and will require further and more persistent attention from the CM and the CoE more generally.[29]

Contested compliance is also observed in other politically sensitive contexts where there is very little or no political will to engage in the process, primarily due to the political motives behind the commitment of violations by the same domestic systems. One such area is ECtHR cases emerging in the context of ongoing conflicts between two CoE member states (also discussed under 6.2.2. as examples of non-genuine dilatory compliance). The current (non) implementation status of the two landmark cases of *Sargsyan v Azerbaijan* and *Chiragov and Others v Armenia*, in which neither state has so far paid monetary compensation to the applicants years after separate ECtHR judgments on just satisfaction were published in December 2017, suggest a strong indication of a 'situation of resistance', particularly given the generally good record of timely payments of compensations by both Governments in the majority of other ECtHR judgments.[30] Such a failure represents a clear violation of their unconditional obligation to abide by the judgments, including a payment of

28 CM Annual Report 2019 (n 26) 20, Committee of Ministers 15th Annual report on Supervision of the Execution of Judgments and Decisions of the European Court of Human Rights (2021) 17.

29 Başak Çalı, 'Byzantine Manoeuvres, Turkey's responses to bad faith judgments of the ECtHR' (Verfassungsblog on constitutional matters 19 February 2020), accessed 23 March 2020; Philip Leach, 'Strasbourg Censures Georgia over Detention of Former Prime Minister – the impact of an Article 18 violation' (EJIL: Talk! Blog of the European Journal of the International Law 2 August 2016), accessed 23 March 2020; Ramute Remezaite, 'Azerbaijan: Is it Time to Invoke Infringement Proceedings for Failing to Implement Judgments of the Strasbourg Court?' (EJIL:Talk! Blog of the European Journal of the International Law, 22 March 2017), accessed 23 March 2020.

30 Ramute Remezaite, 'Introductory Note to *Chiragov and Others v Armenia* and *Sargsyan v Azerbaijan* (EUR.CT.H.R.)' International Legal Materials (American Society of International Law 57(3) June 2018) 405–436; Communication from the applicant (27 July 2018) in *Sargsyan v Azerbaijan* (Appl. no. 40167/06), 09 October 2018.

compensation of EUR 5000 to each applicant, a delay of which is strongly suggestive of resistance to comply. As the ECtHR is increasingly faced with the conflict-related cases, with thousands pending its examination – primarily against the states that emerged after the collapse of the Soviet Union, including all three South Caucasus states, Russia and Ukraine – the CM will likely be faced with more instances of such blatant resistance of compliance in the future.[31] This is particularly likely as the majority of these conflicts remain unresolved or continue escalating, such as those in the Eastern Ukraine and the Nagorno Karabakh territories.

The analysis of the selected ECtHR judgments does not only strongly indicate the existence of partial compliance in the discussed forms; it also suggests that these three forms are not mutually exclusive. They can overlap in particular cases as they are predefined by the various factors and motivations that shape the authorities' behaviour. With minimalistic and dilatory compliance being the most common forms of partial compliance among the three, largely predefined by a mixture of the authorities' lack of will and/or lack of capacities, contested compliance is still relatively rare and is identified in cases that are more overtly resisted. These findings aim to suggest that it is no longer sufficient to see pending cases before the CM as an ongoing process towards full compliance; rather, the Strasbourg supervision system, particularly the CM and the PACE, needs to be able to detect partial compliance instances with vigilant scrutiny and respond adequately. Below I discuss some of the considerations aiding to identify partial compliance in pending cases.

6.3 Identifying Partial Compliance in the South Caucasus States: Methodological Considerations

The Convention system is built on the premise that states are the primary implementers of ECtHR judgments and that they generally enjoy margin of appreciation in deciding how those judgments shall be complied with.[32] Although the idea of 'shared responsibility' for compliance with ECtHR judgments has been increasingly supported among the CoE member states in light of the growing compliance challenges, it is primarily up to the national

31 Steering Committee for Human Rights (CDDH), Draft CDDH report on the effective processing and resolution of cases relating to inter-State disputes, DH-SYSC-IV(2020)04 08/07/2020, accessed 12 August 2020 8–10.

32 *Öcalan v. Turkey* [GC], Appl. no. 46221/99 ECHR 2005-IV [210]; *Scozzari and Giunta v. Italy* [GC], nos. 39221/98 and 41963/98, ECHR 2000-VIII [249].

authorities to identify what individual and general measures are needed for full compliance with ECtHR judgments (except for the monetary compensation, which is normally indicated by the ECtHR, or in rare instances when other measures are prescribed by the ECtHR).[33] Such a system brings ambiguity to the implementation process and its supervision by the CM, which in turn makes it more difficult to measure compliance. Measuring compliance in this context brings several questions to light: who is best placed to decide when judgments are complied with and if the member states act in good faith and put their best efforts to implement judgments; and what factors shall be taken into consideration to assess and identify full compliance. As Donald, Long and Speck suggest, identifying and assessing compliance is crucial to ensure that states' failures are identified and that 'premature termination of follow-up' is avoided, among other functions.[34] I suggest that this is particularly relevant in cases of 'problematic' states such as the South Caucasus states featuring weaknesses in their domestic systems to uphold the Convention standards or, more worryingly, displaying signs of political unwillingness or even bad faith to comply with ECtHR judgments in a full and timely manner. In this Section, I discuss some of the factors aiding to identify instances of partial compliance in such contexts.

6.3.1 *Prescriptiveness of Judgments*

Prescriptive judgments, indicating precisely what measures need to be taken by respondent states significantly simplify the ability of the CM to assess the state's compliance efforts and 'tick off' the relevant boxes when such measures are put in place. Although it is still very rare that the ECtHR, relying on the concept of margin of appreciation, indicates what specific measures need to be taken by the respondent state, it has done so in cases revealing structural systemic problems, including those where implementation of similar/leading cases was met with insufficient willingness or even resistance – which Donald and Speck described as 'evolving and pragmatic remedial approach' by the ECtHR.[35] In cases where the ECtHR does not specify remedies or it is not sufficiently clear what remedies are needed, the issue of compliance is dependent

33 Joint NGO Response to the draft Brussels Declaration on the 'Implementation of the European Convention on Human Rights, our shared responsibility', 27 March 2015.

34 Alice Donald, Debra Long, and Anne-Katrin Speck, 'Identifying and Assessing the Implementation of Human Rights Decisions' (2020), Volume 12 Issue 1, Journal of Human Rights Practice, 1–24 2.

35 Alice Donald, Anne-Katrin Speck, 'The European Court of Human Rights' Remedial Practice and its Impact on the Execution of Judgments' (2019) Volume 19, Issue 1.

on the interpretation of the judgment and the states' willingness to interpret it in good faith, or endorse the interpretation offered by the CM or the DEJ, or the domestic actors such as applicants themselves or the civil society. For example, in the case of *Ilgar Mammadov* of 2014, a leading case in the group, the ECtHR did not indicate any specific measures, and the repeated calls by the CM for his release were met with strong resistance from the authorities for a lengthy period of time (and did not constitute the official reason for his release by the authorities).[36] The authorities argued that the ECtHR did not indicate Mr Mammadov's release and therefore the Government has complied with the judgment by paying the applicant the compensation (see 6.4.2). As the ECtHR continued adjudicating other 'Article 18' cases against Azerbaijan, it indicated in the case of human rights lawyer Intigam Aliyev, in 2018, that the Government shall take measures aimed at 'restoring his professional activities'.[37] It also ruled that they should be 'feasible, timely, adequate and sufficient to ensure the maximum possible reparation for the violations found by the Court' in that way setting the framework for the measures necessary to ensure full implementation.[38] Although in this case, the ECtHR provides a strong indication as to what the compliance with this judgment should lead to, i.e. the restoration of Mr. Aliyev's professional activities, it does not indicate what concrete measures should be taken to achieve it. This in turn may create problems as lack of sufficient clarity on the measures may lead to disagreement between the authorities and the applicant in the highly politically sensitive context of this case.

The judgment also makes strong references to the need to address the wider persecution of the civil society in the country, recognising the existence of the dire situation it is in. The ECtHR found that Mr Aliyev was arrested and detained, and criminally prosecuted in relation to his NGO activities, as a part of 'a troubling pattern of arbitrary arrest and detention of government critics, civil society activists and human-rights defenders through retaliatory prosecutions and misuse of criminal law in defiance of the rule of law'.[39] The necessary measures implied by the ECtHR do not only appear to relate to allowing Mr Aliyev to continue with his NGO activities; the ECtHR's prescribed

36 Appendix to the Interim Resolution of the Committee of Ministers on the execution of the judgment of the European Court of Human Rights in the case of *Ilgar Mammadov v Azerbaijan*, CM/ResDH(2017)429, 5 December 2017, Views of the Republic of Azerbaijan [23].

37 *Aliyev v Azerbaijan*, Appl. nos. 68762/14 and 71200/14 (ECtHR 20 September 2018) [228].

38 Ibid.

39 Ibid [223].

measure includes references for the need to address the wider persecution of the civil society and the existence of the restrictive NGO law. This serves as a strong indication for the CM and others scrutinising implementation as to what steps are expected from the Azerbaijani authorities in this case, however, their adoption will depend on the good will of the authorities and active involvement of all the relevant actors, in absence of sufficient clarity of the judgment.

In the Georgian cases of *Klaus and Yuri Kiladze,* and *Ghavtadze,* relating to compensation to victims of Soviet repression, and failure to provide adequate medical care in prisons respectively, the ECtHR indicated that the Georgian Government should take necessary legislative and administrative measures to address the specific human rights issues identified, which, as discussed in Chapter 5 on Georgia (see 5.3.2.1), has been well received by the authorities as providing clarity as to what measures are expected by the authorities. It has also enabled the CM to assess compliance on that basis, and close the supervision as a result.

6.3.2 *Length of Time*

The *length of time* that ECtHR judgments have been pending implementation before the CM allows the CM to assess the authorities' compliance behaviour and the extent to which it has 'good will' to uphold its obligations. Taken together with other factors, timely implementation is a strong indication of the authorities' willingness and ability to genuinely engage in the implementation process. Conversely, long delays may indicate an absence of good faith. In my researched cases, or groups of cases, as of the end of 2021, the duration varies from 1 year (in one case) to 13 years; on average, cases have been pending implementation for 10 years in Azerbaijan, 6 years in Armenia and 7 years in Georgia.[40] The longest periods of time for implementation are noted in the cases against Azerbaijan: 3 out of 5 selected groups of cases have been pending implementation for 11 to 13 years, with Armenia and Georgia having at least one group of cases pending implementation for at least 10 years.[41]

Azerbaijan

- *Ilgar Mammadov* group (politically motivated arrest and pre-trial detention of Government critics) – pending since 2014 (*7 years*)

40 HUDOC EXEC database as of 1 January 2022.

41 *Mahmudov and Agazade* group, *Muradova, Mammadov (Jalaloglu) and Mikayil Mammadov* group, *Ramazanova and Others* group; *Tsintsabadze* group; *Ashot Harutyunyan* group.

- *Mahmudov and Agazade* group (imprisonment as a punishment for defamation) – pending since 2009 (*12 years*)
- *Muradova, Mammadov (Jalaloglu) and Mikayil Mammadov* group (unlawful actions of security forces and ineffective investigations) – pending since 2007 (*14 years*)
- *Ramazanova and Others* group (failure of the authorities to apply properly the legislation regulating registration/dissolution of NGOs) – pending since 2007 (*14 years*)
- *Sargsyan* case (protection of property of displaced people in the context of the Nagorno Karabakh conflict) – pending since 2015 (*6 years*)

Armenia:
- *Ashot Harutyunyan* group (detention conditions and medical care in prisons) – pending since 2010 (*11 years*)
- *Bayatyan* case (freedom of religion and alternative service for conscientious objectors) – closed after *4 years*
- *Chiragov and Others* case (protection of property of displaced persons in the context of the Nagorno Karabakh conflict) – pending since 2015 (*6 years*)
- *Mkrtchyan* case (exercise of freedom of assembly) – closed after *1 year*
- *Virabyan* group (ill-treatment and/or torture in custody, actions of security forces and ineffective investigations) – pending since 2013 (*9 years*)

Georgia:
- *Gorelishvili* group (amendments to defamation law) – closed after *3 years*
- *Ghavtadze* group (medical care in prison) – closed after *5 years*
- *Identoba and others* case (lack of protection against homophobic attacks) – pending since 2015 (*6 years*)
- *Kiladze* group (compensation for Soviet era repression) – closed after *5 years*
- *Tsintsabadze* group (ineffective investigations into allegations of excessive use of force by police) – pending since 2008 (*13 years*)

Cases where there has been no progress reported whatsoever, as identified particularly in many cases under standard supervision (see 3.2.3.1 and 5.3.1), are strongly indicative of the authorities' failure to engage in a timely manner and adhere to the CM rules. In cases where progress has been reported by the authorities and there is more engagement with the Strasbourg process, which is particularly observed in cases under enhanced supervision, the assessment of timeliness requires further qualitative analysis of the lifespan of cases to assess the justifiability of any delay. In its own categorisation of pending cases, the CM divides leading cases into groups pending implementation for less than two years, between two to five years and more than five years, identifying the latter group as the most problematic one.[42] Although the five year period is a reliable indicator of the state's failure to comply with the judgment in a timely manner, in my research I suggest that partial compliance can also be detected *earlier* if adequately analysed in light of all the factors discussed in this Section. For example, in the groups of cases relating to ill-treatment and torture allegations by security forces concerning all three South Caucasus states where effective re-examination of domestic cases forms a fundamental part of individual measures, a failure to take the necessary investigatory steps within a reasonable time, or the initiation of investigations under charges less serious than ill-treatment or torture, can likely be detected earlier than within a five year period (see 6.2.1 and 6.2.2).[43] This therefore is suggestive of the authorities' preference for minimal or otherwise limited actions.

I further suggest that partial compliance in the authorities' actions can also be detected in cases already closed as implemented by the CM. For example, in the *Bayatyan* case relating to the criminal prosecution of Jehovah's Witnesses as conscientious objectors in Armenia, it took three years for it to be closed as implemented but there was in fact nearly a 10-year delay until Armenia complied with its obligation to adopt a law on alternative service as part of its CoE accession commitments.[44] Upon its accession in 2001, it committed to 'pardon all conscientious objectors sentenced to prison terms ... allowing them instead ... to perform ... alternative service', whereas the 2011 ECtHR judgment concerned the conviction of at least 37 conscientious objectors following Armenia's accession to the CoE.[45] Although the adoption of the ECtHR judgment triggered Armenia's actions towards adopting the necessary mechanism, I suggest that the wider context within which the authorities' adherence to its Convention commitments takes place should be taken into consideration in assessing compliance. This suggests that the CM may have closed the case prematurely, before the law was adopted.

6.3.3 *Engagement with the CM Process*

I propose that the authorities' regular and timely *communication with the CM* and their *observance of basic CM supervision rules* are strong indicators of

42 CM Annual Report 2019 (n 26) 19, CM Annual Report 2021 (n 28) 64.

43 *Muradova, Mammadov (Jalaloglu) and Mikayil Mammadov* group, *Ramazanova and Others* group; *Tsintsabadze* group; *Identoba and Others* group; *Ashot Harutyunyan* group; *Virabyan* group.

44 PACE Opinion 221 (2000), Armenia's application for membership of the Council of Europe, 28 June 2000 [13.4(d)].

45 *Bayatyan v Armenia*, Appl. No. 23459/03, 7 July 2011 [127].

the authorities' willingness to engage with the process, and absence of such engagement indicates partial compliance. As the implementation process is largely based on the concept of socialisation and dialogue between the authorities and the CM, effective communication is key to the effectiveness of the implementation process. The CM's Rules adopted in 2006 put specific guidance and tools in place to facilitate and institutionalise communication, such as the requirements for the domestic authorities to submit action plans and reports within established timeframes, enabling the CM to better assess states' commitment in that regard. Effective communication is therefore a crucial indicator of the states' dedication to achieving full compliance. High percentage of cases under standard supervision where either no information has been provided to the CM or it has been done with significant delays, in violation of the CM Rules, by the authorities of all three states is a good example of the impact of effective engagement with the process (see 3.2.3.1, 4.3.1 and 5.3.1). In other instances, although some communication takes place, often encouraged by the CM's enhanced supervision procedure, state submissions either omit mention of fundamental issues or refer to dilatory processes offering no indications of tangible results. For example, in the Nagorno Karabakh cases of 2015, although both states provided action plans to the CM, with significant delays (in 2017 by Azerbaijan and in 2019 by Armenia), neither of them qualifies as effective communication. The Azerbaijani Government, after having reported on the existence of the necessary property claims mechanism, has failed to respond to the CM's further inquiries on the effectiveness of the mechanism since March 2017, whereas Armenia focused on the reasons why implementation of this judgment is not possible rather than reporting on its efforts to comply with the ECtHR judgment (and its prescribed remedial measure).[46] Furthermore, neither of the states paid monetary compensation to the applicants for more than five years or provided the CM with any explanations for the delay.

In other cases, where communication is observed, the authorities take a selective approach as to what information to communicate to the CM, regardless of the latter's request for specific information. In the *Muradova, Mammadov (Jalaloglu) and Mikayil* group of cases consisting of 20 cases revealing lack of effective investigations into death or ill-treatment allegedly imputable to law

46 Government action plan in the case of *Sargsyan v Azerbaijan* (Appl. no. 40167/06), 6 March 2017; CM decision in the case of *Sargsyan v Azerbaijan* (Appl. no. 40167/06), adopted during its 1280th meeting on 7–10 March 2017; Communication of the Government of Armenia on the actions taken and anticipated concerning the case of *Chiragov and Others v Armenia*, 9 November 2019.

enforcement agents dating back to 2007, in its only action report of February 2018, triggered by the CM's decision of September 2017 urging to provide an update, the Azerbaijani Government chose to report on the adoption of two executive orders aimed to improve the rights and conditions for detained persons, failing to provide any update on such fundamental obligations as effective domestic investigations following ECtHR judgments.[47]

Even in cases where the authorities *do* engage in regular communication with the CM and follow the CM Rules in terms of reporting, the CM is still faced with the challenge of assessing the quality, relevance and sufficiency of the reported progress in order to assess compliance. For example, in the *Virabyan* case, relating to the torture of an opposition member in police custody, the Armenian authorities provided regular updates on the progress of the renewed investigations following the ECtHR judgment, ultimately leading to charges against two police officers; however, they were only found guilty of the lesser offence of exceeding official power accompanied by violence by court, and benefited from the statute of limitations and remained unpunished.[48] In such instances of partial compliance, the CM is faced with the challenge of critically and qualitatively assessing such reported progress by the authorities in the wider domestic context. One effective way to do it is through diversification of sources of information, which I discuss next.

6.3.4 *Diversification of Sources of Information*

As the Strasbourg supervision system is based on the dialogue between the CM/DEJ and the domestic authorities, the CM is primarily bound to assess the implementation progress on the basis of information provided to it by the authorities, often in the contexts of various types of partial compliance as discussed above. Hypothesising that the states' primary objective will always be to have the pending cases closed as soon as possible, with the minimal effort and resources put into it, it is fundamental for the CM to rely on diversified sources of information on implementation as it is the supranational body exclusively tasked to establish states' compliance with ECtHR judgments. In such instances, domestic actors such as victims, the civil society and national human rights institutions, as well as international civil society or other international

47 Communication from the authorities (updated information) (20/02/2018) concerning the cases of *Muradova, Mammadov (Jalaloglu) and Mikayil Mammadov v Azerbaijan* (Appl. no. 22684/05, 34445/04, 4762/05).

48 Updated action plan concerning *Virabyan* group of cases, 24 January 2020 3.

institutions than the CoE play a significant role in filling in this gap.[49] The CM has been gradually increasing transparency of the supervision process through a number of reforms, such as the 2017 launching of the new HUDOC EXEC database storing all official written submissions by the authorities and other actors, and CM decisions and other responses in individual cases. Its annual reports containing valuable statistical data, and the formalisation of the role of victims, the civil society and the national human rights institutions through their right to submit 'Rule 9' submissions, also known as alternative reports, has further contributed to increased transparency.

Their contribution has already proven valuable in enabling the CM to critically assess the authorities' reported compliance progress in cases where they regularly followed the process and provided their input, and where the CM reacted to the contributions. For example, in the *Ilgar Mammadov* group of 'Article 18' cases, in which the ECtHR has found the applicants' arrest and detention unlawful and motivated by ulterior purpose to punish them for their human rights work, activism or criticism towards the Government, the CM's gradual shift in its calls upon the Government is traceable to the fact that several applicants consistently provided submissions on their position as to what compliance with individual measures should entail. Two of the applicant, Rasul Jafarov and Intigam Aliyev, took the position that the ECtHR's findings should be interpreted as entailing the quashing of their criminal convictions as the finding of a violation of Article 18 of the Convention in relation to their arrest and detention meant that the whole criminal proceedings were tainted.[50] While initially, in 2017, the CM limited its position to requesting the Government for information on the re-opening of the domestic proceedings, in December 2019 its calls were extended to include 'the elimination of all other consequences of the criminal charges'.[51] In April 2020, the Supreme Court finally quashed the convictions of Ilgar Mammadov and Rasul Jafarov, however, leaving the cases of all other victims in this group pending before

49 Alice Donald, Debra Long, and Anne-Katrin Speck, 'Identifying and Assessing the Implementation of Human Rights Decisions' (2020), Volume 12 Issue 1, Journal of Human Rights Practice, 1–24, 4.

50 Communication (with appendices) from the applicant (19/01/2017) in the case of *Rasul Jafarov (Ilgar Mammadov group) against Azerbaijan* (Application No. 69981/14); Communication from the applicant's representatives (01/09/2017) in the case of *Rasul Jafarov v. Azerbaijan* (Appl. no. 69981/14); Communication from the applicant (09/05/2019) in the case of *Aliyev (Ilgar Mammadov group) v. Azerbaijan* (Appl. no. 68762/14).

51 CM decision in the *Ilgar Mamadov* group of cases (Appl. no. 15172/13) adopted at its 1362nd meeting on 5 December 2019.

the same court, reaffirming the importance of the victims' engagement in the process.[52]

Similar significant developments are also observed in the *Tsintsabadze* group of cases concerning general measures where a coalition of Georgian civil society organisations and the PDO have actively advocated for the establishment of an independent investigatory mechanism to deal with cases of ill-treatment and torture allegations against law enforcement agents (see 5.3.2.1). Although initially, in 2016, the Government met such a proposal with resistance, arguing that it would be overlapping with the mandate of the Prosecutor's Office, it however gradually committed to exploring this opportunity; this led to the establishment of a State Inspector's Service as a new independent investigative mechanism, whose investigative function became operational on 1 November 2019. While its establishment has been welcomed, it remains under close scrutiny of the CM, with contributions from the civil society and the Georgian Public Defender Office, to assess its effectiveness in practice (see 5.3.2.1).

In summary, all the above-discussed factors have been identified as playing a crucial role in detecting and defining the forms of partial compliance in the analysed cases from the South Caucasus states, and are therefore proposed as criteria by which the CM could adequately assess compliance in contexts of democratizing states, including those featuring increasing trends of authoritarianism in their domestic human rights policies. While assessing compliance and more importantly, identifying partial compliance, is a demanding task for the CM as a supranational body, since they rely primarily on the information received from the authorities and other stakeholders, the development of methodology based on clearly identified factors applied as a multi-layered mechanism would further equip the CM in identifying and tackling instances of partial compliance in such contexts.

6.4 Explaining Partial Compliance in the South Caucasus States

In this final Section of this Chapter, I overview the underlying factors that offer some explanation as to why partial compliance is a likely form of compliance in the South Caucasus states. I identify such factors in each domestic context in the country chapters and in this Section I discuss those factors that are clearly traceable across all three South Caucasus states, thereby offering a regional

52 Action report from Azerbaijan concerning cases of *Ilgar Mammadov v Azerbaijan* (Appl. No. 15172/13) and *Rasul Jafarov v Azerbaijan* (Appl. No. 69981/14), 23 April 2020.

perspective on partial compliance in the South Caucasus (see 3.2.4, 4.2.2.1 and 5.3.2). I submit that it is fundamental to analyse and understand the contexts within which compliance takes place to better enable the Strasbourg supervision mechanism to adequately react and respond to emerging challenges.

6.4.1 *Complexity of Human Rights Issues*

The complexity of human rights issues addressed by the ECtHR in its judgments against all three South Caucasus states require complex structural or otherwise challenging reforms, offering significant explanation to implementation processes in the region. I portray this complexity as two-layered: a) 'case/ issue' complexity and b) 'wider domestic context' complexity. My research findings suggest that they are to be analysed together as they are closely intertwined in the South Caucasus states as states on a spectrum of democratisation.

Firstly, case/issue complexity stems from the fact that all three states emerged as new states, aspiring democracies, with their deeply fragile political and legal systems and weak, if any, human rights protection systems, ineffective justice systems and the judiciary. In this context, where all three states were admitted to the CoE on the basis of their promise to abide by the European standards and integrate them into the domestic systems, the ECtHR individual petition system quite naturally became a part of the CoE support mechanisms to those states in their broader CoE compliance process. As a result, many ECtHR judgments addressed human rights issues that are deeply systemic, with a number of strikingly similar issues across the three countries, requiring substantial reforms, such as the adoption of new laws or amendments of existing legislation, the reinforcement of institutional capacities, and change of mentalities.

Secondly, these complex issues emerge from the contexts that were formed in the states' deep-rooted origins of their totalitarian past, which did not see immediate change with the signing of the CoE accession documents. Strong prevailing cultures of weak separation of powers, authoritarian organisation of the state, lack of authorities' accountability to the public and impunity, high corruption levels, together with poor, turbulent economic situations have shaped the domestic climates of newly accepted CoE member states (see 1.3.1, 3.1.1, 4.1, 5.1).[53] Further to that, all three states suffered from turbulent situations in the conflict-torn areas in Nagorno-Karabakh, South Ossetia

53 PACE Opinion No. 222. (2000) Azerbaijan's application for membership in the Council of Europe [109]; PACE Opinion No. 221 (2000) Armenia's application for membership in the Council of Europe, App I; PACE Doc. 8296, Georgia's application for membership in the Council of Europe, 12 January 1999 [88].

and Abkhazia, halting diplomatic relations between the affected states and affecting the democratisation process as a regional objective (see 1.3.1, 3.1.1, 4.1, 5.1). It is against these complex contexts that ECtHR judgments enter their domestic implementation processes in the South Caucasus states, which they do not face in Western or Central European countries, or at least not to such an extent.

One of the challenging areas of implementation common to all three South Caucasus states, which illustrate the impact of the two-layered complexity relate to ECtHR judgments establishing the absence of effective investigations into the actions of law enforcement and security forces, such as ill-treatment and torture in custody, and lack of accountability. The three groups of cases of *Muradova, Mammadov (Jalaloglu) and Mikayil Mammadov against Azerbaijan, Tsintsabadze against Georgia* and *Virabyan against Armenia* have been pending implementation for extended periods of time varying from 8 to 13 years and face similar challenges both in relation to individual and general measures (see 6.2.1, 6.2.2). Following years of the implementation processes, the states' unconditional obligation to ensure effective investigations have not met the Convention standards and have not offered full and timely remedy to the vast majority of victims. Investigations remain pending without significant progress, perpetrators not brought to justice or brought under charges less serious than ill-treatment and torture, and benefited from expiration of statutory limitations, or investigations have been closed as allegedly having no basis. Similar developments are observed in other Article 3 cases involving an obligation to effectively investigate, such as in *Identoba and Others against Georgia*, in the context of the widespread homophobic bias, discussed in Section 5.3.2.2, and the *Ashot Harutyunyan* group against Armenia, relating to denial of adequate medical care in prison, discussed in 4.2.2.1.

I argue that such challenges stem from the particular domestic contexts affected by the deep-rooted origins of the totalitarian past featuring extensive powers of law enforcement agencies and lack of culture of accountability for such crimes (see 3.2.3, 4.2.2.1, 5.3.2.2). Although an obligation to ensure effective investigations long years after alleged events of ill-treatment and torture may face objective challenges such as inability to obtain evidence, the analysis of these cases and the identified patterns across the three states also strongly indicate the subjective element of the authorities' behaviour, i.e. unwillingness and/or inability of the investigatory mechanisms to effectively investigate and prosecute its members, as discussed in the respective country chapters (see 3.2.3, 4.2.2.1, 5.3.2.2). These findings correspond with literature on compliance establishing that these types of remedies are among the worst implemented across all human rights systems.[54]

6.4.2 *Domestic Political Climate: International Reputation versus Domestic Interests*

It is well recognised in the legal and political science scholarship on compliance that political willingness plays a significant role in upholding states' obligations to comply with the international human rights law, including ECtHR judgments, and I discuss the particularities of this factor in each analysed state in respective country chapters (see 3.2.4, 4.2.2.1.1 and 5.3.2.1). In this Chapter on partial compliance, I further suggest that political willingness in the South Caucasus states should be understood as resulting from a tension between the perceived domestic interests of the state authorities, which may pull away from compliance, and their wish to develop a reputation as rights-respecting states that fulfil their international commitments. I argue that domestic interests often prevail in these states, primarily due to the complexity of solutions that full compliance with ECtHR judgments require. As I discuss in country chapters, the existence of political will is particularly fundamental in politically sensitive, socially controversial or resource intensive cases, and its forms may vary from passivity due to absence of political incentive to more active political resistance, depending on the political, financial or other costs of the measures deriving from the judgment (see 3.2.4, 4.2.2.1, 5.3.2). This is particularly true in the absence of effective domestic implementation mechanisms or procedures that would otherwise institutionalise or 'lock-in' the implementation process and enable other relevant domestic actors to engage in it.

The difference in political willingness to adopt individual and general measures is stark in all three countries. A relatively stable record of timely payments of monetary compensations to applicants in all researched cases may suggest that compliance rate of clear, straightforward and 'easy to implement' measures, such as payments, is high and there is well established political willingness to comply. The monetary expression of this remedial measure involving a

54 Alexandra Huneeus, 'Courts Resisting Courts: Lessons from the Inter-American Court's Struggle to Enforce Human Rights' 2011 Vol. 44 No. 3 Cornell International Law Journal 517, 519; Hawkins and Jacoby (n 23) 58; David C Baluarte,'Strategizing For Compliance: The Evolution of a Compliance Phase of Inter-American Court Litigation and the Strategic Imperative For Victims' Representatives', 2012 Vol. 27(2) American University International Law Review 298; Michael J. Camilleri, M., & Viviana Krsticevic, 'Making international law stick: reflections on compliance with judgments in the inter-american human rights system' 2009 Derecho Internacional y Relaciones Internacionales 241.

rather simple action of a bank transfer to respective applicants does not require any institutional coordination or the involvement of any other domestic actors and consideration of any other actions, which is likely to be a pre-condition to high compliance. The implementation process becomes more complex where other, more 'costly', individual measures, or general measures are required. In cases where additional individual measures are needed, political willingness will vary depending on the political sensitivity or ambiguity of the particular case. For example, in cases of investigation of ill-treatment by security forces in custody, where the state bodies are tasked to investigate the actions of responsible state officials and bring them to justice, the political sensitivity is likely to lead to passivity or even resistance to effectively investigate their counterparts (see 3.2.3, 4.2.2.1, 5.3.2.2). Such passivity in turn carries a risk of objective inability to effectively re-investigate such cases, such as obtaining necessary evidence, given the time lapse since the occurrence of the events.

Political resistance can also be caused, or enabled, by the ambiguity of the case as to what measures are required. One way to avoid it is for the ECtHR to ensure its consistency in its prescriptiveness in its judgments in cases addressing similar issues in similar contexts.[55] For example, if the ECtHR indicates specific measures in one case but does not do so in another similar case, states may exploit the resulting ambiguity to justify its political resistance to adopt the necessary measures. Such behaviour is observed in a highly politically sensitive *Ilgar Mammadov* case, where the authorities complied with the obligation to pay compensation but for a prolonged period refused to release him despite the CM's calls for them to do so. The Government argued that the ECtHR did not indicate such a measure and it therefore did not have an obligation to release Mr Mammadov despite the findings by he Court that he was arrested and detained in absence of any evidence and with the aim to punish him for his criticism.[56] The Government however did comply with the judgment in the case of Mr. Fatullayev (examined as part of *Mahmudov and Agazade* group), where the ECtHR indicated the immediate release of the applicant, journalist critical of the Government, imprisoned under criminal defamation charges. As this case related to a violation of Article 10 of the Convention addressing Mr Fatullayev's freedom of expression rights but

55 Alice Donald, Anne-Katrin Speck, 'The European Court of Human Rights' Remedial Practice and its Impact on the Execution of Judgments' (2019) Volume 19, Issue 1.

56 Appendix to the Interim Resolution of the Committee of Ministers on the execution of the judgment of the European Court of Human Rights in the case of *Ilgar Mammadov v Azerbaijan*, CM/ResDH(2017)429, 5 December 2017, Views of the Republic of Azerbaijan [23].

not the issue of deprivation of his liberty, it is suggested that such an explicit indication of a specific measure of release has played a role in Government's compliance with this measure. Although the payment of the compensation to Mr. Mammadov suggests the Government's recognition of the applicant's violated rights, unravelling the political imprisonment of an opposition politician aiming to challenge the highest leadership of the country in the presidential elections entailed huge political costs to the ruling authorities, prevailing over its damaged international reputation to comply with the CM calls (see 3.2.3). To protect its domestic interests and avoid the release of Mr Mammadov, the Government has relied on the Court's ambiguity in its findings in domestically politically sensitive cases. Such situations lead to instances of minimalistic compliance with ECtHR judgments where payment of compensation often is the only measure fully and timely complied with whereas other measures requiring further actions and involvement of various state bodies lead to dilatory or contested processes (see 6.2).

Such partial compliance is frequently observed in the process of adopting general measures, requiring systemic reforms, such as adopting new law or policies, or improving material conditions. Such measures often require the involvement of multiple state bodies and considerations of balancing the perceived costs. High costs may relate to putting political gains at risk, for example, reforms enhancing political pluralism, such as those required as a part of the Ilgar Mammadov group of cases in Azerbaijan relating to reforms of the justice system that would ensure the independence of judiciary and the law enforcement agencies; or disclosing and effectively investigating alleged wrongdoings of state officials in Armenia, as in the *Virabyan* group; engaging in reforms that may not receive popular support in largely conservative societies in Georgia, such as in the case of *Identoba and Others*. Such costs may also involve the need to create a genuinely enabling environment for media freedom in Azerbaijan, as a part of *Mahmudov and Agazade group*, where tolerance of the current ruling power to criticism and media freedom is very low if existent, due to the exposure of instances of high level corruption and other wrongdoings and zero tolerance for criticism among the ruling elites.[57]

Another example of such phenomenon is observed in cases exposing human rights issues conflicting with the values of highly hierarchical societies of the South Caucasus states with deeply ingrained traditional gender and family

57 CM Decisions H46-3 *Mahmudov and Agazade group v Azerbaijan* (Appl. no. 35877/04) CM/Del/Dec(2017)1294/H46-3, 21 September 2017; '2017 World Press Freedom Index', *Reporters Without Borders*, ranking Azerbaijan with the 162nd place https://rsf.org/en/ranking/2017 accessed 3 August 2020.

values, backed by the prevailing religions and their institutions (see 4.2.2.1.3 and 5.3.2.2). In light of this context, the implementation of general measures in the case of *Identoba and Others* has been met with passivity and, at times, resistance among certain political groups and the public in Georgia due to the controversial nature of the issue in Georgian society. According to the European Commission against Racism and Intolerance (ECRI) report on Georgia published in 2015, in a survey relating to violence against the LGBTI community following the events addressed in the *Identoba* case, 50% of survey respondents said that violence was acceptable towards people who "endanger national values, such as LGBTI persons".[58] The survey also established that nearly 60% of respondents thought that members of Orthodox clergy who participated in acts of violence against LGBTI people should not face trial and that about 50% said that the rights of sexual minorities should never be respected.[59] The same report also refers to the hostile statements of the then Chairman of the Georgian Dream Parliamentary majority who 'blamed the LGBTI organisations themselves for the violence, portraying them as provocateurs'.[60] Such hostile attitudes to human rights issues that remain sensitive to the traditional wider Georgian public explains the dilatory progress with the necessary measures, which remain pending after more than five years (see 5.3.2.2).

Although political will is a key pre-condition to compliance, it is not the 'all or nothing' factor in cases where there is no persistent political resistance and the favourable political climate for reforms can be created or further induced with the support of ECtHR judgments and the CM supervision process, and the involvement of other actors, as discussed in the cases of *Bayatyan v Armenia or Ghavtadze v Georgia* (see 4.2.2.1, 4.3.2 and 5.3.2.1). Existing political will of the executive either enables or allows for compliance with ECtHR judgments. Reforms that are aimed at inducing domestic change without putting the powers of the executive or other domestic authorities at stake may take effect domestically as a result of the ECtHR findings and further assistance from the CM and other CoE bodies in cases of absence of perceived costs. In such instances, the adoption of necessary reforms as a part of implementation of the ECtHR judgments is often the outcome of constructive cooperation of the Government with various actors both domestically and at the CoE level, which ensure the effective adoption of the necessary measures.

58 The European Commission against Racism and Intolerance report on Georgia (8 December 2015), accessed 23 September 2019 [104].

59 Ibid.

60 Ibid [72].

In summary, in the South Caucasus states, where compliance with ECtHR judgments most frequently involves the adoption of general measures in the form of legislative or policy reforms, often aimed at rectifying the existing 'gaps of the Soviet system', as well as individual measures beyond the payment of compensation, full compliance rarely comes without high domestic costs. It often carries political risks to the incumbent authorities, which leaves them at the crossroads of balancing their international and domestic priorities. A good record of paying monetary compensations to victims, but significant delays in adopting contentious individual measures and complex general measures, suggest that the authorities see partial compliance as a way to balance their international-reputational and domestic-political gains. This may include the states' attempts to try to convince the CM to close a case prematurely, even if not all the necessary measures have been adopted.

6.4.3 *Effectiveness of Domestic Infrastructure for Compliance with ECtHR Judgments*

Strong inclusive domestic infrastructure for compliance with ECtHR judgments is an important element of the process in all CoE member states, receiving increasing attention from the CoE as playing a significant role in assisting states with their Convention obligations.[61] This involves not only the necessity 'to set up domestic mechanisms and procedures'[62] but also 'to develop effective synergies between relevant actors in the execution process at the national level'.[63] I submit that in the particular contexts of the South Caucasus states, faced with multiple complex human rights issues requiring complex solutions and turbulent political and social systems, such mechanisms are particularly important. If the implementation of individual measures is often rather straightforward in terms of actions needed and actors involved, effective adoption of general measures entailing legislative and/or policy reforms often require a pool of expertise, effective management and financial resources, and efficient coordination. As issues addressed by those general measures often

61 Brussels Declaration on the 'Implementation of the European Convention on Human Rights, our shared responsibility' (Committee of Ministers, 27 March 2015); Council of Europe Committee of Ministers, 'Copenhagen Declaration', High Level Conference meeting in Copenhagen, 12–13 April 2018.

62 Parliamentary Assembly of the Council of Europe, Recommendation 1764 (2006) Implementation of the Judgments of the European Court of Human Rights (2 October 2006) [1.4].

63 CM/Rec(2008)2 on efficient domestic capacity for rapid execution of judgments of the European Court of Human Rights, adopted by the Committee of Ministers on 6 February 2008 at the 1017th meeting of the Ministers' Deputies [5].

affect the broader public or carry strong political interest, consideration of the public's voice, through national parliaments or the civil society, including media, is essential.

Although the currently existing systems vary in their composition and domestic political leverage in the three countries, none of them sufficiently enable the inclusive horizontal involvement of the relevant domestic actors, with the process primarily being 'directed' by one delegated executive body (see 3.2.2, 4.2.1 and 5.2). Transparency and information sharing by the responsible institution remain limited, or non-existent, with the CM database playing a crucial role in ensuring access to information for domestic actors following the process. Azerbaijan does not publicise any information to the public on its steps taken to comply with ECtHR judgments, whereas Armenia and Georgia have made some progress over nearly two decades of the CoE membership, however, pending further reforms to enable adequate public scrutiny of their efforts (see 3.2.2.4, 4.2.1 and 5.2.2).

Formalised procedures would ensure that the implementation process is not 'held back' by the responsible executive body, particularly in cases where domestic interests of the executive are at stake. The current holding of the top-down 'monopoly' over the implementation process by designated executive bodies, in the absence of any procedures for other state bodies than those 'selected' by the responsible authorities to get involved, prevents inclusive dialogue and cooperation over often very structural political or societal reforms and fails to provide sufficient checks and balances over the executive's actions. For example, in the case of Azerbaijan, the Office of the Government Agent under the auspices of the Presidential Administration holds absolute power to decide on the implementation plan for each judgment, and as no information is available to public, it is not known if and how any other state authorities are involved (see 3.2.2.3).

Where there is sufficient willingness of the designated executive body to take adequate actions, formal procedures would likely assist the executive in solving 'problems' to involve resistant responsible institutions operating in the culture of hierarchical subordination and institutional self-protection to the implementation process as the current status quo offer no adequate scrutiny and accountability of the executive's actions. Such challenges are particularly observed in the Georgian cases in the *Tsintsabadze* group relating to an obligation to effectively investigate ill-treatment and torture allegations by law enforcement agents requiring not only individual investigations but also the reforming of the institutional investigatory framework with regard to such crimes (see 5.3.2.1).

The importance of such procedures is particularly relevant in domestic contexts of younger, aspiring democracies featuring various vulnerabilities in the separation of powers and respect for rule of law, including independence of the judiciary. National parliaments in the South Caucasus states, for example, which undoubtedly can contribute to effective implementation of ECtHR judgments as the 'representation of people', need to be enabled institutionally for them to effectively engage in the process. It is very difficult, if not impossible, for them to get engaged in cases where respective Governments bear no formal duty to report to them on ECtHR compliance, or where it is not effectively used. Whereas the Georgian Parliament was granted a formal role in the implementation process in 2016, the Parliaments' role in Azerbaijan and Armenia is limited to considering legislative proposals submitted by the executive as part of the implementation process (see 3.2.2.3, 4.2.1 and 5.2). They have no formal way to scrutinise the Government's actions relating to implementation of ECtHR judgments or otherwise contribute to it. Without any institutional mechanisms, the national parliaments can do very little, if anything, in the states where the tradition of the overall parliamentary oversight over the executive is very weak and often risks politicising the domestic implementation processes.

The same holds true for the civil society and the national human rights institutions and their ability to engage in the reforms stemming from ECtHR judgments and to subject the authorities to public accountability for their respective actions. Without any type of formalised involvement, either through consultations or presentation of its position, civil society organisations are left with their own ad hoc sporadic attempts to engage in the process or through the communication with the CM in the form of formal NGO submissions on the states' actions relating to a specific ECtHR judgments. In Georgia, where the civil society actively participates in public debates on various societal and political issues and is an engaged contributor to a number of domestic reforms of public matters, or in Armenia where the civil society is gaining the momentum with the recent political changes, establishing a procedure for formalised civil society or national human rights institutions' contributions on the implementation of ECtHR judgments would institutionalise their ability to contribute to tangible changes (see Sections 4.2.1 and 5.2.2). In the Azerbaijani context, where dialogue with the civil society is non-existent, and the national human rights institution has not shown any interest in the implementation process, the mere adoption of procedures may not be sufficient; the creation of a civil society enabling environment, and broader recognition that public dialogue and coordinated actions of various domestic actors shall enhance effective implementation of ECtHR judgments, is needed (see 3.2.2.4).

In summary, I suggest that a combination of these factors offers an explanation for the prevalence of partial compliance in the selected cases from the South Caucasus states. As the analysis of selected cases demonstrates, the South Caucasus states are rarely to feature full compliance in light of the complexity of human rights issues identified by the ECtHR and the high 'costs' for the domestic powers, followed by the necessity for complex solutions to address it in the domestic political and legal contexts short of strong human rights inductive cultures and lacking strong procedures of checks and balances. These factors are particularly important to identify and understand contested compliance as an overt political resistance to certain ECtHR judgments, which my research suggests as a new form of partial compliance, exposing the existing motivations of the domestic authorities.

6.5 Conclusions

The analysis of the selected ECtHR cases and the domestic contexts in the South Caucasus states as states on a spectrum of democratization suggests that partial compliance is a likely form of compliance and this is due to a number of factors. The complexity of human rights issues addressed by ECtHR judgments against all three states, often requiring deep systemic changes, and the political, social or cultural sensitivity to the ECtHR findings and required reforms in the domestic systems often determine the states' compliance behaviour. As a result, the absolute nature of the states' obligation under Article 46 of the Convention to comply with ECtHR judgments has been increasingly challenged by states' selective behaviour, resulting in minimalistic, dilatory or even contested compliance with ECtHR judgments.

It is further suggested that such phenomenon can be explained by the states' balancing of international reputation and their domestic interests. Depending on the nature of the remedies deriving from the ECtHR judgments and the challenges or sensitivities that the implementation of such remedies may cause, the political will to comply with ECtHR judgments ranges from political engagement to passivity to resistance. The existence of the political will is reliant on the balancing of the 'costs' that states incur on the domestic political interests of the ruling authorities and their international performance. The research findings suggest that the ambiguity of ECtHR judgments and the remedies needed for full compliance is a significant factor to the issue of political will. Presence or absence of specific remedial measures stipulated in ECtHR judgments matters, as well as CM's specificity to remedies where they are not specified in the judgment.

The likelihood of partial compliance is further explained by absence of domestic implementation mechanisms in all three states depriving other domestic actors, such as national parliaments or civil society to effectively and systematically engage in the process. Without any effective checks and balances over the executive's compliance behaviour, the adoption of necessary measures is left entirely to the executive's discretion and thus determined by the balancing of domestic 'costs'.

As my research findings suggest that it is no longer sufficient to see compliance as a dichotomous concept on the premise that domestic systems generally accept and socialise with international law, partial compliance in its various forms should be seen as a middle ground in the study of compliance. Following on the earlier research of Hawkins and Jacoby that relies on the limited information of compliance published by the CM before the 2011 reforms, I argue that the concept of partial compliance in the context of ECtHR judgments should be revived and taken into consideration when assessing the states' behaviour. I further suggest that the particular contexts within which ECtHR judgments are implemented must be taken into consideration as it enables the assessment of the potential impact on the domestic level. The wider spectrum of criteria for assessment of compliance by the state allows for the analysis of both the compliance behaviour and domestic motivations that determine it, on the basis of the rich empirical data obtained through interviews. It in turn ensures better understanding of the real impact of the judgments, and the 'how' and 'why' of the compliance by the states (see 2.2 for the overview of compliance theories and the hybrid constructivist and rationalist theory of compliance in particular). This is particularly relevant in younger democracies of the CoE whose political, legal and social domestic environments are rather turbulent and where human rights judgments often serve as socialising tools aimed to improve the states' upholding of the Convention standards. The CM as the main CoE supervisory body, as well as other CoE bodies overseeing implementation, such as the PACE, should consider partial compliance as a possible middle ground and be able to identify and assess the reasons for partial compliance in the wider domestic contexts to get to the roots of the growing implementation challenges. The CM appears to be moving to that direction with the introduction of the concept of 'partial closure' of cases in 2018 (see 3.2.1). I argue that in the 'challenging' contexts such as those of the South Caucasus states, the CM should be particularly rigorous in scrutinising the states' efforts to ensure that partial compliance does not become a normalised status of compliance. This in turn should also enable the CM to identify instances of real impact, which I discuss in the following Chapter.

CHAPTER 7

Beyond Compliance

Identifying Impact of ECtHR Judgments in the South Caucasus States

This Chapter discusses impact of the judgments of the European Court of Human Rights (ECtHR) in the domestic contexts of the South Caucasus states. I start by discussing the concept of impact in my analysis and argue that impact is possible and identifiable in the South Caucasus states even if partial compliance is very likely (see 7.1). I provide an overview of the existing literature on impact of human rights judgments, including the typologies of impact, and move on to discuss the forms of impact of ECtHR judgments I identify in the selected states (see 7.2). I further discuss how my proposed typology corresponds with other existing typologies and offer the contribution of my research to this much needed concept in human rights law studies (see 7.2 and 7.3).

7.1 Concept of Impact of ECtHR Judgments in the South Caucasus States

For the research purposes, I primarily identify impact as any positive change or difference that a particular judgment has made or led to. Although I recognize that ECtHR judgments may also have negative or neutral impact, I focus on any positive impact that judgments may have in the selected domestic contexts as those where implementation of ECtHR judgments is challenging. This is to analyse how ECtHR judgments can contribute to ensuring human rights inducive change in such states as a result of their socialization with the international human rights norms (European Convention on Human Rights (ECHR)) and institutions (the Council of Europe (CoE)). I consider impact from multiple perspectives: primarily from the prism of applicants as victims of injustice and human rights violations and the perception of their individual situations, as well as the civil society and the wider society, but also more conventional impact such as changes in the domestic legal systems and policies. I recognise that it can be difficult to identify and measure impact of ECtHR judgments as the causal link between the judgments and particular changes on the ground, particularly in domestic contexts lacking strong human rights inducive cultures and well established human rights protection systems such

 | DOI:10.1163/9789004538214_008

as the South Caucasus states. I argue, however, that in countries where the rule of law and democratic principles are not well embedded in practice, and the domestic systems fail to offer effective protection of human rights to the same extent that democratic states do, it is particularly important to study all types of impact that ECtHR judgments may have beyond their 'conventional' material impact (e.g. the measures indicated by the ECtHR and prescriptions made by the Committee of Ministers (CM)) as part of the democratization process with the CoE. As the Open Society Justice Initiative (OSJI) study of the impact of strategic litigation in 2018 suggests, while strategic litigation may be more effective in democratic societies, it may be 'more significant in illiberal societies' where it is often one of the few forms of advocacy permitted.[1] In her book *Evidence for Hope*, Kathryn Sikkink argues that human rights laws and institutions more generally have positive impacts, especially in states undergoing political transition to greater democracy.[2] Yuval Shany further argues that impact of ECtHR judgments can take place with or without formal compliance and that the concept may help capture 'the court's more general norm compliance-inducing effect'.[3] The analysis of the rich material obtained through semi-structured interviews with domestic actors in all three states has offered strong conclusions on the significance of such wider impact that ECtHR judgments have beyond the strict normative material perception of compliance. It further suggests that impact is possible in cases of partial compliance and before full compliance is achieved.

7.2 Typologies of Impact

The increased interest in the wider conceptualisation of *impact* of human rights judgments and human rights law more generally by scholars has led to the emergence of discussions on the typology of such effects. In 2010, Rodríguez Garavito argued that the constructivist approach to effects of judicial decisions 'widens the range of research strategies to include qualitative techniques that capture a given decision's indirect and symbolic effects', and

1 Open Society Justice Initiative, 'Strategic Litigation Impacts. Insights from Global Experience (2018)' 17 https://www.justiceinitiative.org/publications/strategic-litigation-impacts-insights-global-experience accessed 16 August 2020.

2 Kathryn Sikkink, *Evidence for Hope, Making Human Rights Work in the 21st Century* (Princeton University Press, 2017).

3 Yuval Shany, 'Assessing the Effectiveness of International Court: A Goal-Based Approach' (2012) Volume 106 Issue 2, The American Journal of International Law 5, 56.

not only the direct, material effects.[4] To explain these two different perspectives, he proposed the following types of effects of judicial decisions concerning socioeconomic rights in the inter-American system:[5]

- *direct material effects* e.g. formulation of a policy or law ordered by the court;
- *indirect material effects* e.g. forming coalitions of activists to influence the issue under consideration; intervention of new actors in the debate;
- *direct symbolic effects* e.g. defining and perceiving the problem as a rights violation; reframing of media coverage; and
- *indirect symbolic effects* e.g. transformation of public opinion on the urgency and gravity of the matter.

OSJI, similarly, highlights the need to identify and assess different types of impact, both direct and indirect, material and non-material in its four different thematic studies of impact of strategic human rights litigation conducted in 2016–2017.[6] It focuses on the issues of Roma school segregation, access to equality education, torture in custody and land rights of indigenous peoples, each examined in three selected countries. Their research discusses such types of impacts:[7]

- material (e.g. restitution or compensation);
- instrumental (such as jurisprudential or policy changes), and
- non-material (such as behavioural or perceptional changes of complainants, policy makers or the wider society).

The CoE itself has been putting increasing focus on identifying impact of the ECHR and ECtHR judgments in light of the growing concerns over implementation challenges. In the recent years, with the financial support of a number of CoE member states, the CoE has started publishing examples of ECtHR judgments that led to the improvement of 'people's lives across Europe', as a

---

4 Rodríguez Garavito, C., Beyond the Courtroom: The Impact of Judicial Activism on Social and Economic Rights in Latin America' (2010) Volume 89, Texas Law Review 1678–1679.

5 Ibid 1681.

6 Open Society Justice Initiative, 'Strategic Litigation Impacts: Roma School Desegregation' (Open Society Foundations 2016), 16 August 2020; Open Society Justice Initiative, 'Strategic Litigation Impacts: Equal Access to Quality Education' (Open Society Foundations 2017), accessed 16 August 2020; Open Society Justice Initiative, 'Strategic Litigation Impacts: Torture in Custody' (Open Society Foundations 2017), accessed 16 August 2020; Open Society Justice Initiative, 'Strategic Litigation Impacts: Indigenous Peoples' Land Rights' (Open Society Foundations 2017), accessed 16 August 2020.

7 Open Society Justice Initiative, 'Strategic Litigation Impacts. Insights from Global Experience (2018)', accessed 16 August 2020, 43.

form of new online communication tools with the public.[8] It focuses both on themes and countries, and aims to demonstrate the impact on both the lives of individual applicants and the wider society. In January 2016, the PACE Legal Affairs and Human Rights Department published a report on the impact of the ECHR in states parties documenting a number of selected examples of positive impact in each member state.[9] Although these sources are mainly concerned with direct material/instrumental effects of ECtHR judgments, the need to demonstrate the impact is apparent at the CoE.

The two typologies offered by Garavito and OSJI are not identical but are similar in that they both identify both material and non-material effects of human rights judgments. Garavito however limits his focus to general measures, falling short of the analysis of impact on individual victims, or any moral impact that judgments may have, whereas OSJI appears to focus exclusively on 'direct' impact stemming from human rights judgments. Building on these approaches, my research offers evidence towards impact in the South Caucasus states and proposes forms of impact that consolidate both the victim oriented and the wider societal approach, and incorporates both direct and indirect, and material and moral types of impact. Some of my case level research into compliance indicates that in domestic contexts of transitional democracies or systems with strong authoritarian policies, both material and non-material impact is possible, including in cases of partial compliance (Chapter 6). The results of the interviews with applicants, lawyers and litigating non-governmental organisations (NGOs) in particular strongly suggest that ECtHR judgments have significant effect that goes beyond material impact that derives directly from the text of the judgments and the CM prescriptions. On that basis, I identify several types of impact of ECtHR judgments in my researched cases.

7.2.1 *Material Impact on Individual Victims*

This type of impact covers both monetary and non-monetary impact of ECtHR judgments on individual victims, similarly to the material effect of human rights judgments proposed by the OSJI. Due to the nature of the ECHR system

8 CoE material on impact available at https://www.coe.int/en/web/impact-convention-human-rights#/ accessed 19 August 2020.

9 PACE Overview 'Impact of the European Convention on Human Rights in States Parties: selected examples', prepared by the Legal Affairs and Human Rights Department upon the request of Mr Pierre Yves-Le Borgn (France, SOC), Rapporteur on the implementation of judgments of the European Court of Human Rights, 8 January 2016, AS/Jur/Inf(2016)04.

built on the subsidiarity principle and the ECtHR policy on remedies, limiting it to monetary compensation to applicants as victims for the incurred damage indicated in its judgments in the vast majority of cases, payment of such compensation is the most easily traceable direct material impact. When the Court orders just satisfaction to the applicant, it indicates a specific amount to be paid by the respondent Government, which it is obliged to do within three months of the judgment becoming final. It is therefore a clearly established obligation both in the operative part of each judgment and under Article 46.1 of the Convention, which enshrines states' unconditional commitment to abide by ECtHR judgments to which they are a party. It enables identifying such material impact for individual victims.

In the majority of the researched cases, the South Caucasus Governments paid the applicants the monetary compensations ordered by the ECtHR, except for the conflict cases of *Sargsyan* by the Azerbaijani Government, and *Chiragov and Others* by the Armenian Government where payments are still due (see 6.2.3). Some delays or partial transactions in payments were also observed in some of Azerbaijan's 'Article 18' cases, however, eventually leading to the Government abiding by its respective obligation (see 3.2.2.1).[10] This generally correlates with the overall statistics on payments of just satisfaction by the three states collected and published by the Department for the Execution of Judgments of the European Court of Human Rights (DEJ) on a yearly basis, with Azerbaijan featuring significant failings in respecting payment deadlines, compared to Armenia and Georgia. For example, in the period of 2016–2019, the DEJ was still awaiting information on payments by the end of each year or for more than six months in either no cases or a single case against Armenia each year, between one to four cases against Georgia, and between 37 to 115 cases against Azerbaijan.[11] Although the DEJ does not publish which cases

10 Communication from the applicant in the case of *Rasul Jafarov (Ilgar Mammadov group) against Azerbaijan* (Appl. no. 68891/14), 19 January 2017; Communication from the applicant in the case of *Rasul Jafarov (Ilgar Mammadov group) against Azerbaijan* (Appl. no. 68891/14), 1 September 2017; Communication from the applicant in the case of *Rasul Jafarov (Ilgar Mammadov group) against Azerbaijan* (Appl. no. 68891/14), 2 May 2019; Communication from the applicant in the case of *Aliyev (Ilgar Mammadov group) against Azerbaijan* (Appl. no. 68762/14), 9 May 2019; Communication from the applicant in the case of *Aliyev (Ilgar Mammadov group) against Azerbaijan* (Appl. no. 68762/14), 14 November 2019; Communication from the applicant in the case of *Mammadli (Ilgar Mammadov group) against Azerbaijan* (Appl. no. 15172/13), 12 November 2019.

11 Supervision of the Execution of Judgments and Decisions of the European Court of Human Rights, 11th Annual Report of the Committee of Ministers (2017) 83; Supervision of the Execution of Judgments and Decisions of the European Court of Human Rights, 13th Annual Report of the Committee of Ministers (2019) 80.

involve such significant delays in payments to identify the possible patterns or factors affecting such delays, it is suggested that such considerable difference in the behaviour of the Azerbaijani Government further corresponds with the research findings of the absence of overall good faith and political willingness to comply with ECtHR judgments and the Convention standards (see 3.2.3 and 3.2.4). A general pattern of deterioration in timely payments has also been observed by the DEJ more generally among the CoE member states, with the percentage of payments made on time 'barely exceed[ing] 70%' in 2017, for example, and increasingly more time needed for submitting relevant information leading to the need for urgent 'remedial action'.[12] The observed trends increasingly raise questions of concern as to the CoE states' dedication to their Convention obligations and the impact of ECtHR judgments, particularly given the very straightforward nature of monetary compensations as remedies secured for victims of human rights violations. As just satisfaction is probably the most uncomplicated material impact to be identified among all forms of tangible impacts of ECtHR judgments, the states' failures to pay it (on time) may point to well identifiable indications of non-compliance or partial compliance compared to more complex measures discussed further below.

Another example of material impact in monetary form identified in the researched cases is the compensation paid to applicants as victims of the Soviet era repressions in the *Kiladze* group of cases, following the Court's order to the Georgian Government to take 'necessary legislative, administrative and budgetary measures' to ensure necessary remedies (see 5.3.2.1). Although the applicants in this case were paid their respective compensation for moral damages indicated in the judgment, which the ECtHR ordered to be paid in case the necessary general measures were not yet in place in Georgia at the time, the creation of a compensation mechanism also established a right for many other victims, estimated by the Court to be around 16,000 people, to seek such a remedy.[13] It was on the basis of this development that the CM closed the case as having been complied with, thereby having a clearly identifiable material impact both on the applicants and many other victims of the Soviet repression who benefitted from the domestic reform.[14]

12 CM Annual Report 2017 (n 11) 14.

13 Action report of the Georgian Government on the execution of the judgment in the case of *Klaus and Yuri Kiladze v Georgia* (Appl. no. 7975/06), 5 December 2014 [10–11].

14 Ibid Annex 1; CM Resolution CM/ResDH(2015)41 on the execution of the judgment of the European Court of Human Rights in the case of *Klaus and Yuri Kiladze v Georgia*, 11 March 2015.

Material impact on individual victims is also observed in other, non-monetary, forms in the researched cases, stemming from other individual measures that ensured meaningful tangible remedies to the applicants. For example, in the *Ilgar Mammadov* group of cases, relating to the criminal prosecution of human rights defenders, activists and opposition politicians for ulterior purposes in Azerbaijan, the quashing of criminal convictions of two applicants, Rasul Jafarov and Ilgar Mammadov, by the Supreme Court in April 2020 as a result of the ECtHR judgments indicate a clear and specific material impact on the two victims in their individual situations (see 3.2.2.1).[15] The causal link between the two respective judgments and the remedies offered to the applicants is noticeable, despite the fact that this group of cases has featured and continues to feature elements attributable to contested compliance, including the fact that the convictions of the remaining applicants in this group have not been quashed without any justification (see 3.2.2.1). In its decisions to quash the two convictions, the Supreme Court explicitly referred to the findings of the ECtHR judgments, thus confirming their direct impact; it ordered the Government to pay compensations to both applications for non-pecuniary damages incurred as a result of the unlawful and politically motivated arrest and detention, and established a right for them to claim for pecuniary damages.[16] Both applicants considered these measures to be sufficient to have their individual cases closed as having been fully complied with.[17]

Similar instances of significant material impact for individual victims would be identifiable were the Governments to fully adopt the necessary individual measures, such as conduct of effective investigations in ill-treatment and torture cases following ECtHR judgments against all three South Caucasus cases. Although domestic investigations have been re-opened in many of these cases in all three countries, very few of them have led to full and timely effective investigations capable of leading to the identification, prosecution and conviction of those responsible. As discussed in Chapter 6 on partial compliance, the majority of the ongoing investigations were either unjustifiably prolonged, with very few investigatory actions taken; or investigations were closed or perpetrators accused under charges other than ill-treatment or torture, leading to milder sentences or no sentence due to the expiry of shorter prescription

15 Communication from Azerbaijan (23/04/2020) concerning the cases of *Ilgar Mammadov v. Azerbaijan* (Appl. no. 15172/13) and *Rasul Jafarov v. Azerbaijan* (Appl. no. 69981/14) 2.

16 Ibid 3–4.

17 Communication from the applicant (03/06/2020) in the cases of *Ilgar Mammadov* and *Ilgar Mammadov (No. 2) v. Azerbaijan* (Appl. no. 15172/13, 919/15); Communication from the applicant (18/06/2020) in the case of *Rasul Jafarov v. Azerbaijan* (Appl. no. 69981/14).

periods (see 6.2.2). Similarly, were the Governments of Azerbaijan and Armenia to establish a property claims mechanism and ensure its effective functioning in practice in the Nagorno Karabakh cases of *Sargsyan*, and *Chiragov and Others*, both the applicants and many other victims of the conflict who were forced to flee would benefit from direct material impact of the respective ECtHR judgments (see 3.2.3 and 4.2.2.1.1). Such clearly identifiable material indicators of the expected outcomes in some of the researched cases allow for credible assessment of anticipated impact, or the absence of such impact, as they leave very little space for any ambiguity in identifying the measures that should stem from the respective judgments.

The above discussed examples of identifiable material impact for individual victims of human rights violations established by the ECtHR indicate the importance of ECtHR judgments in securing particular individual remedies to applicants that lead to tangible change or improvement in their material situation. I further suggest that, on the basis of the evidence offered by the research findings, ECtHR judgments can also have positive moral impact on the individual applicants even in cases where material impact is not (yet) observed.

7.2.2 *Moral Impact on Individual Victims*

My research proposes that apart from the material impact, the positive impact of ECtHR judgments on individual victims can come in other, non-material forms, identifiable through empirical studies (not covered by the Garavito's typology). Some of the interviewed applicants as victims of human rights violations equally appreciated the non-material significance that the ECtHR judgments carried for them in their individual situations. Recognition of the violated rights of the victims and the exposure of injustice by an authoritative international court, often denied by the domestic authorities, were among the most mentioned examples of non-material impacts that the judgments had had on their lives. As one of the applicants in the *Ilgar Mammadov* group said, 'the thought of the European Court examining the clearly fabricated case against me gave me hope in prison that this injustice will finally be disclosed'.[18] Another applicant in the same group highlighted the importance of comprehensive true factual documentation of the case:[19]

> As the authorities pictured us as criminals by abusing the criminal justice system, at times it felt very difficult to refute all the accusations in

18 Human rights lawyer and CSO representative, AZE02, online interview, 27 March 2018 and 13 July 2019.

19 Applicant and CSO representative, AZE06, Brussels, 12 December 2018.

> the eyes of the public and the international community, so the ECtHR exposure and recognition of this abuse of power gave me a strong sense of vindication.

I suggest that such recognition of injustice is particularly significant to victims in countries with authoritarian policies or still undergoing transitions to democracy where often the legal and/or political system is either used to cover up serious human rights abuses and/or is not able to effectively address and remedy such injustice. Being a victim in such a context has additional devastating effects of vulnerability and hopelessness to achieve any justice domestically. Such instances are particularly noticeable in cases of egregious human rights abuses, such as ill-treatment and torture in custody, arbitrary detention and imprisonment and other 'punitive' methods where fundamental rights such as prohibition of torture or a right to liberty are denied. As one interviewed victim of police violence in one of the researched countries noted, 'my vulnerability in the hands of the police and their clear impunity were most victimizing for me so knowing that an international court would recognise this particular nature of abuse and humiliation felt very empowering'.[20] As Duffy writes in the OSJI Strategic Litigation Impacts report focusing on torture in custody, positive non-material impacts for victims can sometimes derive from 'participating in the process of strategic litigation', before the judgment is adopted, as part of the process of seeking justice.[21] International adjudication of human rights abuses does not only provide personal declaratory relief and recognition of violated rights and the incurred suffering, but also serves as a significant tool to properly document such state actions, which I discuss next.

7.2.3 *Documentation and Exposure of States' Human Rights Abuses*

Adequate and comprehensive documentation of human rights violations and injustice is equally significant to the public and not only individual victims. Societies must and need to know of their authorities' actions in seeking their accountability to the public – which Leach describes as part of their 'right to establish the truth'.[22] The establishment of facts or identification of certain abusive or wrongful policies of the domestic authorities in ECtHR judgments, which Garavito describes as 'direct symbolic effect', may be the only way for

20 Applicant, AZE08, email communication, 13 September 2019 and 26 February 2020.

21 OSJI Strategic Litigation Impacts. Torture in Custody (n 6) 27.

22 Philip Leach, 'The Continuing Utility of International Human Rights Mechanisms?' (EJIL:Talk! Blog of the European Journal of International Law 1 November 2017), accessed 2 September 2020.

domestic groups to raise them with the domestic authorities, as a credible authoritative source of evidence of the existence of the violations. As one of the human rights lawyers litigating ill-treatment cases before the ECtHR noted, 'ECtHR litigation is the only way for us to establish the existence of ill-treatment and torture in custody as the authorities withhold all the information and undermine the victims' allegation without any effective review in the domestic courts'.[23] Such documentation and establishment of facts is particularly significant in states such as Azerbaijan, where freedom of information and a right to know is particularly subverted, and there is no culture of public accountability. In cases of more vibrant transitions to democracy such as Armenia or Georgia, ECtHR judgments can create a useful platform for human rights groups and social movements to initiate a public debate and engage with the new authorities on human rights issues as part of their international obligation to comply with ECtHR judgments (see 7.2.5 regarding mobilization of civil society groups and national human rights institutions as a type of impact). This in turn may help depoliticise the human rights narratives in the domestic contexts, which certain political powers or state institutions may unjustifiably politicise, as the ECtHR judgments offer an authoritative judicial assessment of disputed human rights issues.

7.2.4 *Wider Legal and Policy Impact of ECtHR Judgments*

As strategic litigation is intended to establish or advance the rights of wider communities and societies, along with remedying individual victims, actions taken by the authorities as 'general measures' to prevent similar violations in the future is a highly common expected type of impact in the context of implementation of ECtHR judgments. If adequately enforced, the impact of such judgments may include the adoption of the necessary national laws or amendments to the existing ones; the creation or change of policies; or the establishment of new institutions or the reform of existing ones – described by Garavito as 'direct material effect' and 'instrumental' effect by OSJI.

In the South Caucasus states, this type of impact is observed in some of the researched cases. Some ECtHR judgments have led to the adoption of new legislative acts and incentivised Governments to ensure their adequate implementation. For example, in the *Kiladze* group of cases relating to victims of Soviet repression, following the ECtHR judgment of 2010, the Georgian Government amended the existing Law on Victim Status and Social Protection for Persons subjected to Political Repression of 1997 to allow such victims to

23 Human rights lawyer and CSO representative, AZE02, online interview, 13 July 2019.

seek monetary compensation.[24] The legislative amendments, put into force in two rounds in 2011 and 2014, and scrutinized by the civil society organisations that litigated the case before the ECtHR, have led to the establishment of a compensation mechanism aimed to remedy an estimated 16,000 victims of the Soviet repression in Georgia (see 5.3.2.1 and 7.2.1).

The *Bayatyan* case concerning the absence of alternative service for conscientious objectors in Armenia well demonstrates how ECtHR judgments can incentivize the national authorities to advance their international commitments that require legislative reforms. Although Armenia had committed to ensuring alternative service to conscientious objectors upon its accession to the CoE in 2001, it was only after the respective ECtHR judgment in 2011 that it complied with its obligation to adopt a law on alternative service fully, in line with the European standards in 2013, with the support of the Venice Commission (see 4.2.1.3). The existence of this law and its effective application in practice has put an end to the criminal prosecution of conscientious objectors, particularly members of Jehovah's Witnesses, and established their right to alternative service.

Other researched cases involving legislative initiatives, however, failed to generate positive legislative consequences suggesting that they have had no such *tangible* impact, even indirectly. The implementation process of the *Mahmudov and Agazade* group of cases relating to imprisonment of journalists for defamation in Azerbaijan as a violation of freedom of expression involved what appeared to be collaborative consultations of the authorities with the CM and the Venice Commission with the aim to decriminalize defamation in the country in 2012–2013 (see 3.2.2.3). However, this initially promising process has been stalled with the deepening crisis of the relations between Azerbaijan and the CoE since 2014, which I discuss in Section 3.2.4, leading to no legislative progress for more than a decade since the judgment was adopted in 2008. The initiation of this legislative process may create a future basis for action by a more favourable government, and therefore the impact of such steps by the authorities may only become apparent after a considerable time.

The observed examples of wider material impact of the researched cases concern institutional and policy reforms in law enforcement systems, primarily related to medical care in prisons. The extensive measures taken in the *Ghavtadze* group relating to the structural inadequacy of medical care for

24 Action report of the Georgian Government on the execution of the judgment in the case of *Klaus and Yuri Kiladze v Georgia* (Appl. no. 7975/06), 5 December 2014, 3.

detainees suffering from contagious diseases in Georgian prisons, following the Court's prescriptive order to the authorities to undertake the necessary structural reforms, have led to the elimination of the widespread nature of the contagious diseases such as tuberculosis and hepatitis C (see 5.3.2.1). The measures involved the adoption of a new Prison Code in 2010 setting up the normative framework for detainees' right to health care and a complaints procedure (see 5.3.2.1). The legislative steps followed other reforms in the penitentiary health system on the basis of the European Prison Rules introducing prevention, diagnostics and treatment programmes for tuberculosis and hepatitis C, which both the ECtHR in its subsequent judgments and the CM recognised as substantial improvements (see 5.3.2.1). Several Georgian interviewees suggested that the ECtHR judgment created a framework for a comprehensive action plan on the basis of which the necessary reforms were taken, which led to a significant reduction of such cases (see 5.3.2.1).

Similar developments, although still ongoing, are observed in the Armenian *Ashot Harutyunyan* group of cases that concern the state's denial of adequate medical care to prisoners who suffered from various serious medical conditions (see 4.2.2.1.2). With CoE-EU financial support, the Armenian authorities have initiated numerous reforms to improve the prison health care system both in terms of its efficiency and independence, and the material medical conditions provided to prisoners. This involved the establishment of a new Penitentiary Medicine Centre as an independent medical institution for prisons, the purchase of new medical equipment, and training for medical and non-medical staff of prisons in Armenia (see 4.2.2.1.2). Although this large-scale prison system reform continues under the supervision of the CM and other CoE bodies at the time of writing of this book, significant material impact stemming from the ECtHR judgments in this group on prisoners' health care in Armenia is identifiable. This group of cases is also a significant example of how other CoE bodies or international players such as the EU can step in to enhance the implementation process and help magnify the impact of the ECtHR judgments in the respective domestic contexts (see 4.2.2.1.2).

Some of the researched ECtHR cases relating to effective investigations into ill-treatment and torture allegations by law enforcement agents in custody, a deeply systemic issue common across all three South Caucasus states, have also featured some positive signs of wider positive reforms; however, at a significantly slower pace, with material impact still to be observed. While no significant reforms have been observed in the *Muradova, Mammadov (Jalaloglu) and Mikayil Mammadov* group against Azerbaijan, with new ill-treatment and torture cases being continuously reported by the victims or their lawyers,[25] the Armenian and Georgian cases addressing similar issues have shown some positive progress towards such reforms (see 3.2.3, 4.2.2.1.1 and 5.3.2.1). Although individual investigations into victims' cases in the *Tsintsabadze* group feature multiple deficiencies, the authorities have taken some positive steps as general measures aimed at preventing repetition of similar violations in the future. For example, the government reported to the CM that it had adopted legislation establishing the new State Inspector's Service that has become operational from 1 November 2019 as an independent investigatory mechanism to address ill-treatment and torture complaints against law enforcement agents (see 5.3.2.1, 6.3.4). Although it has taken a long time for this new mechanism to be created and it is still to be seen how effective its operation will be in practice, before real impact can be measured, its establishment following close scrutiny of the CM supervision and regular contributions from civil society organisations and the Public Defenders Office may indicate significant progress towards that wider material impact, if effectively enforced (see 5.3.2.1).

Similarly, in the *Virabyan* group of cases, the Armenian authorities have undertaken several significant legislative reforms, the effectiveness of which remains to be monitored. As part of the implementation process of this group, the Criminal Code was amended to introduce the criminalization of torture in Armenia, as a positive step towards adequately investigating torture allegations by detainees and prisoners. Human rights groups, however, report that many such investigations wrongly conclude that the inflicted harm does not reach the threshold of torture; further, ill-treatment is not qualified as a separate crime in the Armenian legislation, often resulting in charges of abuse of official powers (similarly to the observed practice in Georgian cases discussed see 5.3.2.1) against responsible law enforcement agents (see 6.2.2). Such examples well indicate that it can be difficult to establish a real effect of the ECtHR judgments and verify its credibility, and that the inclusive role that other domestic actors may play in this process is significant. Contributions of the civil society and the national human rights institutions have been significant in these cases (e.g. see 4.3.2, 5.3.2.1 and 5.3.2.3). I also identify their active involvement in the implementation process as another type of non-direct impact of ECtHR judgments below.

25 Ramute Remezaite and Ulkar Aliyeva, 'Council of Europe's old pandemic: 'endemic' ill-treatment and torture in custody in Azerbaijan' (European Implementation Network 23 July 2020), accessed 12 September 2020.

7.2.5 *Mobilization of Civil Society Groups and National Human Rights Institutions*

Across all my chapters analyzing selected states' compliance with ECtHR judgments I discuss the significance of contributions of the civil society and the national human rights institutions (NHRIs) to the process (see 4.3.2, 5.3.2.1 and 5.3.2.3). They can play important roles in monitoring the progress of the measures reported by the domestic authorities to the CM on the ground and providing their 'alternative' assessment as to the effectiveness of such proposed progress. As interested groups representing the public interest, they also provide their own proposals as to what additional reforms are necessary, thus enabling the CM to conduct a more comprehensive assessment of the process. Here, I discuss the active involvement of the civil society and NHRIs in the process as a type of impact that I identify in ECtHR judgments in that it enables the mobilization of these groups towards enhancing human rights protection in their respective countries (similar to what Garavito identifies coalitions of activists as 'indirect material effects'). My research findings suggest that it is thanks to the ECtHR judgments as tools for such mobilization that the civil society groups and NHRIs as domestic human rights monitoring groups are able to either engage with the domestic authorities on these matters directly and/or use the Strasbourg supervision process to do it, as in some instances it is the only platform to engage on pertinent human rights issues. As several interviewed Azerbaijani lawyers and civil society representatives noted, the Strasbourg process is the only way for them to engage in the implementation of ECtHR judgments both on behalf of applicants and with regard to general measures as they have no possibilities to engage with the domestic authorities directly due to the hostile approach towards the civil society as critics of the Government's policies (see 3.2.2.4). No engagement of the Azerbaijani Human Rights Ombudsman Office has been observed, either. In Armenia and Georgia, where the domestic environment is more favourable for the civil society, and where the NHRIs take a more proactive and independent stance on human rights issues, the increase in their contributions has been significant. For example, at the time of interviews with the Armenian actors in 2016, the NHRI representative noted that the institution's work did not include any activities relating to implementation of ECtHR judgments and their limited knowledge in the Strasbourg supervision process was observed, whereas in 2019 and 2020, two substantive submissions have been prepared by the Armenian Human Rights Defender's Office in two leading cases under enhanced supervision.[26]

---

26 Communication from the Human Rights Defender of Armenia (21/01/2019) and Reply from the authorities (01/02/2019) in the case of *Ashot Harutyunyan v. Armenia* (Appl.

In one of these cases, the *Ashot Harutyunyan* group, concerning health care in Armenian prisons, the Defender's Office has taken the opportunity to provide its input on the necessary measures, as a domestic monitoring body, by submitting a detailed report with recommendations to the CM, which the CM relied on in its further calls upon the Government. The CM urged the Government to 'vigorously pursue their plans' and 'draw inspiration from the relevant recommendations of the Committee of Ministers ..., together with the indications of relevant domestic monitoring bodies, in particular the Human Rights Defender of Armenia'.[27] In its response to the submission, the Government of Armenia noted to the CM that 'highly appreciating the role and activities of the Ombudsman in ensuring the rights of the persons deprived of liberty, the Government stand ready to continue the active cooperation established to further elaborate result-oriented measures aimed at addressing the shortcomings identified and increasing the efficiency of domestic capacity for rapid execution of this judgment'.[28]

Some increase in employing ECtHR judgments in their advocacy work is observed among Armenian NGOs, although they remain least active among all three countries in using their right to provide submissions to the CM: among all researched cases, 40% fewer reports to the CM were submitted by the civil society in the Armenian cases compared to Azerbaijani or Georgian cases.[29] When interviewed in 2016, a number of them noted, as a weakness, their very limited focus on implementation following successful litigation before the ECtHR, which they primarily explained in terms of the priority placed on litigation, allocating very little time and resources for implementation work.[30] Since 2016, however, an increase has been observed in NGO submissions to the CM in Armenian cases, as well as in the overall awareness and interest in implementation of ECtHR judgments through various coalition-building initiatives.[31] Although the Armenian authorities appeared to be less receptive to

---

no. 34334/04); Communication from an NHRI (Human Rights Defender's Office Republic of Armenia) (31/01/2020) and Reply from the authorities (11/02/2020) in the *Poghosyan group of cases of v. Armenia* (Appl. no. 44068/07).

27 CM decision in the *Ashot Harutyunyan* group v. Armenia (Appl. no. 34334/04), adopted at the 1302nd meeting, 5–7 December 2017 [2].

28 Communication from the Human Rights Defender of Armenia (21/01/2019) and Reply from the authorities (01/02/2019) in the case of *Ashot Harutyunyan v. Armenia* (Appl. no. 34334/04).

29 HUDOC EXEC database as of 1 January 2022.

30 CSO representative, ARM09, Yerevan, 28 April 2017; CSO representative, ARM10, Yerevan, 27 April 2017; CSO representative, ARM11, Yerevan, 27 April 2017.

31 Communication from the European Association of Jehovah's witnesses (11/06/20) concerning the following judgment in *Aghanyan and others v Armenia* (Appl. no. 58070/

NGO contributions than those of the Human Rights Defender in my researched cases, the increasing use of the Strasbourg process by civil society organisations is significant in growing their role in this process and in pushing the idea of it being an inclusive domestic process (see 4.3.2).

What is also observed in the researched cases is the increased use of ECtHR judgments and the implementation process by the respective groups as *one* of their advocacy tools to complement a range of other methods employed to seek for the domestic change, which is particularly noticeable in Georgia. For example, in the *Tsintsabadze* group, the Georgian civil society employed the Strasbourg supervision process as one of the platforms for engagement with and generating pressure on the authorities, alongside its domestic advocacy through a national coalition of NGOs actively involved in the domestic processes[32] (see 5.3.2.3). Similarly, the Georgian Public Defender's Office provided its input on the issue of investigations into ill-treatment and torture allegations both in its submissions to the CM and its annual reports, presented to the Georgian Parliament and the Georgian public more generally, thereby diversifying its channels of engagement.[33] Such a comprehensive approach towards the various strategies to address the pressing human rights issues help ensure both the national and the CoE monitoring of the authorities' actions and better coherence between the CM's and the civil society responses to such actions.

---

12); Communication from a NGO (EHRAC) (02/11/2016) in the cases of *Chiragov v Armenia* (Appl. no. 13216/05) and Sargsyan against Azerbaijan (Appl. no. 40167/06); Communication from an NGO (Open Society Foundations – Armenia) (21/04/2020) in the case of *Mushegh Saghatelyan v. Armenia* (Appl. no. 23086/08) and response from the authorities (05/05/2020); Communication from an NHRI (Human Rights Defender's Office Republic of Armenia) (31/01/2020) and Reply from the authorities (11/02/2020) in the *Poghosyan* group of cases of v Armenia (Appl. no. 44068/07); Communication from NGOs: Open Society Foundations-Armenia, Protection of Rights without Borders NGO, Helsinki Citizens Assembly of Vanadzor, Transparency International Anticorruption Center and Law Development and Protection Foundation (17/06/2020) and Response from the Armenian authorities (25/06/2020) in the case of *Vardanyan and Nanushyan v Armenia* (Appl. no. 8001/07); CSO representative, ARM10, Yerevan, 27 April 2017; European Implementation Network, 'EIN trains Armenian civil society actors in tackling implementation challenges' (12 March 2020), accessed 20 July 2020.

32 CSO representative, GEO08, Tbilisi, online interview, 12 December 2016.

33 Communication of the Public Defender of Georgia to the Committee of Ministers in the *Gharibashvili* group of cases, 28 November 2016; Communication from a NHRI (Public Defender of Georgia) (19/08/2019) in the cases of *Tsartsidze and Others, Begheluri and Others, Members of the Gldani Congregation of Jehovah's Witnesses and Others* and *Identoba and Others group of cases v.* v. *Georgia* (Appl. no. 18766/04, 28490/02, 71156/01, 73235/12), 19 August 2019; 2018 Annual report of the Public Defender of Georgia, accessed 29 September 2019.

In cases where the Strasbourg supervision process is the only platform to engage with the authorities, indirectly, as is the case with Azerbaijan, civil society has been increasingly active in employing this avenue for its advocacy purposes. For example, in the case of all the researched Azerbaijani groups of cases, at least two submissions have been made by the civil society in each group, regardless of the type of classification or supervision by the CM, in contrast to the Armenian and Georgian cases, where not all cases were addressed by the NGOs as of 1 January 2022.[34] One of the reasons explaining this disparity may be related to Azerbaijani civil society organisations' conscious direction of its resources and efforts towards communication with the CM in light of their inability to effectively engage with the domestic authorities. As one litigating NGO representative from Azerbaijan put it, 'we always project our implementation work to be focused on Strasbourg and plan our projects and the related fundraising accordingly, so that when we have a successful judgment in place, we can start our follow up work right away'.[35] Another interviewed Azerbaijani lawyer suggested that their Strasbourg-oriented implementation work is also significantly supported by their international partner NGOs, who 'help them prepare the systematic and good quality submissions' to the CM to assist the CM review process, which is 'invaluable given the dire civil society environment we are operating in, which also affects our ability to work'.[36] The civil society contributions are all the more invaluable as an alternative resource of information for the CM, given the growing difficulties that the CM faces in communicating with the Azerbaijani authorities (discussed in 3.2.3), and the absence of any involvement by the Azerbaijani Human Rights Ombudsman as a domestic monitoring body.

Such non-material impact of strategic litigation resulting in ECtHR judgments that I identify in my research incentivizes the civil society and NHRIS (except for Azerbaijan) to engage with the international commitments of their respective states and take an active role in upholding it domestically. I further suggest that as a result of such non-material effects of ECtHR judgments on the civil society, further impact is likely to be generated as a consequence of their growing involvement in using legal tools in societies of democratizing

34 According to the HUDOC EXEC database, as of 1 June 2020, five NGO submissions have been made in the *Mahmudov and Agazade* group, five in the *Ilgar Mammadov* group, three in the *Sargsyan* case, two in the *Muradova, Mammadov (Jalaloglu) and Mikayil Mammadov* group, and two in the *Ramazanova and Others* group of cases.

35 Human rights lawyer and CSO representative, AZE02, online interview, 13 July 2019.

36 Human rights lawyer, AZE03, Tbilisi, 11 March 2018.

or authoritarian states, which Sikkink recognizes as impact from bottom up.[37] Leach further suggests that establishing a greater role for civil society organisations may be among the innovative tactics to enhance international human rights mechanisms, which, however, necessitates collaboration: 'we need even stronger domestic movements that engage both at the domestic level and internationally'.[38]

7.3 Conclusion

In conclusion, ECtHR judgments can have multiple effects, both as a result of measures directly stemming from the text of the judgments and/or through the CM prescriptions, and the indirect impact identifiable through in-depth empirical studies into domestic contexts. My research proposes expanding the concept of impact that ECtHR judgments may have beyond that deriving from implementation of individual and general measures, as it would allow revealing different levels of effect that the judgments have on the domestic level. It is particularly significant in cases of states in transition, such as the South Caucasus states, where ECtHR judgments do not only aim to put an end to the violations identified by the Court but may have a broader impact in bringing about change and socialising states towards domesticating the Convention standards and practices.

Building on the existing typology of impact of human rights judgments offered by Garavito and OSJI, my research further expands the concept of impact by putting particular emphasis on the 'moral' dimension of such effects. The analysis of the empirical evidence from the South Caucasus states suggests that ECtHR judgments can have strong moral impact on applicants as victims of human rights violations, including in cases where judgments are not yet implemented. International adjudication of human rights abuses from transitional democracies or systems with strong authoritarian policies offer the recognition of violated rights and the suffering of the victims that they are denied in the domestic contexts. Such an exposure of injustice by an authoritative international court, particularly in cases where states act in 'bad faith' as human rights abusers, is significant to victims along the material remedies,

37 Kathryn Sikkink, *Evidence for Hope, Making Human Rights Work in the 21st Century* (Princeton University Press, 2017), Chapter 5.

38 Philip Leach, 'The Continuing Utility of International Human Rights Mechanisms?' (EJIL:Talk! Blog of the European Journal of International Law 1 November 2017), accessed 2 September 2020.

offering them a sense of justice. This in turn reiterates the importance of the debate about the ECtHR's remedial policies as the declaratory relief evidently has value to victims. Along the moral value, my focus on individual measures, which Garavito omits in his typology, stemming from ECtHR judgments and the CM supervision process offers a comprehensive overview of types of impact on individual victims.

Along the identification of impact of general measures as direct effects, empirical studies in my research suggest the wider indirect impact on the affected societies. Among those is the finding that ECtHR judgments inspire and empower local human rights groups to amplify their efforts to seek for change, or serve as an effective lever for change, either on its own or when combined with other advocacy tools.

Finally, my research suggests strong value of putting an emphasis on the whole CoE process when researching impact of ECtHR judgments, from ECtHR findings to the CM and DEJ supervision process to the involvement of the domestic actors, such as the civil society and NHRIs. The impact of the judgments in all three South Caucasus states results from the entire process of the CoE. Such analysis of the impact of ECtHR judgments in its broader meaning contributes to a better understanding of the wider effect of the Convention's objective to harmonise human rights standards across the region and can assist in developing new, much needed responses to the growing challenges of commitment, dedication and effectiveness that the CoE faces.

CHAPTER 8

Conclusions

This book has analysed the compliance behaviour of the South Caucasus states in response to the growing need to understand and address the existing challenges in respect of their non-compliance or only partial compliance with judgments of the European Court of Human Rights (ECtHR), as part of the wider 'implementation crisis' in the Council of Europe (CoE). As such challenges deepened with the accession of the former Soviet Union states to the CoE, it is of importance to conduct qualitative research into the particular contexts of these states as to *why* and *how*, under what conditions they implement ECtHR judgments. The relevance of this research to addressing this problem lies in the discussion of the compliance performance of Armenia and Georgia as democratising states, and Azerbaijan as an increasingly authoritarian state, as well as the elucidation of the underlying reasons why they may sometimes implement judgments in a full and timely way and at other times, slowly, minimally or not at all. This research is state-level and case-level focused and sheds the light on the influence of the particular state contexts and cases, as well as common regional perspectives as the three states share a number of comparable variables.

This research into compliance with ECtHR judgments in the selected states is conducted on the premise that they were all accepted into the CoE with a *promise* to abide by the norms of the European Convention on Human Rights (ECHR) as they emerged as independent states with weak legal and political systems, poor human rights records and low respect for rule of law and democratic principles, with the mutual idea that the CoE would steer them towards democratisation. In this context, the ECtHR's individual petition system became an important support mechanism to building human rights respecting systems in these states. The analysis finds that the Court's influence varies across the countries, and between judgments concerning the same country, and is highly dependent on the political will of the domestic authorities, i.e. their commitment to undertake necessary actions, as well as their domestic capacities to implement judgments. More importantly, it provides some answers as to why this is the case in the particular domestic contexts.

The synergy of two prevailing compliance theories, constructivism and rational choice, on which I based my hypothesis, finds support, although to different extent, in all three domestic contexts. Many researched case examples suggest that constructivism alone, focusing on the way in which international

 | DOI:10.1163/9789004538214_009

law 'socialises' states by exposure to and interaction with human rights norms and institutions, would not find a strong basis in the South Caucasus states' compliance performance. The authorities are often driven by the various domestic interests, preferences and incentives that the rational choice theory relies on, to comply, or rather to not comply in full, timely and effective manner. It is therefore the synergy of the two theories that best explain the states' variable implementation of ECtHR judgments and engagement with the Strasbourg process, as summarised below.

In Azerbaijan, where the compliance rate with ECtHR judgments is the lowest in the whole CoE region, and which increasingly displays authoritarian policies, ECtHR judgments are primarily a reflection of the dire human rights situation and have had very little tangible systemic impact on the ground. For these judgments to act as catalysts for structural systemic domestic change, and foster the establishment of human rights respecting system, would require a more favourable domestic political environment, as opposed to Azerbaijan' present authoritarian organization of the state. The case-level research finds that every analysed ECtHR judgment requiring adoption of both individual and general measures to address complex systemic human rights issues is perceived by the regime as endangering the domestic interests of the state's long-term authoritarian regime, regardless of the nature of the issue addressed by the ECtHR. Cases relating to the ruling authorities' critics, those exposing the very absence of the effective functioning of the state systems and institutions or related to violations stemming from the Nagorno Karabakh conflict with Armenia are perceived to be particularly salient and politically sensitive. The findings offer the pessimistic conclusion that although some socialisation with the international norms and procedures is observed, ECtHR judgments generate very little, if any, tangible domestic change. This is due to the absence of any genuine human rights conducive culture in the domestic politics, on the basis of which ECtHR judgments could generate that change; quite the opposite, judgments often run counter to domestic interests and preferences of the ruling power, which in turn flouts its ECHR obligations, in bad faith, as illustrated by the growing number of 'Article 18' cases (see 3.2.3 and 3.2.4 for the analysis of the *Ilgar Mamma*dov group of cases concerning arrest and detention of a number of human rights defenders, journalists and political activists).

In Georgia, however, which underwent its peaceful democratic change of power back in 2003, a few years after its accession to the CoE, the ECtHR has become a significant anchor in advancing the state's democratisation efforts. Known as a comparatively good case in the South Caucasus, Georgia's compliance performance is notable in that a number of ECtHR judgments have led to significant domestic reforms ensuring necessary legal and policy changes that in turn benefit wider groups of the society. Such reforms did not, however, materialise as a result of political willingness of the authorities alone: it often was possible due to the active and consistent involvement of other domestic actors, such as civil society organisations or the national human rights institution, with the programmatic and financial support of CoE bodies, including the European Committee for the Prevention of Torture and Inhuman and Degrading Treatment or Punishment (CPT) and Departments coordinating the implementation of the CoE-Georgia action plans (see, for example, the *Tsintsabadze* group for the involvement of the civil society and the Public Defender's Office, and the *Ghavtadze* group for measures taken to improve health care in prisons with the financial and programmatic support of the CoE). Other cases created the necessary platform for such advocacy where the domestic authorities were short of sufficient willingness to take initiatives due to certain domestic interests and preferences. Finally, some instances of politicized implementation of certain cases demonstrate the importance of the socialising effect of the Strasbourg processes as a way of dispelling the passivity or reluctance of the domestic authorities to take actions.

Armenia, which only recently underwent a peaceful democratic change of power in 2018, following long years of semi-authoritarian regime since its independence from the Soviet Union, is now seen with high expectations by the international community, including the CoE. The compliance performance of the pre-2018 Armenian authorities is marked by a rather stable and systemic engagement with the Strasbourg supervision process, conducive to the socialising effect of the Convention system. The translation of ECtHR judgments into actual tangible change is, however, largely dependent on the existence of political commitment, which is often insufficient, systemic follow up of the Strasbourg process and the participation of domestic actors, such as the civil society organisations and the national human rights institution, as well as CoE bodies, similarly to the case of Georgia above.

Below, I summarise some of the factors that the research has identified as supporting or hindering compliance with ECtHR judgments in the South Caucasus states.

Multiple factors explain the selected states' behaviour, whether enhancing or obstructing compliance with ECtHR judgments. These findings offer opportunities to both the CoE bodies, primarily the Committee of Ministers (CM) and the Department for Execution of Judgments of the European Court of Human Rights (DEJ), and the domestic actors (the Government, the national parliament, courts, national human rights institutions, civil society organisations) to explore ideas for the most optimal solutions to the challenging compliance situation. The factors vary in their nature and include political, social, financial and societal aspects. Existence of political will as a significant factor is understood as commitment by the responsible state authorities to undertake actions, or create the necessary environment for such actions to be taken by delegated institutions, and vary from insufficient political willingness to passivity to contestation. Some general measures requiring extensive resources, such as prison health care reforms in the *Ashot Harutyunyan* group of cases, have led to minimalistic and dilatory compliance due to the heavy financial burden on the state. Cases addressing human rights issues with strong societal opinions, such as LGBTI rights in the *Identoba and Others* case in Georgia or the rights of conscientious objectors in the *Bayatyan* case in Armenia, have faced compliance challenges due to the confrontation of these groups with traditional values or other deeply entrenched societal views, or pervasive discrimination of certain groups of the society.

Among the factors that enhance compliance is political willingness, largely predetermined by absence of any triggers that would obstruct domestic interests of certain political or institutional powers, as was the case in the *Ghavtadze* group of cases, for example. In such instances, the systematic scrutiny and involvement of the civil society organisations and national human rights institutions have proved significant to ensuring *full* and *effective* compliance in some of these cases (recall the Klaus and Yuri Kiladze case). The empirical research also suggests that the prescription of measures by the ECtHR in these two Georgian cases has played a positive role in enhancing compliance as 'it was sufficiently clear' to the authorities what was necessary in order to comply. In cases where political commitment was sufficient and compliance related largely to capacities and/or resources, the already mentioned programmatic and financial support by the CoE has been significant in fostering adoption of the necessary measures, along the CM supervision process (recall the *Ashot Harutyunyan* group of cases). The research strongly suggests that successful implementation as a process in the South Caucasus states is not an organic continuation of ECtHR judgments and requires systematic 'support' by both domestic actors and the various CoE bodies.

In all three states, the domestic implementation systems fall short of serving as effective means of institutionalizing and enhancing domestic efforts and preventing, or reducing, the politicization of implementation processes, thereby hindering full effective compliance. Problems vary from the complete absence of any such system, as is the case in Azerbaijan, where no information is available as to how judgments are being implemented domestically, to gradual but slow development of domestic systems in Armenia and Georgia. In these states, however, full efficacy is yet to be achieved since the relevant domestic bodies and actors are not effectively included in domestic implementation processes.

For example, in 2016, a procedure for oversight of implementation of judgments of international mechanisms was established entitling the Georgian parliament with a mandate to scrutinize the Government's actions on a yearly basis. It has not, however, been effectively and actively used by the Georgian parliamentarians and the annual deliberations held in the previous years did not involve the responsible executive institutions other than the Ministry of Justice to enable a constructive substantive discussion. The involvement of civil society organisations in Armenia and Georgia is limited to their ad hoc informal initiatives, diminishing their role of public scrutiny to the minimum. In Azerbaijan, civil society organisations have no possibility to engage with the authorities directly, therefore relying primarily on the Strasbourg process in their attempts to enhance implementation of ECtHR judgments.

The CM supervision mechanism plays a significant role in compliance with ECtHR judgments in the three countries. Although the three states' engagement with the formal CM rules and regulations, such as timely provision of action plans and reports, vary significantly, there is strong evidence of the socialisation effect of the CM procedures in all three states, but only where the CM involvement is under the more rigorous 'enhanced' category. In other words, the standard supervision conducted by the DEJ, consisting of expert lawyers, is usually not sufficient to motivate the domestic authorities in the South Caucasus to act as diligent compliers. The research finds that the more regular and frequent the CM follow up is, the more engaged the authorities are and the more likely they are to comply, even if minimally. This tendency is particularly noticeable in the cases of Armenia and Georgia, but is also evident to a lesser extent in Azerbaijan (recall the *Ashot Harutyunyan* group of cases concerning health care in Armenia's prisons discussed in 4.3.1 or the *Identoba and Others* case relating to homophobic violence and a failure to effectively investigate, discussed in 5.3.1). Endorsing the constructivism theory, this finding suggests that regular, formal and public attention on cases from the CM, along with the day-to-day work of the DEJ, is likely to ensure more regular continuous reporting by states, and, in that way, their better socialisation with the Strasbourg norms and procedures. Such increased focus varies from the common CM actions, such as the inclusion of cases on the CM agenda for its quarterly human rights meetings, to debates by CM delegations, followed by formal CM decisions, with recommendations, to less frequently used, such as the discussions at every regular CM meeting (beyond human rights meetings) and submission of specific case related questions to the authorities, to initiation of infringement proceedings as the most rarely used action. The research further finds, however, that such socialisation with the Strasbourg process does not guarantee the achievement of tangible change on the ground; as noted above, other domestic factors come into play, the discussion of which is fundamental to understanding the domestic contexts and the challenges underpinning compliance performance.

This analysis into factors affecting the domestic implementation processes in the South Caucasus states contributes to the literature on compliance with ECtHR judgments in states on a spectrum of democratisation varying from democratising to increasingly authoritarian states, as those that feature less in compliance studies than democratic states. The focus on case level implementation not only helps explain the particularities of the domestic contexts within which ECtHR judgments are being implemented, but also adds to the growing literature on the degree to which, and under what conditions, new democracies of the CoE comply with human rights judgments, and become socialized to international human rights norms and institutions. Although the book's methodological approach combine desk research and empirical studies into the domestic contexts of the South Caucasus states, the empirical evidence is of particular importance to understand the states' motivations and the incentives behind their compliance-related actions that may not otherwise be available.

In light of these findings, the book concludes that ECtHR judgments are often partially complied with in the South Caucasus states, often identified in the forms of minimalistic, dilatory and/or contested compliance, rather than followed by full compliance or non-compliance. For example, to remedy the victims of violence by state agents, the measures were limited to monetary compensations, without any effectively conducted investigations in the *Virabyan* case in Armenia, *Identoba and Others* case in Georgia and in the *Muradova, Mammadov (Jalaloglu) and Mikayil Mammadov* group in Azerbaijan. The analysis of the *Ilgar Mammadov* case, where the infringement proceedings were initiated by the CM, and the twin cases of *Sargsyan v Azerbaijan* and *Chiragov and Others v Armenia* in which the two Governments have taken no actions strongly indicate their contestation over the necessary measures. It is no longer sufficient to see compliance as a dichotomous concept on the premise that domestic systems generally accept and socialise with international law, and the partial compliance in its various forms should be seen as a middle ground in the study of compliance, both by academia and the CoE system. Building on the earlier research of Hawkins and Jacoby, the book aims to revive and advance the so far limited scholarly debate on the concept of partial compliance in the context of international human rights law, and ECtHR human rights judgments, as my research suggests the increasing relevance of this concept in the selected states as states on a spectrum of democratisation. The environment in which such states operate, and which predetermine compliance performance, is rather unique, and needs to be taken into consideration when assessing their compliance efforts, and the underlying problems. The book proposes three forms of partial compliance, minimalistic, dilatory and contested compliance, offering some methodological considerations to establish this phenomenon. The idea of contested compliance is particularly novel, as a new form of partial compliance, in light of growing instances of 'bad faith' behaviour by CoE member states, including Azerbaijan and Georgia, among others.

The empirical studies into particular domestic contexts allows for a discussion of particular factors that explain why partial compliance is likely. The study establishes that the likelihood of partial compliance is predetermined by the complexity of human rights issues addressed by the ECtHR in its judgments against the South Caucasus states, often stemming from the Soviet heritage; the domestic political climate where international reputation is often compromised by domestic interests; and the absence of effective domestic infrastructure that would institutionalise and depoliticise implementation of human rights judgments in these domestic contexts.

Finally, in light of this context, it is particularly significant to study and discuss the wider impact of ECtHR judgments in the selected states, beyond (partial) compliance, and my empirical research offers strong evidence for this phenomenon in the South Caucasus states. The book's discussion of impact is focused on identifying any positive effect that judgments have had in the selected domestic contexts, and goes beyond the measures formally supervised through the CM processes. The research finds that such impact varies in its beneficiaries, from individual victims directly affected by violations, to similarly situated social groups to wider society. Building on the growing academic (see Garavito) and the CoE interest of the conceptualisation of the impact of international human rights judgments in the recent years, the book proposes forms of impact that consolidate both the victim oriented and the wider societal approach, and incorporate both direct and indirect, and material and moral types of impact, to which my empirical research offers strong evidence in the South Caucasus states. For example, a number of analysed ECtHR judgments has enabled and encouraged the national human rights institutions to engage in addressing certain human rights issues domestically, such as in the *Tsintsabadze* group of cases in Georgia or the *Ashot Harutyunyan* group in Armenia, where only a few years ago their reliance on ECtHR judgments in their work was non-existent.

The research findings put particular focus on the 'moral' impact of ECtHR judgments on applicants as victims of human rights violations, including in cases where judgments are not yet implemented. The judgments offer the recognition of violated rights and the suffering of the victims denied by transitional democracies or systems with strong authoritarian policies (recall the *Ilgar Mammadov* group of cases relating to criminal persecution of human rights defenders and other Government critics in Azerbaijan with the aim to punish them and criminalise their activities in the eyes of the public). This in turn reinforces the importance of the debate about the ECtHR's remedial policies as declaratory relief evidently has value to victims. Along with the moral value, my focus on individual measures, stemming from ECtHR judgments and the CM supervision process, which Garavito omits from his typology, offers a comprehensive overview of types of impact on individual victims.

On this basis, the book proposes to expand the concept of the impact that ECtHR judgments may have beyond that deriving from implementation of individual and general measures, as it allows us to reveal the different levels of effect that the judgments have on the domestic level. This is particularly relevant in cases of states in transition, where compliance with ECtHR judgments is not always obvious or easy to grasp. Such 'expanded' analysis of the impact of ECtHR judgments, stemming from the entire process of the CoE, from the ECtHR judgments to CM supervision, to the involvement and enabling of the civil society, will contribute to a better understanding of the wider implementation problem in the CoE and assist in developing new, much needed responses to it.

Appendix

List of Interviews

1. Former Government representative to CoE, AZE01, online interview, 14 August 2019
2. Human rights lawyer and CSO representative, AZE02, online interview, 27 March 2018 and 13 July 2019
3. Human rights lawyer, AZE03, Tbilisi, 11 March 2018
4. Human rights lawyer, AZE04, Tbilisi, 11 March 2018
5. Human rights lawyer and CSO representative, AZE05, online interview, 16 March 2018
6. Applicant and CSO representative, AZE06, Brussels, 12 December 2018
7. Applicant, AZE07, online interview, 17 September 2019
8. Applicant, AZE08, email communication, 13 September 2019 and 26 February 2020
9. Governmental Official, ARM01, Strasbourg, 23 May 2017
10. Government Official, ARM02, email communication, 12 May 2020
11. Armenian MP, ARM03, Yerevan, 28 April 2017
12. NHRI representative, ARM04, Yerevan, 27 April 2017
13. Lawyer, ARM05, Yerevan, 28 April 2017
14. Lawyer, ARM06, Yerevan, 28 April 2017
15. Lawyer, ARM07, Yerevan, 28 April 2017
16. Lawyer, ARM08, online interview, 13 June 2017
17. CSO representative, ARM09, Yerevan, 28 April 2017
18. CSO representative, ARM10, Yerevan, 27 April 2017
19. CSO representative, ARM11, Yerevan, 27 April 2017
20. CSO representative, ARM12, email communication, 9 September 2020
21. Governmental Official, GEO01, Strasbourg, 30 March 2018
22. Former Governmental Official and former human rights lawyer, GEO02, Tbilisi, 15 September 2015
23. Former Governmental Official and former human rights lawyer, GEO03, online interview, 15 October 2016
24. Governmental Official, GEO04, Tbilisi, 15 September 2015
25. Governmental Official and former human rights lawyer, GEO04, Tbilisi, 17 September 2015
26. Georgian MP, GEO05, Tbilisi, 16 September 2015
27. Judge of Georgian Constitutional Court, GEO06, Tbilisi, 9 December 2016
28. NHRI representative, GEO07, Tbilisi, 16 September 2015
29. CSO representative, GEO08, Tbilisi, online interview, 12 December 2016
30. CSO representative, GEO09, Tbilisi, online interview, 15 November 2016

 DOI:10.1163/9789004538214_010

31. CM member state representative, SXB01, Strasbourg, 23 May 2017
32. CM member state representative, SXB02, Strasbourg, 23 May 2017
33. CM member state representative, SXB03, Strasbourg, 23 May 2017
34. DEJ official, SXB04, Strasbourg, 30 November 2016
35. DEJ official, SXB05, Strasbourg, 30 November 2016
36. ECtHR representative, SXB06, Strasbourg, 4 September 2017
37. ECtHR representative, SXB07, Strasbourg, 28 November 2016
38. Former PACE Secretariat member, SXB08, Strasbourg, 2 December 2016
39. Representative of Office of the CoE Commissioner for Human Rights, SXB09, Strasbourg, 4 April 2019
40. CSO representative, SXB10, London, 23 November 2016

Bibliography

Primary Sources

Treaties

Convention for the Protection of Human Rights and Fundamental Freedoms (1950).

Protocol No. 14 to the Convention for the Protection of Human Rights and Fundamental Freedoms, amending the Control System of the Convention, CETS No. 194 (2010).

Judgments and other Documents of the European Court of Human Rights

Judgments v Armenia

Ashot Harutyunyan v Armenia, Appl. no. 34334/04 (ECtHR 15 June 2010).

Bayatyan v Armenia, Appl. no. 23459/03 (ECtHR 7 July 2011).

Chiragov and Others v. Armenia, App. no. 13216/05 (ECtHR 15 June 2015).

Davtyan v Armenia, Appl. no. 29736/06 (ECtHR 30 June 2015).

Mkrtchyan v Armenia, Appl. no. 6562/03 (ECtHR 11 January 2007).

Piruzyan v Armenia, Appl. no. 33376/07 (ECtHR 26 September 2012).

Virabyan v Armenia, Appl. no. 40094/05 (ECtHR 2 October 2012).

Judgments v Azerbaijan

Aliyev v Azerbaijan, Appl. nos. 68762/14 and 71200/14 (ECtHR 20 September 2018).

Anar Mammadli v Azerbaijan, Appl. no. 47145/14 (ECtHR 19 April 2018).

Gafgaz Mammadov v Azerbaijan, Appl. no. 60259/11 (ECtHR 14 March 2016).

Humadov v Azerbaijan, Appl. no. 13652/06 (ECtHR 3 March 2010).

Huseyn and Others v Azerbaijan, Appl. no. 35485/05 (ECtHR 26 October 2011).

Ibrahimov and Mammadov v Azerbaijan, Appl. No. 63571/16 (ECtHR 13 February 2020).

Ilgar Mammadov v Azerbaijan, appl. no. 15172/13 (ECtHR 22 May 2014).

Ilgar Mammadov v Azerbaijan, Appl. no. 15172/13 (ECtHR 29 May 2019).

Insanov v Azerbaijan, Appl. no. 16133/08 (ECtHR 14 June 2013).

Jannatov v Azerbaijan, Appl. no. 32132/07 (ECtHR 31 October 2014).

Khadija Ismayilova v Azerbaijan (No.2), Appl. no. 30778/15 (ECtHR 27 February 2020).

Layijov v Azerbaijan, Appl. no. 22062/07 (ECtHR 10 July 2014).

Mirzayev v Azerbaijan, Appl. No. 50187/06 (ECtHR 3 March 2010).

Namat Aliyev v Azerbaijan, Appl. No. 18705/06, (ECtHR 8 July 2010).

Natig Jafarov v Azerbaijan, Appl. no. 64581/16 (ECtHR 7 November 2019).

Rashad Hasanov and Others v Azerbaijan, Appl. nos. 48653/13 (ECtHR 7 June 2018).

Rasul Jafarov v Azerbaijan, Appl. no. 69981/14 (ECtHR 17 March 2016).

Religious community of Jehovah's Witnesses v Azerbaijan, Appl. no. 52884/09 (ECtHR 20 February 2020).
Sargsyan v. Azerbaijan, App. no. 40167/06 (ECtHR 15 June 2015).
Tarverdiyev v Azerbaijan, Appl. no. 33343/03 (ECtHR 26 October 2007).
Yunusova and Yunusov v Azerbaijan (No. 2), Appl. No. 68817/14 (ECtHR 16 July 2020).

Judgments v Georgia

97 members of the Gldani Congregation of Jehovah's Witnesses and 4 Others v. Georgia, Appl. no. 71156/01 (ECtHR 3 May 2007).
Assanidze v. Georgia [GC], Appl. no. 71503/01, § 202, ECHR 2004-II.
Baghashvili v Georgia, Appl. no. 5168/06 (ECtHR 18 March 2014).
Davit Chantladze v Georgia, Appl. no. 60864/10 (ECtHR 30 June 2015).
Dvalishvili v Georgia, Appl. no. 19634/07 (ECtHR 18 March 2013).
Emzar Kopadze v Georgia, Appl. no. 58228/09 (ECtHR 10 March 2015).
Enukidze and Girgvliani v Georgia, Appl. no. 25091/07 (ECtHR 27 July 2011).
Gharibashvili v Georgia, Appl. no. 11830/03 (ECtHR 29 October 2008).
Ghavtadze v. Georgia, Appl. no. 23204/07 (ECtHR 30 March 2009).
Giorgi Bekauri and Others v Georgia, Appl. no. 312/10 (ECtHR 15 September 2015).
Goginashvili v Georgia, Appl. no. 47729/08 (ECtHR 4 October 2011).
Gorelishvili v Georgia, Appl.no. 12979/04 (ECtHR 5 June 2007).
Identoba and Others v Georgia, Appl. no. 73235/12 (ECtHR 12 May 2015).
Ildani v. Georgia, Appl. no. 65391/09 (ECtHR 23 April 2013).
Irakli Mindadze v. Georgia, Appl. no. 17012/09, (ECtHR 11 December 2012).
Jeladze v. Georgia, Appl. no. 1871/08 (ECtHR18 December 2012).
Jugheli and Others v Georgia, Appl. no. 38342/05 (ECtHR 13 October 2017).
Kartvelishvili v Georgia, Appl. no. 177116/08 (ECtHR 7 September 2018).
Khaindrava and Dzamashvili v Georgia, Appl. no. 18183/05 (ECtHR 08 September 2010).
Klaus and Yuri Kiladze v Georgia, Appl.no. 7975/06 (ECtHR 2 February 2010).
Makharadze and Sikharulidze v. Georgia, Appl. no. 35254/07 (ECtHR 22 November 2011).
Malkhaz Mzekalishvili v Georgia, Appl. no. 8177/12 (ECtHR 10 February 2015).
Mikiashvili v Georgia, Appl. no. 18996/06 (ECtHR 09 January 2013).
Pandjikidze and Others v Georgia, Appl. no. 30323/02 (ECtHR 27 October 2009).
Poghosyan v. Georgia, Appl. no. 9870/07 (ECtHR 24 February 2009).
Ramin Kirizia v Georgia, Appl. No. 4728/08 (ECtHR 11 March 2014).
Sarishvili-Bolkvadze v Georgia, Appl. no. 58240/08 (ECtHR 19 October 2018).
Studio Maestro Ltd and Others v Georgia, Appl. no. 22318/10 (ECtHR 30 June 2015).
Sulkhan Molashvili v Georgia, Appl. no. 39726/04 (ECtHR 30 September 2014).
Tsintsabadze v Georgia, Appl. no. 35403/06 (ECtHR 18 March 2011).
Vazha Gegenava and Others v Georgia, Appl. no. 65128/10 (ECtHR 20 October 2015).

Other Judgments

Broniowski v. Poland [GC], Appl. no. 31443/96, § 194, ECHR 2004-V.

Jehovah's Witnesses of Moscow and Others v Russia, Appl. no. 302/02 (ECtHR 10 June 2010).

Öcalan v. Turkey [GC], Appl. no. 46221/99 ECHR 2005-IV.

Religious Community of Jehovah's Witnesses of Kryvyi Rih's Ternivsky District v. Ukraine Appl. no. 21477/10 (ECtHR 3 September 2019).

Scozzari and Giunta v. Italy [GC], Appl. nos. 39221/98 and 41963/98 ECHR 2000-VIII.

Other Court Documents

European Court of Human Rights Analysis of Statistics 2018.

European Court of Human Rights Analysis of statistics 2019.

European Court of Human Rights Annual Report 2002.

European Court of Human Rights Annual report 2004.

European Court of Human Rights Annual report 2008.

European Court of Human Rights Annual report 2009.

European Court of Human Rights Annual Report 2010.

European Court of Human Rights Annual report 2018.

European Court of Human Rights Annual Report 2019.

European Court of Human Rights Overview of 1959–2019.

Q&A on the European Court of Human Rights award of 'just satisfaction' (ECtHR Press Service 26 March 2019).

Documents of the Committee of Ministers of the Council of Europe

Country Factsheets

Armenia Country Factsheet, Department for Execution of Judgments of the European Court of Human Rights, 5 June 2020.

Azerbaijan Country factsheet, Department for the Execution of Judgments of the European Court of Human Rights, 5 June 2020.

Georgia Country Factsheet, Department for the Execution of Judgments of the European Court of Human Rights, 5 June 2020.

Declarations

Brussels Declaration, High-level Conference on the "Implementation of the European Convention on Human Rights, our shared responsibility" (Brussels 27 March 2015).

Copenhagen Declaration, High Level Conference (Copenhagen 12–13 April 2018).

Decisions and Resolutions

Armenia

CM decision in the *Ashot Harutyunyan* group v. Armenia (Appl. no. 34334/04), 8–10 March 2016.

CM decision in the *Ashot Harutyunyan* group v. Armenia (Appl. no. 34334/04), 5–7 December 2017.

CM decision in the case of *Chiragov and Others v Armenia* (Appl. no. 13216/05), 7–10 March 2017.

CM decision in the *Virabyan* group of cases (Appl. no. 40094/05), 6–8 December 2016.

CM decision in the *Virabyan* group of cases (Appl. no. 40094/05), 7 June 2018.

CM decision in the *Virabyan* group of cases (Appl. no. 40094/05), 3–5 March 2020.

Azerbaijan

CM Final Resolution in the case of *Akimova v Azerbaijan* (Appl. No. 19853/03), 4 April 2019.

CM decision in the *Namat Aliyev* group of cases (Appl. No. 18705/06), 3–5 December 2019.

CM Resolution in the case of *Jafarli and Others v Azerbaijan* (Appl. No. 36079/06), 8 March 2012.

CM decision in the case of *Klaus and Yuri Kiladze v Georgia* (Appl. no. 35877/04), 8–10 March 2011.

CM decision in the case of *Klaus and Yuri Kiladze v Georgia* (Appl. no. 35877/04), 7–8 June 2011.

CM Final Resolution in the case of *Klaus and Yuri Kiladze v Georgia* (Appl. no. 35877/04), 11 March 2015.

CM decision in the *Mahmudov and Agazade* group v Azerbaijan (Appl. no. 35877/04), 6 March 2014.

CM decision in the *Mahmudov and Agazade* group v Azerbaijan (Appl. no. 35877/04), 4 December 2014.

CM decision in the *Mahmudov and Agazade* group v Azerbaijan (Appl. no. 35877/04), 24 September 2015.

CM decision in the *Mahmudov and Agazade* group v Azerbaijan (Appl. no. 35877/04), 8–10 March 2016.

CM decision in the *Mahmudov and Agazade* group v Azerbaijan (Appl. no. 35877/04), 6–8 December 2016.

CM Interim Resolution in the *Mahmudov and Agazade* group v Azerbaijan (Appl. no. 35877/04), 8 June 2016.

CM decision in the *Mahmudov and Agazade* group v Azerbaijan (Appl. no. 35877/04), 19–21 September 2017.

CM decision in the *Mahmudov and Agazade* group v Azerbaijan (Appl. no. 35877/04), 7 June 2018.

CM decision in the case of *Ilgar Mammadov* group of cases (Appl. no. 15172/13), 10 March 2017.

CM Interim Resolution in the case of *Ilgar Mammadov v Azerbaijan* (Appl. no. 15172/13), 8 June 2016.

CM decision in the *Ilgar Mammadov* group v Azerbaijan (Appl. no. 15172/13), 7 March 2017.

CM Interim Resolution in the case of *Ilgar Mammadov v Azerbaijan* (Appl. no. 15172/13), 21 September 2017.

CM Interim Resolution in the case of *Ilgar Mammadov v Azerbaijan* (Appl. no. 15172/13), 5 December 2017.

CM decision in the case of *Ilgar Mammadov* group of cases (Appl. no. 15172/13), 5 December 2019.

CM decision in the case of *Ilgar Mammadov* group of cases (Appl. no. 15172/13), 6 June 2019.

CM Interim Resolution in the *Ilgar Mammadov* group v Azerbaijan (Appl. no. 15172/13), 5 March 2020.

CM decision in the *Muradova, Mammadov (Jalaloglu) and Mikayil Mammadov* group v Azerbaijan (Appl. no. 22684/05, 34445/04, 4762/05), 19–21 September 2017.

CM decision in the *Muradova, Mamamdov (Jalaloglu) and Mikayil Mammadov* group v. Azerbaijan (Appl. no. 22684/05, 34445/04, 4762/05) 13–15 March 2018.

CM Final Resolution in the case of *Rahmanova v Azerbaijan* (Appl. No. 34640/02), 4 April 2019.

CM decision in the case of *Sargsyan v Azerbaijan* (Appl. no. 40167/06), 7–10 March 2017.

Georgia

CM decision in the *Gharibashvili* group v. Georgia (Appl. no. 11830/03), 6–8 December 2016.

CM Interim Resolution in the case of *Gharibashvili* v Georgia (Appl. no. 11830/03), 21 September 2017.

CM Final Resolution in the case of *Gorelishvili v Georgia* (Appl.no. 12979/04), 30 November 2011.

CM Final Resolution in the case of *Ghavtadze* group v Georgia (Appl. no. 23204/07), 5 November 2014.

CM decision in the case of *Identoba and Others v Georgia* (Appl. no. 73235/12), 6–8 December 2016.

CM decision in the case of *Identoba and Others v Georgia* (Appl. no. 73235/12), 7 June 2018.

CM decision in the case of *Identoba and Others v Georgia* (Appl. no. 73235/12), 25 September 2019.

CM decision in the *Tsintsabadze* group of cases (Appl. no. 35403/06), 20 September 2018.

CM decision in the *Tsintsabadze* group of cases (Appl. no. 35403/06), 3–5 December 2019.

CM Notes on Individual Cases

CM notes on the case of *Chiragov and Others v Armenia* from its 1369th meeting, 3–5 December 2019.

CM Notes on the *Tsintsabadze* group of cases from its 1362nd meeting held, 3–5 December 2019.

Annual Reports

CM 4th Annual Report on Supervision of the Execution of Judgments and Decisions of the European Court of Human Rights (2010).

CM 6th Annual Report on Supervision of the Execution of Judgments and Decisions of the European Court of Human Rights (2012).

CM 9th Annual Report on Supervision of the Execution of Judgments and Decisions of the European Court of Human Rights (2015).

CM 11th Annual Report on Supervision of the Execution of Judgments and Decisions of the European Court of Human Rights (2017).

CM 12th Annual Report on Supervision of the Execution of Judgments and Decisions of the European Court of Human Rights (2018).

CM 13th Annual Report on Supervision of the Execution of Judgments and Decisions of the European Court of Human Rights (2019).

Other Documents

CM Information document, Supervision of the execution of judgments and decisions of the European Court of Human Rights: implementation of the Interlaken Action Plan – Modalities for a twin-track supervision system, CM/Inf/DH(2010)37, 6 September 2010.

CM Recommendation CM/Rec(2008)2 on Efficient Domestic Capacity for Rapid Execution of Judgments of the European Court of Human Rights.

Guide for the drafting of action plans and reports for the execution of judgments of the European Court of Human Rights, 16 July 2015.

Rules of the Committee of Ministers for the supervision of the execution of judgments and of the terms of friendly settlements, 10 May 2006.

Documents of the Parliamentary Assembly of the Council of Europe

PACE Opinions

PACE Opinion No. 2009 (1999) ' Georgia's application for membership in the Council of Europe'.

PACE Opinion No. 221 (2000) 'Armenia's application for membership in the Council of Europe'.

PACE Opinion No. 222. (2000) 'Azerbaijan's application for membership in the Council of Europe'.

PACE Reports and Resolutions

PACE Political Affairs Committee report on Georgia's application for membership of the Council of Europe, Doc. 8275, Explanatory memorandum prepared by its rapporteur Mr Terry Davis (UK, Socialist Group), 2 December 1998.

PACE Legal Affairs and Human Rights Committee report, Doc. 8756, Armenia's application for membership of the Council of Europe, 6 June 2000.

PACE Political Affairs Committee Report, Doc. 8747, Armenia's application for membership of the Council of Europe, 23 May 2000.

PACE report 'Azerbaijan's application for membership of the Council of Europe', Doc. 8748, prepared by the Political Affairs Committee and its rapporteur Mr Jacques Baumel (France, European Democratic Group), 23 May 2000.

PACE draft Resolution No. 13011 'The definition of political prisoner', proposed by rapporteur Mr Christoph Strasser, prepared by the Committee on Legal Affairs and Human Rights, 5 September 2012.

PACE Committee on Legal Affairs and Human Rights report, Implementation of Judgments of the European Court of Human Rights – Extracts from the Minutes of hearings, organised by the Committee in April 2012, in June 2012, in October 2012 and in January 2013, AS/Jur (2013).

PACE Committee on Legal Affairs and Human Rights report, Implementation of judgments of the European Court of Human Rights, 9 September 2015.

PACE Committee on Legal Affairs and Human Rights report, The Implementation of Judgments of the European Court of Human Rights, Rapporteur Mr Pierre-Yves Le Borgn, 12 June 2017.

PACE Resolution 2178 (2017), 'The Implementation of judgments of the European Court of Human Rights', 29 June 2017.

PACE Committee on the Honouring of Obligations and Commitments by Member States of the Council of Europe (Monitoring Committee) Report No. 14403 on the functioning of democratic institutions in Azerbaijan, 25 September 2017.

PACE Resolution 2185 (2017) 'Azerbaijan's Chairmanship of the Council of Europe: what follow-up on respect for human rights?, 11 October 2017.

PACE Committee on Legal Affairs and Human Rights report on reported cases of political prisoners in Azerbaijan, prepared by Rapporteur Ms Thorhildur Sunna ÆVARSDÓTTIR, Iceland, Socialists, Democrats and Greens Group, 10 December 2019.

Report of the Independent Investigation Body into allegations of corruption within the Parliamentary Assembly of the Council of Europe, 15 April 2018.

Report of the PACE Committee on the Honouring of Obligations and Commitments by Member States of the Council of Europe, Doc. 10163, Explanatory memorandum, 27 April 2004.

Other Documents and Publications

Letter of the President of Azerbaijan to Lord Russell-Johnston, President of the Parliamentary Assembly of the Council of Europe, 25 March 2000, Appendix 7 of the PACE report 'Azerbaijan's application for membership of the Council of Europe', Doc. 8748, prepared by the Political Affairs Committee and its rapporteur Mr Jacques Baumel (France, European Democratic Group), Appendix 4, Address of President Heydar Aliyev, 23 May 2000.

PACE Recommendation 1764 (2006), Implementation of the Judgments of the European Court of Human Rights, 2 October 2006.

PACE News, 'PACE votes to reject draft resolution on political prisoners in Azerbaijan', 23 January 2013.

PACE Overview 'Impact of the European Convention on Human Rights in States Parties: selected examples', prepared by the Legal Affairs and Human Rights Department, AS/Jur/Inf(2016)04, 8 January 2016.

Other Council of Europe Documents and Publications

CoE Action Plan for Armenia 2015–2018.

CoE Action Plan for Azerbaijan 2014–2017.

CoE Action Plan for Azerbaijan 2018–2021.

CoE Action Plan for Georgia 2013–2015 Final Report, GR-DEM (2016)16 (6 June 2016).

CoE Action Plan for Georgia 2016–2019.

CoE Commissioner opinion article, 'Azerbaijan: an area of darkness' (28 October 2015).

CoE News, 'Azerbaijan: torture, impunity and corruption highlighted in new anti-torture committee publications' (18 July 2018).

CoE News, 'Commissioner Muižnieks intervenes before the European Court of Human Rights on the case of Intigam Aliyev' (18 March 2015).

CoE News, 'Commissioner Muižnieks intervenes in cases concerning Azerbaijan before the European Court of Human Rights' (24 February 2015).

CoE News, 'Azerbaijan human rights inquiry', Secretary General, Strasbourg (16 December 2015).

CoE project infographics 'European Union and Council of Europe strengthening health care and human rights protection in prisons in Armenia 2015–2018'.

CoE/EU joint project 'Penitentiary reform – Strengthening Healthcare and Human Rights Protection in Prisons in Armenia', 2015–2018.

Commissioner for Human Rights report following her visit to Azerbaijan from 8 to 12 July 2019, CommDH(2019)27, December 2019.

European Committee for the Prevention of Torture and Inhuman or Degrading Treatment or Punishment (CPT) Report on the visit to Armenia carried out by the from 5 to 15 October 2015, CPT/Inf (2016).

European Committee for the Prevention of Torture and Inhuman or Degrading Treatment or Punishment (CPT) report on the visit to Georgia from 10 to 21 September 2018, CPT/Inf (2019).

PACE regional seminar on the role of national parliaments in implementing the standards of the European Convention of Human Rights, Tbilisi, 21–22 September 2015 (in attendance).

Steering Committee for Human Rights (CDDH), Draft CDDH report on the effective processing and resolution of cases relating to inter-State disputes, DH-SYSC-IV(2020)04 08 July 2020.

Venice Commission Opinion no. 644/2011 on the Draft Law on Amendments and Additions to the Law on Alternative Service of Armenia (Venice, 16–17 December 2011).

Venice Commission Opinion no. 692/2012 on the Legislation pertaining to the Protection against Defamation of the Republic of Azerbaijan (Venice, 11–12 October 2013).

Government Submissions to the Committee of Ministers on Implementation of ECtHR Judgments

Armenia

Communication from Armenia concerning the *Bayatyan* group of cases against Armenia (Appl. no. 23459/03), Action plan, 25 February 2013.

Communication from Armenia concerning the *Bayatyan* group of cases against Armenia (Appl. no. 23459/03), Updated action plan, 3 February 2014.

Communication from Armenia in the case of *Chiragov and Others v. Armenia* (Appl. no. 13216/05), 6 March 2017.

Communication from Armenia in the case of *Chiragov and Others v. Armenia* (Appl. no. 13216/05), 2 December 2019.

Communication from Armenia concerning the cases of *Ashot Harutyunyan and Piruzyan v Armenia* (Appl. nos. 34334/04, 33376/07), Action plan of 16 April 2015.

Communication from Armenia concerning the *Ashot Harutyunyan* group of cases (Appl. no. 34334/04), Revised action plan, 8 June 2016.

Communication from Armenia concerning the *Ashot Harutyunyan* group of cases (Appl. no. 34334/04), 9 October 2017.

Communication from Armenia concerning the *Ashot Harutyunyan* group of cases (Appl. no. 34334/04), Action plan, 18 January 2019.

Communication from Armenia concerning the case of *Virabyan v Armenia* (Appl. no. 40094/05), 29 November 2013.

Communication from Armenia concerning the case of *Virabyan v Armenia* (Appl. no. 40094/05), 25 February 2014.

Communication from Armenia concerning the *Virabyan* group of cases (Appl. no. 40094/05), Action plan, 14 October 2016.

Communication from Armenia concerning the *Virabyan* group of cases submitted by the Government of Armenia (Appl. no. 40094/05), Action plan, 22 February 2018.

Communication from Armenia concerning the *Virabyan* group of cases submitted by the Government of Armenia (Appl. no. 40094/05), Action plan, 30 March 2018.

Communication from Armenia concerning the *Virabyan* group of cases submitted by the Government of Armenia (Appl. no. 40094/05), Updated action plan, 24 January 2020.

Azerbaijan

Communication from Azerbaijan in the case of *Insanov v Azerbaijan* (Appl. no. 1613/08), 12 February 2016.

Communication from Azerbaijan in the case of *Fatullayev v Azerbaijan* (Appl. no. 40984/07), 26 May 2011.

Communication from Azerbaijan in the *Mahmudov and Agazade* group of cases, (Appl. no. 35877/04), 4–6 December 2012.

Communication from Azerbaijan in the *Mahmudov and Agazade* group of cases, (Appl. no. 35877/04), 4–6 June 2013.

Communication from Azerbaijan in the *Mahmudov and Agazade* group of cases (Appl. no. 35877/04), 3–5 December 2013.

Communication from Azerbaijan concerning the *Mahmudov and Agazade* group of cases (Appl. no. 35877/04), Action plan, 26 February 2014.

Communication from Azerbaijan, Reply from Azerbaijan to the questions pursuant to the decision adopted at the 1250th meeting (DH) in the *Mahmudov and Agazade* group of cases (Appl. no. 35877/04), 20 April 2016.

Communication from Azerbaijan concerning the case of *Ilgar Mammadov v. Azerbaijan* (Appl. no. 15172/13), Action plan, 26 November 2014.

Communication from Azerbaijan concerning the case of *Ilgar Mammadov v. Azerbaijan* (Appl. no. 15172/13), Action report, 2 June 2016.

Communication from Azerbaijan concerning the case of *Ilgar Mammadov v. Azerbaijan* (Appl. no. 15172/13), 14 February 2017.

Communication from Azerbaijan in reply to the communication of the applicant's representative in the case of *Ilgar Mammadov v. Azerbaijan* (Appl. no. 15172/13), 6 March 2017.

Communication from Azerbaijan concerning the *Ilgar Mammadov* group of cases v. Azerbaijan (Appl. no. 15172/13), Action Plan, 20 September 2019.

Communication from Azerbaijan concerning the *Ilgar Mammadov* group of cases v. Azerbaijan (Appl. no. 15172/13), Action Plan, 6 January 2020.

Communication from Azerbaijan concerning cases of *Ilgar Mammadov v Azerbaijan* (Appl. No. 15172/13) and *Rasul Jafarov v Azerbaijan* (Appl. No. 69981/14), Action report, 23 April 2020.

Communication from Azerbaijan concerning the cases of *Muradova, Mammadov (Jalaloglu) and Mikayil Mammadov v. Azerbaijan* (Appl. no. 22684/05, 34445/04, 4762/05), Action plan, 20 February 2018.

Communication from Azerbaijan, Reply of the authorities of 17 September 2014 to the communication from 7 NGOs in the *Ramazanova and Others* group of cases of 5 September 2014.

Communication from Azerbaijan concerning in the case of *Sargsyan v Azerbaijan* (Appl. no. 40167/06), Action plan, 6 March 2017.

Georgia

Action report from Georgia concerning the case of *Identoba and Others* v Georgia (Appl. no. 73235/12), Action report, 10 July 2019.

Communication from Georgia concerning individual and general measures in respect of the execution of the following cases: *Bekauri and Others*, Appl. no. 312/10, *Studio Maestro LTD and Others*, Appl. no. 22318/10, *Chantladze*, Appl. no. 60864/10, Consolidated action plan, 28 October 2016.

Communication from Georgia concerning the case of *Enukidze and Girgvliani* (*Gharibashvili* group) against Georgia (Appl. no. 25091/07), Action plan, 20 January 2015.

Communication from Georgia from Georgia in the *Gharibashvili* group v Georgia, (Appl. no. 11830/03), 17 July 2014.

Communication from Georgia concerning the *Gharibashvili* group of cases against Georgia (Appl. no. 11830/03), 3 June 2015.

Communication from Georgia in the *Gharibashvili* group v Georgia, (Appl. no. 11830/03), 1 March 2016.

Communication from Georgia in the *Gharibashvili* group v Georgia, (Appl. no. 11830/03), 1 June 2016.

Communication from Georgia in the *Gharibashvili* group v Georgia, (Appl. no. 11830/03), 28 October 2016.

Communication from Georgia in the *Gharibashvili* group of cases, Action plan, (Appl. no. 11830/03), 14 November 2016.

Communication from Georgia in the *Gharibashvili* group v Georgia, (Appl. no. 11830/03), 16 August 2017.

Communication from Georgia in the *Gharibashvili* group v Georgia, (Appl. no. 11830/03), 7 September 2017.

Communication from Georgia concerning the execution of cases of *Ghavtadze v. Georgia*, Appl. no. 23204/07, 3 March 2009, *Poghosyan v. Georgia*, Appl. no. 9870/

07, 24 February 2009, *Makharadze and Sikharulidze v. Georgia*, Appl. no. 35254/07, 22 November 2011, *Irakli Mindadze v. Georgia*, Appl. no. 17012/09, 11 December 2012, *Jeladze v. Georgia*, Appl. no. 1871/08, 18 December 2012, *Ildani v. Georgia*, Appl. no. 65391/09, 23 April 2013, Consolidated action plan, 8 January 2014.

Communication from Georgia concerning the *Ghvatadze* group of cases against Georgia (Appl. no. 23204/07), 27 January 2014.

Communication from Georgia concerning the *Ghvatadze* group of cases against Georgia (Appl. no. 23204/07), 30 September 2014.

Communication from Georgia concerning the case of *Identoba and Others* v Georgia (Appl. no. 73235/12), 26 April 2016.

Communication from Georgia in the case of *Identoba and Others* v Georgia, (Appl. no. 73235/12), 15 November 2016.

Communication from Georgia concerning the case *Identoba and Others* v Georgia, (Appl. no. 73235/12), 16 April 2018.

Communication from Georgia concerning the case of *Identoba and Others* v. Georgia (Appl. no. 73235/12), 25 June 2020.

Communication from Georgia in the case of *Klaus and Yuri Kiladze* (Appl. no. 7975/06), Action report, 5 December 2014.

Communication from the Georgia in the case of *Merabishvili v Georgia* (Appl. No. 72508/13), 4 June 2018.

Communication from the Georgia in the case of *Merabishvili v Georgia* (Appl. No. 72508/13), 29 March 2019.

Communication from the Georgia in the case of *Merabishvili v Georgia* (Appl. No. 72508/13), 30 September 2019.

Communication from the Georgia in the case of *Merabishvili v Georgia* (Appl. No. 72508/13), 29 June 2020.

Communications from the Georgian authorities in the *Tsintsabadze* group v Georgia (Appl. no. 35403/06), 5 December 2016.

Communications from the Georgian authorities in the *Tsintsabadze* group v Georgia (Appl. no. 35403/06), 4 June 2018.

Communication from Georgia concerning the case of *Tsintsabadze v. Georgia* (Appl. no. 35403/06), 13 July 2018.

Communications from the Georgian authorities in the *Tsintsabadze* group v Georgia (Appl. no. 35403/06), 25 October 2019.

Submissions from Applicants, NGO*s and National Human Rights Institutions*

Armenia

Communication from the European Association of Jehovah's witnesses concerning the following judgment in *Aghanyan and others v Armenia* (Appl. no. 58070/12), 11 June 2020.

Communication from an NGO in the case of *Chiragov and Others v Armenia* (Appl. no. 13216/05), 1 November 2016.

Communication from an NGO (EHRAC) in the cases of *Chiragov and Others v Armenia* (Appl. no. 13216/05) and *Sargsyan v Azerbaijan* (Appl. no. 40167/06), 2 November 2016.

Communication from the applicant in the case of *Chiragov and Others v Armenia* (Appl. no. 13216/05), 29 November 2019.

Communication from the Human Rights Defender of Armenia in the case of *Ashot Harutyunyan v. Armenia* (Appl. no. 34334/04), 21 January 2019.

Communication from an NGO (Open Society Foundations – Armenia) in the case of *Mushegh Saghatelyan v. Armenia* (Appl. no. 23086/08), 21 April 2020.

Communication from NGOs Open Society Foundations-Armenia, Protection of Rights without Borders NGO, Helsinki Citizens Assembly of Vanadzor, Transparency International Anticorruption Center and Law Development and Protection Foundation in the case of *Vardanyan and Nanushyan v. Armenia* (Appl. no. 8001/07), 17 June 2020.

Communication from an NGO (Rule of Law) in the case of *Virabyan v Armenia* (Appl. no. 40094/05), 25 September 2013.

Communication from NGOs in the cases of *Harutyunyan and Virabyan v Armenia*, Appl. no. 34334/04 and 40094/05, 25 September 2013.

Communication from an NGO (Helsinki Citizens' Assembly-Vanadzor) in the case of *Virabyan v Armenia* (Appl. no. 40094/05), 26 September 2014.

Communication from an NGO (Helsinki Citizens' Assembly-Vanadzor) in the case of *Nalbandyan* (*Virabyan* group) v Armenia (Appl. no. 9935/06), 7 November 2016.

Azerbaijan

Communication from the applicant in the case of *Aliyev* (*Ilgar Mammadov* group) v Azerbaijan (Appl. no. 68762/14), 9 May 2019.

Communication from the applicant's representatives in the case of *Aliyev v. Azerbaijan* (Appl. no. 68762/14), 19 September 2019.

Communication from the applicant in the case of *Aliyev* (*Ilgar Mammadov* group) v Azerbaijan (Appl. no. 68762/14), 14 November 2019.

Communication from the applicant in the case of *Insanov v Azerbaijan* (Appl. no. 1613/08), 22 May 2015.

Communication from the applicant in the case of *Rasul Jafarov (Ilgar Mammadov* group) v Azerbaijan (Appl. no. 68891/14), 19 January 2017.

Communication from the applicant in the case of *Rasul Jafarov (Ilgar Mammadov* group) v Azerbaijan (Appl. no. 68891/14), 1 September 2017.

Communication from the applicant in the case of *Rasul Jafarov (Ilgar Mammadov* group) v Azerbaijan (Appl. no. 68891/14), 2 May 2019.

Communication from the applicant in the case of *Rasul Jafarov v. Azerbaijan* (Appl. no. 69981/14), 18 June 2020.

Communication from NGOs (Institute for Reporters' Freedom and Safety, International Media Support, Media Rights Institute and Legal Education Society) in the case of *Mahmudov and Agazade v Azerbaijan* (Appl. no. 35877/04), 25 February 2014.

Communication from a NGO (Amnesty International) in the case of *Mahmudov and Agazade v Azerbaijan* (Appl. no. 35877/04), 28 November 2016.

Communication from the applicant in the case of *Mammadli (Ilgar Mammadov* group) v Azerbaijan (Appl. no. 15172/13), 12 November 2019.

Communication from the applicant in the cases of *Ilgar Mammadov* and *Ilgar Mammadov (No. 2) v. Azerbaijan* (Appl. no. 15172/13, 919/15), 3 June 2020.

Communication from 7 NGOs in the *Ramazanova and others* group of cases and *Tebieti Mühafize Cemiyyeti and Israfilov v Azerbaijan* (Appl. no. 44363/02 and 37083/03), 5 September 20154.

Communication from a NGO (EHRAC) in the cases of *Chiragov v Armenia* (Appl. no. 13216/05) *and Sargsyan v Azerbaijan* (Appl. no. 40167/06), 2 November 2016.

Communication from the applicant in *Sargsyan v Azerbaijan* (Appl. no. 40167/06), 09 October 2018.

Georgia

Communication from an NGO in the cases of *Bekauri and Others, Studio Maestro Ltd* and *Others and Tsintsanadze v. Georgia* (Appl. no. 312/10, 22318/10, 35403/06), 3 September 2018.

Communication from an NGO (Coalition for an Independent and Transparent Judiciary) in the *Gharibashvili* group of cases against Georgia (Appl. no. 11830/03), 7 March 2016.

Communication from the Public Defender of Georgia in the *Gharibashvili* group of cases against Georgia (Appl. no.11830/03), 28 November 2016.

Communication from NGOs (Identoba, Women's Initiatives Support Group (WISG), Amnesty International and ILGA-Europe) in the case of *Identoba and Others v Georgia* (Appl. No. 73235/12), 16 November 2016.

Communication from a Public Defender of Georgia in the case of *Identoba and Others v Georgia* (Appl. no. 73235/12), 18 August 2017.

Communication from NGOs (Joint submission from The Human Rights Education and Monitoring Center, the Women's initiatives Support Group and ILGA-Europe) in the *Identoba and Others* group of cases v. Georgia (Appl. no. 73235/12), 2 August 2019.

Communication from an NGO in *Identoba and Others* group of cases, and *Jehovah's Witnesses and Others v. Georgia* (Appl. no. 18766/04, 28490/02, 71156/01, 73235/12), 19 August 2019.

Communication by the Georgian Young Lawyers Association (GYLA) and the European Human Rights Advocacy Centre (EHRAC) in the case of *Klaus and Yuri Kiladze* (Appl. no. 7975/06), 24 January 2012.

Communication from a Public Defender of Georgia in the cases *of Makharadze and Sikharulidze, Tsintsabadze, Identoba and Others v Georgia* (Appl. no. 35254/07, 35403/06, 73235/12), 7 December 2017.

Communication from a Public Defender of Georgia in the case of *Merabishvili v Georgia* (Appl. no. 72508/13) on 29 January 2020.

Communication from a Public Defender of Georgia in the case of *Merabishvili v Georgia* (Appl. no. 72508/13) on 13 October 2020.

Communication from an NHRI in the case of *Merabishvili v. Georgia* (Appl. no. 72508/13), 24 January 2020.

Communication of the Public Defender of Georgia to the Committee of Ministers in the *Tsintsabadze* group of cases (Appl. no. 35403/06), 7 December 2017.

National Legislation and other Documents

Armenia

Charter of the Department for Representation before International Human Rights Courts, unofficial translation, provided by an interviewed Government Official, date not indicated.

Law on the Representative of the Republic of Armenia before the European Court of Human Rights, 23 July 2019, HO-141-N.

Azerbaijan

Civil Procedural Code of the Republic of Azerbaijan 28 December 1999.

Criminal Procedural Code of the Republic of Azerbaijan 14 July 2000.

National Program for Action to Raise Effectiveness of the Protection of Human Rights and Freedoms in the Republic of Azerbaijan, 27 December 2011.

Presidential Decree of the Republic of Azerbaijan, 8 December 2013 No 34.

Presidential decree on Plenipotentiary of the Republic of Azerbaijan to the European Court of Human Rights, No. 3, 8 November 2003.

Presidential decree on the appointment of Chingiz Askerov to the position of the Government Agent before the European Court of Human Rights, No. 34, 8 December 2003.

State budget of the Republic of Azerbaijan for 2018.
State budget of the Republic of Azerbaijan for 2019.

Georgia

Civil Procedure Code of the Republic of Georgia (1997) No 1106 IS.
Criminal Procedure Code of the Republic of Georgia (2009) No 1772 II.

Secondary Sources

Books

Brunee J and Toope SJ, Legitimacy and Legality in International Law: An Interactional Account (CUP 2010).

Donald A and Leach P, *Parliaments and the European Court of Human Rights* (OUP 2016).

Franck TM, *The Power of Legitimacy among Nations* (OUP 1990).

Gerards J and Fleuren J (eds), *Implementation of the European Convention on Human Rights and of the Judgements of the ECtHR in National Case-Law: A Comparative Analysis* (CUP 2014).

Goldsmith JL, and Posner EA, *The Limits of International Law* (OUP 2005).

Goodman R and Jinks D, *Socializing States: Promoting Human Rights Through International Law* (OUP 2013).

Guzman AT, *How International Law Works: A Rational Choice Theory* (OUP 2010).

Hillebrecht C, *Domestic Politics and International Human Rights Tribunals: The Problem of Compliance* (CUP 2014).

Korkelia K, *Application of the European Convention on Human Rights in Georgia, Summary in English* (2003).

Risse T, Ropp SC, and Sikkink K (eds), *The Persistent Power of Human Rights: From Commitment to Compliance* (CUP 2013).

Sikkink K, *Evidence for Hope, Making Human Rights Work in the 21st Century* (Princeton University Press, 2017).

Von Staden A, *Shaping Human Rights Policy in Liberal Democracies. Assessing and Explaining Compliance with the Judgments of the European Court of Human Rights*, PhD dissertation (Princeton University 2009).

Contributions to Edited Books

Bowring B, 'Russia and the Council of Europe: An Incompatible Ideology, and a Transplanted Legal Regime?', Sean Morris P (ed) *Russian Discourses on International Law: Sociological and Philosophical Phenomenon* (Abingdon, Routledge 2018).

Gyulumyan A and Melkonyan D, 'The Supremacy of the European Convention on Human Rights: Armenia's path', Motoc I and Ziemele I (ed) *The Impact of the*

ECHR on Democratic Change in Central and Eastern Europe, Judicial Perspectives (CUP 2016).

Hajiyev K, 'Azerbaijan' in I.Motoc and I. Ziemele (Eds.), *The Impact of the ECHR on Democratic Change in Central and Eastern Europe: Judicial Perspectives* (CUP 2016).

Koremenos B, 'Institutionalism and International Law' in Dunoff and Pollack *Interdisciplinary Perspectives on International Law and International Relations* (CUP 2013).

Martin LL, 'Against Compliance', in Dunoff and Pollack, *Interdisciplinary Perspectives on International Law and International Relations* (CUP 2013).

Moravcsik A, 'Liberal Theories of International Law', in Dunoff and Pollack, *Interdisciplinary Perspectives on International Law and International Relations* (CUP 2013).

Neyer J and Wolf D, 'The Analysis of Compliance with International Rules: Definitions, Variables and Methodology' in Zurn M and Joerges C (eds.), *Law and Governance in Postnational Europe: Compliance beyond the Nation-State* (CUP 2005).

Spielmann D, President of the European Court of Human Rights (2012–2015), 'Foreword', in Iulia Motoc and Ineta Ziemele (eds.), *The Impact of the ECHR in Democratic Change in Central and Eastern Europe* (CUP 2016).

Von Stein J, 'The Engines of Compliance', in Dunoff and Pollack, *Interdisciplinary Perspectives on International Law and International Relations* (CUP 2012).

Journal Articles

Baluarte DC, 'Strategizing For Compliance: The Evolution of a Compliance Phase of Inter-American Court Litigation and the Strategic Imperative For Victims' Representatives' (2012) Vol. 27(2) American University International Law Review.

Bates ES, 'Sophisticated Constructivism in Human Rights Compliance Theory' (2014) Vol. 25(4) EJIL.

Çali B and Koch A, 'Foxes Guarding the Foxes? The Peer Review of Human Rights Judgments by the Committee of Ministers of the Council of Europe' (2014) Vol. 14 (2) Human Rights Law Review.

Çalı B and Wyss A, 'Why Do Democracies Comply with Human Rights Judgments? A Comparative Analysis of the UK, Ireland and Germany' (2009) SSRN e-Library.

Çalı B, 'Coping with Crisis: Whither the Variable Geometry in the Jurisprudence of the European Court of Human Rights' (2018) Vol. 35(2) Wisconsin International Law Journal.

Çalı B, Koch A and Bruch N, 'The Legitimacy of the European Court of Human Rights: The View from the Ground' (2011), University College London.

Camilleri MJ, Krsticevic V, 'Making international law stick: reflections on compliance with judgments in the inter-american human rights system' (2009) Derecho Internacional y Relaciones Internacionales.

Chayes A and Chayes AH, 'On Compliance' (1993) Vol. 47 (2) International Organization.

Donald A and Speck AK, 'The Dynamics of Domestic Human Rights Implementation: Lessons from Qualitative Research in Europe' (2020) Vol. 12 (1) Journal of Human Rights Practice.

Donald A and Speck AK, 'The European Court of Human Rights' Remedial Practice and its Impact on the Execution of Judgments' (2019) Vol. 19 (1) Human Rights Law Review.

Donald A, Long D, and Speck AK, 'Identifying and Assessing the Implementation of Human Rights Decisions' (2020) Vol. 12 (1) Journal of Human Rights Practice.

Donnelly J, 'International Human Rights: A Regime Analysis' (1986) Vol. 40 International Organization.

Garavito R, 'Beyond the Courtroom: The Impact of Judicial Activism on Social and Economic Rights in Latin America' (2010) Vol. 89 Texas Law Review.

Grewal S and Voeten E, 'Are New Democracies Better Human Rights Compliers?' (2012) SSRN e-Library.

Hawkins D and Jacoby W, 'Partial compliance. A Comparison of the European and Inter-American Courts of Human Rights' (2010) Vol. 6 Journal of International Law and International Relations.

Helfer LR and Voeten E, 'Do European Court of Human Rights Judgments Promote Legal and Policy Change?' (2010) University of Chicago.

Huneeus A, 'Courts Resisting Courts: Lessons from the Inter-American Court's Struggle to Enforce Human Rights' (2011) Vol. 44 (3) Cornell International Law Journal.

Moravcsik A, 'The Origins of International Human Rights Regimes: Democratic Delegation in Postwar Europe', (2000) Vol. 54(2) International Organization.

Murray R and De Vos C, 'Behind the State: Domestic Mechanisms and Procedures for the Implementation of Human Rights Judgments and Decisions' (2020) Vol. 12(1) Journal of Human Rights Practice.

Nielsen RA and Simmons BA, 'Rewards for Ratification: Payoffs for Participating in the Human Rights Regime?' (2015) Vol. 59(2) International Studies Quarterly.

Remezaite R, 'Introductory Note to *Chiragov and Others v Armenia* and *Sargsyan v Azerbaijan* (EUR.CT.H.R.)' (2018) Vol.57(3) International Legal Materials, American Society of International Law.

Sadurski W, 'Partnering with Strasbourg: Constitutionalisation of the European Court of Human Rights, the Accession of Central and East European States to the Council of Europe, and the Idea of Pilot Judgments' (2009) Vol. 9(3) Human Rights Law Review.

Sandoval C, Leach P and Murray R, 'Monitoring, Cajoling and Promoting Dialogue: What Role for Supranational Human Rights Bodies in the Implementation of Individual Decisions?' (2020) Vol. 12(1) Journal of Human Rights Practice.

Shany Y, 'Assessing the Effectiveness of International Court: A Goal-Based Approach' (2012) Vol.106(2) The American Journal of International Law.

Speck AK, 'The European System of Human Rights Protection: No Rolls-Royce, but a Solid Engine Fit for the Future? In Conversation with Council of Europe Insiders' (2020) Vol. 12(1) Journal of Human Rights Practice.

Vreeland JR, 'Political Institutions and Human Rights: Why Dictatorships Enter into the United Nations Convention against Torture' (2008) Vol. 62(1) International Organisation.

Blogs and other Online Publications

Çalı B, 'Byzantine Manoeuvres, Turkey's responses to bad faith judgments of the ECtHR' (Verfassungsblog on constitutional matters, 19 February 2020).

De Waal T, 'Azerbaijan Doesn't Want to be Western' (Foreign Affairs magazine, 26 September 2014).

De Waal T, 'Is Change Afoot in Azerbaijan?' (Carnegie Europe, 5 November 2019).

De Waal T, 'Why the Long Conflict over Nagorno-Karabakh Could Heat up Again' (World Politics Review 18 October 2019).

European Human Rights Advocacy Centre, 'Georgia amends legislation following European Court case' (13 November 2014).

European Human Rights Advocacy Centre, 'European Court: Former Georgian Prime Minister's pre-trial detention used to exert pressure on him' (14 June 2016).

European Human Rights Advocacy Centre, 'Ten years on, families of those killed during 1 March protests in Yerevan need answers' (1 March 2018).

European Implementation Network, 'EIN launch event: a strong call for collective responsibility over implementation of ECtHR judgments' (6 December 2016).

European Implementation Network, 'EIN trains Armenian civil society actors in tackling implementation challenges' (12 March 2020).

Glas LR, 'The Committee of Ministers goes nuclear: infringement proceedings against Azerbaijan in the case of Ilgar Mammadov' (The Strasbourg Observers, 20 December 2017).

Human Rights Watch, 'Protests erupt in Georgia over failed electoral reforms' (15 November 2019).

Jomarjidze N and Leach P, 'What future for settlements and undertakings in international human rights resolution?' (Strasbourg Observers 15 April 2019).

Kauzlarich RD (former US ambassador to Azerbaijan), 'The Heydar Aliyev Era Ends in Azerbaijan not with a Bang but a Whisper' (Brookings, 13 January 2015).

Leach P and Donald A, 'Russia Defies Strasbourg: Is Contagion Spreading?' (EJIL:Talk! Blog of the European Journal of International Law, 19 December 2015).

Leach P, 'Strasbourg Censures Georgia over Detention of Former Prime Minister – the impact of an Article 18 violation' (EJIL: Talk! Blog of the European Journal of the International Law 2 August 2016).

Leach P, 'Thawing the Frozen Conflict? The European Court's Nagorno-Karabakh Judgments' (EJIL: TALK! Blog of the European Journal of the International Law 6 July 2015).

Leach P, 'The Continuing Utility of International Human Rights Mechanisms?' (EJIL:Talk! Blog of the European Journal of International Law 1 November 2017).

Maggie Murphy, 'Traditional values' v human rights at the UN' (Open Democracy 18 February 2013).

Mchedlishvili G, 'Changing Perceptions of the West in the South Caucasus: Adoration No More' (Chatman House February 2016).

Moxham L, 'Implementation of ECHR judgments – have we reached a crisis point?' (UK Human Rights Blog 7 July 2017).

Netherlands Helsinki Committee, 'Russia's Departure from the Council of Europe Should Be Avoided' (5 December 2018).

Remezaite R and Dahlsen J, 'Explainer: Council of Europe Infringement Proceedings against Azerbaijan' (European Human Rights Advocacy Centre 26 February 2018).

Remezaite R and Aliyeva U, 'Council of Europe's old pandemic: 'endemic' ill-treatment and torture in custody in Azerbaijan' (European Implementation Network 23 July 2020).

Remezaite R, 'Azerbaijan: Is it Time to Invoke Infringement Proceedings for Failing to Implement Judgments of the Strasbourg Court?' (EJIL:Talk! Blog of the European Journal of the International Law 22 March 2017).

Reporters Without Borders, Azerbaijan profile page (accessed 22 August 2020).

Stafford G, 'The Implementation of Judgments of the European Court of Human Rights: Worse Than You Think – Part 1: Grade Inflation' (EJIL:Talk! Blog of the European Journal of the International Law 7 October 2019).

Svensson T and Hon J, 'Attitudes Toward the West in the South Caucasus' (Caucasus Analytical Digest 15 February 2010).

Tweets by Thomas de Waal, Carnegie Europe 15 July 2015.

Tweets by Zaur Shiriyev, International Crisis Group 15 July 2020.

UN Committee Against Torture News, 'UN Committee against Torture to review Armenia' (17 November 2016).

Reports

2018 Annual report of the Public Defender of Georgia.

Amnesty International Report 2017/2018, 'The State of the World's Human Rights'.

Concluding Observations of the UN Committee against Torture on Armenia at its 48th session, 6 July 2012.

Corruption Perceptions Index 2019 by Transparency International.
Europe and Central Asia: Summary of Amnesty International's Concerns in the Region, January-June 2004.
European Implementation Network Handbook for NGOs, injured parties and their legal advisers, Implementation of Judgments of the European Court of Human Rights, 2018, enriched in January 2020.
European Stability Initiative, 'Showdown in Strasbourg the Political Prisoner Debate in October 2012' (February 2013).
European Stability Initiative, Caviar Diplomacy. 'How Azerbaijan silenced the Council of Europe', Part 1 (24 May 2012).
European Stability Initiative, The European Swamp (Caviar Diplomacy Part 2) – Prosecutors, corruption and the Council of Europe (17 December 2016).
Freedom House, 'Freedom in the World 2020, Freedom House Interactive Map'.
Freedom House, Freedom in the World 2001, Azerbaijan.
Freedom House, Freedom in the World 2002, Azerbaijan.
Freedom House, Nations in Transit 2002, Azerbaijan.
Freedom House, Nations in Transit 2003, Azerbaijan.
Freedom House, Nations in Transit 2004: Armenia.
Freedom House Freedom in the World Report 2007, Armenia country report.
Freedom House, Freedom in the World 2017, Armenia.
Freedom House, Freedom in the World 2018, Armenia.
Freedom House report, Nations in Transit 2003: Georgia.
Freedom House, Nations in Transit 2016: Georgia.
Helsinki Citizens' Assembly Vanadzor, Situation of Execution of European Court of Human Rights Judgments by Republic of Armenia, Study (2007–2015), Vanadzor 2016.
Human Rights First, Russia's 'Traditional Values' Leadership (1 June 2016).
Human Rights Watch 'World Report 2016: Russia, Events of 2015'.
Human Rights Watch 'World Report 2016: Azerbaijan, Events of 2015'.
Human Rights Watch Briefing Paper, Cycle of Repression: Human Rights Violations in Armenia (4 May 2004).
Human Rights Watch report 'Democracy on Rocky Ground, Armenia's Disputed 2008 Presidential Election, Post-Election Violence, and the One-Sided Pursuit of Accountability' (25 February 2009).
Human Rights Watch World report 2002, Armenia.
Human Rights Watch World report 2015: Armenia, Events of 2014.
Human Rights Watch World Report 2020: Azerbaijan.
Human Rights Watch, Russia: Escalating Persecution of Jehovah's Witnesses (9 January 2020).

International Crisis Group, 'The Nagorno-Karabakh Conflict: A Visual Explainer' (accessed 23 November 2020).

Media Rights Institute, 'Execution of Judgments of the European Court of Human Rights in Azerbaijan. Status Quo Upon Azerbaijan's Chairmanship of the Committee of Ministers of the Council of Europe' (May 2014).

NGO Article 42 of the Constitution, 'Report on Execution of Rulings of the European Court of Human Rights and the United Nations Treaty Bodies in Georgia' (January 2020).

Open Society Justice Initiative, 'From Rights to Remedies. Structures and Strategies for Implementing International Human Rights Decisions' (2013).

Open Society Justice Initiative, 'Strategic Litigation Impacts: Equal Access to Quality Education' (Open Society Foundations 2017).

Open Society Justice Initiative, 'Strategic Litigation Impacts: Indigenous Peoples' Land Rights' (Open Society Foundations 2017).

Open Society Justice Initiative, 'Strategic Litigation Impacts: Roma School Desegregation' (Open Society Foundations 2016).

Open Society Justice Initiative, 'Strategic Litigation Impacts: Torture in Custody' (Open Society Foundations 2017).

Open Society Justice Initiative, 'Strategic Litigation Impacts. Insights from Global Experience (2018)'.

OSCE ODIHR Final Report on parliamentary elections in Armenia on 12 May 2007 (10 September 2007).

OSCE ODIHR Final Report on parliamentary elections in Armenia on 19 February 2008 (30 May 2008).

OSCE ODIHR Final Report on presidential election in Armenia on 19 February 2008 (30 May 2008).

OSCE ODIHR Final Report on presidential election in Armenia on 19 February and 5 March 2003 (28 April 2003).

OSCE ODIHR International Election Observation Mission Statement of Preliminary Findings and Conclusions, Republic of Azerbaijan-Early Parliamentary Elections (9 February 2020).

OSCE/ODIHR Election Observation Mission Final Report of 11 February 2006 on parliamentary election held on 6 November 2005.

OSCE/ODIHR Election Observation Mission Final Report of 18 July 2018 on early parliamentary election held on 11 April 2018.

OSCE/ODIHR Election Observation Mission Final Report of 25 January 2011 on early parliamentary election held on 7 November 2010.

OSCE/ODIHR Election Observation Mission Final Report, Parliamentary elections, Republic of Azerbaijan (7 November 2010).

Pew Research Centre, 'How do European countries differ in religious commitment? Use our interactive map to find out' (5 December 2018).

Report 'Independent International Fact-Finding Mission on the Conflict in Georgia', established by the Council of the European Union (September 2009).

Report of the UN Committee Against Torture on Armenia, Twenty-fifth session (13–24 November 2000) and Twenty-sixth session (30 April–18 May 2001).

Report of the UN Special Rapporteur on torture and other cruel, inhuman or degrading treatment or punishment on his mission to Georgia, UN Human Rights Council, A/HRC/31/57/Add.3 (1 December 2015).

Reporters Without Borders, 2017 World Press Freedom Index.

The Caucasus Research Resource Center Georgia, 'Knowledge and attitudes toward the EU in Georgia' 2015.

The Caucasus Research Resources Center Georgia, survey report 'Knowledge and Attitudes towards the EU in Georgia: Changes and Trends 2009–2013'.

The European Commission against Racism and Intolerance report on Georgia (8 December 2015).

Transparency International, Anti-Corruption Helpdesk, 'Azerbaijan: Overview of Corruption and Anti-corruption'.

UN Committee Against Torture Concluding Observations on the fourth periodic report of Armenia, CAT/C/ARM/CO/4 (26 January 2016).

Unified List of Political Prisoners in Azerbaijan, prepared by Azerbaijani human rights groups (3 September 2019).

World Bank Economy Overview: Armenia (accessed 15 June 2020).

Media Articles

Agenda.ge, 'PM Gakharia on anniversary of June protests: no matter how many years pass, we prevented destabilisation', (18 June 2020).

Amerikaninsesi.org, Ramiz Mehdiyev, 'We can only be equal in our relations' 29 October 2015 (unofficial translation).

Andrei Beketov, 'Nikol Pashinyan: Armenia will not be authoritarian' (Euronews 8 March 2019).

Anna Ohanyan, 'Armenia's Democratic Dreams' (Foreign Policy 7 November 2018).

APA News, 'President Ilham Aliyev receives Turkish Foreign Minister Mevlut Cavusoglu' (6 February 2020).

AzarTac, 'Ali Hasanov: Azerbaijan travelled a long distance to develop democratic society and no one can deny it' (4 November 2014).

BBC News, 'Georgia protests: Thousands storm parliament over Russian MP's speech' (21 June 2019).

Civil.ge, 'MPs Debate Constitutional Ban of Same-Sex Marriage' (27 May 2016).

Contact.az, 'Ilham Aliyev: There are national traitors in country' (unofficial translation), 28 August 2018.

Radio Free Europe/Free Liberty, 'Ten Years Later, Deadly Shooting In Armenian Parliament Still Echoes' (27 October 2009).

Radio Free Europe/Radio Liberty, 'Armenia's 2019 Budged Approved by Parliament' (22 November 2018).

Reuters, 'Thousands gather in Tbilisi for protest against Georgian government' (20 September 2019).

Washington Post, 'Armenian protesters brought down a prime minister. Here's why they are in the streets' (20 April 2018).

Washington Post, 'Gunmen Take Over Armenian Parliament; Premier Killed' (27 October 1999).

Index